Database and Application Security

A Practitioner's Guide

R. Sarma Danturthi

Addison-Wesley

Figure Credits

Figures 02.01a-b, 03.02, 03.03a-b, 05.01, 05.02, 06.01 – 06.05, 07.07, 07.08, 07.11, 07.15, 08.01, 08.02, 09.03, 10.03, 11.02, 11.05, 11.09 – 11.13, 12.02, 16.02 – 16.05: Microsoft Corporation

Figures 04.02, 05.03, 07.09: Oracle Corporation

Figure 07.10c: The Department of Defense

Figure 09.02: National Institute of Standards and Technology

Figure 11.06: PayPal Holdings, Inc

Figure 11.07 & 11.08: The Apache Software Foundation

Figure 12.03: OWASP Foundation, Inc.

Figure 13.03: The United States Navy

Figure 14.01 & 14.02: The ZAP Dev Team

Figure 14.03 & 14.04: PortSwigger Ltd

Figures 14.05-14.07: Aircrack-ng

Figure 14.08 & 14.15: United States Department of Defense

Figure 14.16: Office of the Director of National Intelligence

Figure 14.17: SLEUTH KIT LABS

Figure 15.01a-b: Okta, Inc.

Figure 15.02: DigitalOcean, LLC.

Figure 15.03: Apple Inc

Library of Congress Control Number: 2024931425

ISBN-13: 978-0-13-807373-2

ISBN-10: 0-13-807373-2

1 2024

Editor-in-Chief
Mark Taub

Director, ITP Product Management
Brett Bartow

Executive Editor
James Manly

Production Manager
Sandra Schroeder

Development Editor
Ellie C. Bru

Production Editor
Mary Roth

Copy Editor
The Wordsmithery LLC

Technical Editor(s)
Brock Pearson

Team Coordinator
Tammi Barnett

Cover Designer
Chuti Prasertsith

Composition
codeMantra

Proofreader
Donna E. Mulder

Indexer
Erika Millen

Dedication

This book is offered jointly into the divine hands of Swami Satyananda Saraswati and Swami Sivananda Saraswati.

Contents at a Glance

Part I. Security Fundamentals

Chapter 1: The Basics of Cybersecurity: In this chapter, the reader is introduced to security fundamentals of CIA-DAD and the authentication fundamentals IAAA. After giving details of hardware, software, and physical security, the roles of users are discussed. A detailed example of security in an organization is then presented to the reader.

Chapter 2: Security Details: This chapter discusses details of encryption, compression, indexing, and archiving. It goes into depth about encryption algorithms, PKI, email security, and non-repudiation. Current and new algorithms are touched on briefly in this chapter as well.

Chapter 3: Goals of Security: The "who is who" in security, RACI matrix, and the goals of security are discussed in this chapter. Events and incidents are also discussed along with risks and breaches. This chapter also stresses the importance of logs and reengineering a project while keeping security as a top priority.

Part II. Database Security—The Back End

Chapter 4: Database Security Introduction: ACID and BASE databases are discussed with examples in this chapter. DDL and DML are shown separately after defining DIT and DAR. Structural and functional security issues in DBs are discussed as well, and a plan for procedural security is put forward for consideration.

Chapter 5: Access Control of Data: Access control with MAC, DAC, RBAC, and RuBAC with roles and privileges is discussed in this chapter. Hashing and checksum examples and how they can be applied to DB are discussed. This chapter also covers monitoring DB with triggers and data protection with various database objects such as views.

Chapter 6: Data Refresh, Backup, and Restore: Data refresh, import, export, backup, and restore methods are shown in this chapter. Readers will learn how the backups and restores should be kept and tested regularly, in addition to daily/weekly/monthly tracking.

Chapter 7: Host Security: A host is a location (such as a Linux server) that keeps the DB and applications. Taking care of host security is important too as the DB is hosted on the server. This chapter shows how to create cron jobs or scheduled jobs on servers and provides numerous examples.

Chapter 8: Proactive Monitoring: Proactive monitoring helps prevent incidents and helps an organization to be fully prepared. Proactive monitoring can be done with logs, triggers, and more. Log file generation and reading are discussed to keep the reader up to date about what to expect.

Chapter 9: Risks, Monitoring, and Encryption: Risks can be mitigated, transferred, or accepted. But before choosing what to do with a risk, the risk needs to be measured. Risk monitoring is discussed in this chapter, along with DB monitoring, encrypting a DB, and generating automated alerts.

Part III. Application Security—The Front End

Chapter 10: Application Security Fundamentals: Application security starts with good coding fundamentals and following an acceptable coding standard. Cohesion and coupling are discussed, and practical examples show server- and client-side security and checking. Change management is introduced in this chapter to help explain why unauthorized changes to code and DB are not allowed and must follow an approved change management process.

Chapter 11: The Unseen Back End: This chapter discusses stored procedures in the back-end DB and how SQL code can be stored on the DB to run queries rather than creating plaintext queries on the front end then passing them to the DB. Stored procedures offer better security and can be easily embedded into many high-level programming languages.

Chapter 12: Securing Software—In-House and Vendor: Requirements to test in-house-developed software and vendor software are different and each should be tested separately to avoid any vulnerabilities. This chapter discusses the SAST tools available and what the tests show. It also shows why patching and software updates are required and should be done as soon as they are released.

Part IV. Security Administration

Chapter 13: Security Administration: The "need to know" and "least privilege" along with clearances given to subjects are discussed in this chapter. Change management is touched on once more to show how the systems all work in tandem to allow only authorized changes. Legal liabilities are discussed in detail as well the benefits of being proactive in maintaining security.

Chapter 14: Follow a Proven Path for Security: A proven path for achieving security in the DB and application is to conduct around-the-clock monitoring after implementing security controls. Proven path includes testing regularly with various tools and conducting audits. Operational security is discussed in this chapter.

Chapter 15: Mobile Devices and Application Security: Mobile devices pose a new threat as they are now widespread and used everywhere. Wi-Fi security, user privacy, and cryptography's role in these devices are discussed in this chapter along with sandboxing and the NIST's directions for mobile devices.

Chapter 16: Corporate Security in Practice: This chapter discusses each aspect of corporate security in detail—physical, software, hardware, and others. It covers how new employees are onboarded and an existing employee can renew their credentials. Attacks and losses are explained, as well as how an organization can recover from an attack. This chapter covers "lessons learned" and how to document the details after an incident materializes.

Contents

Foreword

The computer industry has exploded in a way nobody probably imagined. Along with that explosion came hackers, who utilize the same technology to steal information and cause immeasurable harm. Initially, hackers used viruses to create havoc, either for fun or financial damages. Now, they use innovative methods such as ransomware to lock systems and demand money in huge sums. We are at a point where we do not know what comes next in terms of these exploitations. All we can do is to check our risks, mitigate them to our best possible effort, and do continuous monitoring. By keeping our eyes open for the new threats, we can be better prepared. As you will read in this book, there is no single foolproof method to securing an application of a database. The method to secure these has been, and should always be, a multi-pronged defense method. This is known as defense in depth—employing various possible actions that can detect or even stop an attack.

For this reason, security must start from step zero and should remain a high priority throughout the life cycle of a software or database. In this book, database and application security are discussed in a practical way. Change management, running STIG tests, audits, and creating lessons learned documents are all very important in creating a suitable and secure posture for an IT organization. Each branch of IT, be it networking, operating system, coding, designing etc., has to worry about the security of IT to create a good security posture for the application, DB, or the organization at large. When resources are available, it is also important to isolate DB and application servers.

In the end, security is everyone's responsibility and cannot be achieved by one person. For this reason, we often hear the phrase, "If you see something, say something." Bystanders, or those who think "it is not my job to report," are essentially responsible if they ignore a threat after seeing one. Insider threats are equally dangerous, if not more so, because a disgruntled insider may have more "inside information" that they can pass to others and exploit.

The methods discussed in this book to achieve a good security posture in an organization are only what are known to this day. In other words, this is the research we know now and are currently implementing. We must evolve with a continuous learning curve and implement new methods as hackers and attackers come up with newer techniques to exploit. These methods will continue to get more complex since servers can host more than a simple database and one application. Migration to the cloud is catching up to us too and anything that is transferred to a cloud platform is always considered to be at risk. Mobile devices such as smart phones and tablets will further evolve and all we can do is go with the flow and adapt to new technologies, new threats, and new challenges.

Cybersecurity is both a very challenging and very fun field to work in. The ultimate law to excel in this field remains to be this—keep your eyes open, learn continuously, adapt, and grow with the field. Whether you are an application developer, DB coder, DB administrator, or system administrator, this book will help you achieve a strong security posture in your organization. But remember that cybersecurity is a security posture that can only be achieved by working with everyone around you. The first line of defense in security is YOU.

Godspeed in learning the details of cybersecurity!

Introduction

After working in the IT field for over 20 years, the idea to put into words what I have learned took shape. I started creating my own lists of "to do's" while developing a DB or an application. These to-do lists started to become large and routine processes due to developments in the IT field. Certifications such as Sec+, CISSP, and ITIL have become mandatory requirements in various organizations for developers, DB, and system administrators. After working with various people who implemented security religiously and those who ignored the security part with equal vigor, I felt it was time to put my to-do lists into the form of a book.

The result is the book you have in your hands. Since security details need to be mentioned before they are implemented, the first section goes over the fundamentals of cybersecurity. As you will read in this book, security is never a one-person job. Therefore, after discussing DB security and application security, I added a fourth section on security administration to give details of corporate security in action. All aspects of security are discussed in the last section to give the reader an idea of how cybersecurity aligns with corporate security, IT security, and physical security.

Who Should Read This Book?

This book is for IT professionals who want to learn how to secure their DB or their applications with a multi-pronged stature. System administrators can use this book in securing their hosts, creating firewall rules, and hardening the IIS side of hosting an application. The book might be helpful in learning security of software and DBs and may help with Sec+ and CISSP certifications.

The book should be used at every stage of the software or DB development process to create a strong cybersecurity posture. It also helps in learning the fundamentals for an aspiring student in IT and cybersecurity. The book touches on both Oracle and SQL Server software. Any programming language security can be achieved with applications by incorporating the methods discussed in this book. Students can learn about change management and its process before they enter a corporate environment. Parts of the book also discuss steps for taking care of mobile devices and BYOD at an office. This book could also be used for a general audience to understand the attacks that exist in DB and applications and learn how to prevent those attacks.

How This Book Is Organized

It is recommended that this book be read cover-to-cover to learn about various routes of cybersecurity for DBs and applications that are hosted on Linux or Windows servers.

The book is divided into four sections:

Part I. Security Fundamentals

Part II. Database Security—The Back End

Part III. Application Security—The Front End

Part IV. Security Administration

Parts II and III discuss the security details for DB and applications. Since security cannot be achieved by one single person, Part IV discusses the security administration with the change management process. Various administrative functions—creating roles, granting privileges, and the related paperwork—are included in Part IV. Most of the references are from NIST and organizations such as Microsoft and Oracle. The examples given for Linux were run on the open-source free Linux and express editions of the software from Microsoft, Oracle, and others such as OWASP, Autopsy, etc.

At the end of each chapter, there are chapter-specific questions and answers to those questions to test the readers' understanding. It is recommended that the readers get an account with a cloud provider such as Google or Microsoft Azure (free trial and then very cheap for using on a monthly basis) to create a virtual machine to install free software (SQL Developer, SQL Server Express Edition, etc.) and test the scripts given in this book for hands-on experience.

Command Syntax Conventions

The conventions used to present command syntax in this book are the same conventions used in the IOS Command Reference. The Command Reference describes these conventions as follows:

- **Boldface** indicates commands and keywords that are entered literally as shown. In actual configuration examples and output (not general command syntax), boldface indicates commands that are manually input by the user (such as a **show** command).

- *Italics* indicate arguments for which you supply actual values.

- Vertical bars (|) separate alternative, mutually exclusive elements.

- Square brackets [ ] indicate optional elements.

- Braces { } indicate a required choice.

- Braces within brackets [{ }] indicate a required choice within an optional element.

Register your copy of *Database and Application Security: A Practitioner's Guide* on the InformIT site for convenient access to updates and/or corrections as they become available. To start the registration process, go to informit.com/register and log in or create an account. Enter the product ISBN (**9780138073732**) and click Submit.

Acknowledgments

I'd like to give special recognition to Mr. James Manly at Pearson for providing me the opportunity to put my ideas into writing. When I was working with him on cybersecurity testing questions, we had a casual discussion about the idea of a book where I mentioned that many coding professionals either do not know or just ignore the security aspect in databases and application coding. He encouraged me to put up a synopsis and gave me ample time to write, edit, and bug him at will about the book, the writing topics, and the style. We have developed a great relationship over the past four years and the credit entirely belongs to him.

In my professional life, there are countless individuals who willingly taught me their knowledge, shared their expertise, and allowed me to scale their shoulders to look beyond what I knew. All my current and past employers have been incredibly supportive and gave me opportunity to learn the idea of a "solution-oriented" approach. It would be impossible to repay them with anything in return. As much as I want to thank the people I wanted emulate, it is the group of people, who taught me how *not* to behave, that needs my special thanks. Again, I thank both these groups of people. You made my days, weeks, months, and life a classy one without comparison.

A big "thank you" goes out to the production team that worked tirelessly on this book: Eleanor Bru, Cindy Teeters, Jayaprakash P., Mary Roth, Donna Mulder, and Charlotte Kughen. They have been incredibly professional and a pleasure to work with. I couldn't have asked for a better team than the one at Pearson.

About the Author

Dr. R. Sarma Danturthi holds a PhD in Engineering from the University of Memphis (Memphis, TN) and works for the US Department of Defense. He has several years of experience with IT security, coding, databases, and project management. He holds Sec+, CISSP, and PMP certifications. He has also taught undergraduate and graduate-level courses in Engineering and Information Technology at Marquette University and Gallaudet University as an adjunct professor. He has been a subject matter expert in editing/reviewing IT security books for Pearson, CompTIA, and ISC2 and created test questions for CISSP, CISA, CISM, and CEH certifications. He has published several peer-reviewed papers in engineering, project management's PMI's knowledge shelf. He is the author of *70 Tips and Tricks for Mastering the CISSP Exam* (APress, 2020).

Basics of Cybersecurity

Cybersecurity

The earliest computers, such as the ZX-Spectrum or the original Apple computer designed by Steve Jobs and his colleagues, didn't require login information or user credentials. Anyone could just switch on the machine, open a word processing application, type, and print. Most of those standalone machines did not even connect to a network. At that time, the only thing people wanted was a machine that could print a document and play a few funny games.

The languages used were simple, too—BASIC, C, and so on. Some systems used mostly by government organizations had huge machines called mainframes that ran languages such as FORTRAN and COBOL. A few database programs, such as DBase III and DBase IV, existed. For a desktop computer user who wanted nothing more than a word processing program for documents and a couple of games, all these extra language features did not exist, were neither required nor known.

If you asked most people about computer security in those days, the only answer you would get was about the physical security of the machine in the office or home. Personally identifiable information (PII) such as Social Security Number (SSN) and date of birth did exist in some files, but nobody gave a second thought to losing that information or otherwise finding that it had been compromised. Universities even printed the SSNs on students' primary ID cards. Once in a while, a smart aleck stole credit card numbers in postal mail and used them, but the instances of extensive fraud—like what we have now—were rare.

Then came the era of Windows, Windows NT, and networking. The number of computing machines and the desktop machines exploded. Thanks to the ever-changing and improving technologies, the mainframes that occupied several thousand square feet of physical space slowly gave way to smaller units. As the explosion continued, hackers and attackers have found new ways to steal and smarter ways to dupe users to compromise a single system, a segment of a network, or even a complete network. To counter these attacks or hacking attempts, corporations have started reinventing their systems, reconfiguring software, and updating the login procedures for single computers and networks.

Along the way, new words like *phishing* and *whaling* have been introduced to identify the fraud. Even as governments and computing corporations were busy inventing new antifraud protection and technologies, hackers were getting smarter, too, and they used the same new technologies to invent worse methods to hack and steal. In the early days of Windows, Bill Gates even invited hackers to attend a meeting to share their methods in the hope that Microsoft could design software to avoid those attacks. At one point, people predicted that hacking attempts would end by a particular year, but so far, nothing has stopped hackers. They continue to come up with innovative ways to breach security. New hacking techniques, such as ransomware attacks, continue to be developed and make us wonder when, or even if, these attacks will end.

Although you may be happy with your systems and software with their increasing speeds and evolving technologies, you should never forget that someone is always watching what you do—even if the system is in your bedroom and not physically accessible to anyone. Shopping, checking for an address, finding out where to order a pizza, and almost everything else is online and uses the Internet. The cable that connects your computer to your Internet Service Provider (ISP) is not even required any longer because of the availability of Wi-Fi networks. We now also have more threats than before because most people carry phones and mobile devices such as tablets.

Before we delve deep into attacks, countermeasures, and cybersecurity, let's first talk about a few important terms in cybersecurity. In this chapter, we touch on the basics of cybersecurity: the terms, fundamentals of guarding the data, what to guard, how successful we can become in guarding, and how we can independently decide if the guards we deploy to counter the threats are really successful.

CIA-DAD

Before 1998, the United States Air Force came up with the concept of confidentiality in computing. After several iterations, they introduced a refined model of CIA-DAD to adequately cover topics of current day cybersecurity. But with the cyberattacks becoming increasingly numerous, we needed a set of rules for good security practice in the computer industry. Thus, the first Parkerian Model of six factors, or Hexad, was developed in 1998. The general consensus is that these are the rules for now but they'll continue to evolve as attackers and hacking attempts evolve. We can minimize the risk but may never really eliminate cyberattacks or the risks associated with hacking attempts.

Let's turn our attention to security fundamentals and the elements of the CIA-DAD triad (Figure 1-1).

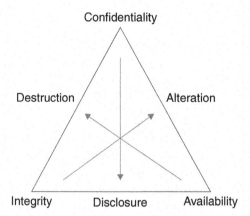

Figure 1-1 *CIA-DAD Triad*

Confidentiality

According to NIST, confidentiality is "preserving authorized restrictions on access and disclosure, including means for protecting personal privacy and proprietary information."

This term dictates that the data, service, or information is provided in a secure way. It does not mean that the information or data is provided to everyone who requests it. The information is provided to those who need it or who have a "need to know." Once such a person requests information or data, their credentials are verified. After credentials are confirmed as currently valid, the data or information is given to the person. For confidentiality to happen, the user must sign a document known as a non-disclosure agreement (NDA), as well as any other documents an organization requires.

The opposite of confidentiality is *disclosure*, which means the data or information is disclosed to everyone without the need to check their credentials. Once information or data falls into the wrong hands, anything can happen, including problems associated with lawsuits and a flurry of financial troubles.

Integrity

Integrity demands that the service is providing the data or files in the original format without any modifications. When modified, the information can become useless or sometimes even harmful. For example, imagine your blood test or other medical test data is available from a lab to your physician. If one or two numbers have changed in the report sent to the physician, the results are inaccurate, which can cause alarm to the patient. Therefore, data transmission—electronic or otherwise—must be correct, accurate, and unchanged. As with confidentiality, the information or data is provided to "need to know" persons. Integrity of electronic transmissions is achieved by adding a hash to files and providing additional metadata.

The opposite of integrity is *alteration* or changed/corrupted data.

Availability

Usually, service providers such as cloud providers or Internet service providers offer some promise for their services, such as whether the service can be provided 24x7x365 or is more limited during some periods like holidays. Availability demands that during the mutually agreed times, data is available without delay. Some information is available at any time of day (hospital service, medical data, websites selling products, and so one), but other information is provided only during office hours (for example, medical billing and auto repairs). Some information is also available via self-service, which means a person can go to the data or information source (online or offline) and use proper credentials to obtain information at any time. For this type of service, it is assumed that the service provider keeps their website active all the time. Amazon.com shopping and Netflix streaming are examples.

The opposite of availability is *destruction* or that the information is not available when requested.

Note that when any one of the three factors is maintained, the other two factors come into play as well. When a service is available, the information is provided confidentially to those who have a need to know, and the provided data is unchanged and is in the original required or requested format.

I-A-A-A

Another important concept in the cybersecurity field is identification, authentication, authorization, and auditing/accounting (IAAA). These words have a lot of significance because if security is weak on a network, anyone can log into the system and hack the data from the files. Identifying a person who has a "need to know" and letting that identified person confirm who they are before giving them access to the files or data are important processes. Earlier technologies allowed anonymous logins and file transfer protocols (FTP), and they were misused greatly to hack important data files, passwords, and such. Then came IAAA, which is described in detail in the following sections.

Identification

Identification refers to finding out who is the person trying to log in to a server or system. Does the person physically exist or is it an anonymous user or an automated program trying to log in with a stolen username and password?

Identification in an organization can usually be done with a corporate ID card or some other credential issued to users after verifying proper government-issued documentation, such as a driver's license, passport, or SSN, and establishing an NDA policy between the issuer and the user. Several other types of physical identification can be issued, such as an access card with a chip or simple picture ID. In the past, identification cards used to have the user's PII, such as SSN, printed on them, but with the increase in cyberattacks based on PII, SSNs are now replaced by random-number employee IDs.

This kind of physical identification falls into the class of *what an employee/user has.*

Authentication

If an employee/user is able to demonstrate with proper identification who they are, next is the step of *verifying or validating that user* to make sure the user indeed exists and the presented identity belongs to that user. This can be done by a human guard stationed at the entrance to the facility or asking the user to supply a personal identification number (PIN) or some other form of proof. Access cards usually require a code of at least four digits to be entered. The code is matched with the issued card to confirm the user's identify and allow the user to log in. In some cases, a second form of authentication is used or required for better protection. A system with this additional step is known as multifactor authentication (MFA). One example is sending a text message with a one-time password/PIN (OTP) to the user's registered phone number. The OTP is valid only for a few minutes and cannot be reused. Any mismatch between the number sent and the number entered results in a refusal to confirm the identity of the user. To prevent damage to the system, the user is disallowed or the account is locked after a few unsuccessful attempts.

This kind of authentication falls into the class of *what the user knows*—a PIN or another number that confirms the user's identity.

Authorization

Once the user has provided proper identity and it has been confirmed and authenticated, a user is allowed to successfully go into a facility physically or log in to a system or network. Now it's a question of what the authenticated user should be allowed to view, read, or write. Or what access should a logged-in user be allowed?

The access allowed to a logged-in user with proper identity and authentication is known as authorization. Authorization depends on what the user really needs to know for their day-to-day work. Simply because a user has a proper identity and has provided proof for authentication, they are not necessarily permitted full access to everything. In other words, users are given access according to the rules of least privilege, which means a user has the access required for their work—nothing less and nothing more. It also means a user may not have administrative privileges to enter a server room physically or go to a system registry to modify settings or install a new program.

Authorization can be given uniformly to all users or at branch/department level as required. Any special authorizations need paperwork completed, background checks done, and signatures taken.

After access is granted, users who log in or enter an area can do what they like—though we expect the users to do what they are only authorized to do per organizational policies. For example, a user who is allowed access to a facility can go to the printer area and collect printed material that does not belong to them or log in to any computer that is not allotted to them in their workspace. Thus, there remains another step to find out what the properly identified, authenticated, and authorized person is actually doing—which is discussed in the following section.

Auditing or Accounting

Tracking what a user does with their given permissions is known as auditing or accounting. Accounting and auditing are done by examining the log files or recorded actions of the user. In a physical building, the recording can be done by a video surveillance camera or the software that records entry and exit times.

Note that the auditing by a third-party person who is not affiliated with the organization is preferred to auditing by a user who works for the organization. By hiring a third-party auditor, any favoritism or partiality can be easily avoided.

Regular reviewing of logs and physical access records demonstrates how a user is correctly using their authorizations and not "moving" vertically or horizontally crossing their given boundaries. When auditing or accounting raises any red flags, the authorizations of users need to be readjusted, and employees are warned of their encroachments into security. Likewise, the organizational permissions or conditions that allowed the user to cross their boundaries—for example, drive or file permissions that allow anyone to read or write—are adjusted not to allow the users to access the files or data.

Defense in Depth

Defense in depth is the term used for employing defense or security for protecting information with multiple controls all the way from the top level to the very bottom level to make sure that the data or information remains safe. The National Institute of Standards and Technology (NIST) defines *defense in depth* as "The application of multiple countermeasures in a layered or stepwise manner to achieve security objectives. The methodology involves layering heterogeneous security technologies, methods or controls in the common attack vectors to ensure that attacks missed by one technology, method or controls are caught by another."

Defense in depth tells users that security needs to be employed at every level so that if security at one level fails, it may be able to catch the intruders at another level. In the corporate world, defense in depth is employed by various means. Physical controls or videos monitor users' entrance and exits, computer log files record the users' login times and actions, programs prevent users from installing unnecessary software, antivirus programs prevent installing or copying of virus files, email programs require identification and verification via public key infrastructure (PKI), and the data or server rooms require users to have an additional access card that is issued with further security clearance. Governmental departments used to give a security clearance by checking the users' activities once a year or so, but as of the beginning of 2020, security clearance is a daily process of tracking users' activities on the Internet in general and on social media websites such as Facebook, Snapchat, and TikTok. Thus, defense in depth works in tandem with a continuous process of tracking a user. Security has no end point or phase because hackers and intruders continue to invent new methods to compromise security as the technology provides newer machines, facilities, and equipment.

Hardware and Software Security

The first line in defense of cybersecurity is always the user (or YOU). Hardware and software come next. Although the two things work independently, they are indispensable to each other.

Hardware security has two parts: individual system security and wired or wireless network security. Individual system security depends on the type of processor, the programs used, and the basic core safety of the operating system that runs with the processor. Known vulnerabilities of a processor, memory chips, and even the additional drive or disks attached to a system are all causes of worry in terms of security. Systems we use at home are connected to our ISP's network either via Wi-Fi or a wired connection. Wi-Fi requires a router and modem, which need to be secure with good passwords to limit or prevent any hacking attempts. Loose and easily guessed or default passwords are a cause for concern. The protocols (WPA, WEP, TKIP, and so on) we use for setting up the Wi-Fi router need to be looked at closely. Likewise, a lack of a firewall on these hardware devices can also make it easy for a hacker to break our individual networks.

Networked systems have their own problems with open ports, default passwords, switches, hubs, the router, balancers, and so on. If the organization maintains its own web servers, how secure are they? How secure are their server and ports? Are there some ports open, or do they allow anonymous logins? If the organization is expecting a large traffic flow on their web server, can their single server manage the traffic or would it need a load balancer to control the traffic? Usually a trusted computing base (TCB) is established with a standard setup for all users. This baseline setup decides which programs are given to the users by default (for example, Word, Excel, Outlook) and which are not. TCB usually consists of fully vetted end-user machines, application servers, web servers, database servers and clients, and so on.

Software security has two distinct problems: bugs arising from bad code are either syntactic or semantic errors and problems from attacks such as SQL injection, bad software design, and memory leaks. Poor coding with errors, weak cohesion and strong coupling between modules, not scanning the software, not testing the software for bugs, and regression errors are also causes of concern in software security. Logic bombs introduced purposefully by disgruntled employees are hard to find, but code reviews can clear those errors.

In general, software security must be included right from the design stage all the way to the very end of deployment in the software development life cycle. If the organization is developing software in-house, how good is the development team with security? Or if the organization is purchasing the software off the shelf, is the third-party software good enough? Is it tested to withstand a vulnerability-based attack? Does the third-party software get regular updates, known as patches and service packs, to fix any vulnerabilities? These factors need to be taken into account to avoid any hacks. A security reference monitor, part of the operating system, usually allows for logins and access between users and systems and the associated log files for auditing.

A generic developmental cycle in software has three different machines or environments known as development, test, and production servers. A programmer writing code or checking a new third-party software to be purchased is only allowed do these things on the developmental machine and servers. Once development is complete, the code in executable form is transferred to a test machine, where an independent tester takes the lead to check functional requirements of the program. Once development and testing have passed, a code review might be conducted to remove any logic bombs or some possibly visible semantic errors in code. At this point, additional security tests for vulnerabilities are performed. Only after these successful phases is the program deployed on the production server.

Firewalls, Access Controls, and Access Control Lists

Firewalls and access control lists (ACL) are either software or hardware. Firewalls have rules that can be set up, edited, or changed depending on the requirements. While blocking traffic, ACLs allow some traffic based on a routing table or some other rule. A default firewall rule that allows all traffic should always be at the bottom of a rules list after filtering out most of the traffic with various other rules. However, you have to make sure the rules are set up rather than assuming that they are already set up. Setting up rules alone would not complete the security of a system or software. The gist is to check the firewall logs on a daily basis to find any activity or noise that is trying to cause any trouble.

ACLs are a set of inbound and outbound rules defined for controlling network traffic to grant or deny access to certain digital environments such as files and networks. ACLs use this set of rules to filter traffic or limit user access.

ACLs are mainly two types: filesystem ACL and networking ACL. Filesystem ACL limits access privileges to files and/or directories, and they work at the operating system level to tell which users can access the system and files and what they can do with those files (read/write/execute). Networking ACLs work on the computer network that contains routers, switches, and other equipment, and they decide which type of traffic can flow on the network and which activity is denied (implicitly or explicitly). In either type of ACL , a log is created when a user tries to access the resources. The log is helpful for the system administrator to check what is happening on the organizational files and network resources.

An organization dealing with various products can also implement an ACL in their offices for physical access. Physical access is decided by the clearance levels required to access an asset ("the need to know"). For example, even the most experienced programmer who worked for 10 years in an organization may not need to enter the data room where the physical machines are stored for data storage. Likewise, most employees don't need to access a plenum space in an office, prohibited areas, print servers, or the fire/water safety controllers or the HVAC room. These factors of who can access what is usually decided by the company, with least privilege and need-to-know rules depending on the policies set by the company's data custodians and its CEO.

Physical Security

Next comes the importance of physical security. Does an organization allow all people to come and go freely into the building? For example, university buildings allow anyone to enter and exit during office hours. There were several reports of panhandlers entering a university building during office hours to steal food and lightweight equipment. In those cases, security wasn't very tight.

Physical buildings also need security from physical attacks by road traffic, which can be handled by installing barriers, placing guards at the entrance, and so on. Contractors or people claiming to be contractors can be a threat when they drive into the office facility in a large truck loaded with explosives, as happened in the bombing of Oklahoma City's Alfred P. Murrah Federal Building in 1995. Video surveillance cameras, recorders, and rotating gates or doors help slow the traffic and avoid piggybacking. Advanced controls with biomedical equipment also provide extra security. Data rooms with automatically locking doors and emergency lights on power failures are important to consider.

If an organization has an office in a state like California where there is a greater threat of earthquakes, floods, and heavy rains, proper physical guards need to be in place to ensure safety of the personnel, assets, data, other equipment, and the office building itself. The design of physical security needs to anticipate even things that may happen without warning, such as pandemics like the spread of COVID-19, because using VPN for virtual offices or teleworking will be the norm sooner or later. In these cases, proper digital or physical signatures are necessary for better safety of both the employees and the organization.

Users are a primary contributor to the downfall of security. It doesn't matter how much cybersecurity is implemented by an organization and how smart the programs employed are if the users aren't vigilant. This is the basic reason why the first line of defense is always YOU.

It is important that you keep your eyes open at all times to make sure you know what is happening around you and report any suspicious activity. This is known as "if you see something, say something" rule. When an organization employs a person and gives access to that person, they assume that employee is honest and will follow the mutually agreed upon rules. The organization also assumes that the employees follow the rules they read and sign in the NDA. Employees, contractors, and vendors entering the facility have to apply due diligence and not allow piggybacking and misuse of resources and assets.

Everyone has a role to play in security, although the CEO, chief security officer, and information and protection security officers often get the blame when something goes wrong. However, each of us is an equal stakeholder, and we need to practice, advise, and learn every day about unexpected attacks and contribute to help the organization. We should remember that objects/assets (what) have permissions (how), and the users (who) have rights (how). These terms mean we design a secure environment for how assets/objects use permissions or how the objects and assets are used and what rights a user has when accessing a resource—IT or otherwise.

No matter how hard a corporation tries to help with security, users have a limited memory and can only remember a few things on a permanent basis. Therefore, it is very important to train employees regularly about security, including active shooters, terrorist attacks, natural disasters, and fire drills. Training helps people remember what they've learned when an attack actually happens. Training also should be enforced with strict rules, and it is important to remove both computer and building access from employees who do not follow the policies of training and retraining.

Practical Example of a Server Security in an Organization

Let's consider an example of how corporate security is set up. Tables 1-1 through 1-5 illustrate how we can set up layers of security to achieve defense in depth. Each layer has an extensive framework of rules and regulations that must be followed. Though each layer is cohesive and acts independently, all units in a corporation work with each other with a common goal of a highly secure environment because security is everyone's responsibility. Note that this is a simplified example and can expand and shrink depending on the size of the corporation, needed security, the location of the site, and many other factors—both locally and on a larger scale.

Table 1-1   *Physical Security Aspects in an Organization*

Item	Why Is It Important?	Remediation
Gate and door entries	Avoids forced entries and piggybacking, helps block unwanted intruders.	Implement access cards with a PIN, station a guard to check manually.
Server rooms	Protection of servers, data, and personnel.	Implement additional card access, closed doors at all times.
Lock and key for files or records	Corporate data protection, theft of PII.	Use locks and keys and advise users to always lock unused cupboards or overhead storage bins.
Computers, printers, phone, or fax	Equipment is expensive and valuable for daily work, and it isn't easy to replace.	Buy insurance for equipment, locks and keys with a chain, electronic lock protection.
Fire and smoke	Danger for all working people, suffocation, hardware parts can be damaged from change in humidity levels.	Install alarms, avoid storing flammable and unapproved items in office.
Lighting inside	Bad lighting can cause physical eye problems for employees and may encourage theft.	Install adequate lighting, automatic lighting that turns on and off when people enter and exit premises.

Item	Why Is It Important?	Remediation
Inventory and store-rooms	Missing or stolen equipment can be a problem. Bad log records cannot trace inventory—who is borrowing what from the inventory and where the equipment is used and to whom it is allotted.	Use closed-circuit cameras, video and audio recordings, up-to-date logs/records of equipment being checked in and checked out with proper signatures of customers.
Door locks/blind spot mirrors	Dangers of being locked in or out or having secure doors unlocked due to power failures, shootings, and other dangers to human lives.	Make sure the correct type of doors are installed. Regularly check mirror and video camera (pan/zoom) alignments.
First aid kits and emergency supplies	Not being installed, or regularly checked, or not restocked results in danger to human lives.	Check regularly, update with portable pacemakers. Educate employees how to use them.
Alternate sites	If not up to date, disaster recovery is difficult. Data can be lost. Can result in financial burden.	Keep data up to date on all alternate sites. Check regularly with a tabletop or live exercise.
Other physical assets	These help run the business smoothly.	

Table 1-2 *Software Security Aspects in an Organization*

Item	Why Is It Important?	Remediation
Software copies, if any (repositories)	Lost copies are hard to restore. Can fail an independent audit. Loss of copyrights and possible duplication.	Install software repositories, update and maintain copies by version regularly. Save hard disks or USB drives with software copies. Label drives correctly.
Removable media	Loss can cause data loss and financial penalties, jail time, and other repercussions.	Protect data in transit and at rest. Maintain a secure safe and bank for removable media.
Firewalls	Weak or default rules can allow viruses and malware to get in.	Update/create firewall rules, update software, watch the logs daily.
Development/test copies	Loss can destroy basic software design idea, requirements, testing rules, and results.	Maintain separate repositories by version, check repositories for safety regularly.

Item	Why Is It Important?	Remediation
Production copy	Loss can result in financial doom and piracy. Hard to recover and involves lawsuits and lengthy legal processes.	Maintain separate repositories by version, check repositories for safety regularly. Patent or copyright the software as required.
Antivirus	Not installing up-to-date protection and new patches leaves software vulnerable against new viruses and attacks.	Choose good antivirus software, update regularly with patches, watch logs daily.
Log files	Loss of log files or not maintaining time synchronization can result in attacks being ignored.	Create code to send email to system administrators when there is any log file change. Track daily.
VPN, networking software	For teleworking and remote personnel, VPN should be up to date with enough connections and security to prevent risk loss/theft of data.	Update the software. Install patches. Invest in a good software package with signed contracts.
Trusted baseline image	Users install unnecessary software, exposing more vulnerabilities. Trusted baseline image allows least privilege uniformly across all machines.	Create the baseline after all tests are complete. Update accordingly but keep checking individual machines randomly and warn users about excess privileges.
Data and other PII files	Loss of data can derail a corporation with a flurry of problems from law enforcement, government, and lawyers.	Maintain due diligence and due care; keep security up to date, watch data in transit, at rest, and in use. Take all precautions as required per local and federal laws.
Other software assets	Vendor supplied, in-house software is hard to replace and may need more spending.	Keep vendor contracts up to date. Maintain all assets per regulations and expect the unexpected to happen and be ready.

Table 1-3   *Hardware Security Aspects in an Organization*

Item	Why Is It Important?	Remediation
Laptops and desktops	Loss, degradation, replacement, and updates are expensive, time-consuming, and need several hours of labor/contracts.	Keep equipment locked with physical locks and keys. Obtain and maintain up-to-date signed agreements from users for accepting the equipment.
Cables, bricks, and chargers	Loss can result in a minor financial burden. These also often need replacement due to heavy use.	Be ready with additional inventory for replacement, for non-functioning or burned out units.

Item	Why Is It Important?	Remediation
Access card or other readers	Unauthorized access can result in various issues like tampering with email and files. Access should be only for permitted and approved users who sign NDAs. Card readers and associated software must be up to date.	Lock systems when not used with access cards or passwords/PINs.
Printers or plotters	Important papers can be stolen. Printers/plotters/supplies are at a risk for damage/theft.	Allow printer access with access card or login only. Use chains and locks for expensive printers/plotters and supplies.
Special phones	Video phones and VOIP are hard to set up, are expensive, and have messages stored in memory. People with disabilities may use special phones that are very expensive.	Install good versions; maintain and update software required regularly. People with disabilities may need extra care of their communication equipment.
Office supplies	Though sometimes cheap, some are expensive, such as the plotter supplies, ink, and cartridges.	Track with logs who is using what and check logs regularly of the needed and depleted supplies.
Servers (DB, network, and so on)	By far, these are the most expensive to replace or buy new. They also need special software.	Invest in a separate team that works on these machines and their security.
Routers, modems, and so on	These network components are the bread and butter of the network.	Should regularly be checked and updated. Logs should be read daily for any possible trouble and malware attacks. Passwords should be enforced and maintained with strict corporate password policies.
Other hardware assets	Hardware will continue to evolve and need investment to keep pace with the future.	Update as required, but do take care of data on older hard disks and other devices and follow corporate policy for data protection, preservation, and destruction.

Table 1-4   *Network Security Aspects in an Organization*

Item	Why Is It Important?	Remediation
LAN/WAN	Broken network inhibits data flow and causes financial losses, data loss, and innumerable other related issues.	Invest in good networking infrastructure and topology and update regularly.
Antivirus	Not installing up-to-date antivirus protection and new patches does not protect against methods of attack. This software is different from normal antivirus software installed on each machine.	Choose good antivirus software, update regularly with patches, watch logs daily.
Firewalls	Network firewalls, routing tables, and other safety features need to be updated regularly to avoid loss or theft of data.	Implement firewall rules, update regularly, and watch the logs.
Other network security	Networks will continue to evolve and need investment to keep pace with the future (fiber optics, new topologies and networks, and so on).	Update as required and follow corporate policy for data protection, preservation, and destruction.

Table 1-5   *Environmental Security Aspects in an Organization*

Item	Why Is It Important?	Remediation
Barriers all around the building	Vehicles can ram into a building or crash, either accidentally or intentionally.	Barriers protect the building from severe damage. Orange or red paint warns users to stay away and not to park around these items.
Surroundings	Dark, empty, dimly lit surroundings are a cause for concern for attacks, theft, and shootings.	Install light fixtures (solar powered, auto shut off) around the building. Alarms should be available to be activated in case of dangers. Regularly check the alarms and make sure they work through all seasons of the year.
Roads to the building	Clear and drivable roads without potholes or thick plant and tree growth on either side. No long and winding roads.	Visibility should be clear with straight roads without hindrances. Regularly check and re-surface.
Video surveillance	Serves as evidence or proof in a court of law. Can record very important information without human interaction.	Adjust pan and zoom of the camera, examine the recordings daily. Update broken lenses, dysfunctional cameras (due to weather or otherwise).

Item	Why Is It Important?	Remediation
Fire extinguishers	Help control fires and save human lives and equipment.	Should be examined, updated, or replaced per local fire department laws—usually once every six months or year. Work with the local codes and regulations to update.
Water sprinklers for fire	All rooms must have functional sprinklers to save human lives and buildings in case of fire.	Test these regularly, replace dysfunctional units and update.
Natural disasters	These are unexpected and unavoidable but risk and damage can be minimized with proper plans.	Buy insurance for these events; establish a chain of command to make sure all human lives are safe.
Unexpected attacks	Terrorist or pandemic attacks cannot be expected ahead.	Be prepared for active shooters and terrorist attacks. Train employees regularly.
Physical safety	Human life is irreplaceable and the first priority. Ensuring physical safety reduces financial burden on the corporation.	Establish a chain of command; train and retrain users regularly, conduct tabletop exercises to make sure all human life is protected.
Parking lot/signs/fences	Fences, signs, and lot numbering help users find their vehicles; they also discourage intruders from entering the premises and otherwise help with safety.	Posted signs and warnings should be stern and clear. Fences and borders should be checked regularly and damages fixed.
Other environmental	Rules can change from time to time and from county to county or state to state.	Discuss with local municipalities and counties/districts to see what is required to ensure safety.

In this book, we only discuss the database and software security in detail, but it is important to know that factors such as those listed in the preceding tables contribute to security for software and databases because a single lapse can directly affect databases or software regardless of whether they are small or big or developed in-house or acquired off the shelf. Remember, security is the responsibility of *everyone*. Failing to educate and train can be the fault of a corporation, but the fault rests equally on each person if they fail to report anything suspicious. As we previously stated, the rule in security is, "if you see something, say something." Sometimes following simple rules can make a lot of difference in our lives.

Summary

Cybersecurity is everyone's responsibility and has the basics of confidentiality, integrity, and availability. Secure access to assets is defined with the process of identification, authentication, and authorization. Once access is given to a user, they are audited for their accountability in their day-to-day work. Several layers of security are put in place in an organization with various controls to achieve defense in depth. Defense in depth helps in such a way that if one or more controls fail, another control can possibly detect a breach or threat.

Security considerations for hardware and software are different. Physical security of the hardware and software assets is important too. Access control decides who can access what assets in an organization. Access controls can be for files on an operating system, inbound and outbound traffic on a network, or physical access to buildings and assets. The roles of users are important too because a corporation decides what role each user is given and access can be dependent on that given role. In this chapter, we also demonstrated various aspects of security in an organization.

Chapter 1 Questions

1. What are the three factors of a security triad? What are their opposite factors?

2. If a company has lost all its data from repositories and cannot find backup copies, what factor or security triad does the company violate?

3. If an approved and authorized user requests a file and finds that the contents of the file have been modified, what security factor have the changes in the file violated?

4. Who is the best person to do accounting or auditing in a corporation?

5. Why is authentication required when a user can scan their identity card to enter a secure building?

6. What is the importance of logs in IT and cybersecurity?

7. When natural disasters are unavoidable, why should a corporation worry about them?

8. How should a corporation implement physical fire safety for its buildings?

9. Do corporations really save development, test, and production copies of software?

10. Who is ultimately responsible for security in an IT organization?

Answers to Chapter 1 Questions

1. Confidentiality, integrity, and availability (CIA). The opposite factors of the security triad are disclosure, alteration, and destruction (DAD).

2. Availability. Because all the data is destroyed, the company cannot supply information or data to legitimate users.

3. The integrity factor is violated because the file contents were modified.

4. A third-party independent, certified, and licensed auditor is the best person to conduct an audit. Such a person can ensure that the audit is frank and devoid of favoritism.

5. Authentication helps double-check the person as the genuine person who was issued the identity card. Usually this involves the user remembering a PIN or code to enter and a way to prove that the person who entered the PIN is indeed the person who was issued the access card.

6. Logs and log files provide entries and details of intruders, attacks, and the time of entry and exit. Examining logs daily can demonstrate details of who is entering with authorization and who is an intruder. Firewall, database, and network logs also show any entries to demonstrate excessive logins, denial of service, or attacks coming from external IPs.

7. It is true that natural disasters cannot be avoided but the first priority of any disaster is to save human life. Establishing a chain of command, training and retraining employees regularly regarding how to handle natural disasters, and contacting employees when a disaster strikes to make sure of their safety are all very important.

8. Fire safety can be achieved by installing extinguishers and a sprinkling system but you must also consult local fire departments to determine their codes and laws. The fire department can advise the best possible solutions to be implemented.

9. Yes, corporations really save their development, test, and production software copies separately on code repositories by version and subversion numbers. All are well documented in each environment.

10. Corporate cybersecurity is the responsibility of everyone, although CEO and security officers are the owners and custodians who take care of implementing the policies and rules. This is the main reason why corporate security follows the rule of "if you see something, say something."

Security Details

The Four Attributes: Encrypt, Compress, Index, and Archive

Data or information falling into the wrong hands is the biggest worry for any corporation because such spillage can cause a lot of trouble from customers, local and federal governments, and hungry lawyers. Protect the data encryption or changing the format of data—without modifying the data itself—has become a necessity. Many operating systems allow files to be encrypted, compressed, indexed, and archived for various reasons, such as security, disk space, easy retrieval, and storage. When managed correctly, these four processes are important components of cybersecurity. In this chapter, we discuss each of these factors in detail.

Figure 2-1 shows properties of a file in the Windows operating system. If you click the **Advanced** button on the General tab, advanced attributes of a file are pulled out. The right side of Figure 2-1 shows the four attributes for a file and the information in the file. Every operating system or program can implement these four attributes to a file structure for data protection. Some of these are applied automatically by the system when a file is created, whereas the user needs to add some as required.

We will now turn our attention to these four attributes.

Encryption

Encryption, which addresses the confidentiality factor in the security triad (see Chapter 1), is a form of mixing and mingling actual data contents with other known contents, such as a key, to make the data unreadable to hackers and attackers. Some simple encryption methods use an algorithm and may not even use a key. The earliest form of encryption was used by Julius Caesar, who used a "plus three" shift method. In that method, he added three letters to each letter of his messages. For example, A became D, F became I, and so on. But when he reached X and added three, the result was out of bounds of the alphabet.

Caesar made that up by rolling back to A after the plus-three character reached Z. X became A, Y became B, and Z became C. Caesar's system worked until the system was found out. Since Caesar's time, encryption has come a long way with a variety of algorithms, the introduction of salt, and many other details that address the problems associated with the algorithms. Windows BitLocker is an example of full-volume encryption for data protection. (Read more in the "Encryption, Algorithms" section later in this chapter.)

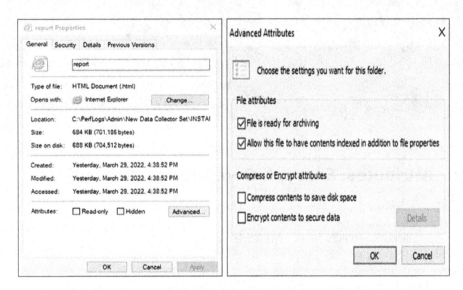

Figure 2-1   *Properties and Advanced Attributes in the Windows Operating System*

Compression

By definition, compression is a mechanism for using fewer bits to process or store information. Compression is generally lossless or lossy. Lossless compression removes bits by identifying and eliminating statistical redundancy. As the name implies, it does not lose any bits or information such as unnecessary metadata. Lossy compression removes unnecessary bits or information from original data.

For data in transmission or for data at rest, compression is very useful because with smaller file sizes, the transmission and storage can be much faster. There is a trade-off in lossy compression for reducing the size and removing the information. Compression in general has a negative effect on the processing power. Every file we read from the system or write to the system needs to be uncompressed and compressed, respectively.

Windows NTFS file system is Lempel-Ziv compression. This is a *lossless* compression algorithm, which means that no data is lost when compressing and decompressing the file. Compression on a NTFS file system is also done transparently, which means the applications that use the files would not recognize a file as compressed. The other problem with compression is the size and time required to compress. Microsoft warns that trying to compress files that are very large is time consuming and may result in errors.

NTFS file system provides compression attributes for each file, which can be used with a checkbox, as shown in Figure 2-1.

Indexing

Indexes help find a file or a group of files that contains specific information. A typical index one might be familiar with is the thumb index in a dictionary, which helps you move through the order of alphabet. Instead of going through the pages one at a time to find a word starting with the letter K, a thumb index enables you to jump directly to the start of words that begin with K.

Databases use indexes to pull out information quickly. Indexes can be single or multiple indexes. Some databases have clustered indexes in which the data is completely sorted per that created index. Others use non-clustered indexes, which means the database remains unsorted and in arbitrary order, but the indexes are applied to pull the data quickly.

Indexes use logical ordering, and the physical ordering of the data in tables of a database is different from the logical ordering of the data per the index. Indexes gather the cataloging information with metadata to pull a file or data from a file. Explained in another way, a clustered index is used to define the order or to sort the data by alphabetical order as in a dictionary. A non-clustered index keeps the index data at one place and records at another place. The index has pointers to the position of the database records.

Notice in Figure 2-1 that indexing is an automatic choice applied to all NTFS files on Windows. It is easy to disable an index on the NTFS file system, but once it's disabled, it will be harder and more time consuming to find the files that are not indexed. There are a variety of indexes such as bitmap, sparse, dense, reverse, primary, secondary, and so on.

Archiving

Assume you have a number of files created on your machine either at your office or home, and you don't use those files regularly. They can be temporary files and one-time-use and destroy-type files. Because the hard disk capacity on most computers these days extends to gigabytes and terabytes, we do not give much consideration to the size of files we create or the files we don't even use.

Unused files can be combined into one folder called the archive folder, and several archive folders can be further consolidated into another folder. In Windows OS, the folder can be assigned the archive option for that folder only or for that folder and all subfolders below that level. Archiving can also save the space on disks and uses the lossless and lossy compression methods discussed previously.

In short, by archiving, we condense or zip all unused (or not frequently used) files/folders into another folder to be saved for the future. Once archived, the files can be easily retrieved at any time. A variety of programs like zip, gzip, tar, and 7zip are available for use on various operating systems for archiving and zipping/unzipping files.

Encryption, Algorithms

As discussed earlier, the main purpose of encryption is to create a ciphertext or jumbled up unreadable text from the plaintext. The ciphertext can be transmitted or stored for future use. When plaintext is converted to ciphertext, normally a key or some value like "salt" is used. When the data is retrieved, the end user has to employ a decryption method to convert the ciphertext back to plaintext. A great variety of algorithms, methods, and types are available to do this ciphering and deciphering.

There are two basic types of encryption or cryptographic methods: symmetric and asymmetric. In both these methods, a "key" or a string of numbers generated randomly is used to create ciphertext.

Symmetric algorithms use one key to encrypt and decrypt. Data encrypted by one key can be decrypted with the same key. It also means everyone dealing with the data must know the key, and all those who know the key must keep it secret. In other words, in symmetric algorithms, the secret key holds all the important information for both encryption and decryption. Once the key is lost or known publicly, everything is exposed and the data can become public. Trust between parties is a very important factor in symmetric encryption. Examples of symmetric encryption include Digital Encryption Standard (DES), 3DES (an improved version of DES), and Advanced Encryption Standard (AES). In symmetric encryption for N uses, a total of $N*(N-1)/2$ keys is required to maintain secrecy.

Asymmetric algorithms use two keys, known as public and private keys, which are mathematically connected/related to each other. The private key and public keys are given to each person who needs to know the data or information. The public keys of all people are put on a global address list (GAL), but the private keys are secretly held by users and never disclosed. The gist of asymmetric algorithms is that the data that is encrypted with one key can only be decrypted with the other key. If Bob is encrypting data with his private key, anyone can decrypt the data with Bob's public key. But assume for a moment that Bob encrypts the data with his public key. In this case, to decrypt the data, someone needs Bob's private key, which is known only to Bob. It implies that nobody, except Bob, can decrypt the data and read it. In the asymmetric method of encryption, because each user has two keys, we need only $2*N$ keys for N number of users. If Bob wants to encrypt data for David only, then Bob can encrypt the data with David's public key. Now, if this encrypted data (that used David's public key) falls into the wrong hands of Mary or Susan, they will not be able to decrypt the data because they need David's private key. Rivest-Shamir-Adleman (RSA) algorithm is one example of the asymmetric method, which is used in emails and other ways of exchanging information. RSA is also called public key encryption algorithm. How the public key infrastructure (PKI) implements the keys is described in detail in the following section.

Public Key Infrastructure

Public key infrastructure (PKI) in a broad sense consists of roles, policies, software, and procedures that are used to create, manage, distribute, use, store, and revoke digital certificates (X.509 standard). PKI also is used in public key encryption that helps in transfer of data or information that is widely used with personally identifiable information (PII) in e-commerce, Internet banking, and email. It can also be implemented in situations where simple passwords are currently used with weak authentication methods and where second or third proof is needed to confirm the identity of senders and to validate the data in transit. When used in cryptography, a PKI *binds* public keys with respective entities (people or organizations). The binding is done with registration and issuance of certificates from a certificate authority (CA). Certificate binding can be either an automated or manual process. If it is done automatically, it uses secure certificate enrollment or certificate management protocol (CMP).

A certification registration body is called a *registration authority* (RA). An RA is responsible for accepting requests for digital certificates and checking the person or organization making the request before authenticating the applicant. After the applicant is authenticated, the request is approved or rejected. The requesting person or organization should have credentials that are uniquely identifiable within the CA domain before a certificate can be issued. Note that the RAs do not have the same signing authority as a CA and only manage the vetting and provisioning of certificates.

Microsoft has a different PKI situation. The RA functionality is offered by Microsoft Certificate Services or through Active Directory Certificate Services, both of which may use certificate templates. Solution providers and others who are not associated with Microsoft PKI solutions have their own RA component.

Invalidation of previously issued invalid or lost certificates is done by certification revocation. In general, a PKI dealing with digital certificates has a CA; an RA; a centrally located directory where keys are stored; a management system to retrieve, store, and deliver certificates; and the policy governing all these rules. The certification validation authority uses a certificate revocation list for checking and verifying the validity of the certificates. The policy should be made public so anyone who wants to test vulnerabilities of the PKI structure can analyze, test, and check the associated certificates. PKI is used in encryption, email with digital signatures, authentication, smart card login with a PIN (what you have and what you know), and many other applications.

Email Security Example

When two parties use a symmetric key to securely exchange information, both parties use the same key and depend on trust between both. The key holds the secrecy for confidentiality. If the key is disclosed or known to others, the data is considered disclosed. Also, as users increase, the number of keys in symmetric encryption becomes large $[N*(N-1)/2]$, and the effort to keep a large number of keys becomes extremely difficult for both users and the organization. For example, for 250 users exchanging email, symmetric encryption demands 31,125 keys. This is where asymmetric key structure can work much better.

In asymmetric key structure, each user needs just two keys: one private key for the user's personal use (kept secret) and one public key that everyone can know. The public key of any user is put on a GAL and can be accessed by anyone. A large company that issues access cards usually makes them work for the building entrance and computer use. Such cards have digital certificate details embedded by design for the user. The certificate contains the public and private keys. When a user is issued a new certificate, the user has to publish their public key on the GAL. Once that is done, secure email communication becomes easier.

Figure 2-2 shows how this is done. Assume Tom and Robert are exchanging email messages in a secure way. Tom and Robert both have valid certificates that hold two keys per person. The private key is secret, and neither Tom nor Robert discloses their private keys to anyone. However, both Tom and Robert share their public keys on a database named GAL. In other words, every person has their public key published on GAL but they hold their private key in secret. Now, we know that when a message is encrypted with one key, it can only be decrypted with the other key. As shown in Figure 2-2, there are two ways Tom can send a message to Robert. In the first way (noted with number 1), Tom uses Robert's public key to encrypt the message he wants to send. This is possible because Robert's public key is already published on GAL and is available to all. Because Tom encrypted the message with Robert's public key, only Robert can open the message to read it if he uses his private key. Robert has his private key stored on his computer or access card along with a PIN. When he tries to open the encrypted message, the software asks for the PIN and uses Robert's private key to decrypt the message.

Let's assume that the message went to David's email box. Can David read the message? To read the message David would need Robert's private key. Because the private key is never shared, David cannot open the message or read it. It also means nobody except Robert can read the message, thereby guaranteeing confidentiality of the message. In another scenario, what if Tom encrypts a message with his own public key? To read that message, a person would need Tom's private key. That means nobody but Tom can read that message. This is the gist of PKI with private and public keys.

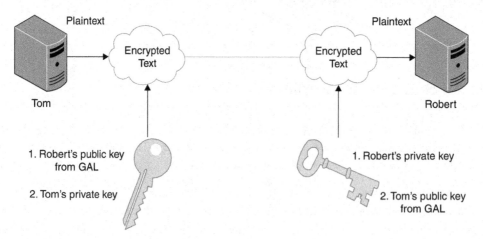

Figure 2-2   *Secure Email Exchange with PKI*

But what if Tom is trying to send a message to a group of people who should all be able to read the message? That is the second scenario shown in Figure 2-2 (numbered with 2). Instead of encrypting the message with everyone else's public keys, Tom now simply encrypts the message with his own private key. When the group of people get that message, they need Tom's public key to read the message. Because Tom's public key is available from GAL, anyone can read the message.

Imagine Tom is actually sending the message to 10 different colleagues. It would be impossible for Tom to encrypt the message with all 10 people's public keys, and it would look ridiculous. In this case, PKI uses a combination of asymmetric and symmetric key encryption, which is described in the next few paragraphs.

First, a random symmetric key is generated for all recipients. The message is encrypted with this symmetric key. Then the random symmetric key is encrypted with the public keys of recipients. Each user is then sent the encrypted message and the encrypted symmetric key. When a user opens the message, they would first decrypt the symmetric key with their own private key. With the decrypted symmetric key, the recipient can now decrypt the message itself. Assuming that we have a file named "myData.dat," with openssl we can do the following:

```
Openssl cms -encrypt -in myData.dat -out encryptedData.cms -recip
David.cert -recip John.cert -recip Friend3.cert
```

This can add as many certificates as required.

Then just email the "encryptedData.cms" to David, John, friend3, and others whose certificates you included in the **openssl** command shown. Note that the certificates are the public certificates of John, David, and other friends you know.

When your friend John receives the "encryptedData.cms" file, John could do the following to decrypt.

```
Openssl cms -decrypt -in encryptedData.cms -recip john.cert -inkey
john-private.pem -out myData.dat
```

In this case, john-private.pem is the certificate that contains the private key of John. John is then able to get the original :myData.dat" file. David and the other friend can run a similar command with their own private keys to decrypt the message.

There are dozens of other options, such as including your digital signature, available with the **openssl** command. You can find out more from the openssl.org website.

Nonrepudiation, Authentication Methods (K-H-A)

Private keys also offer a way to apply an authenticated digital signature to the message. When such a signature is used for sending the message or signing a document, one cannot deny they did not send that message or create that signed document. This is also known as "nonrepudiation." Digital signatures are admissible and can be used in a court of law as a proof for nonrepudiation purposes.

Once identity is shown, authentication can be done in three different ways. These are known as K-H-A: what you know (K), what you have (H), and what you are (A). What you know usually falls into some kind of password or PIN. What you have is associated with an access card, ID card, or some other form of identification like a passport or driver's license. What you have types of cards are universal and inexpensive, and they can be programmed for use with some or all facilities, data access room entries, computer access via USB card reader, and so on. What you are is usually a biomedical recognition of a facial picture, a fingerprint, a voice recognition, or a combination of allowed biomedical systems that checks the presented identity with a second way to authenticate a user. For the best identification and authentication, usually more than one method of these presents the best case scenario.

Current and New Algorithms

You now know you have to use some sort of encryption and either symmetric or asymmetric key encryption to protect your data, messages, and everything electronic. But how do you pick which algorithm is better? Or how would you know if the algorithm or program you picked has a better way of protecting the data? The National Institute of Standards and Technology (NIST) invites applications, allows people to test, and filters the algorithms regularly to arrive at a better solution. They have Federal Information and Processing Standards (FIPS) and Special Publications (SP) where everything is defined for block cipher techniques, digital signatures, hash functions, key management, and a host of other programs like Cryptographic Algorithm Validation Program (CAVP) that validates algorithms submitted every few years. AES was selected as the standard by NIST, but now they are into quantum cryptography and looking at future needs since attacks can generate from those areas.

The best option you can pick is to use what NIST recommends. That way, you do not have to reinvent the wheel. Programs such as Outlook and other emailing systems use certificates and private and public keys seamlessly, and a normal user is never even aware of these techniques happening behind the software. You can find a great amount of information about the algorithms and how they work and how they are filtered at www.nist.gov and csrc.nist.gov.

Summary

Security details are concerned with attributes for compression, encryption, indexing, and archiving. Most operating systems provide these attributes to be applied effortlessly. Encryption can use a variety of algorithms, from the simplest Caesar encryption to the most up-to-date AES. Windows BitLocker is an example of full volume encryption for data protection on media such as a hard disk. Compression can be lossy or lossless. Indexing comes in two ways: clustered and nonclustered. The indexing methods are used for relational databases generally. On operating systems index attributes for files help in locating the files quickly with search commands or methods. Archiving is for storing files that are old or large and need to be moved to a special location. This is usually achieved with the zipping commands of various operating systems. Archiving can be combined with passwords to protect the archived files.

Encryption with symmetric and asymmetric methods uses a variety of algorithms. Symmetric encryption uses one key to encrypt and decrypt, whereas asymmetric encryption uses public and private keys. Public key infrastructure (PKI) uses asymmetric encryption and a GAL for sharing messages (email) and files. PKI consists of roles, software, policies, and so on. It uses X.509 digital certificates. A certification authority (CA) and a revocation authority (RA) help keep the certificates active or revoked. Nonrepudiation is a way of saying that a user cannot deny they did an act (like sending a signed email or document). Authentication methods generally use what you know, what you have, and what you are for verification. Current new algorithms approved by NIST are generally recommended for use because NIST invites experts to test and validate those algorithms.

Chapter 2 Questions

1. What are the four attributes for security of a file or data?

2. Which two file security attributes are automatically applied or checked by default in the Windows operating system?

3. Which software is an example of full volume encryption for data protection?

4. What are the two types of compression algorithms?

5. How does encryption help secure data?

6. What are the two forms of indexing in databases?

7. Which are the basic types of encryption or cryptographic methods?

8. How do users using symmetric keys use their keys and protect communication?

9. How many keys will be required among 50 users who decide to use symmetric encryption? If the same number of users switch to asymmetric encryption, how many keys will be required?

10. What standard do the PKI digital certificates follow?

11. Using PKI, if David wants to send an encrypted email to Tom so that only Tom can decrypt and read that email, what key should David use?

12. If Sarah uses PKI and her own public key to encrypt and send email to Jessica, how should Jessica be able to decrypt and read that email?

13. What command-line tool in Linux is helpful to encrypt and decrypt messages with users' certificates?

14. What is a GAL that is used with PKI?

15. If one needs to send encrypted email to several users, what encryption mechanism is best suited in PKI?

Answers to Chapter 2 Questions

1. Encryption, compression, archive, and indexing.

2. Archiving and indexing.

3. BitLocker.

4. Lossless and lossy algorithms.

5. Encryption is a form of mixing and mingling actual data contents with other known contents such as a "salt" to make the data unreadable to hackers and attackers.

6. Clustered and nonclustered indexing.

7. Symmetric and asymmetric.

8. Symmetric algorithms have one shared key between users, and trust is very important between parties to maintain security of the key and communication using that key.

9. In symmetric keys, 50 users need 50*49/2 or 1225 keys. In asymmetric keys, they would need 2*50 or 100 keys.

10. Public key infrastructure uses X.509 standard for digital certificates.

11. David should use Tom's public key.

12. Jessica would need Sarah's private key to decrypt and read that email. Because Sarah cannot share her private key with anyone, Jessica will not be able to read the email she received from Sarah.

13. The openssl tool in Linux.

14. GAL stands for global address list. When used with PKI, GAL has all the users' public keys to be shared among all users.

15. When sending email to several users, PKI uses both symmetric and asymmetric keys. A symmetric key is randomly generated for that message only, and the message is encrypted with this symmetric key. The symmetric key is then encrypted with receivers' public keys.

Goals of Security

Goals of Security—SMART/OKR

When does the first step—taking care of security in information technology or in a project—start, and when does it actually end? The short answers to these questions are from the day the project is initiated and never, respectively. However, those answers need further explanation.

Vulnerabilities in IT security can start from the very beginning, and ignoring them can cause them to escalate and become huge problems to fix later. This is the reason security for the project—whether an IT project or otherwise—needs to be considered from the beginning. As the project progresses, vulnerabilities are tested for at regular intervals during the development, testing, and deployment phases. Even after a successful deployment there is no guarantee that the application is safe from attacks. Attackers are smart people who can find a previously unknown vulnerability and exploit it, something known as a zero-day attack. Zero-day attacks can happen even several years after software has been deployed. A few years ago, we'd never heard about ransomware attacks, but now this threat takes a priority. Any deployed application needs to be monitored continuously; consequently, there is no end point that can be called "the end of security monitoring."

After applications and operating systems are decommissioned, organizations that devised the software advise the users that "support for the software no longer exists or will be discontinued." In other words, users may continue to use the software, but if any attacks or breaks happen, the creator of the software will not fix the software or send a patch to fix that vulnerability. So even though the application is decommissioned, if we continue to use it, the risk of attack always exists. Deciding to use a decommissioned application implies that we accept the risks that continue to exist. We will learn more about risks and their details in Chapter 13.

The acronyms SMART and OKR stand for "Specific, Measurable, Attainable, Realistic, and Time bound" and "Objectives and Key Results," respectively. SMART goals basically set a plan for achieving future objectives, whereas OKRs are concrete objectives and the key results. When applied to security, SMART goals must take into account specific risks and attacks and how they can be measured and mitigated. When doing that risk mitigation, the results should be attainable, realistic, and time bound. It also means the goals are not vague. SMART goals are usually tactical and designed to be accomplished in a short time span; they can be adjusted accordingly as new threats surface and new fixes are warranted. When no common consensus happens on the team working on the project, the goals of security can fall short or bypass security steps. This is the main reason to set up SMART goals for the team. When a database or application is being created, often the group of programmers and the database administrators (DBAs) concentrate on the structure and function of the program or database (DB), putting security on the back burner—or even sidestepping the security details. But these problems will backfire at a later date when data is being inserted or when the application is found to have a vulnerability that can be easily exploited. Every change in requirements, the function of an application, or the database needs to be considered in tandem with the security and possible vulnerabilities. In the realm of security, it is often said one should think like an attacker to anticipate and fix a possible vulnerability.

Table 3-1 shows an example of how to create SMART goals in security. In fact, the example can apply to any IT project. As previously mentioned, SMART goals concentrate on short-term planning. These goals continue to change after a project starts, when it is in progress, and when it ends, but the goals of security remain in force throughout as "continuous process improvement."

Table 3-1   *SMART Goals Example with Questions and Answers*

Goal Item	Questions to Ask	Answers
Specific	What is to be accomplished? (Ex: Prevent data loss, protect from viruses)	Application security, DB security, installing firewalls.
	Who is involved?	People, teams, resources.
	How are we going to accomplish it?	Software updates, buying a firewall.
	When is the goal going to be met?	Design, test, or deployment phases.
	Do we have enough resources?	Money, people, devices, servers.
	What could happen if we ignore the goal?	Attacks, ransomware.
	What requirements does this meet?	Main goals of application/DB security.
	What obstacles do we have?	Continuous involvement, time, money.
Measurable	Can we show the concrete results?	Test what was implemented.
	Can we show that the results are relevant?	Tests conducted have relevance to security.
	Can we show the evidence that results are good?	Results show security improvement.
	Can we show that results help progress (rubric)?	Demonstrate results with the rubric.

Goal Item	Questions to Ask	Answers
Attainable	Can we really reach security goals we set in "specific and measurable" areas?	The answer should be a definite YES.
Realistic	How credible are our expectations?	Must have real proof that security risk mitigation is working.
	Do results align with security values and goals in the long term?	Results align with long-term goals and possibly prevent zero-day attacks and provide needed security.
Time bound	Are we able to set up timelines for the security tasks?	Create deadlines for development, testing, and deployment tasks. Coordinate with all staff and dev/test/deployment/ security groups.
	Are the tasks and dates prioritized?	Dates are communicated in advance and reminders issued regularly. Stress timelines and accomplishments by the dates and their priorities.

OKRs are a different story after we agree to implement SMART goals. OKRs provide immediate attainable goals to be done by a deadline, and they're implemented corporate wide. The OKR is like creating and enforcing a new corporate-wide password policy to use longer passwords, not using the previously used passwords, and requiring all passwords to contain some numbers and special characters. Note that when such a policy objective is set, it often goes with a short time span like 20 or 30 days. If any user does not follow the new policy, their accounts will be locked automatically. Thus, OKRs show key results by the date set in the objectives. Once the OKR is achieved almost completely, some adjustments will be required to address some blips in the policy and realign the goals. These adjustments often are necessary because of employees who were lazy and did not follow the rules or were on vacation or on leave when the policy was implemented. Also, key results are not personal achievements of each employee, but they indicate corporate-wide success and results.

An example of a SMART goal for database security would be to implement an Oracle or SQL Server database with good password policies and in the next six months to migrate all existing access applications to the new database. An OKR for the same might concentrate on checking the password policies and having timely and regular installation of the correct patches or service packs of the Oracle or SQL Server software to avoid problems with recognized or known vulnerabilities. Both SMART goals and OKRs almost always apply to everyone in the company rather than a single unit or a person.

Who's Who in Security: RACI

In the SMART goal of "specific," you need to know who will work on the security aspect. RACI stands for responsible, accountable, consulted, and informed, and the RACI matrix is used to decide the people or human resources required for achieving the necessary security. Generally speaking, the following personnel have security roles and responsibilities:

- **CEO:** The chief executive officer is the person known as the data owner. The CEO works with their branch chiefs and other C-level officers to make policies and take responsibility of the entire organization's data. Any loss of data due to breaches, misuse, spillage, and so on is always blamed on the CEO. The CEO may explain lapses occurred in security due to mistakes of others, but the CEO is considered the owner of data and the security. This is the main reason security implementation starts in the beginning with the ownership and support of management and extends through everyday planning and continuous improvement.

- **COO:** The chief operating officer is the person who looks after the day-to-day operations of the organization and reports directly to the CEO. The COO can replace the CEO if necessary and when required, but the COO would not be the sole data owner in security.

- **CSO:** The chief security officer oversees all aspects of security in the company. Security encompasses the electronic exit and entrance controlling mechanisms, access card control, physical control with closed-circuit cameras that pan and zoom, or even the fire and water sprinkler systems that provide safety and security in case of a natural disaster.

- **CISO:** The chief information security officer oversees the inflow and outflow of information in the company. The CISO has the duty to provide data to legitimate users on the basis of the CIA security triad, discussed in Chapter 1. Information accessibility and management are the sole responsibilities of the CISO. The CISO also has to make sure that data does not fall into the wrong hands due to loopholes or vulnerabilities in security policies implemented by the organization. The position of a chief technology officer (CTO) is sometimes confused with the CISO, but a CTO oversees the acquisition, development, and maintenance of technology—both hardware and software—within the company. A CTO can also work as a CISO, but the reverse is not necessarily the case.

- **Data custodian:** Data custodians usually are the people who implement the security policies organization-wide and make sure that the policies are enforced on time with the rules of OKR. Custodians can translate the policy into rules that can be implemented in software and databases for security and report to the CISO about how the rules were created and implemented.

- **Administrator:** This role, which is also known as database administrator (DBA) when involved with data and DBs, is responsible for maintaining the DBs; ensuring that the DBs are up, running, and functioning as required; and meeting the needs of end users. DBAs also oversee account usage, data file overages, illegal logins, account lockouts, and backups and data restores as required. System administrators take care of the systems, and network administrators work with the Internet, local network, WAN, and the external-facing demilitarized zones (DMZ) of the company network.

- **Processors and controllers:** Data processors are those who deal only with the data and may not need to exercise private controls. An example is a third-party pay stub printing and check issuing agency for a company. Research institutions that use huge quantities of data are another example of data processors. The third-party agency processes the data provided to them with caution but would not be the responsible party for data loss that occurs in the parent organization. Controllers, on the other hand, own the data and have the responsibility of taking care of the privacy of it. In this example of a third-party check issuing agency, the agency would be a data controller for their own staff and their own data privacy.

- **CPO:** The newer role of chief privacy officer (which may also be known as chief data privacy officer) sprang to life with the passing of the European data security law—GDPR—which is a comprehensive legislation about data protection and the movement of private data that applies to companies of all sizes. A CPO develops and implements the security policies of a company. The CPO must have the knowledge of both corporate laws and privacy laws and must also be able to effectively communicate the policies to all users, vendors, contractors, and everyone else in the organization.

Creating the RACI Matrix

When security is being developed, the first step is to create a RACI matrix based on SMART and OKR goals. Depending on the roles of people who are involved in the RACI matrix, effective results can be obtained to reach the goals. In some cases, one person can have more than one role in the RACI table. For example, a programmer beginning to write code for an application may have to consult with the DBA to get the DB structure and other details. The DBA role in that task will be "consulted," but the DBA also has the role of "responsible" because the DBA has to provide the correct DB and make sure that the programmer's code works in tandem with the provided database.

Table 3-2 shows an example of a RACI matrix for a project that has a single MS-SQL Server database and an application that uses the database to create an external-facing corporate website for vendors. Once ready, the vendors can look for tenders being invited for any specific work, submit their own tenders, see the results of bidding, submit receipts for money, get payment details, and so on. Like in every project, various people are involved to make this a successful project without any security loopholes.

Table 3-2 *An Example RACI Matrix in an IT Project for Vendors*

Item/Goal	CEO	CISO	Programmer	DBA	Network Admin	System Admin	ISP	Users or Vendors
Requirements	I	I	R	R	C	C	I	R
Secure design	I	R	A	A	A, R	A	R	I
Firewalls	I	R	R	R	A	A	R	I

Item/Goal	CEO	CISO	Programmer	DBA	Network Admin	System Admin	ISP	Users or Vendors
DB design	I	I	A, R	R, A	I	I, R	I	I
DB patching	I	A	R	A	I	I	I	I
Software security	I	R	R	R	A	A	I	I
Website	I	I	R, A	R	R	R	A	I

R - Responsible, A - Accountable, C - Consulted, I - Informed

Planning—Strategic, Tactical, and Operational

Three basic types of planning are required for secure design of an application and its maintenance. Note that each of these types of planning is required for security in databases and applications. As said earlier, security is a never-ending work that should be taken care of with utmost care. Neglecting or ignoring the slightest vulnerability is inviting an accident to happen.

The three types of planning are described in detail:

- **Strategic planning:** As the name implies, strategic plans are long-term plans of an organization. For implementing security, strategic planning typically considers what may come in the next 5 to 10 years and anticipates what an innovative attacker or hacker might do. Such thinking also involves expecting the unexpected and trying to be ready for it. One example is the fast proliferation of ransomware attacks. A few years ago, few people had not even heard this word, but now this attack, which is often supported by other countries and their political parties, is becoming common. Strategic planning has to consider how a company can be ready quickly in the event of such an attack as well as how to thwart such attacks and any other attacks that can occur as an offshoot of larger attacks and data loss. Putting imagination to work and considering due diligence and due care are not completely sufficient, but they should go hand in hand with strategic planning while designing security. Organizations also use strategic planning for upcoming new software packages and new hardware devices to avoid possible security loopholes. Strategic plans also work at the top level and identify problems as a whole, working down the corporate ladder to find solutions.

- **Tactical planning:** Tactical plans are usually for a time that is shorter than strategic planning timelines. Companies like Microsoft, Oracle, and Google often issue patches and service packs for their devices and software when they find a vulnerability. These are usually released once in a quarter, twice a year, or several times a year. Security loopholes that are patched quickly when they are discovered, and software is sent to users to install. These kinds of quick fixes often take a few days' to few months' time and are considered tactical ways to fix issues.

■ **Operational planning:** This is the day-to-day execution of some work based on a pre-created policy or law. Checking daily for account lockouts, helping customers with their day-to-day login problems, confirming the transactions are correct, and totaling and reporting at the end of business day fall under operational planning.

In general, tactical plans fall somewhere in the middle between strategic and operational plans. An example of these plans is shown in Figure 3-1, where policy creation, procedures for enforcing the policy, and execution of those procedures are shown.

Figure 3-1 *Three Types of Planning in Security*

If we consider the policy as a corporate-wide security policy, it is created for a long-term plan or strategy. To implement that strategy, IT staff, DBAs, network and system administrators, human resources, and others across the company create rules in the software, firewalls, paperwork, and so on and work with the end users as a tactic to enforce the policy. In the operational planning of day-to-day work, DBAs and system administrators set, reset, and correct security loopholes and remind users about the policy and the rules that are in force. Similar lines of planning must happen in every type of application, like software, hardware, external-facing attacks, system design, and network design for better security of applications and databases. Such planning also helps organizational security at large in the long run.

Events and Incidents

As a rule, in security, an event is defined as an activity that can be observed. Such an observable activity may or may not cause harm. Events happen because of some scripts that run or some process that was automatically set up to run at a predetermined time. For example, anyone trying to log in with an incorrect password is recorded and considered as an event. An abrupt restart to Windows due to an update can also be an event.

On the other hand, incidents are events that cause an unwanted negative effect. All incidents are events but not vice versa. Incidents are a cause for concern and need to be investigated. A generic user attempting to log in as a system administrator, a firewall not blocking an infected data packet, and anyone viewing confidential data without proper authorization are all considered as incidents. Incidents often cause violations of policy and the three security factors (confidentiality, integrity, and availability). In the field of security, an Incident Response Plan (IRP) is usually created and updated at least once a year by an organization. The IRP has detailed procedures to deal with incidents and recovery.

Risks, Breaches, Fixes

As a general rule, risks exist in everything we do. Even after we do everything under the sun to protect ourselves from risk, some risk always remains, and that part of risk is what we have to live with or accept. Risks are usually mitigated by applying a countermeasure, transferred to another party with insurance, ignored if they are small, and accepted if they are tolerable. The risk appetite of an organization is the total value a company is willing to forfeit if something unwanted happens. It is like buying car insurance to transfer risk in case of an accident, but the insurance company asks for a deductible payment, coinsurance, a copay, or some such thing. This is the amount you are comfortable to pay to avoid paying the full dollar amount of the vehicle.

When security risks actually materialize they may result in varied amounts of damages. That is why the risks need to be considered in depth, much more in advance. Sometimes, we just ignore the risk when the countermeasure is more expensive than the value of our asset or when we know that the materialization of a risk is unlikely. For example, flood insurance is almost always mandatory in Florida due to hurricanes, but people in states like Michigan, Texas, or Colorado may be able to consider that floods are less likely and ignore the risk. But heavy rains can still cause floods in those states, and the risk can never really be zero. In security, if we install a firewall with the latest signatures of all viruses, we have mitigated most of the risks, but the risk of a new virus attacking our systems always remains. In that case, we bank on the idea that the company selling the firewall would find a fix, patch, or a service pack and send it to us for protection.

Breaches can happen in a variety of ways: password guessing to hack someone's account, finding open ports to cause a denial of service attack, and social engineering to woo someone to give personal details of company staff are all considered breaches of security. Attackers causing a breach always try to create two possible outcomes: stealing the data and creating a system account on the machine, if possible. Creating an administrative account gives a hacker more freedom to come back repeatedly to steal data, cause crashes, or create a denial of service (DoS) attack. While many breaches happen for financial gains, some can happen to cause fear, for fun, and for intimidation. Data and security breaches at large organizations such as credit card companies and multinational banks can cause widespread disruption to users and the banks' resources—financial, human, or otherwise. Note that any unauthorized viewing of data or information is also called a breach or incident because at the time of viewing, there might not be any danger, but we can't know how the data may be used later by unauthorized users.

Fixes to security problems are often via hardware upgrading or software patching. The company that sells software or hardware sends the patches or fixes to known security problems to the customer via the Internet. New attacks that occur and new vulnerabilities that have been found but not yet exploited are patched ahead of incidents and sent to customers who bought the software or hardware. In this way, customers can avoid an exploitation, and the vendor continues to support a version of software or hardware. Those rules we create with firewall software are in our hands to modify and adjust, but the signatures stored in the firewall itself need to be updated by the company that sells the software. This is why patches, fixes, and service packs that contain several fixes at one time are required to avoid breaches and incidents. Most software and operating systems can be set up to download automatic patching and updates as well. These days, even smart TVs can download new software and updates to fix any vulnerabilities. Automatic updating avoids the hassle of manual updating and forgetting to update.

Security Logs—The More the Merrier

Now we come to a stage where we want to know how a breach or an incident even occurred and how we found it out. Logs give us that information.

Every software, hardware, or network component has the ability to generate a log and store an incident or an event. It is the responsibility of the system administrators to watch these logs closely and regularly. For a firewall, one can log in as a system administrator, set up a rule, and prioritize that rule on how it should work and in what order. For example, Figure 3-2 shows the firewall properties from a Windows server that has a built-in firewall. On the left side of the figure, notice that the firewall has different rules, such as inbound rules, outbound rules, and connection security rules. On the right side, a new rule can be created, viewed, or edited. Once created, each rule can be either enabled or disabled as required by the administrator. More details of customizing a firewall log, setting up the log file size, establishing what to log (dropped packets, connections, and so on), and giving the log file a location and required name are shown in Figure 3-3.

In Figure 3-3, notice that different rules can be applied to different traffic. In the figure, inbound connections are blocked by default, and outbound connections are allowed by default. The firewall itself can be set to On or Off. There are also tabs to set up in private and public profiles. Customization of logs can be done with the click of a button, which produces what you see on the right side of Figure 3-3. The log file is by default pfirewall. log but can be renamed to anything. While logging, we can also set rules for what we want to keep as a record in the log itself. We can record dropped packets, successful connections, and so on. The log file can have a predetermined size and can be increased or decreased as the need arises. Once we decide on these details, the log will continue to grow.

So, what is in the log file? Example 3-1 shows a listing of the log file. The top part of the table is the header, and the bottom part is the line-by-line listing of the log. From the header, we notice what fields are being displayed. Any null field is displayed as a - in the table. The action that shows "DROP" means the packet is dropped, but the source and destination IPs are recorded in the log, as well as the size of the packet and whether the packet is going out or coming in. The type of packet is also indicated in the table as UDP, TCP, ICMP, and so on.

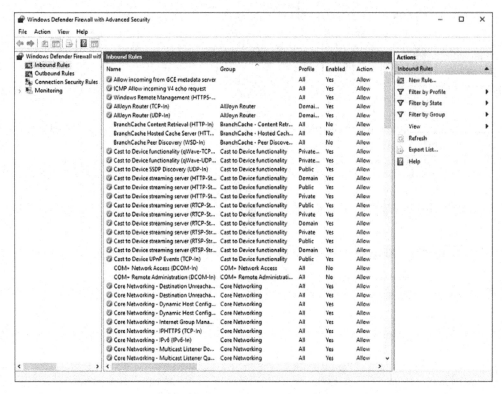

Figure 3-2   *Windows Defender Firewall with Advanced Security*

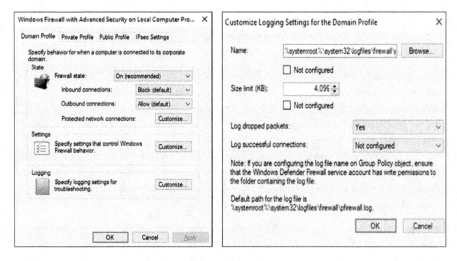

Figure 3-3   *Firewall Set Up*

Example 3-1 *Example of Firewall Log Listing*

```
#Version: X.X

Software: Microsoft Windows Firewall

Time Format: Local

Fields: date time action protocol src-ip dst-ip src-port dst-port size tcpflags
  tcpsyn tcpack tcpwin icmptype icmpcode info path


2022-12-19  09:53:22  DROP UDP  142.108.12.165   216.58.201.37    61782   5355 0
  - - - - - - - RECEIVE

2022-12-19  09:53:12  DROP TCP  122.08.32.157    216.58.201.37    61782   1434 40
  - - - - - - - RECEIVE

2022-12-19  09:53:02  DROP ICMP 142.108.12.165   170.96.151.150   - -     64 - - - -
  0 0 - RECEIVE

2022-12-19  09:53:01  DROP ICMP 142.108.12.165   170.96.101.150   - -     64 - - - -
  0 0 - RECEIVE
```

Note that from the fields listed we can decide what fields we want to display and what we can ignore. Similarly, we can set the time to match another machine in another location so the timing of an event or incident can be recorded. All this is an example of a firewall from Microsoft Windows. Logs can be created from a wide variety of applications, software, hardware devices, and more. The more logs we have, the merrier our security will be because we can easily find any problem from the log. There are also software packages available that dig into these logs and display them in a more readable format than the listing shown in Example 3-1. Logs also can be exported as XML files for use in dozens of applications. There is more to logs with Windows PowerShell commands, which are operating system–level commands (like Linux commands). With PowerShell, you also can create rules for firewalls, set up the size of the log, read the logs, and do much more. In the end, one should understand that though logs can give us details of an event or incident in an expert manner, if we fail to monitor or read the logs regularly, there is really no point in creating the logs themselves. A good system administrator is adept in reading the logs to find a problem quickly and fix it before it escalates to something more troublesome.

Re/Engineering a Project

As we discussed in Chapter 1 and the Introduction, the early computers and software packages did not have a lot to worry about in terms of security because people either didn't connect their computers to networks or use them extensively for financial transactions as we do today. Many of the software or applications that were created earlier or are being created now need constant worry about security and how hackers can attack. Vulnerabilities known and unknown keep cropping up as hackers get smarter with new technological tools. The natural questions we get now are at what stage of the database or application do security considerations need to be addressed and where would be the ending point of security consideration be for a project. To answer these questions, we need to first consider what a zero-day attack is.

Any attack that exploits an unknown, unpatched vulnerability is considered as a zero-day attack. A zero-day attack has no known fix, at least not yet. Can a zero-day attack happen on Windows XP or Windows 8 version computers, although Microsoft ceased support for these operating systems and there are not well-known populations or groups that might be using these operating systems? The answer is yes because a smart hacker with all the time in the world on their hands can continue to exploit vulnerabilities and spring a surprise at some point. Thus, zero-day attacks can happen on any systems old or new. For example, in many hospitals, older equipment continues to work, but if it is exploited, a zero-day attack still can happen on it. Now we need to come back to the question of at what stage does security consideration start for any software or hardware? Because security needs to deeply integrate into IT, it should start as early as possible and remain an important consideration throughout its life. Security never ends for any software or hardware system. Thinking that security has been already taken care of and there is nothing more to be done would be the start of our downfall because we will never know or can guess what vulnerability a smart hacker can find and exploit. How would we know what vulnerability a hacker is going to exploit and what vulnerabilities have we not already addressed? For this, we can use the Internet and find known vulnerabilities people have been recording at cve.mitre.org website. Common Vulnerabilities and Exposure (CVE) for websites, software packages, databases, and all such things are recorded on this website. The website also provides a link where a fix can possibly be found. For example, an Oracle database error or vulnerability shown on the mitre.org website shows a solution Oracle corporation has developed to patch. One can go to the Oracle website and get the patch installed for better security. But we must understand that installing such a patch would not free us from that vulnerability 100% because, like we are trying to fix a vulnerability, the hackers are hard at work to find a new vulnerability or to break the fix we just obtained.

This is the reason for keeping eyes open for security problems throughout the life of an IT product—from the start to the end. This process is also known as continuous process improvement until a product is decommissioned or its support discontinued.

Keeping Security Up to Date

For the software we create, we may already be aware of vulnerabilities or may find and possibly fix vulnerabilities, but what about software or database products we buy from a vendor? If the product is popular—like Oracle or SQL Server—users report vulnerabilities directly to the company or can register them on mitre.org with a numerical score. Oracle Corporation and Microsoft look at these, find fixes for those vulnerabilities, and roll out a patch soon. Oracle Corporation, for example, releases patches once in every quarter of the year. People who buy the software from Oracle download these free patches from the Oracle website. Patch fixing is usually very straightforward and takes less than 20 minutes. There are various versions of patches for different platforms.

Any vendor software that has announced a patch should be patched as soon as possible because the vendor has found a solution and closed that vulnerability. Leaving that vulnerability open is inviting an accident to happen. When there are too many fixes,

Microsoft and other companies release what is known as a service package, which contains updates, new releases, and patches to the vulnerabilities.

Summary

The basic rule of security is to remember that the first line of defense is always YOU, meaning we end users have to be careful about the problems and the attacks that may surface. It would be wise to learn from our own mistakes but would be wiser to learn from mistakes of everyone in the IT field and build a system that has defenses in several layers. This is also known as defense in depth.

Security considerations start from day one on a project and virtually never end because taking care of security is a continuous process. The main goals are SMART (specific, measurable, attainable, realistic, and time bound) and OKR (objectives and key results). The RACI (responsible, accountable, consulted, and informed) matrix details who's who in security. Each organization can create its own RACI matrix and designate people for each role.

There are three types of planning for security: strategic, tactical, and operational. Events are observable activities, but incidents are events that cause negative effects. Once security fixes are in place for known and expected vulnerabilities, logs are created for administrators' use. The more logs we have, the better prepared we are to take care of incidents or see events. Logs must be created very regularly and should be in a readable format or in a format that can be easily exported to various types of files.

In re-engineering a project, the developers and the organization have to consider vulnerabilities in the older system as well as the newer one. Patching and applying service packs promptly is an important part of keeping security up to date for hardware and software.

Chapter 3 Questions

1. What does the acronym SMART stand for?

2. What does the acronym OKR stand for?

3. What does the RACI matrix indicate?

4. What is the main job of a data custodian?

5. What are the three types of planning?

6. What is the difference between an event and an incident?

7. What kinds of entries are recorded in a firewall's log file?

8. What type of rules can a user create in Windows firewall?

9. At what stage of the project can risk be reduced to zero?

10. What is the best way to keep security up to date when you purchase software or hardware from third-party vendors?

Answers to Chapter 3 Questions

1. Specific, measurable, attainable, realistic, and time bound.

2. Objectives and key results.

3. RACI stands for responsible, accountable, consulted, informed. The RACI matrix gives details of who deals with what to ease the burden of work.

4. Data custodians usually are the people who implement the security policies.

5. Strategic, tactical, and operational.

6. An event is any observable change that happens on a system or software. An incident is an event with negative impact.

7. Security logs can be made to record both the events and incidents.

8. Windows firewall can create inbound, outbound, and connection security rules. It can also be set up to keep an entry in the log file for dropped packets.

9. Risk will never be zero. It can be minimized or transferred, but there is always some risk left over that has to be accepted. This is also known as a company's comfort zone for accepting a certain level of risk and absorbing any losses.

10. The best way to keep security up to date is to get the latest patches from vendors that regularly fix the vulnerabilities.

Database Security Introduction

ACID, BASE of DB, and CIA Compliance

Modern databases (DBs) have moved beyond basic tables and simple Structured Query Language (SQL) versions of simple Excel sheets and tables. Now a DB can have tables, relations, XML data, JSON objects, and more. However, the basic idea behind a DB still remains as the ACID principles: atomicity, consistency, isolation, and durability. ACID is the gold standard for databases that use a relational structure. Databases called "noSQL" databases follow the BASE principles: basically available, soft state, and eventually consistent.

Since security is important for databases and their applications, the transactions that happen on a DB must conform to the basic security triad principles of CIA (confidentiality, integrity, and availability). Consider a large corporation such as Meta Inc., which owns Facebook. Per one estimate, the data on Facebook is projected to be 2.5 billion pieces of content each day. Facebook posts also register 2.7 billion "Like" actions and 300 million photos per day. The company's engines regularly scan about roughly 200 terabytes of data each hour. This is equivalent of 4 petabytes or more of data per day. And the transactions are increasing exponentially. Assume that everything is stored in a database, each transaction has to be discrete, transactions should not interfere with other transactions, and all data should be available when required to needed users. This is where the basic ACID principles of a DB spring to action.

ACID, BASE, and CIA

We will now consider each of the ACID and BASE principles in detail. Atomicity of a database transaction can be described as "all or none." It means when we execute a transaction—a read or write—it executes as a whole or not at all. A partial transaction is never done on the database. Atomicity helps in keeping the database integrity intact because a partial transaction may modify database contents to an undesirable level. If a transaction is not completed in its entirety, it is automatically rolled back.

Consistency of the database indicates that the database must be available in a consistent mode before and after a transaction. It also means if a transaction fails, the database should not crash. Data can be modified in tables and updated by good or bad transactions, but the state of the database should be stable and be ready before and after such a transaction. In other words, consistency ensures that all transactions bring the database from one consistent state to another, preserving data properties. Any data written to the database must be valid according to all defined rules.

The isolation property essentially states that every transaction acts independently on the database. No two transactions can collide or interfere with each other and cause trouble. It also means each transaction maintains its confidentiality on the database and works by itself. One transaction may call a second transaction, but they each work in isolation of the other, or the second transaction must be completed in isolation before the control returns the first.

Durability of a database means the effects of a transaction are permanent. Suppose that a computer system crashes due to a bad event. After a database transaction is complete on the same system, the database changes made by the transaction are permanent. An example can illustrate this better. If we book a hotel room on the Priceline website, even if the Priceline website and their databases crash, our hotel reservation remains in the database and can be retrieved later when the system is back in action.

Table 4-1 is a comparison of ACID and BASE database properties.

Table 4-1   *ACID and BASE Properties of Databases*

ACID	BASE
Atomicity: A database transaction is completed in full or it is discarded or rolled back. There are no partial transactions. Also known as "All or none."	Basically Available: NoSQL databases. Availability of data is achieved by spreading data across the nodes of database cluster.
Consistency: Database remains in a consistent state. If the database is consistent before a transaction, it should remain consistent after the transaction. Also known as "no adverse effects."	Read/Write functionality is available for all transactions, but it is possible to have data that is not persistent, or the data read by a query is not up to date.
Isolation: Each database transaction works in isolation and does not interfere with the other transactions. Also known as "parallel transactions."	Soft State: Lacks immediate consistency. Data values may change over time. Data consistency is the responsibility of developers.
Durability: A committed database transaction holds even if the system fails or restarts. Data saved is durable. Also known as "permanent."	Eventually Consistent: Immediate consistency is not guaranteed, but at some point the database is consistent after data goes through all clusters and nodes. It's possible to read data before that final state is reached.

BASE properties are generally applied to noSQL databases. BA means the database is basically available; read and write are available at the least level but the consistency of the data is not guaranteed. This is because data being read could be older than the data written into the DB by another transaction. This leads to the next letter, S, which means that the database is in soft state. At the exact time of transaction, the database may not reflect the up-to-date data and lacks consistency. The responsibility for consistency does not fall on the database side but falls on the developer side. It is understood that the data is preserved, but at the time of a transaction, the consistency is not guaranteed. Would the data be consistent at all? The last letter, E, addresses that question. Data will eventually be consistent when it spreads across the clusters and nodes. Consistency happens over time, and the time is not fixed in stone or by rules. Sooner or later, the data will become consistent, but at the exact microsecond the transaction ends, the data might not be consistent. If you agree this kind of delayed consistency is acceptable, you can use BASE databases; otherwise, you should choose to go with ACID databases.

Regardless of whether you use ACID or BASE databases, a database has to conform to the security goals of the CIA triad. Database confidentiality is achieved by various methods, such as creating accounts with passwords for those who have a "need to know." Usually, the need to know is determined by filing a signed form (digital or otherwise), getting it signed again by the supervisor, and forwarding it for final approval. Need-to-know forms are not simply sign-and-approve processes. Those authorities who check the forms also check the background of the applicant and look for any violations in security, problems in human resources, and training required before granting access. Violations need to be corrected before those forms are signed. Need-to-know forms also mention what kind of access is required for the database or application. Providing simple read access with grants may be an easier solution, but keep in mind that giving even read access can be a problem for prior violators because they can copy the data and violate the policies again. These forms must mention the kind of access required, which tables or data will be accessed, the name of the person, where that person works, and what they intend to do with the data. For read-only access, a database can be supplied as a view, which the end user can read but can't modify. But occasionally they are also given access to a materialized view (view physically stored as a table). The usual password policies apply to these users after an account is created. Importantly, the credentials created are supplied to the users with further conditions. One such condition is to ask the end user to accept a database group policy that they won't misuse the data, will inform the database administrators of any discrepancies, and sign these papers or send a signed email accepting these details. These procedures may sound harsh and difficult to cope with, but such rules are required to protect the corporate data adequately.

In the following section, we further consider a few more database terms, and what data is presented to an end user and how it is presented.

Data in Transit, Data at Rest

Data is the most important asset to any organization. Loss of data can lead to a limitless number of problems from law enforcement agencies, hungry lawyers, federal and state regulators, and hundreds of complaints from end users, customers, and vendors. Typically, what is considered a valuable asset to an organization must be always guarded well and secured, whether that data is in storage, moving, or temporarily at rest.

At-rest data can be in the system disks, tapes, small USB drives, a large server, or even on the hard disk of the computer itself. There are dozens of ways to protect data at rest. Encrypting the data is obviously one solution, but physical safety is another consideration, along with many other factors.

Data can be backed up regularly—daily, weekly, monthly, or at any designated time—and can be treated as the data at rest. Full backups help restore the entire data, but full backups can cause issues of size and the time it takes to do a full restore. Differential backup, as the name indicates, is the backup of data since the last full backup. To restore full data with a differential backup, one would need two copies—the latest full backup and the current differential backup. Another option is an incremental backup, which saves data in increments by the day, week, and so on. If an incremental backup is done daily, restoring data requires the latest full backup and the copies of the recent incremental backups. Figure 4-1 shows the backup methods.

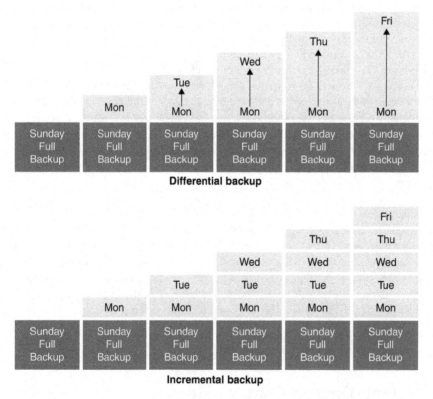

Figure 4-1 *Different Types of Backups for Data at Rest*

The backed-up data can be stored in an encrypted manner with a secret key or by using an encryption algorithm such as AES256. Data in databases is usually updated with each transaction on individual tables or objects. It's also updated every day and through ETL (Extract-Transform-Load) processes, with files supplying data and the database scripts copying the data from files to tables quickly. Any temporary unused data in the ETL files (in any format such as CSV or Excel) needs to be encrypted and/or removed and should not persist on the disks or storage since it was copied to the database tables. Data in database tables also can be encrypted, or scripts can track who is modifying the data to send an alert to the system or database administrators.

Data in transit is a different story. Data can move on email, as network traffic, or from one host to another in various ways. Various protocols like HTTPS, SSL, TLS, and IPSec are available for protecting sensitive data. Network security with firewalls with a good access rules list that is continually upgraded helps protect the data. It would be unwise to rely on default safety measures, regardless of whether they're provided by third-party vendors or built in house. Measures must be taken to block, prompt for encryption, or implement automatic encryption when any egress is in play. The basic mantra is ZERO TRUST, which means not believing anyone or anything blindly.

The advent of cloud data storage brought a new problem to worry about in terms of the safety of data. A few considerations are to check whether the cloud is private, public, or hybrid, what measures the cloud provider follows for data security, and how the data is backed up in case of a system crash. Again, it would be unwise to rely completely on the cloud provider for data backup. One should always take measures to have a data copy on hand just in case the cloud provider cannot restore the latest version of full data.

It is important to note that even with all possible precautions, data can be lost, compromised, or breached, normally because of loose data protection policies. An organization needs not only to create strict policies but also to enforce the policy with an iron fist. Enforcing the policies involves identity management—who can access data, how access is supplied, and how the user given access is identified and authenticated. Also note that any actions taken after a breach has been detected are almost useless because the breach has already occurred. These so-called "reactive solutions" do not normally yield great results because data loss prevention (DLP) is something that should happen as the policies are created and rules are made to protect data.

Data at rest or data in transit needs the following rules and policies:

1. Create rules for data/asset classification.

2. Create a policy based on the rules and enforce the policy strictly. An unenforced policy is as good as no policy at all.

3. Do not assume the default rules are adequate. Update the access rules regularly.

4. Encryption of data on email should be made mandatory.

5. Implement proper IAAA rules for identity management and authentication.

6. Train and retrain the staff regularly to implement policies.

7. Back up data regularly in any format that is affordable.

8. Encrypt the data in disks and on the database if possible.

9. Keep the encrypting algorithm and any associated keys secret.

10. Audit the operations to check that policies are implemented correctly.

11. If a cloud data provider is used, do not assume that the provider will do the data backup for you.

12. Follow zero trust when working with confidential data, whether it is data at rest, data in transit, or data in use.

The bottom line is any data loss can quickly escalate as a violation of federal, state, or local regulations and result in legal troubles with lawyers and erosion of the customer base. These may ultimately even lead to the complete demise of an organization. Pretending that the organization exercised due diligence and feigning ignorance is not an excuse, and no courts or laws agree to exonerate the data owner for any data loss or lapses in implementing the data loss prevention measures.

DDL and DML

Data manipulation language (DML) deals with how to edit the data in a database—be it in an Oracle database, an SQL Server database, an XML file, or a simple Excel table that can be easily read or transmitted over the wire. Data definition language (DDL) is for building tables, views, structures, and other database objects that consist of the database itself. Table 4-2 shows some differences between these languages.

Table 4-2 *Data Definition Language (DDL) Versus Data Manipulation Language (DML)*

Data Definition Language (DDL)	Data Manipulation Language (DML)
Has commands to create tables, views, and other database objects.	Used for changing data inside database objects.
Does not have where, having, group by, or other such clauses.	Uses all clauses like where, having, group by, in, not in.
Does not have any variations.	DDL can be procedural or non-procedural.
Can define primary keys and foreign keys when creating the objects.	Needs proper understanding of relationships among tables before DML is executed or the statement could result in an error for violation of a relationship.
Can have default values, auto incrementing a column value in DDL.	Values must be implicitly supplied with the SQL statement for data changes.
Does not need a commit statement and DDL commits automatically (if there are no constraints already defined).	Needs a commit statement to make changes or the changes may roll back.

Data Definition Language (DDL)	Data Manipulation Language (DML)
Used basically to create columns of a database object. The columns are attributes of the data.	Generally used to change a database tuple (row). Can change/update a group of rows or a single row.
Typical commands are **CREATE, ALTER, DROP, RENAME, TRUNCATE**, etc.	Commands include **SELECT, INSERT, UPDATE, DELETE, MERGE, JOIN**, etc.
Wildcard operators are not generally allowed.	Wildcard operators such as % are widely used.
Used for creating, dropping, or altering one database object at a time.	Can combine various objects with joins, additions, and subtractions to extract complicated data based on various rules.
Several DDLs can be put in one file and can be run at once to create all objects.	Can be run with more than one file with one procedure in a file calling another in a different file.

Example 4-1 shows a generic example of a complicated DDL for creating a table. Notice that the table DDL contains constraints, primary key, and foreign key definitions. Various other definitions for auto increment, default values, and so on are shown in the table, too. Note that the IDENTITY (1, 1) works with SQLServer database, but with other databases such as mySQL, you can use AUTO_INCREMENT statements for giving a starting and increment numbers. The default value is inserted into the table when the user does not supply any data for the ZipCode column. Note that these are hypothetical examples and may not yield perfect results because each database has a different format for DDL/DML, and the results also depend on the data that exists in the tables individually.

Example 4-1 *DDL Example*

```
CREATE TABLE Finance.Employees
(
Sr_Number  NUMBER IDENTITY (1, 1),
Employee_ID NUMBER  CONSTRAINT   Id_Check  PRIMARY KEY,
Employee LastName VARCHAR2(100) NOT NULL,
Employee MiddleName VARCHAR2(100),
Employee FirstName VARCHAR2(100) NOT NULL,
EmployeeDept NUMBER  CONSTRAINT Dept_Check  REFERENCES Finance.Branch(Dept),
EmployeeSalary NUMBER,
EmployeeClass CHAR(1) CONSTRAINT Class_Check  EmployeeClass in ('A', 'B', 'Z')),
EmployeeJobDesc VARCHAR2(60),
EmployeeHireDate DATE,
ZipCode NUMBER DEFAULT 20090
);
```

Example 4-2 shows an example of DML that inserts data into a table "Three," after finding rows existing in table "One" and removing the rows that are in table "Two."

Example 4-2   *DML Example*

```
INSERT INTO Finance.Three (Sr_Number, LastName, FirstName, Zipcode)
(
SELECT Sr_Number, LastName, FirstName, Zipcode
FROM Finance.One WHERE ZipCode NOT in (20090, 43091, 90021)

minus

SELECT Sr_Number, LastName, FirstName, Zipcode
FROM Finance.Two WHERE ZipCode in (53090, 62891, 84025)
);
```

Designing a Secure Database

Per CIA triad rules, data is or should be always accessible to deserving and need-to-know users in an unchanged original form. Therefore, security of the database (physically or otherwise) is important. Administratively, access control is mandatory and should be done in a format that is agreeable and signed. End users can work from a secure office or from home on a VPN, which requires secure VPN connections and in-office security of the networks with proper firewalls, access control lists, and good bandwidth for smooth data transfer. Data encryption is a must inside the DB software suite or on the disk. The backups must also be secured with encryption, and the physical rooms where the backups are stored should be locked and provided with adequate HVAC. They should be accessible only for privileged and authorized personnel. While the database itself can be guarded this way, end users can still steal, modify, corrupt, or manipulate the data if they have access in any way. Implementing end-user security should also be considered important.

Auditing must be implemented to find out which user or employee is going "out of zone" to create trouble. Generally, there are three different ways a breach can happen: an internal attack by a disgruntled employee, an outside hacker who obtains access by securing credentials of another user through social engineering methods, friendship, or threats, or a negligent employee or insider who does something they do not recognize as serious. This last error is a human weakness in judgment. Also, people who leave an organization can try to log in to the organizational infrastructure after they leave and exploit information they can obtain. For this reason, credentials of employees for access should be immediately suspended if the employee is terminated or they quit. Here are a few things to consider:

■ **Separate the database servers from application servers.**

Installing and setting up databases on a standalone server not only provides security but also speeds up operations because the server does not have to work on various software packages and applications. Also, any virus attacks that happen to applications do not automatically propagate to the databases if databases are hosted separately.

■ **Guard the database server rooms physically.**

Keeping the database server machines in a room under lock and key offers an additional layer of security from insider threats. Keeping the servers under proper HVAC controls and backup AC power allows the servers to align with 7x24x365 availability. Anyone who does not have privileges to enter the room has no access, and those who have privileges should not carry electronic devices such as their cell phones, watches, and tablets into the secure rooms.

■ **Close the unused ports and do not use default setup ports.**

When a software suite such as Oracle or SQL Server is installed, they come with default ports for the databases, which are already set up or can be set up for the user. Any such default ports set up already should not be used and preferably disabled. Any other ports that are open but not used should also be closed to deny access to anyone.

■ **Create scripts for real-time database event monitoring.**

A database package may or may not come with event monitoring software. For example, if your organization wants to monitor for excessive logins on a database, you can easily create an SQL script to monitor such events and send an email to alert the database administrators. Dozens of scripts to check activities such as user logins, failed logins, password changes, account lockouts, and account unlocks can be created to monitor the database activity.

■ **Create an invited IP address list and do not allow connections from other IP addresses.**

Database packages such as Oracle allow a DB administrator to create a list of IP addresses that are accepted for DB transactions. These are also static IPs that allow connections to go through. Dynamic IP addresses can be noted with a universal * character as substitution for access. Any IP that is not in the invited node list will be rejected for DB access. In this way, DB administrators can limit access to the database to only known users.

■ **Use data encryption protocols provided in the DB suite.**

Does your database software suite come with a built-in encryption protocol for the database? If so, use it with a good password or access key. Do not share the key with everyone, and keep it a secret among trusted and known people in the organization.

■ **Update your DB with new patches as soon as they are released.**

Almost every kind of attack that has been recorded on a database is already documented and can be found at https://cve.mitre.org. The attacks are checked, and the vulnerabilities are regularly fixed by the software manufacturers. The vendors fix these vulnerabilities and release a patch. It is imperative that the database be patched regularly with the patches the vendor supplies. For example, Oracle and SQL Server supply patches every quarter or four times a year.

- **Create daily backups in more than one way—full, incremental, and differential.**

  Since "zero trust" is the law we are mostly interested in following, always create a backup of your data in more than one way, even if you trust all your employees. Backing up data has two distinct advantages: if data is lost or breached, you always have a copy to get back to normalcy and backed-up data can be transported to another location (for example, a secondary site) for restoring operations. Creating more than one way of backing up data is important because if one kind of backup fails to restore, we will always have another way to get the data back.

- **Create scripts to generate reports daily on usage, logging, DML, and DDL changes.**

  SQL scripts should be created to track who is logging in, when the user last logged in, the contact information for the user, what the user does, and so on. If the users or DBAs change data in the tables, those changes also should be recorded. Audit logs of databases show these details along with the username, date, and time. These logs serve a great purpose in the event there is a problem with database operations.

- **Watch the logs daily for any suspicious events/incidents.**

  Although creating logs is a great way to go, never reading those logs makes the entire effort a waste of time. Reading those logs regularly and, fixing any bugs that exist are important to do before any of those bugs escalate and cause trouble for access.

- **Create strong password policies—days of validity, length, complexity, and so on.**

  User authentication should be via passwords that follow a strict policy. The passwords should have good complexity (a combination of uppercase letters, lowercase letter, symbols, and numbers), they should be valid for a limited period of time (45, 60, 90 days), and a few older passwords cannot be re-used (password history). Accounts not used for a few weeks should be locked to prevent unauthorized access.

- **Allow access to anyone only after proper forms are signed and checked.**

  While authentication is important, access should be given only after proper identification, completion of forms, valid signatures, and checks by the appropriate authorities, supervisors, or branches. A supervisor asking for database access for their employee must also sign the form indicating that the employee is authenticated and will follow the rules set forth by the database administrators. You can find an example access form at https://www.commerce.wa.gov/wp-content/uploads/2016/08/COM-CMS-Online-A19-External-User-Request-Form.pdf.

■ **Train users to implement policies. Disable accounts of people who do not comply.**

Having considered all of these, it is imperative to train the employees, database administrators, end users, data owners, and everyone dealing with the database to enforce the policies. As said earlier, an unenforced policy is a plain useless paper. Enforcing policies tells the users that the organization takes its work very seriously.

In the end, security is the duty of everyone in the organization. This is the reason a rigorous structure is required for data control. All these measures may seem lengthy, boring, and time-consuming to complete, but it is better to do these procedures first and follow a standard than lose the data and be dragged into a court of law.

Structural Security

The structural security of a DB depends on the how it is designed and what objects comprise the DB. The basic idea of a DB structure is to start with a schema and create tables, views, procedures, functions, and so on. A schema is created in a database, and tables and other objects remain in that schema. A table has rows (or tuples) and columns (attributes or fields). Each tuple generally has a primary key to keep the data unique to that tuple. In other words, a row of data can be pulled up with a unique primary key. The primary key itself can be one column or a combination of columns. Where required, it may be better to use a surrogate key as the primary key than a column with personally identifiable information (PII). A surrogate key has no known use for data but will work as a key to pull data out via an index. Naming conventions for various database objects dictate how well the database is planned and designed.

For easy access of data reading and updating, stored procedures should be used. Complex data operations also need stored procedures created. Generic stored procedures for various tables, views, and other objects should be readily available for end users and programmers who can use them rather than creating their own on the front end with SQL. There is a distinct disadvantage for end users or programmers to create their own functions. The programmers may or may not be good with SQL coding. They also expose the SQL scripts should their libraries get hacked. For those reasons, DBAs should have stored procedures created to be supplied to the need-to-know users.

Permissions via grants should be given to end users for only those objects they need to know and not on every possible data object. This can be done by creating roles. Role creation in a database allows people to be attached to roles, and permissions are given to roles, rather than permissions given directly to the people. For those people who have just the read privileges, it is always better to create a view to give data than give access to the entire table. Stored procedures and functions should have proper read and execute (but not write) grants to the end users.

Any changes to the data objects—be it changing a column of a table, changing the view script, or creating a new table—must happen with the permission of change management and should be adequately documented with a reason to explain why such a change is warranted. This change is usually coordinated with the database managers, database administrators, and the end user who requested the change. Once the change is implemented, it should be on the development database, and a tester will validate the change before it is deployed on the production database. Read more about change management in Chapter 13. Figure 4-2 shows an example schema and database structure of a database.

Figure 4-2   *An Example of Schema, Tables, Views, and Other Database Objects*

Figure 4-2 contains partial screenshots from the SQL Developer tool, which is owned by Oracle corporation. Notice the left side listing shows the connection to HR Database, which is the main name of the database. The middle listing shows the details of a schema named Salaries, which has tables, views, and others. The right-most picture is for database administrator functions that include backing up, exporting, and so on. The DBA screen also shows roles, profiles, and users who have accounts in the database. Various other DBA functions and utilities are also listed in that picture.

Example 4-3 shows a listing of an Oracle table, a view, a role, and how roles are given permissions and the users attached to roles.

Example 4-3   *SQL Script That Shows Table, View Creation*

```
CREATE TABLE Finance.Employees
(
Sr_Number  NUMBER GENERATED BY DEFAULT AS IDENTITY,
Employee_ID NUMBER(10)  NOT NULL,
Employee LastName VARCHAR2(100) NOT NULL,
Employee MiddleName VARCHAR2(100),
Employee FirstName VARCHAR2(100) NOT NULL,
EmployeeDept NUMBER(5)
EmployeeSalary NUMBER(10),
EmployeeClass CHAR(1),
EmployeeJobDesc VARCHAR2(60),
EmployeeHireDate DATE,
ZipCode NUMBER DEFAULT 20090,
CONSTRAINT Emp_PK PRIMARY KEY (Employee_ID),
CONSTRAINT empl_FK
      FOREIGN KEY (EmployeeDept)
      REFERENCES Dept(Dept_ID)
);

CREATE OR REPLACE VIEW EmpView AS
SELECT
Employee_ID,
EmployeeHireDate,
SUM( 12 * EmployeeSalary ) amount
FROM
Finance.Employees
INNER JOIN Finance.Dept
On Dept_ID
WHERE
UPPER (EmployeeClass in ('A', 'F')
ORDER BY
Employee_ID desc;
```

If we assume we have the table and a view shown in Example 4-3, we can create a role to which people as users can be added later as required, as shown in Example 4-4.

Example 4-4   *SQL for Creating a Role*

```
CREATE ROLE Human_Resc_Read;

GRANT SELECT on Finance.EmpView, Finance.Employees to Human_Resc_read;

CREATE ROLE Human_Resc_Write;

GRANT DELETE, INSERT, UPDATE on Finance.EmpView, Finance.Employees to Human_Resc_read;
```

Now add the users to these roles as required. By using these roles, it is easier to grant and revoke permissions to users than granting permissions individually and hiding details of user privileges. Example 4-5 grants or revokes privileges for human resources user DAVIDJL. These roles also help create a role-based access control list.

Example 4-5 *SQL for Attaching Users to Roles*

```
GRANT Human_Resc_Read to DAVIDJL;

REVOKE Human_Resc_Write FROM DAVIDJL
```

Functional Security

Openarchitecture.org defines functional security as services that need to be achieved by the system under inspection. Examples could be authentication, authorization, backup, server-clustering, and so on. In another way, the basic definition of a functional require-ment can be said to be one that *specifies "what a system should do," given proper setup and operation.* If we examine our daily life, a functional requirement for an every-day object like an umbrella would be "ability to shield the person holding the umbrella from moderately falling rain." Note that the same umbrella cannot hold the function when there is a tornado or hurricane. So, an object or a function fails when the proper preset conditions or assumptions change.

Extending this to security, we can define functional security as a particular security function of the system when certain conditions are met. Here is an example: "Sending an encrypted email when the email contains PII or any confidential information such as a password." This example assumes the preset conditions as ability of an email program (such as Outlook) to use encryption, authentication, and certificates for the sender and receiver. The functional security of a program or database therefore demands that there are requirements before you can implement security. Some of these requirements are

- Organizational rules and regulations set by business policies.

- Transaction rollbacks, commits, or cancellations.

- Identification venues—both physical and nonphysical (username/password).

- Administrative functions (creation, deletion of accounts, etc.).

- Authentication methods—manual, automatic, or biometric methods.

- Authorization—what a user can do or cannot do.

- Audit tracking—are the users going out of zone of permitted authorized levels?

- Licensing body and or certification requirements for both users and systems.

- Reporting requirements.

- Backing up of data, ability to bring up a particular version depending on date/time.

- Federal, state, and local legal or regulatory procedures.

The functional security's first step is to formulate organizational policies—also known as best practices for security—and the CIA discussed earlier. Note again that the formulated policies should be strictly enforced and fit with all regulations. Functional security of a software is achieved for users by allowing the users to create or update accounts, set up minimum needed (need-to-know) privileges (authentication and authorization), check for two- or multi-factor authentication, block accounts when user is going "out of zone," not allow a generic user to access security setup details, and so on. Separation of duties can be implemented for software development as well, where a programmer is not allowed to test the code or a tester is not allowed to write the code. Neither a programmer or a tester should be allowed to deploy the executable on a server. In a database, the functional security can be achieved by limiting user access to tables but providing them data read via a view or read-only grant. When all is said and done, the database or the software must continue to function despite how the users' accounts are set up and what they can read or write. The accounts and functions of the database software need to be monitored on a daily basis. One avenue for monitoring is to set up an automatic alarm email to the system administrator when a user is going out of zone. One example is to generate an email to the system administrator (SA) when the user tries several login attempts. These login attempts could be from a hacker trying to do a brute force attack or a trusted user with a forgotten password. In either case, the user account is blocked and disabled after N (usually 3 to 5) unsuccessful attempts, to alert the SA. When the SA reviews logs they would easily find out who was trying to log in, and the SA would resolve the situation.

Data Security

No matter how hard we try, we know that there always exists a risk of data breach because as technology is progressing, adversaries such as hackers and attackers use the same technology to exploit the new applications and the security we deploy.

The main reason for a data breach is unauthorized access. Unauthorized access can come from an insider—usually a disgruntled employee—or an outsider, and the attack can be on data at rest or data in movement. Some of the following can cause a breach and loss or change of data:

- Leaks, spillage, or accidental exposures

- Social engineering attacks (phishing, whaling, spear-phishing)

- Backdoor manipulation

- Physical stealing or manipulation

- Distributed or simple denial of service (DoS) attacks that deny data availability

- Losing encryption keys

- Intellectual property theft

So, how do we protect our data? First, we need to keep in mind the regulations we have to follow, such as credit card industry laws (PCI-DSS), medical information protection (HIPAA), European Union's data protection laws (GDPR), financial disclosure information laws new and old (Sarbanes-Oxley or SOX), and any other rules that govern an industry or area in which our organization operates. The laws on these acts or regulations pose very strict fines and penalties for data breaches and irregularities in keeping the data safe. Note that data needs to be secure in both movement and at rest, but you don't need to use the exact same methods to secure data in both cases.

Government and industry use different definitions for data protection. Table 4-3 provides details. The damages that could happen are listed in the last column of the table.

Table 4-3   *Government and Nongovernment Definitions of Data Classification*

Level/Class	Government/ Military	Non- government	Effect of a Breach
Class 0	Public/Unclassified	Public	No damage (recruiting information, budget numbers)
	Sensitive but unclassified		Minor damage (medical information records, skill level of soldiers, scores)
Class 1	Confidential	Sensitive	Some damage (departmental secrets, computer code)
Class 2	Secret	Private	Serious damage (war details, general office facility access, locker keys)
Class 3	Top Secret	Confidential	Exceptionally grave damage (stolen plans, nuclear facility codes)

Note from Table 4-3 that not all government/military classifications are mapped for private or nongovernment entities, but they both share some levels. Depending on the data to be protected, a control is selected. The following are some of the methods we use for data protection, and they can be used in combination:

- Encryption of data by using various methods such as hashing, parity, salting, and so on. Symmetric and asymmetric key encryption can be used.

- Data masking with methods such as using a surrogate key in database designs for replacing the PII. Creating views for read only access of need-to-know data only is another way of controlling privileges. Data masking techniques also involve scrambling with a known algorithm, substitution, shifting, shuffling, nullifying, and so on.

- Preventing data loss by employing proper privileges and authorization controls. Employ roles and grants to tables, views, and programming modules. Data loss prevention also can be employed by regular comparison of data with archives, data change patterns, analysis, and trends of changes to see if anything is particularly disturbing.

- Backing up data regularly in more than one way (incremental, full, and differential), and restricting the database or software backup access to only a few individuals.

- Controlling physical access with access cards or keys. This method also means programming the access cards individually and granting access to buildings, offices, and general areas but not allowing access to server rooms, database servers, and web servers.

- Separation of duties allows only database administrators to make changes to DBs and programmers to make changes to their own code. This also indirectly means DB administrators cannot alter written code, and a programmer cannot make changes to a database—either DDL or DML—unless special roles are granted.

- In the end, data security and protection measures dictate how we can protect the privacy of data we collect. And those protection measures ultimately must keep in mind all the federal, state, and local government laws and regulations.

Procedural Security

In the process of procedural security, we are mostly concerned with the steps we take to control access to people or systems. The following list describes several of these steps:

- If possible, employ a central clearance facility to get security clearance for people. The background investigations and checks cannot be done by people who work in programming, database, or human resources and must be done by a separate entity that specializes in the clearance process.

- Get the employees or contractor to sign access forms—one for coding, one for database access, and so on—explaining the role of users for access. Before granting access, make sure that the access forms are current and valid. Employees or contractors also must have completed proper training on how to access and use the systems and database in a secure way and sign to agree to the organization's terms and conditions when using the facilities. If employees are allowed to work from home, a separate training program is required to declare that they know how to access the VPN and abide by the rules set forth for using the VPN.

- Access cards or identification badges must be visibly worn all the time while in the office to avoid any confrontation with security. While in the facility, an employee must always accompany visitors.

- Document the work done by employees or contractors and process the documents on a share drive for sharing among the department staff on a need-to-know basis.

- DB administrators check the submitted forms for accuracy before creating an account and giving role grants to a user. Any discrepancies in the signed forms must be corrected before access is given.

- Desktop support or any other department that installs required software checks a different access form signed by requesting users before installing software.

- When an employee leaves or is fired, all the accounts are blocked first and are deleted immediately to block access for the departing or fired employee.

- Make sure that the documents transmitted among staff are properly signed electronically to avoid nonrepudiation and are encrypted if they contain any PII.

When we follow these security measures, we can adequately protect the data to make sure a breach does not happen easily, but we always accept the fact that risk can never be reduced to zero.

Summary

Databases come in a variety of modes, and most relational databases conform to the ACID (atomicity, consistency, isolation, and durability) rules. BASE databases are basically available, are in soft state, and eventually consistent. BASE properties generally apply to noSQL databases. Both types always comply with the CIA security fundamentals.

Data can be in transit or at rest and needs to be protected in both cases. Backup copies of data can be termed data at rest. Backing up can be handled in three ways: full, incremental, and differential. Data transit can happen on various protocols, such as HTTPS, TLS, SSL, and so on. DDL (data definition language) is a set of database language scripts or commands that is used for creating DB objects and building structures. DML (data manipulation language) uses scripts or commands to manipulate data in the database objects (tables, views, and so on).

There are various steps to create and keep a database secure. Most important of these steps is to separate the database servers from application servers and keep them as standalone. Physical security of the databases and the HVAC to keep them functioning are also important because any overheating of the servers can shut down the databases. Structural security of the database depends on how the DB is designed with primary keys and foreign keys. Functional security comes from policies, transactions, and other functions. Data inside the databases need data security so that nobody can change, corrupt, or manipulate the data. Government and nongovernment organizations categorize their data into various classes from 0 to 3, where 3 indicates the highest level of damage (grave damage). Procedural security of the database comes from how the DB is connected to applications and/or users. Users need vetting and must sign forms to be approved to get access.

Chapter 4 Questions

1. What are the basic principles on which modern databases are built?

2. What does the isolation property of databases indicate?

3. What is meant by soft state of a database in the BASE database model?

4. In what states can data exist?

5. What are the possible ways of backing up data?

6. A DB is backed up incrementally with Sunday as full backup and every day as an incremental backup. If on a Thursday morning you want to restore the entire backup, how many copies of backup would you need? How would the situation change if you do a differential backup instead of incremental backup every day?

7. What is the SQL language method known as when we update a couple of rows of data in a table using a where clause in an SQL statement?

8. If we have twenty massive databases and six applications that use these databases, which will be the best way to host these DBs and applications on servers?

9. How often should you patch your applications and databases?

10. Administrative functions, backup, audit tracking, and authentication processes fall into which type of security?

11. What processes or countermeasures can help maintain data security in general?

12. What level or class of government data can cause serious damage when disclosed without authorization?

13. If a visitor is entering a secure facility, what should be the procedure for security?

14. Which department should normally be engaged to do background checks and security clearances of an employee?

15. What is the best way to make sure employees and contractors are following the rules and regulations set by organizational policies?

Answers to Chapter 4 Questions

1. ACID (atomicity, consistency, isolation, and durability) and BASE (basically available, soft state, and eventually consistent) are the modern database principles.

2. Isolation states that each database transaction works in isolation and doesn't interfere with other transactions, also known as parallel transactions.

3. A soft state indicates that the DB lacks "immediate consistency," and data may change over a short period of time. Data consistency is the responsibility of developers and does not rest with DB administrators. Data will be eventually consistent.

4. Data can exist in three states: data at rest, data in movement, and data in use.

5. Data can be backed up in full, differential, or incremental modes.

6. Because the backup is done as full a backup on Sunday and incremental backups every day, by Thursday morning, you will have one full backup and three incremental backups (Monday, Tuesday, and Wednesday). You need all four copies to restore full data on Thursday.

   For a differential backup, you will need the full backup from Sunday and the differential backup done on Wednesday to restore full data on Thursday.

7. The SQL statement with the where clause is updating data; therefore, it is DML (data modification language).

8. For security, it would be best to separate applications and DBs to be put on separate servers with different access controls.

9. The best protection we can give to our DBs and applications is to install vendor-released patches as soon as possible. But we need to make sure that the vendor-released patch is genuine and works well before installing on the production servers.

10. Administrative functions, backup, audit tracking, and authentication processes fall into functional security.

11. Avoiding leaks or spillage, controlling social engineering attacks, keeping the encryption keys secret, guarding against intellectual property theft, and not giving a chance for anyone to physically steal data are some of the countermeasures for data security.

12. Class 2 or secret classification.

13. A visitor must have a visitor badge and must always be accompanied by an employee.

14. A separate departmental entity must be assigned with the duties of background checks and security clearances because these are time-consuming functions and cannot be done by HR or people dealing with data or technology.

15. Strictly enforce the organizational policies and audit everyone.

Access Control of Data

Access Control—Roles for Individuals and Applications

Access to the database of an application is usually done by permissions given to the users or applications. The most general form of access given is the username and password set. However, before access is given, it is important to determine what access should be given, what privileges will be granted, and the user's need to know. These depend on the trust an organization places in their employees. Trust may require a background investigation and security clearance details to be obtained for the user. Access is given to people and applications with system accounts but only after proper forms are signed by responsible individuals.

Interestingly, access control spans more than one level and goes from top to bottom or sideways. Vertical privilege violation is when access privileges are violated from one level to another level. Horizontal privilege violation is when access privileges are violated at the same level. An example of vertical privilege violation is an employee can access the files of his supervisor or other C-level managers and modify those files, or an employee can enter a server room without proper authentication because the server room is open for all because of a broken lock. These types of escalations pose a great danger when they occur in financial industries, such as credit card companies or a Wall Street stockbroker's office.

When a customer service person in the credit card industry can access full details of files and modify the numbers therein, that can wreak havoc and cause trouble to both the company and the customer. This is one reason why the customer service representatives often transfer calls to their supervisors when a customer asks an important question regarding raising the credit limit or a refund to be issued. Horizontal privilege escalation is equally dangerous in that one customer service representative can change what a previous customer service representative modified on a customer file. This is why access control has to determine what control a person or a system has to have (read, write, execute, update, delete, or a combination of these) after access is granted. Thus, access control determines three factors: who (the person or an application or system account), what (the functions a user or application account can perform on the system or object), and how (whether the access is full, read, write, or something else). Once we decide these, our next step is to choose what type of access control we can grant and audit these accounts to check that the user or application account is not going "out of their permitted zones" at any time.

Access control generally works on the subject-object relationship. Subjects are those people or systems that can perform some action (read, write, delete). Objects are the entities or resources (a database, file storage location, or a server room) to which access is required. Subjects usually have background checks, clearances, and proper training already done and file a signed form (either digitally or in ink) for access. Objects have labels of what level of clearance they belong to. For example, a person can have top security, security, classified, or unclassified clearances depending on their need and background checks. Objects have labels like classified, top secret, and so on. Access is granted to subjects when the subject clearance matches the object labels. As an example, a person holding top security clearance can mostly access whatever is labeled top security and anything below (security, classified, and unclassified), but a person holding simple classified clearance cannot access levels above the classified level.

Tables 5-1 to 5-4 show an example of data recorded in a hospital setting. For simplicity, not all fields recorded are shown in the example. Table 5-1 gives access clearance to subjects, and Table 5-2 is what access is allowed to each type of clearance. If Table 5-3 is an example of data recorded for a patient, a subject with unclassified clearance level can only see two columns: patient name and balance unpaid. Note that these clearances do not automatically mean the subject can read, write, delete, or execute anything. Each clearance level defines what a subject can do or cannot do. Refer to Table 5-2 to see what columns in a table a subject with a particular clearance type can see. But if the same table is accessed by secret clearance personnel (such as a CEO or COO), they can see everything in a patient record and may even be able to modify details in the table data. In some cases, the COO may be able to read but not modify, and the access to write/delete may still be with the accounts department.

Table 5-1 *Clearances Granted for Staff in a Hospital Setting*

Who/Subjects	Clearance
Top-level managers (CEO, COO)	Secret
Doctor, nurse	Sensitive
Billing department staff	Private
IT staff	Unclassified

Table 5-2 *Clearances Granted for Admitted Patient Details in a Hospital Setting*

Type of Clearance	Access Allowed To
Secret	All columns and all fields
Sensitive	Surgery details, admission, discharge dates, symptoms
Protected	Contact phone, name, employer details, symptoms
Private	Admission, discharge, days in ICU, days in general ward
Unclassified	Patient name, balance unpaid, total charged, payment plans

Table 5-3 *Example Patient Details Recorded in a Hospital Setting*

Patient Name	Admission	Discharge	Surgery Details	Balance Unpaid
David Joshua	12/03/2008	12/09/2008	Thyroidectomy	$2,675.86
Vivian Edwards	02/18/2001	03/14/2001	Appendicitis	$12,538.37
Angela Mathews	05/30/2020	06/07/2020	Cardiomyopathy, valve replacement	$56,325.00
Thomas Driller	10/02/2021	10/22/2021	Lung cancer, COVID-19, deceased	$35,690.56

Table 5-4 *The Actual Data an "Unclassified" Subject Can Access (Read Only)*

Patient Name	Balance Unpaid
David Joshua	$2,675.86
Vivian Edwards	$12,538.37
Angela Mathews	$56,325.00
Thomas Driller	$35,690.56

Thus, various levels' access options can be defined by an organization as they deem fit and enforce those options on their employees. Access control is important because data needs to be protected at the database level or at the application level, as well as at data-at-rest and data-in-movement states. It is also important because data protection is based on the "zero trust" assumption in which no person or system is trusted blindly. Without such access controls and policies being enforced, data can be lost or stolen easily.

Now let us talk about the types of access controls that are well known.

MAC, DAC, RBAC, RuBAC

The various types of access control are discussed in this section. Mandatory access control (MAC) is dependent on the rules that a subject's granted security clearance level dictates what object they can access. MAC is often enforced in government and military agencies where a subject is first sent to get a particular form of clearance from a separate entity. Generally, the entity or organization that grants the requested clearance is different from the organization where the subject works.

Here is an example: An employee hired by the income tax department has to get secret clearance. The employee files for clearance by signing the required forms. The forms are then countersigned by the income tax department's supervisor who is hiring the new employee, affirming that the new employee does need access (confirming the "need to know"). The papers are then sent to one or more departments, such as Homeland Security, Department of Defense, and Central Intelligence Agency, depending on the type of clearance required. MAC therefore is heavily dependent on various factors and can be revoked at any time by those separate departments that granted the clearance.

MAC is also enforced by the hiring agency or department by subjecting the person to more rules, such as using a baseline security computer, not allowing them to install additional software, not installing more than required software, and enforcing password policies. These rules apply to every single person in the organization and are put on every single desktop or laptop. The MAC rules also differ from one operating system to another and to the mobile devices or Bring Your Own Device (BYOD) policies, but are all uniform for all employees from CEO level to the most bottom rung in the corporate structure. Giving access does not mean that a subject is free to do what they like; instead, a clearance is granted, and the subject will be watched closely to see if the access control is violated in any way. If any violation is observed, access can be revoked, lowered, or restricted with more rules and restraints. For this reason, MAC is also called nondiscretionary access control.

Discretionary access control (DAC) comes into play after MAC is implemented. DAC is based on ownership of an object—typically a piece of software or a system. The owner decides who should get access and what access should be given. It also means a person who was granted security clearance at the MAC level may not get DAC for a particular system or software.

Here is an example: The income tax employee who was hired and given MAC and a laptop may not be able to access a particular database hosted by the income tax department—say, the lawmaker's database (LDB)—because the owner of that database does not think the new employee needs access to the LDB. If the new employee does actually need access to the LDB, they have to request it specifically with their local branch supervisor, who will attest to the need for the LDB access and file a signed form to request access. Then the database administrators of the LDB would examine the filed papers for accuracy and grant or reject access. Permitting access involves creating a new username and temporary password for the employee and following separate password policies (discussed in the next section of this chapter) for that LDB account. DAC is also called branch-level access where the local supervisor or boss decides if access can be granted.

Discretionary rules are implemented with files and folders easily in the Linux or Unix operating system with read (r, has a numerical value of 4), write (w, numerical value 2), and execute (x, numerical value 1) for three different areas: owner, group, and others. The permissions for files can be seen with the long listing command (**ls -l**). Example 5-1 shows a hypothetical listing of files and folders with the **ls -l** command.

Example 5-1   *File Listing on Linux Showing Files and Directories with Permissions*

```
-rwx --x -w-    root    root    9037    Jul    05    13:24    helloWorld.c
drwx r-x r-x    root    root    4097    May    02    09:23    PerlFiles
-rw- --x -w-    root    root    9037    Jul    05    13:24    a.out
```

In Example 5-1, you can see three blocks of letters rwx mixed in various ways. The very first letter in the listing of each line is either a "d" (directory) or a "-" (file). The first block of rwx belongs to the owner of the file or directory. The second rwx belongs to the group, and the last and third rwx belongs to everyone else (not the owner or the group). From the listing for helloWorld.c file, we notice that owner can read, write, and execute, but group can only execute the file (r and w are missing), and others can only write to the file. Permissions can be changed with the **chmod** command, and the command can be given with a solid number or a "+" and "-" sign as demonstrated in the following example. Note that only the owner of the file can give a successful **chmod** command to change permissions of files or directories/folders. When issuing a **chmod** command, the value supplied for each block (user, group, or others), the values of r, w, and x are summed up. In the case of helloWorld.c file, the mode becomes 712 because the owner has rwx totaling to 7 (r+w+x = 4+2+1), group has 1 (x only), and others have 2 (w only).

```
Chmod o+r helloWorld.c
```

```
chmod 000 helloWorld.c
```

The first command changes the file permissions as "add read privileges to others" and the mode now becomes rwx - - x rw- or 715. In the second **chmod** command, all permissions to all people—owner, group, and others—are removed, and nobody can read, write, or execute that file. In this way, DAC can be achieved by the owner at their own level and discretion. In the Windows operating system, the option to allow or deny is pretty straightforward. As an owner, you can right-click the filename, go to the **Security** tab, and allow or deny privileges. Figure 5-1 shows the Windows operating system permissions setup. This dialog box can be brought up by right-clicking any folder or file in the Windows operating system and choosing the **Properties, Security** tab and the **Edit** button on the **Security** tab.

Users can be added with the **Add** button and deleted with the **Remove** button by highlighting a user. The **Add** option further offers assistance in finding the users with a **Find** button on the server. Once the user is selected, the privileges of allow or deny can be adjusted for read, read/execute, and other options like "full control."

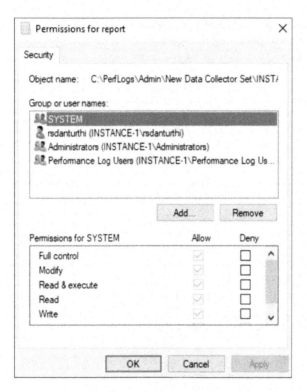

Figure 5-1   *Windows Operating System File Permissions*

Role-based access control (RBAC) happens after DAC is approved. Assume that the newly hired income tax employee applies for DAC on the server where the LDB is stationed. Now the database administrator gives access to the employee by creating a username and password, but the access is not exclusively given. There already might be some users in the department who are using the LDB and have the same access rights as the new employee. All these employees are grouped into a common RBAC, and a new role is created. For example, in an Oracle database, the following statement creates a role that gives access for security-cleared users with a read access (select):

```
Create role Sec_Users_Select_Role;
```

Now the users are added to or deleted from the role as required. In the following statement, "Senator_Data" is a table of the LDB. Notice that the table reading access is given to the role but not to the user directly because there are already existing groups of users who have the same or similar access rights on the LDB as the new user:

```
Grant select on Senator_Data to Sec_Users_Select_Role;
```

Now the database username THOMSONRK that was created is added to the role so that he gets the access grants of "select" on the "Senator_Data" table in LDB:

```
Grant Sec_Users_Select_Role to THOMSONRK;
```

What if after a few years, the user THOMSONRK leaves the department for good? Then the local RBAC is revoked simply without disturbing a lot of other settings:

```
Revoke Sec_Users_Select_Role from THOMSONRK;
```

Note that the role created is only for the Select statement in Oracle or for just reading the data of one table, Senator_Data. For writing and deleting, separate roles must be created and users added. Table 5-5 illustrates how an Oracle database uses privileges to roles that can be given with the following statement:

```
Grant "options" on "Object" to "Role_name";
```

Table 5-5   *Options in Oracle DB Command to Create Roles*

Option	Details
SELECT	Read data by executing SELECT statements on the table
INSERT	Put new data with INSERT statements on the table
UPDATE	Modify existing data with UPDATE statements on the table
DELETE	Remove data with DELETE statements on the table
REFERENCES	Create a constraint that refers to the table
ALTER	Modify the table with the ALTER TABLE statement; changes table definition
INDEX	Ability to create an index on the table with the create index statement
ALL	All possible options on table

The following are some statements that will create privileges on the "Senator_Data" table of the LDB. Note that one or more options can be included in the same Grant statement:

```
Grant SELECT, INSERT, UPDATE, DELETE on Senator_Data to Allowed_Role;

Grant ALL on Senator_Data to All_Powerful_Role;
```

Likewise, we can run a Revoke statement to remove all privileges:

```
Revoke SELECT, INSERT, UPDATE, DELETE on Senator_Data from Allowed_Role;

Revoke ALL on Senator_Data from All_Powerful_Role;
```

Rule-based access control (RuBAC) kicks into play like RBAC but can work with a variety of rules an organization implements. The rules can be local, global, or temporarily implemented. The rules can and do change regularly as well. One example of RuBAC is to allow people to work in only eight-hour shifts. Once the shift time is completed, no more access is allowed for an employee. It also means an employee who works the morning shift cannot log in to a system after their shift is over. So, the shift employee who works from morning 8:00 a.m. to 5:00 p.m. cannot enter the building after 5:00 p.m. because the entry access to the front gate will be blocked to the employee. Would the employee be allowed to work from home in the after-shift hours? That also is determined by the organizational rules that are in force.

The greatest disadvantage of this access control is that there is a lot of work required to implement new and changing rules to work with all employees and the RuBAC access control. And the rules can be static (fixed forever) or dynamic (due to a situation like COVID-19). One RuBAC that is implemented on databases and login processes is the number of attempts a user is allowed to try their username and password to log in. A rule can be set up to allow a user to try three attempts to log in, and after the third unsuccessful attempt, the account will be locked out. Some organizations can change the number of attempts from three to five or more and, if a situation warrants, even remove the rule and create a new rule. But for every rule to be implemented, the system needs to be reprogrammed, and the workload on the staff will increase with changing rules because it involves understanding and decoding the rule.

Passwords, Logins, and Maintenance

The easiest way to get into any system is to have no login information for starting up a system and shutting it down when not required. But this offers a great vulnerability for attacks. Anyone can open and use the system and then they would be the owners of the system, its files, and security. This kind of open system has a great vulnerability of losing data, programs, and files. To overcome this vulnerability, we now have a login method in every operating system with a username and password. There are better ways to log in with a two- or multifactor authentication with an access card and biometrics, but username and password still remains the most common way to allow a user to log in easily. Once logged in, the authorization privileges kick in, and the user is either allowed or denied further access to files, folders, databases, and so on.

Each database may need a username and password that are different from the username and password that are used to log in to the system. As more access or higher privileges are granted to a user, the user is entrusted with higher responsibility with the database. The logging mechanism of the DB has to make sure that after a stipulated period of inactivity (for example, 30 days), a DB account is locked out automatically. There are reasons to lock out an account on inactivity and on wrong password entries because to protect the data, an organization has policies in place. The number of attempts allowed for a successful login, the type of password used—its length, complexity, and so on—along with how long they can be used is spelled out in the password policies of the organization.

History, length, and complexity of a password dictate how hard it is for a hacker to break the password with a brute force attack or rainbow attacks. Length of a password should be at least eight characters, but common passwords should be longer because the reason is a password like "qwerty123" or "TomHanks22" can be easily cracked. For this reason, a general rule is to require password length to be a minimum of 12 to 15 characters and maximum of 24 characters. (The maximum length needs to be mentioned because a very long password can be hard to remember or recall even for the owner.) Password history dictates how many of the earlier used passwords can be reused. If the history is set as five, it means the last five passwords used earlier cannot be reused. In the Windows operating system or in any database software, the administrators can adjust this number. The complexity of a password dictates what the actual password of 15 or more characters must have. It should always be a combination of upper- and lowercase letters, numbers, and some permitted symbols like $, @, #, =, and so on. But note that some database software packages use $ and @ as reserved symbols for database operations. Therefore, what password complexity in a password policy works perfectly for system login may or may not work for accessing a database. For this reason, the policies for database passwords are always different from those of login passwords.

Defining the password policy is only the first step, but to make sure of the data safety and security of an IT system, it is mandatory that the organization creating the policies enforce those policies with a strict authority. Any unenforced policy is useless, and there is no point in having a policy that is never enforced. A common way to have a password policy is shown in Figure 5-2, which is an example of how the Windows operating system's password policy is set up using the Group Policy Management Editor. The group policy editor can be brought up by typing the **Group policy editor** in the Windows operating system and choosing **Computer configuration**, **Policies**, **Windows Settings**, **Security settings**, **Account policies**, **Password policy**. The details of password policies for history, age, and so on are listed in Table 5-6. In the password policy options on the right side, password age tells how many days a new password is valid. And always remember that any password policy that is drafted but never strictly implemented is useless and serves no purpose. Therefore, any policy audits must strictly focus on the policy enforcement and implementation by every single user logging into the system or using the database software or an application.

Also note that like the operating system, other applications and database packages have similar password restrictions that can be easily set and changed as required. But in the end, it is the administrator's duty to watch and enforce the policies.

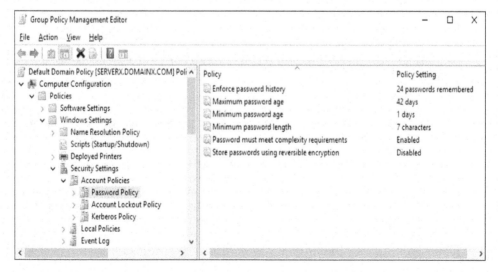

Figure 5-2 *Windows Operating System's Password Policy*

Table 5-6   *Password Policy Details and Their Meaning*

Policy Item	What It Means
Age	Maximum number of days a password can be used before it expires. A value of 0 implies that passwords never expire.
Length	Minimum length is the number of characters the system accepts for a good password.
Complexity	A combination of upper- and lowercase letters, numbers, and symbols such as $, @, #, and so on.
History	The number of older passwords the system remembers and cannot be reused.
Reversible encryption	Option on how to store passwords.

Note: Any policy that is drafted for use but never implemented is *useless*.

Hashing and Checksum Methods

Passwords, whether long or short, are stored in a specific location for the system to remember. If that storage area of the passwords is accessible to everyone, anyone can read and modify those passwords, or worse yet, reuse the user account and cause unfathomable damage. For this reason, passwords are stored as hashes. Hashing is a one-way function that encrypts the passwords into an unreadable stream of fixed-length characters. There is absolutely no way any one can get a plain text password from the unreadable hashed password text. The reason is that hashing is done with complex algorithms that are never disclosed to the public. Generally hashing offers the following advantages and properties:

- Hash algorithms are fast and always work one way and have fixed length.

- The range of hash values produced by a hash algorithm is huge.

- Similar or close to similar input to the same algorithm produces different hashes.

- A hash value cannot be reversed because the functioning of a hash algorithm is secret.

- Two different hash values do not follow any pattern or similarities.

- When hash values produced are identical, it is called a hash collision, but collisions in a hash algorithm are very rare.

- Hashes can be used for message integrity as well as encryption.

Common hash functions include MD5 (Message Digest, 128 bits), SHA-1 (Security Hash Algorithm, 160 bits), SHA-2 (or SHA256 with 256 bits), and SHA-3 (224 to 512 bits). These are also designated by their bits as SHA256, SHA512, and so on. The strength requirements are dependent upon data classification.

For unclassified data, where cryptography is required, the following is recommended:

- AES 128 for encryption
- SHA 256 for hashing

NSA has established the suite B encryption requirements for protecting National Security Systems (NSS) as follows:

- AES 128 for Secret
- AES 256 for Top Secret
- SHA 256 for Secret
- SHA 384 for Top Secret

National Security System is defined as

(OMB Circular A-130) Any telecommunications or information system operated by the United States Government, the function, operation, or use of which (1) involves intelligence activities; (2) involves cryptologic activities related to national security; (3) involves command and control of military forces; (4) involves equipment that is an integral part of a weapon or weapons system; or (5) is critical to the direct fulfillment of military or intelligence missions, but excluding any system that is to be used for routine administrative and business applications (including payroll, finance, logistics, and personnel management applications).

The following is a demonstration in the Linux operating system of how plain text can be used to generate a hash followed by a compression of a file and generation of a hash for the compressed file. Note that the commands **md5sum** and **sha256sum**, **sha512sum** are the hash-producing functions. Let us first create a variable named "Var":

```
[root@localhost ~]# export Var="A quick brown fox jumped over a lazy dog!"

[root@localhost ~]# echo $Var
A quick brown fox jumped over a lazy dog!
```

Once the variable is created, the same can be used to create a md5sum. In the following snippet, | is the piping character. The echo command produces the variable value and feeds it to the **md5sum** command to create a hash or MD5 checksum:

```
[root@localhost ~]# echo -n "$Var" |md5sum
8cea297fa8e0b669951a729b707df436  -
```

Let us now create another variable "Var2" with a slight change in one word, but keep the sentence as it is. In the following listing, Var2 has the word as "brawn" instead of "brown":

```
[root@localhost ~]# export Var2="A quick brawn fox jumped over a lazy dog!"
```

```
[root@localhost ~]# echo $Var2
A quick brawn fox jumped over a lazy dog!

[root@localhost ~]# echo -n "$Var2" |md5sum
42f5504200293febe4db5d402d33d386  -
```

Observe from the previous that change of one single letter in the entire sentence has produced an entirely different hash output. The following two commands produce different hashes of different lengths with SHA256 and SHA512 algorithms on the variables Var and Var2:

```
[root@localhost ~]# echo -n "Var" |sha256sum
60529803e0f91fc27260bc1e41b06d589df686290d0298b473a8f3a6c999ebe6  -


[root@localhost ~]# echo -n "$Var2" |sha512sum

6e5301699e1c1d5c25d6d50eab07c4d53ece58ec15530161b1b8b6f41409b9256043f-
36354627334fa4e92db59a4be67247f0e66b5e40cc3ea780eebd97a86b6  -
```

We can also create a hash for a file. First, we will zip our existing two files "bench.py" and "hello.c" into a tar file named myFile.tar:

```
[root@localhost ~]# ls -1


-rw-r--r--  1  root  root  114    Dec 26  2020   bench.py
-rw-r--r--  1  root  root  10240  Dec 12 13:16  hello.c

[root@localhost ~]# tar -cvf myFile.tar bench.py hello.c
bench.py
hello.c


[root@localhost ~]# ls -1


-rw-r--r--  1  root  root  114    Dec 26  2020   bench.py
-rw-r--r--  1  root  root  10240  Dec 12 13:16  hello.c
-rw-r--r--  1  root  root  20480  Dec 12 13:18  myFile.tar
```

With the tar file created, use that tar file and create a message digest for that tar file. We use the filename md5sum.txt for storing the generated MD5 hash:

```
[root@localhost ~]# md5sum myFile.tar > md5sum.txt
[root@localhost ~]# ls -1


-rw-r--r--  1  root  root  114    Dec 26  2020   bench.py
-rw-r--r--  1  root  root  10240  Dec 12 13:16  hello.c
-rw-r--r--  1  root  root  45     Dec 12 13:25  md5sum.txt
-rw-r--r--  1  root  root  0      Dec 12 13:19  myFile.tar
```

Because the file size now shows as zero (very small), what is in the newly created hash file? We can check that with another Linux command and display the contents:

```
[root@localhost ~]# more md5sum.txt
d41d8cd98f00b204e9800998ecf8427e  myFile.tar
```

The md5sum.txt file has the filename for which the hash is generated and the hash itself as 128 bits (or 32 hexadecimal numbers). Likewise, we can create another file for the SHA 512 hash, which is shown here:

```
[root@localhost ~]# sha512sum myFile.tar >sha512.txt

[root@localhost ~]# more sha512.txt
cf83e1357eefb8bdf1542850d66d8007d620e4050b5715dc83f4a921d36ce9ce47d0d1
3c5d85f2b0ff8318d2877eec2f63b931bd47417a81a538327af927da3e  myFile.tar
```

Now let us turn our attention to checking the generated hash for accuracy. Can the hash generated be checked to make sure that it belongs to the myFile.tar and is accurate? In Linux, we can use the same commands md5sum, sha512sum etc., with an option -c for checking:

```
[root@localhost ~]# md5sum -c md5sum.txt
myFile.tar: OK
```

What happens if we feed a wrong hash file to sha512 algorithm? Does it validate correctly? We will feed the MD5 (128 bits) hash to SHA512 (512 bits) and observe results:

```
[root@localhost ~]# sha512sum -c md5sum.txt
sha512sum: md5sum.txt: no properly formatted SHA512 checksum lines found
```

We can see the hash is wrong, and the command shows it is an error or the hash generated does not belong to the file as checksum. But when we feed the 512 bits hash to the correct algorithm, it should validate accurately, as shown:

```
[root@localhost ~]# sha512sum -c sha512.txt
myFile.tar: OK
```

The previous listing demonstrates how a checksum or hash can be generated. There is a practical use for this hash or checksum. Assume that we have a website or server from where users after proper authentication can download an important file. The users should have a way to know that the file they download is not changed, and it conforms to the integrity factor of the CIA security triad. Therefore, when putting a file on a site for downloading, the administrator of the site also generates a hash (or checksum) and makes it available as a separate file for users. Users who download the file also download the message digest or the hash file. When they have the hash file and the actual file, they can quickly check, as demonstrated previously, whether the file contents are intact. Any change in the contents of the file or the hash file would generate an error. As the hash checks for errors in the file, it is also called "checksum," which checks the total contents of the file.

Table 5-7 contains hash contents reproduced from Oracle Internet pages where one can download the Oracle virtual machine box. The file comes with a md5sum as well sha1sum. The file details and checksums are provided for the user to check the file size downloaded and match the checksum to verify the file's integrity.

Table 5-7   *Oracle File Download on Internet with Checksum*

Download	Release Notes
Oracle DB Developer VM	7,817,064,448 bytes, md5sum: 20b5a5bd91cfe9d4f5acf5128f06146e, sha1: e0b9f8af8158664139b9ca970c3500752fc15fd2

(from URL: https://www.oracle.com/database/technologies/databaseappdev-vm.html)

Hashing is very helpful in storing passwords (as hashes) and for maintaining integrity of files. And always remember that hash is a one-way function. If a hash is supplied to a hacker, it is impossible for the hacker to find the original plain text password. It also means on an operating system such as Windows 11, where user passwords are stored as hashes, if the password is lost or forgotten, virtually nobody can retrieve them. Many database and software applications use hashing to store passwords as hashes in the backend.

Following is a hypothetical listing from the Oracle database when you read the SQL used for creating the account. Notice the password stored as a very long hash:

```
create user "JDBIDEN" identified by values 'S:3218d581f92716e0826aec78
9431093a782312798be809097266edc8299272927eba36782'
default tablespace "USERS" temporary tablespace "TEMP" profile
"GENERAL"
```

If the password is lost or forgotten, another administrator can log in and reset the passwords but cannot retrieve an older password in plain text. Hackers sometimes use rainbow tables—a pre-compiled list of hashes for all known and common passwords—to attack a system if the system allows a hash to be used as a password. Rainbow tables are available for free and purchase on the Internet as well, making the life of hackers easy.

Locking, Unlocking, Resetting

A lot of time in a system administrator's work is usually spent creating, locking, unlocking, and resetting of accounts, whether they are system login accounts, database, or application accounts. People tend to forget passwords, ignore maintaining accounts, or never even use their accounts when they have no time after they are given privileges. Automatic locking of accounts on N (usually less than five) unsuccessful attempts is also recommended to avoid any attacks a hacker might try as a brute force. Sometimes a user, unaware that their account is locked, can retry the same expired password on a locked-out account dozens of times to create an event named "excessive logins." These excessive logins need to be monitored by a system, database, or application administrators regularly to avoid any impending trouble. As observed earlier, password policies dictate how long the account is active, how complex a password should be, and how many days a password can be used.

Figure 5-3 shows how Oracle software sets up password policy for locking, unlocking, and so on. Notice the **Number of failed login attempts to lock after** field. This can be adjusted and usually set up as 3 to 5 for better security. Attempting to use bad passwords, brute force attacks, and such can be prevented with this setup.

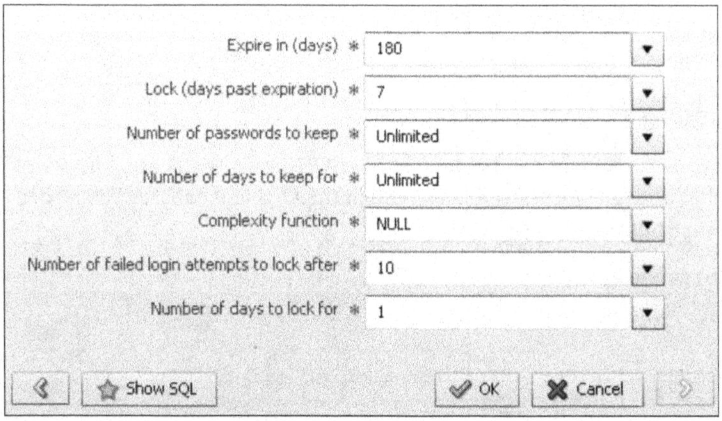

Figure 5-3   *Oracle Password Policy Setup*

But what if an authorized genuine user forgot their password and is locked out? In such cases, users request a password reset via a proper channel with a DB administrator or system administrator. The following listing demonstrates how a password can be reset, set, or modified in both Oracle and MS SQL Server databases. For the example, assume the account name is "JDBIDEN."

Oracle PL-SQL Listing

Let's see in action the actual SQL scripts that create the accounts and can be locked, unlocked, or reset with a new password.

To unlock the user account but leave the password intact, use this:

```
alter user "JDBIDEN" account unlock;
```

If the user knows their password, the following can reset the password to a new one:

```
alter user "JDBIDEN" identified by "NewPassWord" replace "OldPassword";
```

If the user does not remember their password, a DBA can use the following to create a new password. It can also be combined with the unlock option to both reset the password and unlock the account at the same time. The second line lists the hash for the password if the DBA needs to do it via a hash. Note that even the DBA will not know the plain text password when they use the hash:

```
Alter user "JDBIDEN" identified by "NewPassWord" account unlock;


alter user "JDBIDEN" identified by 'S:3218d581f92716e0826aec789431093';
```

If a user is fired, on long leave, or needs their account suspended temporarily, use the following:

```
alter user "JDBIDEN" account lock;
```

MS SQL Server Listing

What was achieved earlier in Oracle can be done in MS SQL Server with ease. The script is slightly different but does the identical job as it did in the Oracle database. The reader can compare the commands easily as well.

```
ALTER LOGIN   JDBIDEN ENABLE;
GO


ALTER LOGIN   JDBIDEN WITH PASSWORD='NewPassWord' OLD_
PASSWORD='oldpassword';
GO


ALTER LOGIN   JDBIDEN WITH PASSWORD='NewPassWord' UNLOCK;
GO


ALTER LOGIN   JDBIDEN WITH PASSWORD=0x3218d581f92716e0826aec789431093
HASHED;
GO
```

But remember, before you reset any account or create one, you must verify proper identification, do background investigations, and make sure papers requesting an account are signed in good faith. Any discrepancies should be first corrected before granting privileges per the IAAA process discussed in earlier chapters. Almost all the systems, software packages, and database software have settings to follow the locking mechanism and send an email to the administrators when something goes wrong. It is the responsibility of the administrator to read those incidence or event alarms in the logs and take appropriate action. In the next section, we talk about how to monitor and set up system or application accounts.

Monitoring User Accounts, System Account

Remember that the last step in the IAAA process is auditing to see what the user is actually doing with the granted privileges. Assume that a user has an authorized ID and password to log in to an Oracle database. Because they have either forgotten or mistyped the password, they are unable to login. But per the rules of password policy, the system will reject the password after three to five attempts and locks the account. However, the user continues to try on their end with the same password. How does a system administrator find this event or discover the unsuccessful login is from a hacker who found the username and is trying to get into the system with various possible passwords. There is a simple way the database is equipped to provide the login information; the login information and the events or incidents are always recorded in an audit file. Oracle stores the audit data in two different tables, namely sys.aud$ and system.audit_data, for 30 days. These tables have the following information and more.

Oracle stores the audit data in the database audit trail, stored in the SYS.AUD$ table, with different types of information. The following information is included in each audit trail record:

■ Operating system login username

■ Username

■ Session identifier

■ Terminal identifier

■ Name of the schema object accessed

■ Operation performed or attempted

■ Completion code of the operation (return code)

■ Date and time stamp

A return code of 1017 indicates an unsuccessful login with an invalid username password combination. There are other codes, such as 28000, that indicate a user is trying to log in too many times and can show a brute force attack or unsuccessful login. Return code 0 often is associated with success with a command, login, and such. It is possible to easily check these audit tables to find details with script lines such as the following:

```
select  timestamp#, userid, userhost from system.aud$;
```

```
select * from system.audit_data where returncode in (1017, 28000);
```

Various other combinations of SQL scripts can be executed to find users. Clauses such as "order by" or several "where" conditions can be added to the script as well. When "group by" and "order by" options are added to the script, they can narrow the searches. All these options can display the user(s) with their login details and cause of these error codes.

Monitoring—Triggers

Assume you have a database with tables and data and of course your data needs to be safe and protected. You take every precaution with users and exercise extreme security measures to protect data, but still data can be manipulated by some user either knowingly or by mistake. How would you track such changes? The answer comes from database triggers, which are like small built-in programs that fire on a given condition. For example, if you create a table and a trigger to watch any indexes created, modified, or deleted on that table, the events of such changes can be tracked in a log via a trigger. Example 5-2 is a sample in MS SQL Server database. IDX_Change_Log is the table you create to store any changes. TR_IDX_Change is the trigger itself, which stores data into the log table when invoked. On what event would you create an entry in the table? Those events are mentioned in the "for" part—on creating new index, altering an index, or removing an existing index. The data stored comes from MS SQL Server's EVENTDATA() block, which is the XML block.

Example 5-2 *Creating a Trigger That Creates a Log Entry on Table Changes in SQL Server*

```
CREATE TABLE  IDX_Change_log (
    Entry_Nbr INT IDENTITY PRIMARY KEY,
    Log_Data XML NOT NULL,
    UserName SYSNAME NOT NULL
);
GO


CREATE TRIGGER TR_IDX_Change
ON DATABASE
FOR
    CREATE_INDEX,
    ALTER_INDEX,
    DROP_INDEX
AS
BEGIN
    SET NOCOUNT ON;

    INSERT INTO IDX_Change_log (
        Log_data,
        UserName
    )
    VALUES (
        EVENTDATA(),
        USER
    );
END;
GO
```

The XML block in the table would look somewhat like that shown in Example 5-3 (shown only the shortened version).

Example 5-3 *Sample of XML Data Column in a Table*

```
<EVENT INSTANCE>
    <EventType>ALTER INDEX</EventType>
    <PostTime>2022-12-20</PostTime>
    <SPID>321832</SPID>
    <LoginName>DavidMJ</LoginName>
    <DatabaseName>HR_Test</DatabaseName>
    <SchemaName>Employees</SchemaName>
    <ObjectType>INDEX</ObjectType>
    <TargetobjectType>TABLE</TargetobjectType>
    <TSQLCommand>
        ...
    </TSOLCommand>
</EVENT INSTANCE>
```

Note that the conditions when you need to create a table entry can be modified. In Example 5-3, we used alter, drop, and create, but it is not necessary to include all. It can have one or more. In Example 5-3, the trigger only creates a log entry but continues to allow the user to alter, modify, or create an index.

What if you want a check for insert or remove data in a table that may have some safety concerns? You can use the clauses "for Insert" and "for Delete," as shown in Example 5-4.

Example 5-4 *Raising Errors with a Trigger on Changes in a Table in SQL Server*

```
CREATE TRIGGER TR_DoubleCheck
    ON HR.Employees
FOR DELETE
    AS
    IF (SELECT Count(*) FROM HR.Paystubs where employees like 'CODERS') > 0
    BEGIN
        RAISERROR 50009 'Cannot remove a coder that easily')
        ROLLBACK TRANSACTION
        RETURN
    END
GO
```

Example 5-4 checks whether an employee can be deleted from the HR.Employees table and fires an error (RAISERROR) if there are coders in the HR.Paystubs table. The Select statement can be any type with any clauses as well.

Note that there can be three different ways to create a trigger: one for DDL (firing on create, alter, or drop), one for DML (firing on insert, update, or delete), and one for logon events (login and logout). Example 5-5 is a shortened version of a trigger in Oracle created for insert, update, or delete event on a table—all in one trigger.

Example 5-5   *Trigger Script in Oracle for Insert, Delete, and Updates on a Table*

```
CREATE OR REPLACE trigger Trg_Employees
BEFORE INSERT OR DELETE OR UPDATE ON HR.Employees
FOR EACH ROW
ENABLE
-- Declare required variables
DECLARE
    curUser  VARCHAR2 (20);
    curDate  VARCHAR2(30);
    curVersion VARCHAR2(10);
BEGIN
    SELECT user, sysdate, INTO curUser, curDate FROM dual;
    IF INSERTING THEN
        INSERT INTO HR.InsertAudit (InsUser, InsDate, InsVersion, command)
        VALUES (curUser, curDate, 1.12.1.2x, 'Insert');
    ELSIF UPDATING THEN
        INSERT INTO HR.UpdateAudit (updUser, updDate, updVersion, command)
        VALUES (curUser, curDate, 1.13.1.2x, 'Update');
    ELSIF DELETING THEN
        INSERT INTO HR.DeleteAudit (delUser, delDate, delVersion, command)
        VALUES (curUser, curDate, 1.10.1.2x, 'Delete');
    END IF;
END;
```

Triggers can cause serious trouble if not used correctly. If a database is updating automatically on some nightly run or needs manual update, these triggers can prevent DB updates in a nasty way. For that reason, when a DB is being updated, triggers are disabled first and are re-enabled when the update is complete. These need to be done by a responsible DBA who knows what they are doing, rather than randomly enabling and disabling. As much as a trigger can cause trouble, disabling a trigger can easily cause a bigger trouble and data loss.

Data Protection—Views and Materialized Views

If you have a lot of data and lots of users, you know for sure that data cannot be exposed at will to everyone. For those people who do not need to read all tables or all columns of a particular table, the DBA often creates views and allows data access via the views. A view is like a small program that runs only when the user executes a select operation to read data. In other words, a view does not hold any data but just holds another select statement to pull data from one or more tables. For that reason, a view is always up to date because the data is pulled when the users ask for it. The main purpose of a view is to create a temporary table to show partial data from a real physical table to users. If we grant read only privileges to a user on a table, the user can still see all columns of that table. By creating a view, we can restrict what columns a user can see. The view also never has the data as a physical table but fetches the data when the view is queried. The fetched data is stored in a temporary table that vanishes when the user stops querying the view. Example 5-6 shows a view created in Oracle on a table HREmployees. The view has a different name as HR.vw_Employees.

Example 5-6 *Oracle View Object Created from a Table*

```
CREATE OR REPLACE FORCE VIEW HR.vw_Employees
(ID, firstName, lastName, hseNumber, Address, City, State, Zip, payGr, Dept, stDate)
AS
SELECT  ID,
    empFirstName,
    empLastaName,
    empHNbr,
    empAddr,
    empCity,
    empSt,
    empZip,
    empPayGr,
    empDept,
    empStDt
FROM HR.Employees ORDER BY empSt, empStDt desc;
```

The view has a select statement to pick only a few select data items (columns) from table HR.Employees. The select statement does not have to pick all columns of the table but can also pick all columns as well. It means those columns that are not picked in the view are hidden from the users who are granted read permissions on the view. The permissions on the view are granted as shown in the following for individual users or roles.

```
GRANT SELECT ON HR.vw_Employees TO READ_SW_USERS;
GRANT SELECT ON HR.vw_Employees TO DAVIDJ;
GRANT SELECT ON HR.vw_Employees TO READ_DBA;
GRANT SELECT ON HR.vw_Employees TO READ_HR_USERS;
```

Then the actual grants for users happen in the role privileges such as

```
GRANT READ_SW_USERS TO MILLERK;
GRANT READ_DBA TO MICHAELJ WITH ADMIN OPTION;
```

Sometimes users need data from more than one table and are not required to have write privileges. Creating two views for two tables is not a bad idea, but can we create a view to have data with more than one table? No problem. Here it is, as demonstrated in Example 5-7.

Example 5-7   *An Oracle View Created from More Than One Table*

```
CREATE OR REPLACE FORCE VIEW HR.vw_EmpSalData
(ID, firstName, lastName, payGrade, Dept, startDate, monthlySal,
yearlySal, raiseDate, CONSTRAINT id_pk PRIMARY KEY (ID)
)
AS
SELECT  e.ID
    e.empFirstName,
    e.empLastName,
    e.empPayGr,
    e.empDept,
    s.empStDt,
    s.salPaidMon,
    s.salPaidYr,
    s.raiseDt
FROM HR.Employees e  INNER JOIN HR.SALARIES s on e.ID=s.ID
ORDER BY empStartDept, empStartDate desc;
```

In other words, any select statement with any number of clauses like where, group by, order by union, minus, or any complex select statement to fetch data from many tables (and other views as well) can be included in creating a view. When such complicated statements are written inside a view, the only problem would be the time the view takes to execute the statement to fetch the data. Note from Example 5-7 that if the HR.Employees table has some data like Social Security Numbers, they need not be shown to the public and excluded from the select statements defined inside the view. The tables that supply the data to the view are known in Oracle as "base tables." Usually before creating a view, the select statement must be run separately by the DBA to make sure there are no errors in the statement—either syntax or semantic.

Assume that the views HR.vw_EmpSalData and HR.vw_Employees are created and ready for users. A user named MICHAELJ who is given permissions via a role as indicated would see data from the view as shown in Table 5-8.

Table 5-8   *Data from Views HR.vw_EmpSalData (Top) and HR.vw_Employees (Bottom)*

ID	firstName	lastName	payGrade	Dept	startDate	monthlySal	yearlySal	raiseDate

ID	firstName	lastName	hseNumber	Address	City	State	Zip	payGr	Dept	stDate

Because the user MICHAELJ can now read the data from these tables, does he have to read all columns of the view? No need. MICHAELJ can run his own select commands on these views (temporary tables) as the following or with any combination of select statements, joins, order, where clauses, and so on.

```
Select ID, payGrade, Dept from HR.vw_EmpSalData order by raiseDate;
```

```
Select a.firstName, a.lastName, b.payGr, b.stDate from HR.vw_
EmpSalData a INNER JOIN HR.vw_Employees b on a.ID=b.ID ORDER BY
a.Dept asc;
```

All users who have the read privileges (who have the "select" grants) on the views can treat it as a table and run any combination of select statements to fetch data from the view. In other words, a view is designed for users to give just the "need-to-know" data and disable them from erasing or deleting the actual data in a table. The users who have read access on the view can further restrict themselves to read a select few columns of the data rather than reading all the available data columns.

Materialized views follow a different route than the normal views. Normal view as discussed earlier is a virtual table with no storage, but a materialized view actually has its results stored in a cache as a solid table—thus, the word *materialized*. If the users are performing a lot of queries on production tables, causing downtime or expenses (as in the cloud), a local materialized view may be a better option that can be created once and queried repeatedly. Also, in a materialized view, an index can be set to any column, which is really not an option in a normal view. Two example definitions for a materialized view are given in Example 5-8.

Example 5-8 *Script for Creating a Materialized View*

```
CREATE MATERIALIZED VIEW  mv_Employees
AS
(
    SELECT
        ID,
        SUM(Salary) AS TotalSalary
    FROM    HR.Employees
    GROUP BY Dept
);


CREATE MATERIALIZED VIEW  mv_Employees
WITH curSelection
AS
(
    SELECT
        ID,
        SUM(Salary) AS TotalSalary, Avg(HrsWorked) as AvHrs
    FROM HR.Employees
```

```
)

SELECT sum(AvHrs), COUNT(*) AS counter
FROM curSelection
GROUP BY AvHrs;
```

Like the select statements in the normal views, a great variety of select statements with complicated joins, groups, and where clauses can be included in materialized view too. In fact, materialized view has an advantage for using the complicated select statements in that a normal view's script can spend a lot of time getting results from a server every time it is executed, but the materialized view will quickly pull the results from a cached table without spending a lot of time. When using a cloud DB server that bills the customer by the minute, a materialized view is more advantageous cost-wise.

Refresh procedures are in the Oracle package DBMS_MVIEW. There are three types of refresh operations.

DBMS_MVIEW.REFRESH: Refreshes a given materialized view

DBMS_MVIEW.REFRESH_ALL_MVIEWS: Refreshes all existing materialized views

DBMS_MVIEW.REFRESH_DEPENDENT: Refreshes all table-based materialized views

The refreshing commands can be invoked to run when the server is not busy or when a lot of users are not logged in (say between 9:00 p.m. to 3:00 a.m.) and can be set up to run automatically or run manually on demand by the DBA or authorized personnel.

PII Security—Data, Metadata, and Surrogates

Personally identifiable information (PII)—such as Social Security Numbers, credit card numbers, home address, medical data, and names of family members—poses a great challenge for protection. Dozens of laws, both at the federal and state level, exist that impose extreme penalties when PII is exposed, stolen, or spilled. To protect data in motion and data at rest, databases offer encryption capabilities, but hackers are too smart and break those encryptions and succeed in stealing information.

To protect the data stored in the tablespaces and files, DB packages use various encryption methods and algorithms such as AES. These algorithms use a key to encrypt the data. Before going further down the encryption route, let us briefly touch on Kerchoff's law in security. The hacking world is so smart, it can usually find the environment we work in, the databases we use, and the network to which we connect to reach our databases and applications. They may even break the firewall and get into the network and steal. In general, everything about our systems is or can be known except the key. Therefore, Kerchoff stated that if we can keep our key confidential, we can probably protect our data. The most significant step we can implement to shield our data is to protect our encryption key. Most database packages follow this rule and allow the DBA and DB owners to create a key and keep it secret. The algorithms implemented can be different, but they are adapted from the NIST's recommended algorithms such as AES. Example 5-9 is a simple listing of how Oracle and SQL Server implement encryption and how we can find out details. Note that these queries work only for users with appropriate privileges.

Oracle has the table by name—"v$encrypted_tablespaces"—to store information for the key and algorithm. Example 5-9 shows the table that has the data columns and how to select required data from the table.

Example 5-9   *Oracle's v$encrypted_tablespaces Table Data and a Corresponding Select Statement*

```
TS#,
ENCRYPTIONALG,
ENCRYPTEDTS,
ENCRYPTEDKEY,
MASTERKEYID,
BLOCKS_ENCRYPTED,
BLOCKS_DECRYPTED,
KEY_VERSION,
STATUS,
CON_ID


Select ENCRYPTIONALG, ENCRYPTEDTS, MASTERKEYID, BLOCKS_ENCRYPTED, STATUS
   from v$encrypted_tablespaces;



        AES256      YES      1AE1….B1F       74293       NORMAL
        AES256      YES      D02E…D96        67923       NORMAL
        AES256      YES      623C…7A2         1547       NORMAL
```

SQL server has similar encryption algorithm and can be found from sys schema and encryption keys as follows from the system table sys.dm_database_encryption_keys:

```
SELECT  db_name(database_id), encryption_state
FROM    sys.dm_database_encryption_keys;

            HRdb                        3
        PayrollDB                       3
```

Another table by name sys.databases has more information, which can be displayed with a query, as shown in Example 5-10.

Example 5-10   *SQL Server Sample for Database Encryption Details*

```
SELECT
Sdb.name AS Name
Sdb.is_encrypted AS IsEncr,
sdek.encryption_state, AS State,
sdek. key_algorithm Algorithm,
sdek.key_length AS KeyLength
FROM
sys.databases    Sdb


LEFT OUTER JOIN sys.dm_database_encryption_keys    sdek


ON Sdb.database_id = sdek.database_id;


Name             IsEncr        State    Algorithm    KeyLength
---------------------------------------------------------------------
-----

HRdb             1             3        AES          256
PayrollDB        1             3        AES          256
```

Note the status of encryption in Example 5-10, given by the column "encryption_state."
It has the following details per MS SQL. The column actually indicates whether the
database is encrypted or not:

> 0 = No database encryption key present, no encryption
>
> 1 = Unencrypted
>
> 2 = Encryption in progress
>
> 3 = Encrypted
>
> 4 = Key change in progress
>
> 5 = Decryption in progress
>
> 6 = Protection change in progress (The certificate or asymmetric key that is
> encrypting the database encryption key is being changed.)

From the list, we note that there is a state numbered "6" that indicates the key is being
changed. SQL server supports symmetric algorithms, asymmetric algorithms, and X.509
certificates. Here are the ways to get more details of these encryptions.

```
SELECT * FROM sys.symmetric_keys;
```

Or if we are using asymmetric keys and certificates, we can use

```
SELECT * FROM sys.asymmetric_keys;
SELECT * FROM sys.certificates
```

While querying, if we find some binary data in MS SQL server tables, note that they may not be encrypted data but just normal binary data. This is so because SQL Server can store binary data in different ways (binary, varbinary, image). It would be a good idea to find those columns that are defined as binary types before assuming that those columns are actually encrypted. Binary data type of columns can be found by doing a select statement on the following tables with various joins, unions, and so on.

```
sys.columns
sys.types
sys.tables
sys.schemas
```

After we exercise adequate measures to protect our data, we now concentrate on the metadata. In a simple definition, metadata is "data about data." Metadata is not about what is in a column or table of a database and never talks about the contents of a DB. Rather, it gives a trend of the data and can indicate interesting details. Here is an example. Two days before a winter storm, you go the store and want to buy supplies, such as salt pellets, snow or ice melting sprays, a shovel, and maybe even gloves and snow boots, but you find that these are all already sold out and the shelves are empty. The stores did not expect this to happen and were not prepared—at least for the first time. But by the next year, the data analysts have analyzed the data for the previous year and arrived at the conclusion that these winter items must be stocked ahead of time between dates of November 1 and March 31. The stores now use this derived data to stock items and increase their sales. Likewise, online retailers like Amazon analyze their data and use it to better serve customers during the holiday season. A simple example of metadata can be normally found in picture files with the file properties in Windows and Mac operating systems. The data indicates the file type, size, format, what camera was used, and location the picture was taken. Sometimes, hackers can use this data to find out the whereabouts of people taking the pictures, and if the users used a smartphone, they can easily find out whether that phone is an iPhone or an Android phone. The National Information Standards Organization (NISO) defines metadata as different types, as listed in Table 5-9.

Table 5-9   *Types of Metadata per NISO*

Type	Details	Example
Descriptive metadata	To find a source	Title, author, genre, and so on
Administrative	Decoding, rendering	File size, type
■ Technical metadata	Long-term management	Checksum, encryption
■ Preservation metadata	Intellectual property	Copyrights
■ Rights metadata		
Structural metadata	Relationships	Navigation
Markup languages	Metadata and flags in tags	Navigation, interoperability

Metadata is stored in a variety of ways in a DB, an XML format file, or in other ways. XML provides a great way to define metadata because the user has freedom to generate any number of tags and is not limited to a few reserved words. Sharing of metadata, if required, is usually done with an application programming interface (API). In the open web, https://www.schema.org has the details of schemas, validation, and related documents.

So far, we have discussed data safety and encryption. Data items such as PII and medical information are usually unique, and DB owners sometimes can make a mistake of defining those attributes as primary keys and foreign keys. This can be a problem because PII is easily exposed to anyone who has access. With "zero trust" policies, it would be a good idea to replace the PII with something else that serves as the primary key, but the PII data may be important and should be often kept in the tables. Another way is to create a data attribute or column in a table that serves no other purpose as valid data but can be a unique number or name for each row of the table. This new attribute can serve as the primary key, but because it is not useful as a data item to anyone, it is called the surrogate key. The surrogate key is not dependent on the current data of a table or other tables. Neither is it derived from other attributes of the data. It is an internally generated number that can serve as the primary key. Universally unique identifiers (UUIDs) are an example of a surrogate key. Table 5-10 shows a table with a surrogate key that serves as the primary key of the table.

Table 5-10   *Data from Table with a Surrogate Key*

SK	firstName	lastName	HrsPerWk	stDate	endDate
0000127	Tom	Donaldson	42.5	03-01-2022	03-31-2022
0053603	Tom	Donaldson	30	03-01-2022	03-31-2022
0105364	Tom	Donaldson	25	03-01-2022	03-31-2022

Note that the table has three employees with the same name and same pay periods but different hours worked per week. If the table were to use SSN as a primary key, it would expose PII. Thus, the surrogate key (SK in the table) is introduced as a primary key. In this table, SK serves no other purpose and is not dependent on any other attribute of this table or any other table. Surrogates help protect data but should be generated with caution and privileged users should be informed how they work, and why and where they are situated or introduced in the tables. Many database packages can generate, auto-incrementing numerical values for a column that can serve as a surrogate key.

Summary

Access is given to users and applications based on their requirements, needs, and approval. Usually, these are decided by the subject-object tables that indicate what type of clearance each subject has and what access each clearance allows. Data can be shown as read-only format for individuals who should not have write access. MAC and DAC rules decide these permissions and accesses. Both Linux/Unix and Windows operating systems have commands to control access of files by users. Passwords inside a database (or operating system) are stored as hashes that cannot be broken because hash is a one-way function. Linux has various functions built in for MD, SHA256, and so on. Files also can have hashes to provide integrity. A file available for download from a website can come with a downloadable hash. When the file is downloaded, the downloaded hash can be compared to the file hash to make sure the file is intact. Locking, unlocking, and resetting of the database accounts is done by the DBAs, but they cannot give the original password back to users due to hashing. Monitoring the use of end-user and system accounts is important because the monitoring activity might reveal something about the users and what they are doing. Views and materialized views help save the data in tables because views only provide read-only access and views are always up to date. Metadata is data about data. When protecting PII, surrogate keys can work as primary keys in a database. Surrogate keys have no inherent value for data but only are added for a database to protect sensitive data such as SSNs.

Chapter 5 Questions

1. What two entities does an access control depend upon? Give examples for those entities.

2. When mandatory access control (MAC) is enforced, who grants the clearance for access?

3. What type of access control is dependent on ownership of the object?

4. What is role-based access control (RBAC)?

5. An employee granted access for "works night shift only" tries to enter the office building during the day shift, and she is denied entry. What kind of access control is this known as?

6. What factors contain a password policy in an organizational setup, and how should the policy be used?

7. A web server stores passwords as hashes. If you have lost your password, how can you use the hash to get the plaintext password?

8. What is the main use of checksum algorithms such as MD5 and SHA-2?

9. What is the main purpose of a trigger in database?

10. What is a view and the purpose of a view?

11. What is a materialized view?

12. What is Kerchoff's principle in data/information/cybersecurity?

13. What does the value of 6 indicate in the "encryption_state" column in the "sys. dm_database_encryption_keys" MS SQL server table?

14. What is metadata?

15. What is a surrogate key in a database?

Answers to Chapter 5 Questions

1. Access control is based on subjects and objects. Subjects are people or systems that can perform an action such as read, write, delete, and so on. Objects are resources such as a database of file storage area.

2. The entity or organization that grants the requested clearance for MAC is different from the organization where the subject generally works.

3. DAC is based on ownership of an object—typically a piece of software or a system.

4. Role-based access control (RBAC) is given to a group of people who all do the same type of work. A role is created for the group of people, and all people in the group inherit the permissions given to the group. No individual access privileges are granted. What is granted to the group applies to every person in the group because all people in the group are expected to do the same type of work. Example: All human resources staff are granted privileges to see employee salaries. All programmers have access to Microsoft Visual Studio libraries.

5. Rule-based access control (RuBAC) because a rule of "works night shift only."

6. Password length, history, age, and complexity dictate a password policy. A password policy must be strictly and uniformly enforced without exception to anyone.

7. Hash is a one-way function, and it is impossible to get the plaintext password.

8. Checksum algorithms are used to preserve integrity of a file or contents of a message.

9. A trigger is like a flag that switched on, when a condition—such as deleting a row or inserting a row—is met. Triggers alert the DB administrator that something is going on, and a log entry is created.

10. A view is a virtual table. It contains SQL script to pull data on demand. The script is not executed until the user initiates a select command. A view is also always up to date because the script runs only when a request is made.

11. A materialized view is a view that can store data in cache like a physical table. Materialized views are useful when lengthy SQL operations on DB tables consume time, effort, and employee resources.

12. Kerchoff's principle says that everything about data can become public but by keeping the encryption key private, data can be protected.

13. The state value of 6 indicates "protection change in progress (The certificate or asymmetric key that is encrypting the database encryption key is being changed.)"

14. Metadata is defined as "data about data."

15. Surrogate key is a nondata item column/attribute. It can be used as a key on the table but has no value as a data item. It is not based on other table data or data in the table where the surrogate key is defined. It is usually an auto-incremented value.

Data Refresh, Backup, and Restore

Data Refresh—Manual, ETL, and Script

A typical corporate IT environment usually has three different environments—namely development, test, and the production. A development environment is what the coders and database administrator (DBA) use as the playing field for development of their application or database (DB). Tests will be conducted later on a test environment, and if everything works well, the final product will go to the production environment on a demilitarized zone that faces the Internet and the public end users.

Note that when we have separate environments, large databases are usually hosted on different servers that are usually dedicated to hosting the databases; applications are on a different server. This setup protects the data and the database servers from any internal or external attacks. The databases also have backup schemes to back up data regularly (daily, weekly, monthly, and so on), and the backups are used to restore any missing data on the original database. Any changes to the database software (such as Oracle, SQL Server) are first made on the development and test databases. Once these changes are deemed successful, the final step is to modify the production database. In this sense, the production database is a sacred, not-to-be touched precious asset of the organization.

The backup or data refreshes can be at various levels: at the individual table level, a group of tables, a schema with hundreds of tables, or even the entire database with all the schemas. Once a backup is made, restoring the database from a backup can again be at a single table, a single schema, an entire schema, or the complete database. In other words, even if we back up the entire database, we do not have to use the entire database to restore. We can use the full backup copy of a database to restore one table, one or more schemas, or the entire database. The types of backups were discussed in Chapter 4.

Let's think about a local database that gets daily updates from another location or server. The server may send files in some format—text, binary, encrypted, and so on—to the local database. We do not have to know how the server creates and sends these files; it's enough to know that we get those files on a known file location or via email. How do we use those received files to update the local database? There are several ways.

Let's first examine how we can actually insert data into one table and move forward to multiple insertions and the related problems. In Chapter 5, we use a SQL command to insert data with simple values such as

```
INSERT INTO HR.InsertAudit (InsUser, InsDate, InsVersion, command)
VALUES ('DMILLER', 01-Dec-2021, 1.12.1.2x, 'Insert');
```

Usually, corporate database tables have dozens of columns, and few columns are null. This means an insert statement can become very long, and values to insert into each column are cumbersome to type. Not only that, when such lengthy insert statements are typed, data is prone to typing mistakes, missing or mismatched quotes for strings, and much more. Also, if we are inserting just a few tuples (or rows), say 20 rows of data, these simple insert statements will be sufficient and will not take a lot of time or cause trouble. However, a corporate database usually gets a few million or more inserts a day on a single table, and such a process needs to be automated. If the database actually needs to be refreshed, we need to truncate the existing table and repopulate it with incoming new data. This would be even more time-consuming if the number of rows grows daily. This is where the ETL (extract, transform, and load) process—which we discuss in the next section—comes in handy. SQL Server database has GUI tools that can be used for import and export as shown in Figures 6-1, 6-2, and 6-3.

Figure 6-1 *Starting the Import/Export Wizard from Windows Menu*

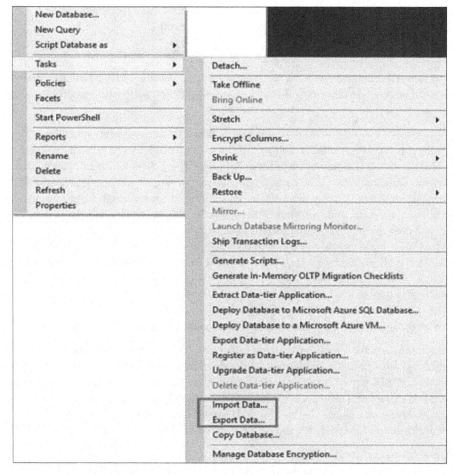

Figure 6-2 *Import/Export Option from Within the SQL Server Management Studio (Right-Click on Any Database Instance and See This Menu)*

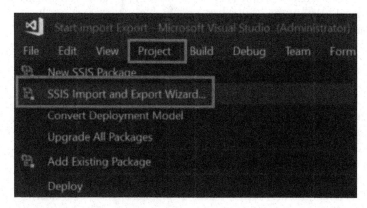

Figure 6-3 *From Within Visual Studio's SQL Server Integration Services (SSIS)*

The import/export wizard of SQL Server can also be started from the command-line interpreter in the DOS window with the following command:

C: \Program Files\Microsoft SQL Server\..\DTS\Binn>dtswizard

This **dtswizard** command line has a path that shows "..." because many installation path names can be different depending on where and how the SQL Server was installed on the disk.

Data import is a breeze. The user is guided through tables, data, viewing sample data, choosing row numbers, excludes, and so on. The entire process can be saved as a job for repeated use or can possibly be included in Windows Task Scheduler for automating the process at a required time of the day. The Import/Export wizard accepts a wide variety of files including text, Excel, and more. Before copying data into the table, the table can be truncated, dropped, and recreated. What is more, the table can be created as a new table, and even the SQL script that creates the new table can be edited right inside the GUI tool to define keys, add rows, and so on. The process of importing the data is quite similar (and more detailed with options) to how one imports files into an Excel sheet from text, XML, and other files. Importantly, the SSIS package can be ingrained into the Visual Studio suite to use with coding and database, as shown in Figure 6-3. The advantage of this GUI tool is that the user can abort and cancel the process at any time and stay with the same database without committing to new changes.

Several third-party tools exist for copying from one table to another, one database to another, and one schema to another within the same database or among various databases. The TOAD suite of software packages by Quest Inc. for Oracle provides a way to import and export data (also known as import dump **impdp** and export dump **expdp**). The SQL Developer tool can do this as well. However, it may be easier on the operating system with simple files to do the import/export as discussed later in this chapter.

ETL is a way to transform unformatted or raw data into database tables by making it compatible with the rules and constraints we set for the database and tables, such as primary keys, foreign keys, constraints, and so on. It is important to know that before we load our raw data into the database tables, we should be aware of these constraints when we run our own scripts. When data is simply loaded without worrying about constraints, the triggers that control the data can fire and stall the process. It is for that reason all foreign key constraints and triggers are disabled before data is loaded, and then these triggers are enabled back for the DB.

ETL Jobs

Assume you have a table and want to load data into the table with some kind of insert statement. If there are many columns, a single insert statement can take a few milliseconds to load data, and that would be fine for loading a row or two. As the number of rows increases, there are two main problems. First, creating an insert statement for each row with different data will be cumbersome to type or generate the statements. Second, corporate data is always huge—on the order of petabytes or more—resulting in each table having millions of rows of data. Assuming that each row takes 1 millisecond, 2 million rows can take 30 minutes or more. What if we have a process to load 400 or 600 tables, each with 2 million rows? Do we want to keep the database going during this load time? It would be unreasonable to load data that way.

To solve these problems, Oracle database has built-in utilities such as SQL Loader (**sqlldr**) to load data into a table. SQL Loader works at the operating system level (Linux or Unix) and can load these 2 million rows quickly. The format to create the loading process is slightly different from SQL statements. The **sqlldr** utility looks for a few files: the incoming data file, a log file to store the log of the loading process, a bad file to store bad records that cannot be loaded (corrupted data in the incoming file), and a control file that tells how the data should be loaded. An example of a control file is shown in Example 6-1.

Example 6-1   *SQL Loader Control File*

```
-- OPTIONS
-- CTL File location is at  '/FirstFolder/One/anyFolder/ControlFiles/TableOne.ctl'
OPTIONS(DIRECT=TRUE, ROWS=25000, SILENT=(FEEDBACK, ERRORS))
LOAD DATA
INFILE   '/FirstFolder/../../DataFiles/TableOne.dat'
DISCARDFILE   '/FirstFolder/One/anyFolder/DiscardFiles/TableOne.txt'
TRUNCATE
INTO TABLE HR.EmployeeSalaries
-- SORTED INDEXES (SSN_PK)
FIELDS TERMINATED BY '|'
TRAILING NULLCOLS
(SSN,
START_DT,
LAST_RAISE_DT 'YYYY-MM-DD',
YEARS EMPLOYED ,
DT_QUIT 'YYYY-MM-DD')
```

Notice that the control file has an extension of "ctl" and tells the utility how to load the file and what fields are inside the plain text file that has the actual data. And how is the data organized in the text file? Each field is separated by the pipe character (|), which can be changed by users as well. However, putting a space, comma, dash, or a period as separators may not be a good idea because text fields may contain spaces too. The 'TRUNCATE' statement in the control file also tells the SQL Loader that the table must be truncated before inserting new data. Instead of truncating, an append statement can be used to add data to existing data without truncating. If the SQL Loader command encounters any errors while running, these errors and bad data if any are reported in a log file. The log filename and path are usually mentioned in the SQL Loader command.

To use the control and load data, we use the following SQL Loader script. This loader script is run from the Linux or Unix operating system command line with a username and password. The username used in the following example is a database account and is generally different and unique only for the ETL process and not for anything else.

```
-- SQL LOADER command that uses a control (CTL) file
$ sqlldr ETLUserName/"PasswordHere" control=/FirstFolder/One/
anyFolder/ControlFiles/TableOne.ctl log=/FirstFolder/One/anyFolder/
LogFiles/TableOne.log
```

Security in Invoking ETL Job

Once the **sqlldr** command with all supplied parameters is executed, data from the file is loaded to the table quickly, and the data definition language (DDL), and data modification language (DML) metadata can be checked to see if the table is up to date. Examine the **sqlldr** command line closely and notice that the password is typed directly in the command. Usually, that is not a great idea for security purposes because shoulder surfing and screenshots or text persistence on screen can expose the password very easily. Hard-coded passwords are also against best practices and pose a security threat because the password is available to anyone who has access to full code or code statements. Since we are basically involved in database security, we will need to modify this command line to suppress or encrypt the password.

A Perl language command is an easy way to hexify (convert to hexadecimal) a password. We will first hexify the password and store it in a file named Enc_pwd.txt. The following command line works for the purpose:

```
$ perl -e 'print unpack "H*","PasswordHere"' > /FirstFolder/One/
anyFolder/Enc_pwd.txt
```

To see what is inside the hexified password, use the following:

```
$ export myword=`cat /FirstFolder/../anyFolder/Enc_pwd.txt`
$ echo $myword
457926c5430937d3135733475322324
```

The hexadecimal text displayed is our encoded password. As long as our password and file permissions are kept well-guarded, we can avoid password theft. But how do we use the encoded password in the SQL Loader? We can create a shell file to do that job and run the SQL Loader. In Example 6-2, the password is converted back to the plain text but is given to a shell variable named "mtxt." The other definitions for the log file path, control file path, and bad and data files' paths are mentioned before the SQL Loader is invoked. Before creating the shell script shown in Example 6-2, check that the **sqlldr** utility should normally be available in $ORACALE_HOME/BIN folder. Also, before running the SQL Loader command (**sqlldr**), make sure the "ETLUserName" database account has privileges to run that loader. It should be noted that the sql loader and commands to run data pump exports and imports (discussed in the next section) are not for every user. Usually, only DBAs are allowed to run these commands to protect the database integrity and the data itself.

Example 6-2 *Shell File Created for Running the SQL Loader with Hidden Password and Usernames*

```
export myword=`cat /FirstFolder/../anyFolder/Enc_pwd.txt`
export mtxt=`perl -e 'print pack "H*",'\"$myword\"''`
etluser='ETLUserName'
ctrlFolder=/FirstFolder/One/anyFolder/ControlFiles
logFolder=/FirstFolder/One/anyFolder/LogFiles
badFolder=/FirstFolder/One/anyFolder/BadFiles
dataFolder=/FirstFolder/One/anyFolder/dataFiles

$ sqlldr ${etluser}/${mtxt} CONTROL=$ctlFolder/TableOne.ctl LOG=$logFolder/TableOne.
log BAD=$badFolder/TableOne.bad DATA=$dataFolder/TableOne.dat
```

Notice from Example 6-2 that now the **sqlldr** command doesn't show any password or usernames on the screen as you run the shell script. Rather, it uses the variables created from the encoded password text file. The Enc_pwd.txt is the encoded file for our password for the user "ETLUserName." Again, keep in mind the following details while creating the shell and ETL script: ETLUserName is a database-level account, and Enc_pwd.txt is the encoded password for the database account "ETLUserName." The shell file (.sh or .ksh) is an operating system shell/BASH shell script that can be created to invoke the SQL Loader. For safety, Linux and Unix operating systems do not create a new file with executable privileges. Therefore, before running the shell script, change the privileges of the shell file with a command such as **chmod +x sqlloader.sh**, where sqlloader.sh is the file that contains the script given in Example 6-2.

We should remember a few things when creating the encoded text file for the password and running the SQL loader shell script. First, remember we have used the following line to encrypt a password. Assume that your password is pa$$word2023@:

```
$ perl -e 'print unpack "H*"," pa$$word2023@"' > /FirstFolder/One/
anyFolder/Enc_pwd.txt
```

This Perl command line might not work if the Linux or Unix operating system fires a warning that the password contains special characters because operating systems use $ and @ characters for special purposes. How then can we use these characters in a password? The way is to put an escape character to tell the operating system that we want to use the special character. So, the following will work nicely:

```
$ perl -e 'print unpack "H*"," pa\$\$word2023\@"' > /FirstFolder/
One/anyFolder/Enc_pwd.txt
```

Notice the escape character as a backslash. The slash only appears in the Perl command, and our password is not affected. It still remains pa$$word2023@. This can be verified with the following:

```
$ export myword=`cat /FirstFolder/../anyFolder/Enc_pwd.txt`
$ export mtxt=`perl -e 'print pack "H*",'\"$myword\"''`
$ echo $mtxt
```

The second problem is finding out whether we have any referential integrity keys (foreign keys) and triggers that would fire when we load data with ETL. If our database does have a few such triggers, we need to disable those triggers before invoking the SQL Loader script. Once loading is complete, remember to turn those keys and triggers back on for the database integrity. In general, this enabling and disabling of foreign key triggers should be done in any mass data loads on a database, and the [enabling and disabling of] triggers can be included in the script shell file.

Data Pump: Exporting and Importing

Oracle data pump has two exclusive commands, **impdp** (import dump) and **expdp** (export dump), for importing and exporting data into tables. They can be used to restore data in a database, a single table, schema, or multiple data objects. The commands are simple to use but need some parameters quite similar to the control parameters discussed in the earlier section. Though all these parameters can be put in the **impdp** or **expdp** commands, it would be wise to use these parameters in a separate file for better clarity. An example of a simple parameter file is shown in Example 6-3 for an export dump. A parameter file usually has an extension of .par, though it is not necessary and can have any extension.

Example 6-3   *Various Parameters for Exporting Data (myexpdp.par file)*

```
JOB_NAME=EXP_TABLES_JOB
DIRECTORY=IMP_EXP_DIRECTORY
DUMPFILE=EXP_TABLES_%U.DMP
LOGFILE= EXP_TABLES.LOG
SCHEMAS=HR, PAYROLL, TRANSFERS
TABLES=HR.EMPLOYEE, PAYROLL.PAYSCALES, HR.RETIREMENTS
ORACLE_HOME=/Databases/currentDb/MyDatabase/Product/21.0.0.1
ORACLE_SID=MyDatabase
QUERY=HR.EMPLOYEE:"WHERE FIRST_NAME in ('DAVID', 'MILLER')"
QUERY=PAYROLLS.PAYSCALES:"WHERE DEPT_NBR > 05 AND SALARY > 75482"
EXCLUDE=GRANT
EXCLUDE=REF_CONSTRAINT
EXCLUDE=STATISTICS
EXCLUDE=TRIGGER
EXCLUDE=INDEXES
PARALLEL=16
```

Notice in Example 6-3 that the dump files created have an extension of DMP and will be named as EXP_TABLES. %U in the filename indicates that the dump files will be named as **EXP_TABLES_01.DMP, EXP_TABLES_02.DMP**, and so on. The parameter file also indicates what to export and whether any of the tables can be limited by a query instead of exporting everything in the table. For example, *QUERY=PAYROLLS. PAYSCALES:"WHERE DEPT_NBR > 05 AND SALARY > 75482"* indicates that the number of rows in the table Payrolls.Payscales is not imported in full. Rather, only data rows that satisfy the condition *"WHERE DEPT_NBR > 05 AND SALARY > 75482"* from the table are exported. The parameter file also indicates what schemas or tables are to be excluded, whether triggers and indexes can be excluded, and so on. The PARALLEL parameter specifies the maximum number of processes of active execution operating on behalf of the export job, and the default value is 1 but can go up to 16. Oracle also refers to the export dump as "unloading the schema or tables." Once a parameter file is created, a single command can create the export dump, as shown in Example 6-4, as a shell file.

Example 6-4   *Script to Run the expdp Command with Options in the myexpdp.par File*

```
export ORACLE_SID=MyDatabase
logFolder=/FirstFolder/One/anyFolder/LogFiles
ParFolder=/FirstFolder/One/anyFolder/ParFiles
expdp Username/Password PARFILE=$Parfolder/myexpdp.par
```

There is more to the expdp parameter file. The file size for each file can be set, and files generated can have compressed data only, metadata only, or no data. If compression is chosen, a compression algorithm can be chosen too, as shown here:

```
FILESIZE=2G
COMPRESSION=METADATA_ONLY - -  data_only or none
COMPRESSION_ALGORITHM=LOW - - basic, low, medium, high
```

If we now get dump files, anyone can use those files and may be able to use the **impdp** command to extract our data. Thus, our data needs to be secure with a password and encryption algorithm. We can also protect security of the exported data with encryption using the following parameters. Various encryption algorithms are available that can use a given password:

```
ENCRYPTION=data_only -- all
ENCRYPTION_ALGORITHM=AES128 - - AES256 etc.
ENCRYPTION_PASSWORD=YourEncryptingPassword
ENCRYPTION_MODE=DUAL
```

Let us assume for a minute that we do not really want to export first but want to know the estimated file sizes and files only. After seeing the estimate generated, we may decide later whether to export data. The following option in the parameter file can do that. When this option is included in the PAR file, Oracle generates an estimation only and does not create the dmp files:

```
ESTIMATE_ONLY=YES
```

Again, we can include or exclude a few schemas or tables or use a query to export data with various statements or clauses of the SQL:

```
EXCLUDE=SCHEMA:"='HR'"
INCLUDE=TABLE:"IN ('EMPLOYEES', 'DEPARTMENTS')"
INCLUDE=PROCEDURE
INCLUDE=INDEX:"LIKE 'EMP%'"
```

Recall that we used a single command to export our data/tables or schemas with

```
expdp Username/Password PARFILE=$Parfolder/myexpdp.par
```

After this command is run, where can we find our EXP_TABLES_01.DMP, EXP_TABLES_02.DMP, and so on files? Oracle defines a specific location for DATA_PUMP_DIRECTORY, but we can change that with an SQL command. We also need to change read and write permissions to that folder to the database user (Username) who is running the **expdp** and **impdp** commands:

```
SQL> create or replace directory DATA_PUMP_DIRECTORY as '/
FirstFolder/One/DmpFolder/;
SQL> grant read, write on directory DATA_PUMP_DIRECTORY to Username;
```

DBAs with privileges often run a command similar to the following for exporting data across databases or platforms. Because DBAs are granted privileges to see DATA_PUMP_DIRECTORY, this command would not require any username or password:

```
expdp \"/ as sysdba\" parfile= PARFILE=$Parfolder/myexpdp.par
```

Again, let us go back and examine our expdp PAR file in Example 6-2 from a security point of view. The username and password are specified in clear text. And if we assume that dmp files are password protected, then the PAR files also mention that pass as clear text in the PAR file. To overcome this, we can remove those lines from the PAR file and create the **expdp** shell script as shown in Example 6-5. This is almost similar to what we did with control files.

Example 6-5   *Script to Run the expdp Command with a Hidden Password*

```
export myword=`cat /FirstFolder/../anyFolder/Enc_pwd.txt`
export mtxt=`perl -e 'print pack "H*",'\"$myword\"''`
currentuser='UserName'
ParFolder=/FirstFolder/One/anyFolder/ParFiles
expdp \"/ as sysdba\" PARFILE=$Parfolder/myexpdp.par ENCRYPTION_ALGORITHM= AES256
ENCRYPTION_PASSWORD=${myword}
```

The last line in the shell script shown in Example 6-5 can also be used with a username and password, as shown in the following listing if the specific username has privileges to run the **expdp**:

```
$ expdp ${currentuser}/${mtxt}   PARFILE=$Parfolder/myexpdp.par
ENCRYPTION_ALGORITHM= AES256   ENCRYPTION_PASSWORD=${myword}
```

Import dump is the opposite of export dump and uses similar parameter files with the **impdp** command. Example 6-6 shows the parameter file for **impdp**:

Example 6-6   *Parameter File for impdp Command*

```
JOB_NAME=IMP_TABLES_JOB
DIRECTORY=DATA_PUMP_DIRECTORY
DUMPFILE=EXP_TABLES_%U.DMP
```

```
LOGFILE= IMP_TABLES.LOG
SCHEMAS=HR, PAYROLL, TRANSFERS
CONTENT=DATA_ONLY
TABLES=HR.EMPLOYEE, PAYROLL.PAYSCALES, HR.RETIREMENTS
TABLE_EXISTS_ACTION=TRUNCATE
EXCLUDE=SCHEMA:"='HR'"
EXCLUDE=TABLE: "IN ('HR.PAYROLLS', 'EMP.EMPDATA')"
```

Notice that the parameter file for **impdp** can specify %U to indicate files such as
EXP_TABLES_01.DMP, EXP_TABLES_02.DMP, and so on. But what if our files are
not numbered and are like EXP_TABLES_First.DMP, EXP_TABLES_Second.DMP, and
EXP_TABLES_Third.DMP? We can specify individual files when filenames are different,
as in the following listing:

```
DUMPFILE= EXP_TABLES_First.DMP,  EXP_TABLES_Second.DMP, EXP_TABLES_
Third.DMP
```

To actually import the data, we use a script file similar to what we used before for expdp.
This is illustrated in Example 6-7:

Example 6-7 *Script to Run the impdp Command with a Hidden Password*

```
export myword=`cat /FirstFolder/../anyFolder/Enc_pwd.txt`
export mtxt=`perl -e 'print pack "H*",'\"$myword\"''`
currentuser='UserName'
ParFolder=/FirstFolder/One/anyFolder/ParFiles
impdp \"/ as sysdba\" PARFILE=$Parfolder/myexpdp.par ENCRYPTION_PASSWORD=${myword}
```

Note that the logfile specified in the parameter file is the log for importing. There is no
need to include the export log. But the dump files listed in this PAR file must exactly
match the export dump files we create with **expdp** command. Lastly, the exported dump
files can be transferred to another database or location and loaded to the same database
or to another database if the table structure matches. These kind of imports and exports
are normally done from production to either development or test databases, subject to
the company policies on things like personally identifiable information (PII). These files
can be small if only one or two tables are required but can go beyond Gigabyte storage if
everything needs to be saved. In such cases, export dump and import dump are considered weak strategies.

Backup and Restore

The first thing any corporation gives priority to, after saving human lives either in a disaster or to be safe, is the data. We have seen how tables can be exported and imported, but
they are for shorter versions or partial import and export of a few data tables, schemas,

or objects. If we want to back up an entire database, the process is different. A backup can be full, differential, or incremental, and also can be done once a day, more than once a day, or at any time frames one prefers. Depending on the frequency of data backup required, the changes that happen to the corporate data, and the type or importance of the data, the system administrators automate these schedules. In SQL Server, backing up a database is made easier and one can use a GUI for the purpose. Simple database backup can be done without writing a line of a SQL script, and SQL Server Management Studio (SSMS) takes care of these steps when we run them through the GUI. Figure 6-4 shows the starting point. Figure 6-5 shows the dialog box that shows up when the **Back Up** option is chosen from the tasks submenu.

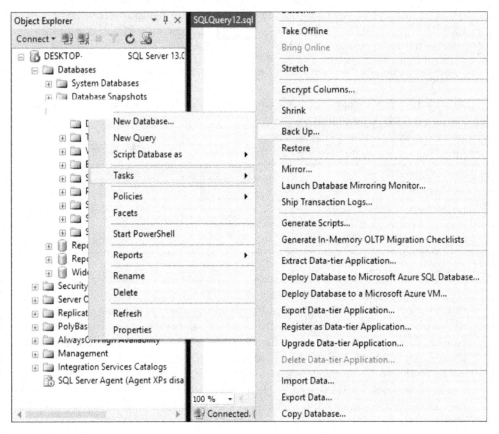

Figure 6-4   *Back Up Selection Within SSMS (Right-Click on Any Database Instance and See This Menu)*

The location, type of backup, and various other options are ready to be picked up with a click of a button and various GUI options. Also notice that the **Add** button allows as many locations as one desires to be added for backup, and there also are options for encryption. Any names can be chosen for files.

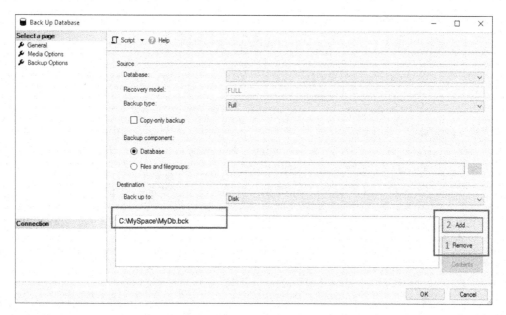

Figure 6-5 *Back Up Options from Within SSMS*

The following list shows other ways to back up with a SQL script. The four basic steps required are simple and straightforward. Because we are concerned about security throughout this book, we will demonstrate how the secure backup is done:

1. Generate a master key.

2. Create a certificate.

3. Export the certificate.

4. Back up the database using the certificate.

The database master key is a symmetric key used to protect the private keys of certificates and asymmetric keys that are present in the database. Creating a master key is straightforward with the following:

```
-- Create a new master key
CREATE MASTER KEY ENCRYPTION BY PASSWORD = 'MyS3cureP@$$_{3204}';
```

What if we already have the master key saved earlier? Then we can open the key and use it:

```
-- Or use an existing one
OPEN MASTER KEY DECRYPTION BY PASSWORD = 'MyS3cureP@$$_{3204}'
```

The script in the following statement now creates a certificate:

```
-- Create the certificate encrypted by the master key
CREATE CERTIFICATE MySecureDBCert
    WITH SUBJECT = 'My New SQL Server Backup Certificate'  EXPIRY_
DATE = '20241231';
GO
```

At this point, SMSS warns the user to save the certificate. The certificate and the encryption are in asynchronous mode, and without saving the certificate, it is impossible to get the database if a restore is ever required.

The following script saves the certificate. The certificate defined here is encrypted by the master key we defined earlier, but the certificate itself has a different password. Also "DECRYPTION BY PASSWORD" is an option. If that option is removed, encryption and decryption can be done by the same password specified:

```
-- Export the certificate to a file

BACKUP CERTIFICATE MySecureDBCert TO FILE = 'C:\MyDBCert\
MySecureDBCert.cert'
WITH PRIVATE KEY (
FILE = ' C:\MyDBCert\MySecureDBCert.key',
ENCRYPTION BY PASSWORD = 'C3rT_[p@$$_203}'
DECRYPTION BY PASSWORD = '{p@$$_302]_CerT''
)
```

The next step is to do the actual database back up. Here is the script:

```
-- backup the database with encryption
Use MySQLDatabase
GO

BACKUP DATABASE MYSQLDatabase
TO DISK = 'C:\MySpace\MySQLDatabase.bak'
WITH
ENCRYPTION (ALGORITHM = AES_256, SERVER CERTIFICATE = MySecureDBCert)
MEDIANAME = 'ALLSQL_Backup',
NAME = 'Full_Diff_Incr_Backup of MYSQLDatabase';
GO
```

That's all there to the SQL Server backup. If you feel this is not the route to take and would rather use the GUI, you can choose that as well; the files you create will be similar. SQL Server Object Explorer and other menus show the certificates, backup areas, and keys easily, and everything is visible to the user by a click of a button.

Let's assume that we carry our database backup files to another server where we want to restore our database. Remember that we encrypted our database with a certificate and encrypted the certificate with a master key. If we try to restore the database without using those keys, obviously SQL Server will throw an error. Let's first restore those keys and certificates to the new server:

```
-- Create a new master key
CREATE MASTER KEY ENCRYPTION BY PASSWORD = 'MyS3cureP@$$_{3204}';


CREATE CERTIFICATE MySecureDBCert FROM FILE = 'C:\MyDBCert\
MySecureDBCert.cert'
WITH PRIVATE KEY (
FILE = ' C:\MyDBCert\MySecureDBCert.key',
ENCRYPTION BY PASSWORD = 'C3rT_[p@$$_203}'
DECRYPTION BY PASSWORD = '{p@$$_302]_CerT''
)
```

Note that these CREATE statements are similar to what we used before encrypting the database earlier. Once we have these in place, the restore can be a snap, as shown in the following script. The "FROM DISK" path needs to be changed, depending on from where the database backup is being restored, which is the easy part:

```
RESTORE DATABASE MySQLDatabase
FROM DISK = 'C:\MySpace\MySQLDatabase.bak'
WITH
        MOVE N'MySQLDatabase' TO N'C\MyData|Old\EncryptionDemo.mdf',
        MOVE N' MySQLDatabase_log' TO N'C:\MyData|Old\EncryptionDemo_
log.ldf'
```

Now we can turn our attention to Oracle. Oracle databases that are installed on Linux or Unix mainframe machines have a different way of backing up databases. The Oracle tool called Recovery Manager (RMAN) can simplify the job for users. To enter RMAN, use the following at the command prompt:

RMAN target /

There are dozens of parameters RMAN uses, and they can be checked with the following command at the RMAN prompt, as shown in Example 6-8. The results will be long and take time to understand. Notice that the listing is annotated with the word **# default** to show how RMAN sets a default value to the parameter.

Example 6-8 *Manager Parameters in an Oracle Setting*

```
RMAN> SHOW ALL;


RMAN configuration parameters for database with db_unique_name MyDataBase are:


CONFIGURE RETENTION POLICY TO REDUNDANCY 1; # default
CONFIGURE BACKUP OPTIMIZATION OFF; # default
CONFIGURE DEFAULT DEVICE TYPE TO DISK; # default
CONFIGURE CONTROLFILE AUTOBACKUP ON;
CONFIGURE CONTROLFILE AUTOBACKUP FORMAT FOR DEVICE TYPE DISK TO '/disk1/oracle/
  dbs/%F';
```

```
CONFIGURE CONTROLFILE AUTOBACKUP FORMAT FOR DEVICE TYPE SBT_TAPE TO '%F'; # default
CONFIGURE DEVICE TYPE DISK PARALLELISM 1 BACKUP TYPE TO BACKUPSET; # default
CONFIGURE DEVICE TYPE SBT_TAPE PARALLELISM 1 BACKUP TYPE TO BACKUPSET; # default
CONFIGURE DATAFILE BACKUP COPIES FOR DEVICE TYPE DISK TO 1; # default
CONFIGURE DATAFILE BACKUP COPIES FOR DEVICE TYPE SBT_TAPE TO 1; # default
CONFIGURE ARCHIVELOG BACKUP COPIES FOR DEVICE TYPE DISK TO 1; # default
CONFIGURE ARCHIVELOG BACKUP COPIES FOR DEVICE TYPE SBT_TAPE TO 1; # default
CONFIGURE CHANNEL DEVICE TYPE 'SBT_TAPE'
  PARMS "SBT_LIBRARY=/usr/local/oracle/backup/lib/libobk.so";
CONFIGURE MAXSETSIZE TO UNLIMITED; # default
CONFIGURE ENCRYPTION FOR DATABASE ON;
CONFIGURE ENCRYPTION ALGORITHM 'AES128'; # default
CONFIGURE COMPRESSION ALGORITHM 'BASIC' AS OF RELEASE 'DEFAULT' OPTIMIZE FOR LOAD
  TRUE ;
  # default
CONFIGURE RMAN OUTPUT TO KEEP FOR 7 DAYS; # default
CONFIGURE ARCHIVELOG DELETION POLICY TO NONE; # default
CONFIGURE SNAPSHOT CONTROLFILE NAME TO '/disk1/oracle/dbs/cf_snap .f'
```

We can change any of these RMAN parameters as shown in the following listings, but know that when you change the disk format path to another location, such as '/ MyBackUp/15Days/RMAN', make sure that the folder there is writable or issue a change mode command (**chmod +w**):

```
RMAN> CONFIGURE CHANNEL DEVICE TYPE DISK FORMAT '/MyBackUp/15Days/
RMAN/full_%u_%s_%p';
RMAN> CONFIGURE RETENTION POLICY TO RECOVERY WINDOW OF 15 DAYS;
RMAN> CONFIGURE ENCRYPTION ALGORITHM 'AES256;
```

To reset the value of any of these parameters to the default values, which are visible with the **SHOW ALL** command, use the following as an example:

```
RMAN> CONFIGURE RETENTION POLICY CLEAR;
```

Once we set up our parameters, the backup can be done with a single command or by running a group of commands as follows:

```
RMAN> BACKUP AS BACKUPSET DATABASE;
```

Do we want to do a backup with archive logs? Then the command is as follows:

```
RMAN> BACKUP AS BACKUPSET DATABASE PLUS ARCHIVELOG;
```

We know that tables store data into tablespaces, and there could be dozens of table-spaces on a single database. Can we actually back up only a required tablespace rather than backing up everything? The answer is yes. The following example takes the backup of a tablespace named MyTableSpace2023. Usually, a tag can be attached to the backup to identify it easily. This can be done as follows:

```
RMAN> BACKUP AS BACKUPSET TAG 'FIFTEEN_DAYS_MYTABLESPACE2023_BK_
ONLY'  TABLESPACE MyTableSpace2023;
```

At this point, we know we have an encryption algorithm, and we have the encryption switched ON, but how about putting an encryption password for the backup files? The following can do that with a specified password:

```
RMAN> SET ENCRYPTION ON IDENTIFIED BY 'NewP@55dr0W{2014]' ONLY;
```

If we have one disk or mount point named as /MyBackUp/15Days/RMAN with plenty of room for backup copies, we can create channels to run the Recovery Manager. Notice that the following example backs up the database as a compressed set, archive logs, and the control file all in the same location but in different folders:

```
run{
ALLOCATE CHANNEL CH1 DEVICE TYPE DISK;
ALLOCATE CHANNEL CH2 DEVICE TYPE DISK;
ALLOCATE CHANNEL CH3 DEVICE TYPE DISK;
ALLOCATE CHANNEL CH4 DEVICE TYPE DISK;

BACKUP AS COMPRESSED BACKUPSET DATABASE FORMAT '/MyBackUp/15Days/
RMAN/DB /FULL_%d_%u_%s_%T.bkp';
BACKUP AS COMPRESSED BACKUPSET ARCHIVELOG ALL FORMAT '/
MyBackUp/15Days/RMAN/LOGS/Archivelogs_%d_%u_%s_%T.bkp';
BACKUP CURRENT CONTROLFILE FORMAT '/MyBackUp/15Days/RMAN/CONTROL/ /
CONTROLFILE%d_%u_%s_%T.bkp';

RELEASE CHANNEL CH1;
RELEASE CHANNEL CH2;
RELEASE CHANNEL CH3;
RELEASE CHANNEL CH4;
}
```

The notations mentioned in the RMAN script for "FORMAT" need explanation. %d is for specifying the database name, %u is for system generated filename in short form, %s is for backup set number, %p is for piece number within that backup set, and %T is the date format in YYYYMMDD. There are many other parameters that can be added as well.

The following RMAN and SQL commands on the database show details of the backup. They can be checked frequently to make sure the backups are in correct format and date as well as to keep track of the disk space:

```
RMAN> LIST BACKUP SMMARY;

SQL> SELECT OPERATION, STATUS, MBYTES_PROCESSED, START_TIME, END_
TIME from V$RMAN_STATUS;
```

Instead of using a single disk or mount, we can also allocate *CHANNEL DEVICE TYPE DISK FORMAT* to distribute the backups among different mount points. The channel disk format is as follows:

```
run{
ALLOCATE CHANNEL CH1 DEVICE TYPE DISK format '/MyBackUp/15Days/
RMAN/DB/01/%U';
ALLOCATE CHANNEL CH2 DEVICE TYPE DISK format '/MyBackUp/15Days/
RMAN/DB/02/%U';
ALLOCATE CHANNEL CH3 DEVICE TYPE DISK format '/MyBackUp/15Days/
RMAN/DB/03/%U';
ALLOCATE CHANNEL CH4 DEVICE TYPE DISK format '/MyBackUp/15Days/
RMAN/DB/04/%U';
BACKUP AS COMPRESSED BACKUPSET DATABASE;
RELEASE CHANNEL CH1;
RELEASE CHANNEL CH2;
RELEASE CHANNEL CH3;
RELEASE CHANNEL CH4;
}
```

An alternative is to issue an **RMAN** command in one line as follows:

```
Run{
ALLOCATE CHANNEL CH1 DEVICE TYPE DISK;
ALLOCATE CHANNEL CH2 DEVICE TYPE DISK;
ALLOCATE CHANNEL CH3 DEVICE TYPE DISK;
ALLOCATE CHANNEL CH4 DEVICE TYPE DISK;
CONFIGURE CHANNEL DEVICE TYPE DISK FORMAT '/MyBackUp/15Days/RMAN/
DB/01/%U',
, /MyBackUp/15Days/RMAN/DB/02/%U', /MyBackUp/15Days/RMAN/DB/03/%U',
/MyBackUp/15Days/RMAN/DB/04/%U';
BACKUP AS COMPRESSED BACKUPSET DATABASE;
RELEASE CHANNEL CH1;
RELEASE CHANNEL CH2;
RELEASE CHANNEL CH3;
RELEASE CHANNEL CH4;
}
```

Recovery of a database is also simple in Oracle, but since we already encrypted the database with a password, the password must be used before the database is restored. The following commands show how to issue the password for decryption, restoring a database, restoring a control file, and restoring a tablespace instead of a complete database:

```
RMAN> SET DECRYPTION IDENTIFIED BY 'NEWP@55DR0W{2014]';
RMAN> RESTORE DATABASE;
RMAN> RESTORE CONTROLFILE FROM "'/MyBackUp/15Days/RMAN/CONTROL/File
-12345-20141003-03";
RMAN> RESTORE DATABASE
RMAN> RESTORE TABLESPACE DEV1, DEV2;
```

One final note for the Oracle backups: Once the backup files are ready, we know we have encryption in place for them, as mentioned in the RMAN parameters. Some organizations keep these backup files for one week, some for a month, some for a year, and some forever. As the files grow, more and more disk space is required. The best practice at that time is to zip or compress a group of these backup files (control and archive logs, too) and store them in a different location. Usually, operating systems such as Linux offer commands like **tar**, **gtar**, and so on, and Windows offers compression readily. Data upkeep is not an easy job and must follow retention policies defined by the data owners in an organization. Collecting data, keeping the data, and even destroying data all need different specific policies and are subject to audits.

Keeping Track—Daily, Weekly, Monthly

We now know how we can securely keep our data, back it up with a protected password, and restore databases or tablespaces of individual databases. How often we back up or restore depends on how often our company policies dictate. However, it is important to watch what errors might occur. As surprising as it sounds, simple bad weather or another environmental event such as an earthquake can destroy a data center quickly. We often hear services are down for a particular Internet service provider (ISP) or a website in demand. When an ISP cannot restore services within minutes, there can be huge complications, lawsuits, and other problems. Customers also demand financial compensation for a service that did not work and caused troubles in everyday life. For avoiding any catastrophic events, data is backed up daily, weekly, monthly, or even more than once a day. But how do we know or keep track of whether our backups are going well and we can restore at any time we want should problems occur? The most important avenue to find out is to check the log files. It must be stressed that watching the log files regularly without fail is the best way to keep tracking the backup activities and checking the data integrity.

Restoring a backup is usually done manually because we do not know in advance which backup version we need to restore our database. Usually, when daily and hourly backups are going well, organizations choose to remove any backup copies older than N days (7, 15, and so on). Even when the data is restored, a log is kept of when the data was restored and the date of backup used for the restore. These dates and frequencies of the backup, restore, and destroying activities must always follow the organizational policies, or they need to be corrected per policies if the audit teams later identify any gaps.

Before concluding, we want to reiterate that the security of data, files, and anything that is inside the database starts with *you*. You are the first in line to be alert to notice anything that may go wrong or to find any vulnerability and promptly patch those if a fix is available. But in reality, patches are released by organizations (that sell database software) in an organized manner, such as once every few weeks. If the organization does not care to fix a particular vulnerability, the customers have to wait. In the meantime, we should do our part to protect data. Defense in depth calls for multilayered security, whereby one applies several methods to protect data and assets at various levels. Considering the defense-in-depth concept, we can take the following steps. These steps would not completely eliminate the attacks but do greatly minimize the attack surface:

1. Separate the database servers—the machines that host the databases—from the hosts that have applications. Applications only need database client software to connect to a database server. Separating applications and databases on different hosts helps protect them from each other in case one is attacked or exposed.

2. Keep passwords safe, have a password policy, *and* enforce it strictly with options and utilities provided by the software packages. An unenforced policy is as good as no policy. In this method, we must make sure passwords meet the age, length, history, and complexity rules. Create rules in such a way that users cannot connect to DBs without following the policies. Users either follow the rules or stay out.

3. Use available encryption like AES256 in database software both for backing up and for keeping the data in tables. Most operating systems and database software packages provide this encryption as a built-in option.

4. Back up regularly and look for any failures in backups with the help of log files. Look both at the onsite and offsite backups. Make sure the offsite backup is usable and up to date. Assuming an old backup will work can be an accident waiting to happen.

5. Keep the log files in a readable format, zip the log files by the month, and store them in a separate area or disk. Log files help defend your actions in an audit.

6. Make sure the server, database, and system date and time formats are the same and in sync when working to avoid time and time zone differences.

7. For import and export of files, encrypt the files with a separate password and store them in a different location. If encryption is allowed here, use it.

8. For backing up files, decide how long to keep the files based on your organization's retention policy. When retaining, zip the backup files and also encrypt the zipped file with another password. This can be done with OpenSSL commands in Linux, as discussed in Chapter 2.

9. Do read all the logs—both the system-generated and user-generated logs. Remember that creating log files with every process is a good idea, but if you do not read those logs, they are as good as useless. Reading and monitoring the DB transactions can be handled both with security monitoring functions and manual methods.

10. Patch your database software promptly when a new patch is released by the organization that sold the software. Consider high-level patching strategy and the usual manual methods, whichever fits the organization in a better way.

11. In the end, remember that it is your everyday responsibility to exercise due diligence, take due care by being alert, and keep track of the updates and new attack methodologies that surface regularly.

All these steps may look to be too much work, but to protect your database, it is important to follow a methodical and logical approach to spot an unwanted activity. One cannot simply assume that since the organization implemented good controls, looked at vulnerabilities, and exercised due care, everything would be fine. In other words, the methodical and logical approach of "look and be prepared for trouble before it happens" falls into the scope of due diligence and should become a daily habit.

Summary

Data in the databases can be refreshed in various ways, such as manual methods, extract transform, and load, which also can be done by script. Windows GUI offers easy methods to export and import data from SQL Server DB. ETL jobs are more complicated because they need parameters, passwords, and schema details of what is being imported or exported. However, ETL works at the operating system level with SQL Loader and is very fast compared to a manual insert of data into a database. ETL also can be used with a password for protection.

Import and export of files can be done with dump pump utilities. Backing up can be handled with a GUI or, in the case of Oracle, with Recovery Manager (RMAN). All these need higher privileges and only authorized personnel, such as a database administrator, can perform these. RMAN dump utilities can specify filenames, the size of each file, and the number of channels the utility can use. On a multiprocessor machine that is hosting the DB, channels can be as many as the processors present on the host machine.

Reading logs is important to quickly find problems if any exist. However, creating logs with every DB operation might be a good idea, and tracking the user activity can help fix problems before they arise. Several suggestions were given in this chapter to minimize the attack surface.

Chapter 6 Questions

1. What is an advantage of the ETL process as compared to an insert statement in updating a table in a database?

2. What are the advantages in SQL Server software for data imports?

3. Why are data import and export important in databases?

4. What is the purpose of the control (CTL) file in the Oracle import or export process?

5. What is the purpose of the ESTIMATE ONLY parameter in the Oracle expdp parameter file?

6. If we are exporting data in two schemas named HR and EMP in Oracle with expdp and want to exclude two tables HR.PAYROLLS and EMP.EMPDATA in the schemas, how does the parameter file (*.par) define those table exclusions?

7. A parameter file in expdp of Oracle defines the following line. What would the output files look like when **expdp** runs successfully?

```
DUMPFILE=EXP_TABLES_%U.DMP
```

8. What are the four basic steps of the SQL Server database backup procedure?

9. What command is useful in finding the current parameters in Oracle Recovery Manager (RMAN)?

10. How can we configure a new retention policy and encryption algorithms in Oracle Recovery Manager (RMAN)?

11. How can we reset any RMAN parameter to a default value in Oracle Recovery Manager tool?

12. If we are using six different mounts to backup, what does the **rman** command look like?

13. Is it possible to restore only a few tablespaces from a full backup copy when restoring on a different machine?

14. What is the best way to retain backup and expdp files?

15. What are the best options for logs created by export and backup processes?

16. What do you need to do to take care of data with defense in depth?

Answers to Chapter 6 Questions

1. ETL helps load huge data in a known format (such as a .txt or .csv) quickly to tables at the operating system level, whereas an insert statement needs to be typed with column names and data for those columns for each tuple. In a large table with several million rows and columns of data to load, ETL can finish the process a lot quicker than individual insert statements.

2. SQL Server has a user-friendly GUI tool. Also, the Import/Export wizard tool can be embedded in other software packages such as Visual Studio as SSIS. It also can be started with a command line with dtswizard.

3. They preserve the older data before new data is replaced into the tables. If at any time older data is needed, we can restore the selected tables, schemas, or other objects. Import and export processes also help in updating data from one database to another if the table structures are the same. The same is not true with backups. With backups, we restore the entire database.

4. Import or export parameters are defined in the control files for the SQL Loader utility. The controls also tell the software where the original unformatted data is and what form it is in. It mentions what columns are going to be loaded and whether the table should be appended or truncated before loading.

5. When *ESTIMATE_ONLY=YES* is mentioned in the parameter file, the **expdp** command does not really export but gives an estimated size of disk space required for exporting the data in schemas or tables mentioned in the parameter file.

6. Use the following two lines to exclude tables:

```
EXCLUDE=SCHEMA:"='HR'"
EXCLUDE=TABLE: "IN ('HR.PAYROLLS', 'EMP.EMPDATA')"
```

7. The files will appear as EXP_TABLES_01.DMP, EXP_TABLES_02.DMP, EXP_TABLES_03.DMP, and so on.

8. The four basic steps of the SQL Server backup procedure are

   a. Generate a master key.

   b. Create a certificate.

   c. Export the certificate.

   d. Back up database using the certificate.

9. RMAN target / to enter into RMAN and then SHOW ALL; at the RMAN prompt.

10. Use the following:

```
RMAN> CONFIGURE RETENTION POLICY TO RECOVERY WINDOW OF 15 DAYS;
RMAN> CONFIGURE ENCRYPTION ALGORITHM 'AES256;
```

11. Use Clear, as shown in this example:

```
RMAN> CONFIGURE RETENTION POLICY CLEAR;
```

12. An example for six different mounts can be as follows:

```
run{
ALLOCATE CHANNEL CH1 DEVICE TYPE DISK format '/MyBackUp/15Days/
RMAN/DB/01/%U';
ALLOCATE CHANNEL CH2 DEVICE TYPE DISK format '/MyBackUp/15Days/
RMAN/DB/02/%U';
ALLOCATE CHANNEL CH3 DEVICE TYPE DISK format '/MyBackUp/15Days/
RMAN/DB/03/%U';
ALLOCATE CHANNEL CH4 DEVICE TYPE DISK format '/MyBackUp/15Days/
RMAN/DB/04/%U';
ALLOCATE CHANNEL CH3 DEVICE TYPE DISK format '/MyBackUp/15Days/
RMAN/DB/05/%U';
ALLOCATE CHANNEL CH4 DEVICE TYPE DISK format '/MyBackUp/15Days/
RMAN/DB/06/%U';
BACKUP AS COMPRESSED BACKUPSET DATABASE;
RELEASE CHANNEL CH1;
RELEASE CHANNEL CH2;
RELEASE CHANNEL CH3;
RELEASE CHANNEL CH4;
RELEASE CHANNEL CH5;
RELEASE CHANNEL CH6;
}
```

13. Yes, use the following in RMAN. It is not required to restore everything from a database, although you can do that.

14. To retain several backup files, it is advised that you zip them in the operating system and store them in a separate location. This helps in a quick recovery if the main database location is down and cannot be restored quickly.

15. Keep logs in a readable format, sync the system, database, and application times, and read the logs daily and regularly to find problems. Zip older logs, and store them in a separate location for audit purposes.

16. Encrypt the database, encrypt the import and export files, encrypt the backup files, zip the backup, or export and import files and again encrypt the zipped files. Patch databases regularly, and continue to watch for vulnerabilities. Remember that the first line of defense starts with you.

Host Security

Server Connections and Separation

So far, we have discussed protecting the database, the data in tables, the objects inside the database, backing up, importing, and exporting. Let's now turn our attention to the host where the database binaries and database applications (Oracle, SQL Server, and so on) are hosted. These databases can be hosted on Linux, Unix, and Windows. While installation itself is a breeze, maintenance of the database package (known as relational database management systems or RDBMS) takes time, regular patchwork, viewing the logs, and so on.

Assume that we want to host databases and applications on the same server. It means our web application running on Internet Information Server (IIS), our database required for the application hosted in the IIS, and everything else are on the same host, and that host has sufficient memory for all these databases, applications, and so on. Figure 7-1 shows what this scenario looks like. The server in the picture is S1. The database on the server has everything related to our data. The applications on the same machine can access the DB easily. End users, employees, groups from outside (vendors), or the internal database group can be granted to have access to the DB or applications on the server. Notice that if a hacker obtained credentials, they may access the database or applications on the server.

If you closely study the scenario depicted in Figure 7-1, end users get an "instance" of the web page from the web server and deal with it directly on databases. Likewise, vendors, employees, and DB group staff also deal with the same database with various applications. Unfortunately, a hacker can also come in and break the security, send unlimited attack commands, and try to cause denial of service (DoS) with too many requests, thereby negating service to the legitimate users. When the only existing server goes down during such an attack, it's a DoS attack, but when we have a distributed attack on all our servers, every server will go down in the Distributed DoS attack (DDoS). Although the server going down is not good, the danger of an attacker accessing an application, database, and everything else can be even worse. In other words, we do not want to give away everything to an attacker because of an error in an application or the database. We want to protect our data and the applications separately.

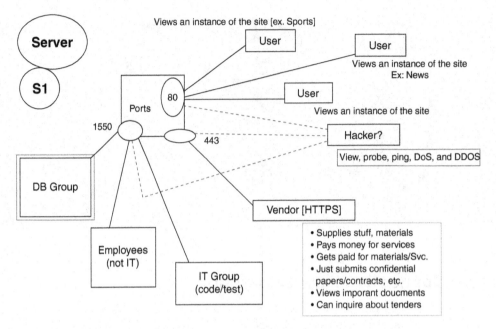

Figure 7-1   *Web Server with Databases and Applications*

Also, in a large corporation, one server or a couple blade servers are barely enough. As the number of end users increases, we need more and more servers to meet the demand. The redirection of user requests to each server is usually done by a load balancer. F5, the vendor for load balancers, can encrypt the network traffic and provide an additional protection layer for the servers from attackers. A typical F5 setup is shown in Figure 7-2.

Notice from Figure 7-2 that the database servers are not necessarily directly connected to the Internet with F5, although they can be. The main logic is to separate the databases and keep them on separate servers for better protection. We set up connections in a way that our applications are accessible from the Internet, but when the application needs the database, it communicates to the database on its own. Therefore, our database IP isn't exposed to a demilitarized zone where an attacker can access and send attack commands or requests.

Another major advantage in creating and hosting the databases on separate servers is that in a single server, if one application goes down, a hacker can take down the entire database. The result is other unattacked applications will fail because the database is down. However, when we separate the databases and applications on separate servers, even if one application is down, others continue to function normally.

Figure 7-3 shows how the DMZ can be set up. There is more than one firewall with various rules set up to filter the traffic and possibly avoid an attack. Users connecting to the LAN/WAN have their traffic filtered twice: once at the perimeter and once with an internal firewall, as shown. Between the firewalls sit various servers that filter traffic for the corresponding servers. Each firewall has its own rules for inbound and outbound traffic.

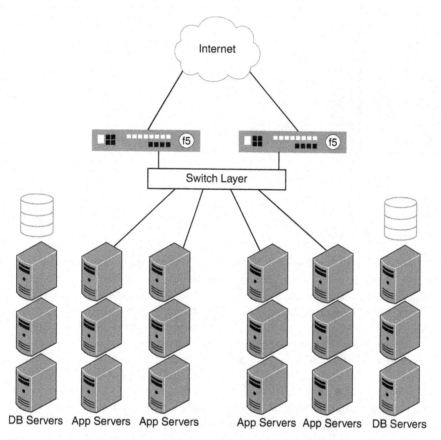

Figure 7-2 *Application Servers and Database Servers Connected to the Internet with F5*

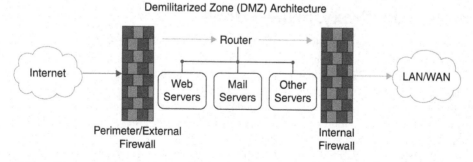

Figure 7-3 *DMZ in a Corporate Environment*

Figure 7-4 shows a corporate structure that has a DMZ followed by servers for applications, databases, and so on. Each layer can have its own firewall and specific inbound and outbound rules set up.

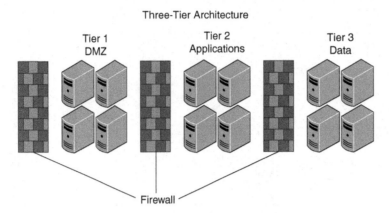

Figure 7-4 *Three-Tier Architecture*

In a nutshell, this is how the corporate structure should be set up. Create servers for databases and applications separately. To access the databases, all application servers have a database client installed on them. Separating applications and databases on different servers and keeping them up to date is the first step in host security. The second step is downloading and installing any new patches or service packs required for the database or for the clients. Without patches, any newly found vulnerabilities remain open for possible exploitation. Note that when a new patch is available, it is not instantly downloaded and installed on all servers or database engines. Rather, the patches or the service pack is tested on a machine, and when the patching is successful, they are applied to the development and test machines. Then with the help of network/host/Unix/Linux administrators, the patches are applied on production database engines. Installing patches in this order protects the integrity and security of servers and the data itself. In the next section, we discuss connections to the databases and servers.

IP Selection, Proxy, Invited Nodes

First we'll discuss a few details about the Internet Protocol (IP) address of a server. Once we have a server—used either for a database or an application—we can register a domain name and IP address, and we may even create a website with the help of our Internet service provider (ISP), if required. When users want to connect to these servers, they use the IP with a port or the URL. But knowing the IP can reveal the geo-location of the server and thereby the address (the IPv4 or IPv6 address). Once these are known, anyone can use an Internet search engine to find more details and vulnerabilities or open ports and initiate an exploitation. Firewalls help filter attacks to some extent, but they may still expose the IP address. Therefore, we want to protect our server IP address for better security. This can be accomplished by proxy servers. Proxies help prevent exposing the server IP to the world. Some advantages of proxies are that they offer enhanced security, allow private browsing or going to shopping websites, and prevent users from accessing inappropriate content. Proxy servers can be implemented as either hardware or software.

In this chapter, we mainly discuss two types of proxy servers: forward and reverse. A forward proxy server sits immediately in front of users. As users send requests, a forward proxy examines each request and either sends it forward or blocks it. In this way, forward proxy servers decide whether to make a connection to the server depending on the user requests. In other words, proxy servers are a single point of entry, and they accept connections from computers on a private network and forward those requests to the public Internet. This setup also makes it hard for a company to meet the individual needs of end users. Figure 7-5 shows a diagram of a forward proxy setup. Notice that a forward proxy can be set up without connecting to the Internet and as a private network. But when an Internet connection comes into play, a VPN is better suited because VPN encrypts the traffic.

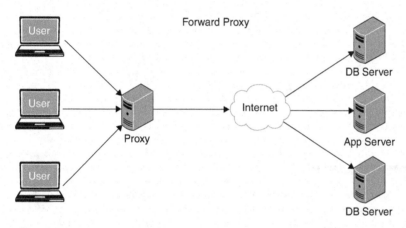

Figure 7-5 *Forward Proxy*

In the forward proxy connections shown in Figure 7-5, there is an advantage with cache. When a request is received from the user, the proxy first checks whether the requested information is cached. If cached, the proxy sends the information directly to the user, thereby eliminating the connection to the Internet, and then on to server. If no cached information is available, the proxy decides on two things: first, if the request is valid. If it is, the proxy sends the request to servers. Second, the proxy examines the request and denies it if the request is not legitimate or allowed. This is how the proxy protects both the users and the servers. Notice that if the forward proxy has cached information of personally identifiable data somehow, any user can request it, and the proxy is able to provide it without blocking. Sensitive information can be stolen by a disgruntled employee (an end user) even with a forward proxy in place.

A reverse proxy, shown in Figure 7-6, is the opposite, as its name indicates. The proxy sits one step before the servers as a gatekeeper. A reverse proxy eliminates the problem mentioned in the discussion of forward proxies: stealing sensitive information. In other words, a reverse proxy acts as a single point of entry for external systems to access resources on a private subnet. User requests now have to go through a firewall and the Internet before they land in proxy. If any of the requests are illegitimate, they are blocked by firewalls; however, a legitimate request is examined by the proxy. The reverse proxy also has a cache of stored information and doesn't need to contact the server for every request. If the cache doesn't contain the requested information, the request is then delivered to the servers.

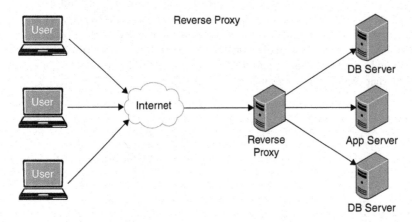

Figure 7-6   *Reverse Proxy*

Access Control Lists

We have so far examined two ways to protect our servers: separating the database and application servers and using a proxy. Both can offer protection, but as we discussed, we want defense in depth to address all possible security issues. The next step for host security involves employing an access control list (ACL) of allowed IP addresses, also known as an invited node list. Each database allows a list of allowed nodes or IP addresses that it can accept. Any IP address that is not in the allowed IP address list, ACL, or invited node list is rejected, and no information is sent for any requests. In an Oracle database, this information is stored in the sqlnet.ora file under the /admin/network folder. The node list part of the sqlnet.ora file typically looks like Example 7-1.

Example 7-1   \ *SQLNET.ORA File in an Oracle Database for Invited and Excluded Node List*

```
# SQLNET.ORA Network Configuration general format file


# File: /myDatabase/product/Version/22/2023/network/admin/sqlnet.ora
# Generated by Oracle configuration tools.
#NAMES.DIRECTORY_PATH = (TNSNAMES, ONAMES, HOSTNAME)


TCP.VALIDNODE_CHECKING = YES
TCP.INVITED_NODES=(sales.us.example.com, hr.company.com, 192.168.*,
  2001:DB8:200C:433B/32)
TCP.EXCLUDED_NODES=(12.9.2.198, 112.65.245.234)
```

```
SQLNET.EXPIRE_TIME = 1
SQLNET.INBOUND_CONNECT_TIMEOUT=7


DIAG_ADR_ENABLED=OFF
DIAG_DDE_ENABLED=FALSE
DIAG_SIGHANDLER_ENABLED=FALSE


SEC_USER_AUDIT_ACTION_BANNER=/myDatabase/AuditWarningBanner.txt
SEC_USER_UNAUTHORIZED_ACCESS_BANNER=/myDatabase/AuthAccessBanner.txt


SQLNET.ENCRYPTION_TYPES_SERVER = (AES256)
SQLNET.ENCRYPTION_SERVER = REQUESTED
SQLNET.ENCRYPTION_TYPES_CLIENT = (AES256)
SQLNET.ENCRYPTION_CLIENT = REQUESTED


SQLNET.AUTHENTICATION_SERVICES=(BEQ, TCPS)     ## (for TNS entry for SSL).
SSL_VERSION=1.2    #To ensure TLS use

## Note - The following is TRUE on server, FALSE on client (in sqlnet.ora file)
SSL_CLIENT_AUTHENTICATION=TRUE
SSL_CIPHER_SUITES=(SSL_RSA_WITH_AES_256_CBC_SHA384)


###  WALLET-DIT(DATA IN TRANSIT)
WALLET_LOCATION=(SOURCE=(METHOD=FILE)(METHOD_DATA=(DIRECTORY=/myDatabase/Wallet-
  Folder/DataInTransit)))


### ENCRYPTION WALLET-DAR(DATA AT REST)
ENCRYPTION_WALLET_LOCATION=(SOURCE=(METHOD=FILE)(METHOD_DATA=(DIRECTORY=/myDatabase/
  WalletFolder/DataAtRest/$ORACLE_SID)))


SQLNET.CRYPTO_CHECKSUM_TYPES_SERVER=(SHA256, SHA384, SHA512)
SQLNET.CRYPTO_CHECKSUM_SERVER=REQUESTED
SQLNET.CRYPTO_CHECKSUM_TYPES_CLIENT=(SHA256, SHA384, SHA512)
SQLNET.CRYPTO_CHECKSUM_CLIENT=REQUESTED


##SQLNET LOGON_VERSION
#minimum client password version allowed
SQLNET.ALLOWED_LOGON_VERSION_SERVER = 12
SQLNET.ALLOWED_LOGON_VERSION_CLIENT = 12
```

Notice the following from the sqlnet.ora file listed in Example 7-1:

```
TCP.VALIDNODE_CHECKING = YES
TCP.INVITED_NODES=(sales.us.example.com, hr.company.com, 142.128.*,
2001:DB8:200C:433B/32)
TCP.EXCLUDED_NODES=(12.9.2.198, 112.65.245.234)
```

The first noncommented line in Example 7-1 tells the DB that nodes are being checked for validity. The second line specifies the locations' URL or a global IP address in either IPv4 (142.128.*) or IPv6 versions (2001:DB8:200C:433B/32). It also includes locations that are excluded. These excluded nodes mean any requests from those IP addresses are rejected or not serviced. An organization usually includes IP addresses or the URLs of reliable websites and other IP addresses they know are good in the invited node list. Typically, invited node lists also contain developers', testers', and SA's individual IP nodes—either dynamic or static—to control the traffic to DB servers. The reason is that when we use these lists (ACLs), we want to leverage static IPs from the relevant servers within the applicable environment. We don't want to give the "test" servers the ability to communicate with production DB servers and vice-versa. The list of invited and excluded nodes needs to be updated regularly to add or delete items to keep the database servers safe and up to date from any new attacks. In the next section, we discuss how to generate a log when the invited node list or the excluded node list changes.

A typical setup with Windows firewall can be as shown in Figure 7-7. Notice from the figure that firewalls can be set up for inbound and outbound rules for a port and IP. Once created, the rule can be updated, edited, or even disabled/deleted.

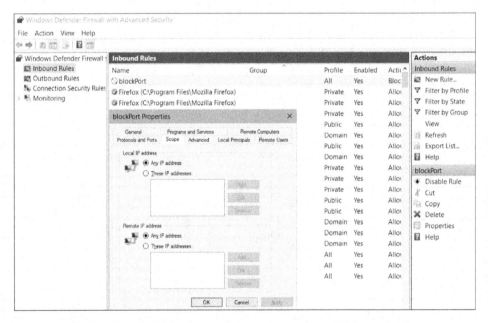

Figure 7-7 *Windows Defender Firewall Setup for an IP and Port*

The solution for an allowed node list and excluded node list is different in SQL Server. By default, the typical ports used by SQL Server and associated database engine services are TCP **1433**, **4022**, **135**, and **1434** and UDP **1434**. If SQL Server is set up with a default port of TCP 1433, and if we do not know the IP addresses of clients who may connect to the DB server, then there are two different things we can minimally do to protect the database:

■ Ensure that accounts accessing the SQL Server have very strong passwords (typically this password policy can be easily set up for length, history, age, and complexity requirements)

■ Make sure that security patches for SQL Server are up to date on the server operating system where you have the database

But if we do know the details of IP addresses of your clients, the built-in Windows firewall can be easily set up to allow access to port TCP 1433 with only the client IPs. A simple PowerShell script to set up such a privilege can be done as follows:

```
New-NetFirewallRule -DisplayName "SQLServer default instance"
-Direction Inbound -LocalPort 1433 -Protocol TCP -Action Allow

New-NetFirewallRule -DisplayName "SQLServer Browser service"
-Direction Inbound -LocalPort 1434 -Protocol UDP -Action Allow
```

Connecting to a System/DB: Passwords, Smart Cards, Certificates

In Chapter 2, we briefly discussed the authentication factors based on what you know, what you have, and what you are. To keep and maintain security of our data, we need as many layers as possible, but we also know that too many layers will increasingly push even legitimate users away from the connections. Thus, one-factor authentication and adding another factor would be sufficient if all other layers are already protected. At least this is the best information we know at the current time in the progress of technology. Of course, everything is subject to change depending on how the technology evolves. Let's first talk about passwords. As common as it is in practice, the username-and-password combination is the weakest link for authentication, but it's also the easiest tool to implement for various platforms and applications. Username and password fall into the category of what you know. Passwords are or should be governed by a policy; otherwise, users tend to implement anything they like, making it easy for an attacker to steal passwords. In fact, most commonly used and easily guessed passwords are stored in cache as hashes in a list known as a rainbow table. These tables can be purchased for a fee or are free for hackers. Knowing a person and their interests from social media websites such as Facebook, an attacker tries to guess a possible password after starting a phishing email to confirm or find a username and/or email to initiate an attack. Therefore, the stronger the password, the better our protection will be.

Password policies are real documents that are enforced across the organization in real time. They are governed by several rules:

■ Password history: Determines how long you need to wait before you can re-use an earlier password. If your new password is the same as the last N passwords you already used, the password policy should reject those N passwords. N can be any adjustable number, such as 3, 5, 8, or 10.

■ Password age: The validity time for the current password. Some passwords are good for 30 days, some for 90 days, and some for a year. This time is adjustable depending on the needs of an organization.

■ Password length: Dictates how many characters your password should be at minimum. Notice that the length is "minimum." Observe that most websites and trusted corporations often ask users to create passwords of at least eight characters. Is the length of eight characters sufficient for a password? The answer depends on what account the password is used for and what the purpose of the account is. If you are registering for a free account for a newspaper website just to read news (but not to pay for any services with a credit card or give any other personally identifiable information) or to comment on a public discussion board such as Reddit, it may be relatively safe to use an eight-character password, but any lengthy password is always a better bet than a shorter one. One point though is worth mentioning. A longer password is a great idea, but lengthy passwords exceeding 20 or 30 characters become a problem because the users cannot easily type or even remember them.

■ Password complexity: Passwords must have special characters like @, $, #, % or even the braces like {, (, [and so on. A password like TomCruiseSummer2024 is easily guessable (even though it is long), and adding complexity with special characters makes it more secure. Again, when we come to this stage we have to follow the four rules to make our password policy successful. Note that characters like @ and $ have special meaning in SQL, PowerShell, Linux/Unix operating system variables, and so on. This is why the password policy should state what special characters are allowed. Consider the following passwords:

Password created by a user for Windows log in: JohnDavidson_2023

Password generated by software: mIP|\{8qmFqXD:.

It is easy to see the complexity of the password generated as one or more lowercase letters, one or more uppercase letters, special characters, and symbols like the colon and the period.

■ Password attempts: Allowing an infinite number of attempts to use a password to get in proves detrimental for data centers because an attacker who gained access can implement a million passwords with software to log in. For this purpose, data center password attempts are limited to N, which can be 3, 5, or anything an organization chooses to implement. If we implement N as 5, after five unsuccessful attempts, the username is locked out. It would need an account unlock, and if the user still cannot remember or recall their old password, a reset with a new password is required. Some corporations provide self-service account resets and unlocks, but that service requires additional resources to maintain and work out how users can access that service. Again, note that once a password is reset, it should follow the rules of complexity, age, history, and length.

Another variation of database security is to lock unused accounts. For example, if a user who was given access to a database never used their account in the past N days, it would be safer to lock their account than let it remain open and risk an attack. It may even be worth first reminding users via email about an impending account lockout before actually locking out their account. Do we then keep the locked accounts if the user has not still used the account and not requested an unlock and/or password reset? That again depends on the organization's policy. Some organizations keep the accounts for 90 days and some delete after 30 days. Accounts of fired or laid-off employees or those who resigned from the organization may be disabled on the same day of the layoff or resignation and locked for 30 days to check for any unusual activities. There may be required procedures to be followed before permanently deleting the accounts.

Passwords need to be stored in a system that authenticates the users and can provide a way to retrieve forgotten passwords. The system should also have a reset if a user says they cannot recall their earlier passwords. This further complicates the situation and demands that we store the passwords as plaintext on the disk or backup. Storing passwords as plaintext is problematic because anyone may be able to open the file and steal those passwords if they gain access to the file.

How then should we be storing passwords? The answer lies in hashing, which we touched on in Chapter 5. Hashing is a one-way function. Passwords are stored as hashes in a reliable system and even in the Windows operating system. The password a user enters is converted to a hash to compare with the stored hash to make a decision for allowing the user to log in or have access. If the user loses or forgets the password, Windows operating system, Microsoft corporation, or anyone on the face of the Earth, for that matter, cannot get that password back from the hash. The only way is to give the user a hint about the password and refresh their memory to see if they can come up with it. Many users think that database administrators who work at a different level than front-end users can easily read the passwords of end users and can supply them back in plaintext. In reality, DBAs or data owners, custodians, or anyone else would never be able to read passwords in plaintext because they are stored on the database as hashes. All the DBA or owner can do is to reset the account with a new password if required, or, if the user can still recall their password, unlock the account for another N attempts.

Hashing is another reason why a person creating accounts on a Windows or other machine needs to create a separate administrative account with a different password but use a nonadministrative account for general email, web browsing, and so on. If the normal user password is forgotten, the user still has access to the system as an administrator with the admin account and can reset the password for the normal user.

Again, remember that with all these rules and policies, the username-password combination is still a one-factor authentication method and is weak. Figures 7-8 and 7-9 show the password policy in a Windows server and database and different aspects of the password policy and how they can be easily implemented are discussed. Note that each password policy is different and needs to be implemented separately. For example, the Windows password policy is a uniform mandatory implementation for every employee, but the database password policy applies to those who have DB privileges. Other software packages can have their own rules as well.

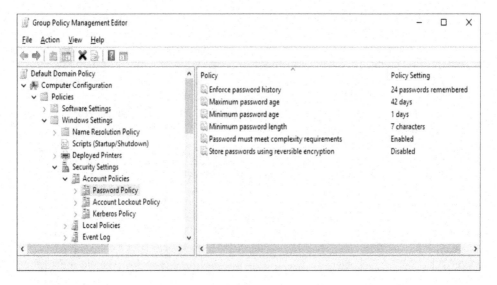

Figure 7-8   *Windows Server Password Policy*

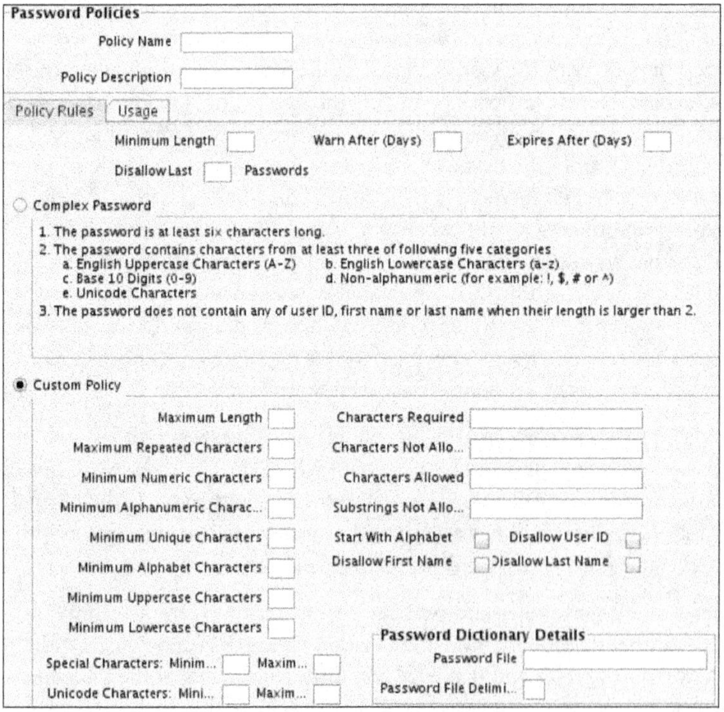

Figure 7-9   *Database Password Policy*

The second factor of what you know can be a PIN, but it should only work in combination with another factor; a PIN by itself is or weak. The PIN can be fixed or dynamically generated for each login attempt. Once the username and password are correct, the system can send a phone text message and demand that the PIN sent on the text be entered accurately to confirm the user trying to log in is authentic. Also notice that the PIN has a lifetime. It does not work forever. The time can be decided by the administrators as anything from 5 minutes to 30 minutes depending on the importance of data and what the user is trying to attempt. The PIN also usually works with another factor known as what you have, which is an access card. Access cards are similar to credit cards with a chip. Figure 7-10 shows an example of a common access card (CAC) as released by the Department of Defense. Notice the chip, barcode, photo of the user, and various other details such as pay grade and rank. The same card is used for physical access to a facility, logging into a computer, identification, and so on.

Figure 7-10 *An Access Card with a Chip and the Chip's Inside Details (U.S. Government and a Typical Credit card)*

The card, sometimes referred as a smart card, can be used for a variety of purposes—logging into a computer system, gate entry at the entrance of a facility, entry privileges into a data center room, access to highly privileged discussion or meeting areas, ATM access for cash withdrawals, and more. Each of these privileges can be programmed into the card, edited, or deleted. The card can be made unusable if it's reported as stolen. Keyboards with a card reader or USB card readers can be connected to a system for end users to log in with the card. Once the card is recognized, the second authentication factor would require the user to input a PIN, which is normally fixed and does not change. Like everything else in life that has an expiry date, the access card has an expiry date and should be reissued or reactivated.

Figure 7-10 also shows the magnified example of the chip on the right side. A great many varieties of the chip design are possible, with lines running across on the yellow area in a variety of ways. Each area indicates some particular function (ground, I/O, clock, and so on). The access card can also store a user's private and public key certificates, such as X.509 used for other information and privileges on a variety of operating systems and software packages.

The card must remain in the slot of the card reader for the user to work on a system. If the user moves away from the system (computer, ATM, or any other system), the card must be pulled out, which automatically locks the system. In other words, the access card must be present in the reader as long as the user needs access to the system. Other newer varieties of these cards for ATM access and use in the payment industry work with wireless scanning and do not need to be scanned or inserted. A few seconds of proximity to the reader allows access for card reading, and payment is made. These kinds of wireless or proximity access cards are not suitable for data center security.

The next idea of data security lies in asynchronous encryption with X.509 certificates where a private and public key is involved. The asynchronous encryption with private and public keys is also discussed in Chapter 2. They can be used for signature, encryption, and authentication. Windows Device Manager can automatically detect these cards with built-in software, as shown in Figure 7-11.

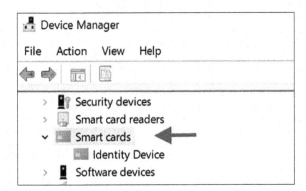

Figure 7-11 *Windows Device Manager Detecting Smart Cards*

Linux/Unix systems can also use the same private and public certificates to control user access. Because each user has one public and one private key, the process typically works as follows on these systems:

1. Send this public key as a text to the system administrator (SA).

2. The SA adds the public key to the user's login account. As an example, for OpenSSH server, the public key is added to ~/.ssh/authorized_keys file.

3. The system asks for the user's private key when OpenSSH is executed and matches the stored public key with the entered private key (usually validated along with the PIN associated with the keys).

4. If the user authentication works at this point, SA can usually disable other types of user authentications for better security of your server that is hosting the database.

5. The SA can also keep your password as an alternative access for logging in. If this is the case, the password policies discussed earlier need to be strictly followed.

Creating certificates and smart cards is beyond the scope of the book, but once the certificates are known, this implementation usually works for the security of the database that is hosted on the server (Windows or Linux/Unix). Red Hat Linux and Ubuntu also have GUI versions of identity management screens that can be used for setting up passwords and certificates.

Cron Jobs or Task Scheduler

One of the biggest problems in an attack or illegal and excessive use is to find out who did the attack and generate a log. This can be done by setting up a job that alerts the DBA or SA about what is happening on the database or system. A program or a script that can run at a predetermined time, date, or month is greatly useful when it detects unusual activity and sends an email to that effect to the administrators. In Linux and Unix systems, a crontab, which runs a programmed job at a predetermined time, is considered the best method. The word *cron* is short form for *chronos*, which is the Greek word for *time*. *Crontab* is short for *cron table*. Cron tables use a job scheduler named cron to execute tasks. Cron is a system process that performs a task to a set schedule. The schedule is referred to as the crontab in Unix/Linux. Crontab is also the name of the program used to edit that schedule of jobs. A crontab is defined for each account and runs for that account if privileges are given correctly. A typical crontab entry looks like this:

```
30  05  14  07 * /home/myDatabase/HR/refreshPayScales.ksh
```

At first look, the entry may look puzzling, but it is fairly simple to understand the Linux crontab format with the fields explained in Table 7-1.

Table 7-1 *Crontab Fields Explained*

MIN HOUR DOM MON DOW CMD

Field	Description	Allowed Value
MIN	Minute	0 to 59
HOUR	Hour	0 to 23
DOM	Day of month	1-31
MON	Month	1-12 (1-Jan, 2-Feb, and so on)
DOW	Day of week	0-6 (0-Sunday, 1-Monday, and so on)
CMD	Command	Any command to be executed
MIN	Minute field	0 to 59

Looking back at the command, now we understand that the Linux shell script refresh-PayScales.ksh under the folder /home/myDatabase/HR/ will run at 05:30 AM (24-hour format) on July 14 and on every day of the week. In other words, the command numbers can be explained as

> 30 – 30th Minute; 05 – 05 AM; 14 – 14th Day; 07 – 7th Month (July); * – Every day of the week

Note that several crontabs can be added to an account, and all can have the same time and date of execution or can have different times and dates. The following commands can be used to list and edit crontab entries for an account:

- **crontab -l** lists all the jobs for the account (the account with which the user is logged in currently).

- **Crontab -e** allows the user to edit the crontab entries (add/delete/modify).

Here are a few examples:

- **To schedule a job for every minute using Cron:**

  ```
  * * * * * /home/myDatabase/HR/refreshPayScales.ksh
  ```

  It may be hard to find someone needing to schedule some job every minute, but this example helps you understand how a crontab entry can be made. * is a universal substitute that we use for files. In this example, it indicates all possible values, which means every day, every month, every year, every hour, and every minute.

- **To schedule a job twice a day:**

  The following script runs the same command twice a day and every day at 10:00 (10 AM) and 18:00 (6 PM). Notice that the second field (hour) has a comma-separated value—which is to indicate that the command needs to run at the given time.

  ```
  00 10, 18 * * * /home/myDatabase/HR/refreshPayScales.ksh
  ```

- **Running a job only on weekdays:**

  If a job has to run every weekday at the top of every hour during the working hours of 8 AM to 4 PM (Monday to Friday):

  ```
  00 08-16 * * 1-5 /home/myDatabase/HR/CheckForErrors.ksh
  ```

  Cron also has special keyword values that allow us to give a short word instead of mentioning the entire line with numbers:

  ```
  @yearly  /home/myDatabase/HR/CleanupDB.ksh
  ```

The other keywords that can be used are shown in Table 7-2, along with the actual equivalents of the keywords. Some additional sample schedules are shown following Table 7-2. Finally, note that the crontab listing is different for each user or account. Each user can have their own crontab listing to run anything on a schedule.

Table 7-2 *Keywords*

Keyword	Equivalent
@yearly	0 0 1 1 *
@daily	0 0 * * *
@hourly	0 * * * *
@reboot	Run at startup.

```
@monthly /home/myDatabase/HR/CleanLogs.ksh
@daily /home/myDatabase/Payroll/Accounting/Attendance.ksh
@reboot /home/myDatabase/HR/SendRebootEmail.ksh
```

Microsoft Windows has a utility named Task Scheduler that can use used to schedule an update just like the crontab work we just discussed. Setting up a job to run at a particular time is a straightforward process with the GUI, as shown in Figures 7-12 through 7-15. One can create a basic task (say restarting the computer or running a virus scan or doing one after another) as a user or group, configure for an operating system to tell the job what to do (run a command) and how often to do it (daily, weekly, etc.), and give it a name. It's easy to know that the job can be either disabled or enabled or can even be deleted when not required. Once a job is created, it can be saved and let it run on schedule, or one can go to the job and run it manually immediately by clicking the **run now** option. An interesting thing with the task scheduler is that the command that is run can have parameters supplied. The setting up of a task is easy and has the following tabs for the user: General, Trigger, Actions, Conditions, Settings, and History. The **History** tab shows whether the job actually ran as required.

The task scheduler, along with the Windows Defender firewall, can work in tandem to take care of the database security in a Windows server. As an ending note, remember that the first line of defense always starts with us; how we maintain the security of our servers depends entirely on us. Notice that besides daily, monthly, or any other schedule, the task can be scheduled to run depending on another event. The event can be a reboot, start up, or any other activity we can run or define.

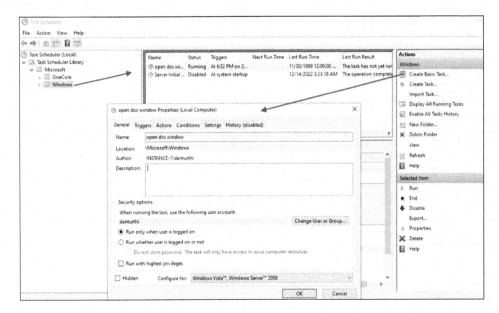

Figure 7-12   *Task Scheduling in Microsoft Windows with GUI*

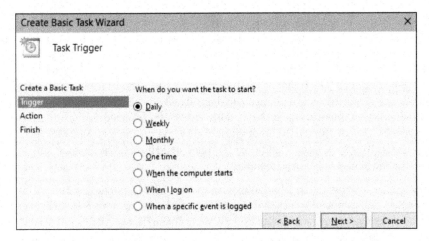

Figure 7-13   *Task Scheduling Trigger in Microsoft Windows with GUI*

An interesting thing about the task scheduler needs to be mentioned. A task can be written and saved as an XML file. Thus, anyone who knows the correct syntax of XML can easily create a text file instead of going through all these smaller windows and GUI and quickly import that file into task scheduler. See the Import Task, Export Task, Run, and End on the right side of Figure 7-12.

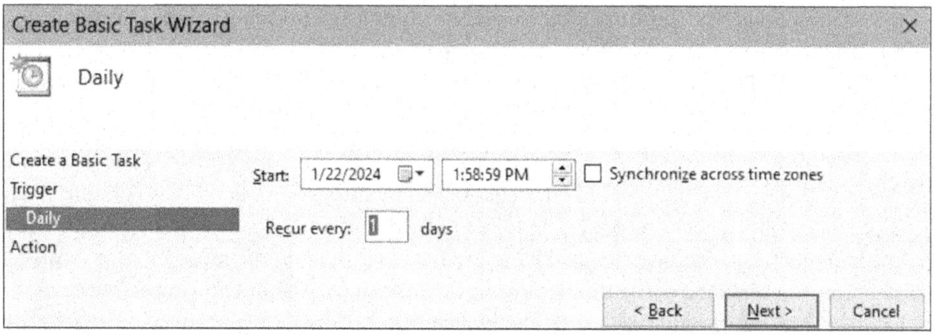

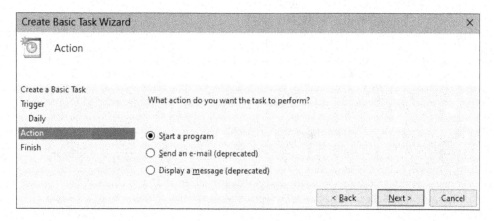

Figure 7-14   *Task Scheduling Timing in Microsoft Windows with GUI*

Figure 7-15   *Task Scheduling Action in Microsoft Windows with GUI*

Regular Monitoring and Troubleshooting

Public and private organizations, units, and branches of government almost always have a great policy drafted and put in place. Yet we see that there are failures, and an external auditor always finds some items or people that do not align with the policies or, worse yet, move far away from the policies. The simple reason is human negligence to implement or follow the policy. Hence, the adage "an unenforced policy is good as useless." If an organization tells the employees to use at least 10-character passwords at minimum, most passwords can be like "ILoveMyJob," or "I_hate_this_policy." These passwords are so easy that an attacker can guess them or get them from password generators or password crackers (for example, John the Ripper or L0phtCrack) available on the Internet. The password policy is fine but lacks complexity and other rules. When the password is checked for complexity, users must use an uppercase and lowercase letter combinations, numbers, and symbols. Not only that, it should also exclude repeated and consecutive numbers, such as 9999 or 54321. The policy must be uniformly enforced, and that is just the starting point. By uniform enforcement, we mean it is a mandatory access control at the organizational level that applies to everyone from the CEO level to the lowest-level employee. Further rules can apply at the branch level with discriminatory access control that make systems and databases better from the security point of view. Regular auditing and checking of these policies and reporting are important to avoid future problems.

We then come to the question of who checks and monitors these activities. A branch can allot these policy checks to a few employees who do other things as well. For example, a programmer who is coding can check the log files first thing in the morning to review the activities of users on a software they previously deployed. The monitoring activity takes an hour or so but greatly helps keep the branch in good shape. We need to create logs for every single activity, regardless of whether the activity is good or bad. Even the firewalls that we buy examine the packets and generate a log entry when a packet is found suspicious and dropped. If the system administrator has no time or interest to read the firewall logs, it is just an accident waiting to happen.

The cron jobs we discussed earlier usually run a shell script, such as a Linux/Unix shell or a Bourne shell script. The script can easily send an email to the administrators. An example with the following line in a shell file can demonstrate how email can be sent.

```
mail -s "Daily Morning Log" username@UserOrganization.com <  /
MyFolder/Logs/Feb25.log
```

The -s option indicates the subject line of an email, and the email will be sent to the user at the address of *username@UserOrganization.com*. It can enclose a file such as */MyFolder/Logs/Feb25.log*. But in the end, it is the responsibility of the branch or organization to read those files and find any abnormal, or even normal, activity. Microsoft Task Scheduler has a similar option to send email to a user in its GUI part. Newer versions of Windows may have deprecated the Send Email Message option in the Task Scheduler, but that can be easily overcome by a small PowerShell script block. Task Scheduler can run a batch file that has several smaller jobs executing one after another. All the jobs can be put into a PowerShell file with an ending command line such as the **Send-MailMessage** command, and the scheduler can invoke this PowerShell script directly from a PowerShell (.ps1) file. Various options are available in the **Send-MailMessage** PowerShell command for emailing, like CC, BCC, subject, body, priority, attachments, and so on.

Sending a message to a single user, enclosing a file, can be done as follows:

```
Send-MailMessage
        -From 'CurrentUser <cuser@SomeCompany.com>'
        -To 'someReceiver <someReceiver@SomeCompany.com>',
                'secondReceiver <secReceiver@SomeCompany.com>'
        -Subject 'Daily log with an attachment'
        -Body "Please read - Daily morning firewall log"
        -Attachments .\dailyFW.log
        -Priority High
        -DeliveryNotificationOption OnSuccess, OnFailure
        -SmtpServer 'smtp.SomeCompany.com'
```

For sending a message to a user and to a group of people who share a common email account, use this:

```
Send-MailMessage
        -From 'CurrentUser <cuser@SomeCompany.com>'
        -To 'NetworkSAs <NetSysAdmins@SomeCompany.com>'
        -Cc 'secondReceiver <secReceiver@SomeCompany.com>'
        -Bcc 'ITSupervisors <AllSupervisors@SomeCompany.com >'
        -Subject "Cancelled - Today's auditing visits due to inclement
         weather"
        -Credential localDomain01\sysAdm01 -UseSsl
```

Remember that for achieving optimal security, enforcing a policy is a job half done. The other half is to monitor, track, and troubleshoot problems promptly as they occur rather than waiting for someone to complain. When these security and troubleshooting rules are in place, the following important steps are worth noting to avoid a painful audit or an attack:

1. Create a log entry for every activity—user creation, user login, user logout, user daily activities, user lockout, and so on.

2. Make sure that the log entry created is saved and emailed to the administrators.

3. Designate someone to read the logs and emails and take corrective action promptly.

4. Report unusual activity, even if it is from a known employee or a customer.

5. Make everyone understand that the rules apply to all users, without exception.

6. Lock expired and unused accounts after a few days (30, 60, and so on) of inactivity.

7. Promptly delete the accounts and usernames when a person has left the organization.

8. Document any unusual activity and save for future audits.

9. Apply security filters at the database level and user level for both users and system accounts.

10. Make sure that the system accounts used by groups or branches, if any, have strong passwords as well and must be maintained like normal usernames.

11. Inform users to change passwords regularly, or the accounts will be locked.

12. Maintain documentation—even if it is just an email request—of who is asking for database access and who is recommending the user for such access.

13. Automate log creation and emailing of the logs to required personnel at least once a day or as required.

14. Train and encourage people to take security seriously and make retraining a mandatory step to remind users about the dangers of a breach.

15. When using database calls from a program, let the programmers know that closing a DB connection is important after a transaction is complete, or the DB will be stuck with several open transaction connections.

16. Be mindful of shoulder surfing and passwords being stolen by users, and do not display passwords (or mask them) when a user logs in.

17. Continue to monitor who is creating daily or regular tasks and who is modifying the existing tasks, so as not to generate any regression errors in email logs or log files.

18. Track the database file sizes, disk sizes, and limits, if any. Set up a process to clean or remove unwanted files on the machines that host an application or database.

19. Have more than one person check the logs and activities or create a second set of eyes that can quickly do the job of the primary when reviewing logs.

20. Anyone who wants access to databases must follow through a process of background check and be reminded of the dire consequences in case of data breach/loss/spill.

However hard we try to take our security seriously, remember that the first line of defense of security always starts with you. Taking care of data is everyone's responsibility.

Summary

For better security of databases, they need to be separated from where applications are hosted. In other words, applications stay on the application servers with a database client, and the databases stay on the database servers. A demilitarized zone with firewalls helps protect a corporate network. When the end users are expected to be large in number, a load balancer is used for controlling and stabilizing the traffic. Thus a three-tier application is more helpful for protecting the data layer and the data itself.

Database engines can be staged with either forward or reverse proxies and can use static or dynamic IP addresses. These IP addresses are usually stored in an "invited node list" to preserve connections from only trusted IPs. Databases also use multifactor authentication and strict password policies to protect user accounts. When multifactor authentication is required, a smart card would be more helpful because it can be used for email, digital signatures, photo identification, and logging into a network. Smart card setup is easy and comes with built-in tools for various operating systems. Cronjobs or Task Scheduler on Linux/Unix and Windows, respectively, help organize jobs that can detect unusual traffic and alert the administrators in a timely manner. There must be a designated group of people who read the logs daily to take action on what the logs show.

Chapter 7 Questions

1. Why is it necessary for databases to be on separate servers on a large corporate network?

2. How do we update the RDBMS software with new patches when new releases of the software come out?

3. What are the two types of proxy servers, and how do they differ in their action?

4. Where is the access control list or invited node list for Oracle database and SQL Server?

5. What constitutes a password policy?

6. Why are unused accounts normally locked out by database administrators?

7. If a system stores passwords as hash values and if a user on the system forgets the password, how can the user get back their plaintext password?

8. If your system uses two-factor authentication of an access card and a PIN, how are these factors identified?

9. How are access cards, known as smart cards, with X.509 certificates that store asynchronous encryption used?

10. What is the function of a cron and crontab in Unix/Linux?

11. What is the format of a crontab in Unix/Linux?

12. What is the Task Scheduler in Windows Server?

13. How can one compensate for the deprecated function of sending email in Windows Server's Task Scheduler?

Answers to Chapter 7 Questions

1. For protecting the data from unwanted attackers and to keep the data unexposed. Any application server that needs access to data will have a database client installed on it to access databases on DB servers

2. Update the database servers with DB server patches and DB clients with client-side patches. Companies like Oracle provide patches for servers and clients separately on various platforms.

3. Proxy servers are either forward or reverse. A forward proxy server sits immediately in the front of users. As users send requests, the forward proxy examines each request and either sends it forward or blocks it. A reverse proxy sits one step before the servers as a gatekeeper. User requests have to go through a firewall and the Internet before they land in the proxy.

4. In Oracle database, invited node list information is stored in the sqlnet.ora file under /admin/network folder. It can also contain an entry for "Excluded nodes." In SQL Server, it is achieved with two possible options: an inbound firewall rule and allowing only known IP addresses. In both Oracle and SQL Server, these rules and files can be updated regularly as circumstances warrant.

5. Password policy constitutes a) password history, b) password age, c) password length, d) password complexity, and e) number of attempts the user can try before getting locked out of their access to an application, database, or system.

6. To avoid access to systems from users who quit or are fired from using these accounts, it is necessary to lock out unused accounts.

7. It is impossible to get plaintext from hashed passwords because hashing is a one-way function. System administrators can only generate a new password and reset the account but not get the plaintext passwords from hashes.

8. An access card is what you have, and a PIN is what you know. The third way of authentication is what you are, which is usually biometric authentication systems that use fingerprints, handprints, and so on.

9. They can be used for authentication, digital signature, and encryption with files, emails, or any other communication.

10. Cron is a system process that performs a task to a set schedule. The schedule is referred as the crontab in Unix/Linux. Crontab is also the name of the program used to edit that schedule of jobs. A crontab is defined for each account and runs for that account if privileges are given correctly.

11. Crontab has the following details:

MIN HOUR DOM MON DOW CMD

Field	Description	Allowed Value
MIN	Minute	0 to 59
HOUR	Hour	0 to 23
DOM	Day of month	1-31
MON	Month	1-12 (1-Jan, 2-Feb, and so on)
DOW	Day of week	0-6 (0-Sunday, 1-Monday, and so on)
CMD	Command	Any command to be executed

12. Task Scheduler has a similar function in Windows, akin to the crontab in Linux/Unix. Task Scheduler is a GUI tool that can be used to set up a recurring job and create a log.

13. A simple PowerShell script can be scheduled to run from Task Scheduler of the Windows Server to send email to the user.

Proactive Monitoring

Logs, Logs, and More Logs

There are at least two routes to maintain data's confidentiality, integrity, and availability. The first is a well-known idea to take care of a problem after it occurs. A problem detected might be in need of an easy fix, or it might have progressed beyond a quick repair. You will not know the consequences until you research further and find the root cause. Root cause analysis has its own methods to find details and follows a systematic route that results in using more time and resources. The second way is to proactively monitor the database for any possible or expected problems. In proactive monitoring, you're always prepared and "expect" a problem to occur. You also have a solution ready if that problem were to occur.

Consider this scenario: An organization has set up its database and added users both as end users with least privileges and database administrators with more privileges. Everything is working fine, and one day the organization found that an unknown user logged in. The unknown user might have used an anonymous username that might have been provided as default in your database's basic installation with a default password. Oracle has such an account named Scott/Tiger for fun purposes. Oracle also provides a simple script file to create this account in all the Oracle latest releases. If your database installation created such an account, anyone can try their hands to get into the database. In the worst-case scenario, if the DBA or other administrative users had weak passwords or their passwords had been stolen, an unwanted hacker could get into the database and steal data or do more harm than you can imagine. The main aim of hackers would first be to create an administrative account for themselves, so they can come back whenever they want. Here is a question for this situation: Do you want to wait until this person causes damage, or would it be better if you caught them earlier? Also, have you tracked your database regularly to find who is logging in and what the users are actually doing? The answers to these questions (and more like these) can drive your security posture with your database.

With proactive monitoring, you always know ahead of time what to expect and, if anything goes wrong, where to check. This is where the importance of logs comes in. Almost every program, every executable code and operating system procedure, installation or patch upgrade creates or an create a log of the process. It does not matter if the process is successful or a failure; the log is always created to show what happened.

Creating logs is only half the process in proactive monitoring. If the logs created are not read or monitored regularly, there is no reason to call yourself proactive. Regular reading of logs can be time-consuming and needs a trained eye to catch errors quickly. Training and experience for spotting issues such events and incidents come with practice and daily monitoring. It is advisable to delegate a couple of people to watch the logs regularly and inform others who can take action.

In this chapter, we will discuss what actions on a database need a log and how that log can help us quickly detect a possible error or hacking attempt on a regular basis. Various transactions and operations that can happen simultaneously on a database (refer to the ACID and BASE rules we discuss in Chapter 4, "Database Security Introduction") and can create a plethora of logs. Some database transactions can be DML, DDL, data audits, backups, imports and exports, changes to meta data and so on.

Data Manipulation Monitoring

In an earlier chapter, we noted the differences between DML and DDL. In DML some example SQL commands can be as follows:

- **INSERT:** Inserts a data row or partial row (or column) into a specified schema table
- **UPDATE:** Updates an existing row or partial row (or column) within a specified schema table
- **DELETE:** Deletes/removes one or more records from a table
- **MERGE:** Merges data, or performs an operation consisting of an insert or update
- **CALL:** Calls a PL/SQL or Java program to run a specific procedure
- **EXPLAIN PLAN:** Though not a direct DML, explains access path to data
- **LOCK TABLE:** Not a direct DML but helps control concurrency

Notice that an end user or a hacker posing as an end user may be able to execute these commands once or more than once. The select statement is of course the most used because it retrieves data quickly with an option of specifying columns or shows all columns with a wildcard like the *. A trigger can be created for checking who is using the database and their purpose. Think about whether you should create a trigger that fires, since you want to proactively track your database, for every select statement. If there are 100 users, at any time, at least 100 select statements can be expected, which means you will have 100 triggers firing simultaneously. Instead, you can use an easier method by not allowing access to everyone on the table. (We discussed roles and grants in an earlier chapter.) But if you still decide to create a trigger that fires, the SQL Server script in Example 8-1 can work. Notice that select is technically not a DML command since it does not modify or manipulate anything. For this reason, there is really no need to create a trigger on a select statement.

If we read the script in Example 8-1, it shows there is a simple error-raising event after any insert or update operations on the Salaries table of the HR schema. But how does the HR staff know about this? They may not, unless they are specifically notified. Thus, we need to tweak the script to send an email.

Example 8-1 *Script for Triggering Creation with a Raise Error Notice*

```
CREATE TRIGGER NotifyHR
ON HR.Salaries
AFTER INSERT, UPDATE
AS RAISERROR ('Notify Human Resources', 16, 10);
GO
```

The script in Example 8-2 can send an email message to a specified person when there are insert or update changes on the table HR.Salaries. Note that, for the following script to work, Database Mail needs to be configured and enabled to work. The SQL Server Management Studio's (SSMS) GUI can easily accomplish this, as shown in Figure 8-1.

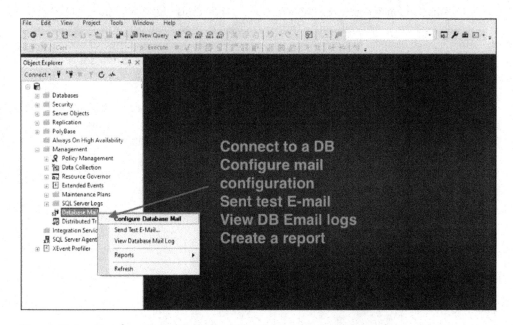

Figure 8-1 *Database Email Setup in SQL Server Management Studio*

The script shown in Example 8-2 now is modified to send an email to HR staff members at a group email address (CustomerServiceAtHR@OurOrganization.com) that can be accessed by more than one person in the HR department. Multiple email addresses can be included as well (similar to the way we discussed in the PowerShell script in Chapter 7, "Host Security").

Example 8-2 *Trigger Creation with Email Notification*

```
CREATE TRIGGER NotifyHR
ON HR.Salaries
AFTER INSERT, UPDATE, DELETE
AS
    EXEC msdb.dbo.sp_send_dbmail
        @profile_name = 'DataBaseAlertAdministrator',
        @recipients = 'CustomerServiceAtHR@OurOrganization.com',
@body = 'Note that there was a change in HR.Salaries table. If you do not recognize
  the changes made, please report to the database group and your security office.',
        @subject = 'Notice on Salaries table insert, update or delete';
GO
```

Once this trigger is created, for any DML changes on this particular table, there will be an email sent to the HR email address specified. But if the database is set up correctly and access is given only to a specified group of people you trust within the organization, this email may not be required. The reason is that this trigger will fire even if the smallest change is made. If can be further tweaked to send email only when the modifications exceed a specified count. Say a hacker got into the system and tried to update the first 100 (or any predetermined number of) rows with an invalid value into a specified column or an entire row itself. A trigger created for this purpose can alert the HR staff, as illustrated in Example 8-3. The **Rollback** command in the script is for removing any changes done by the end user. But the same script works when an authorized HR person is updating the table. In such a case, you need to remove the Rollback line, run the insert as required, and put the **Rollback** back into the trigger to prevent any end user from making changes. Of course, the end user can also have definite rights/grants to write or read the tables. What we are doing in this situation is creating a trigger that would fire if a hacker made an attempt to create a privileged administrative account and insert data into the table.

Example 8-3 *Trigger Creation with Email*

```
CREATE TRIGGER NotifyHR
ON HR.Salaries
AFTER INSERT
AS
    IF (SELECT  COUNT(*)  FROM INSERTED > 100)
     BEGIN
     ROLLBACK;
```

```
        EXEC msdb.dbo.sp_send_dbmail
        @profile_name = 'DataBaseAlertAdministrator',
        @recipients = 'CustomerServiceAtHR@OurOrganization.com',
        @body = 'Note that there was a change in HR.Salaries table. If you do not
      recognize the changes made, please report to the database group and your security
      office.',
        @subject = 'Notice on Salaries table insert, update or delete';
        END
GO
```

Example 8-4 shows a different type of trigger in Oracle SQL. Assume that a particular user is inserting data rows in a table. You do not know the username or whether the transaction is good or bad. You record every insert as a new entry into the table HR.Salaries and store the details of who made the inserts in a different audit table (HR.Salaries_Audit). The audit table will have a new entry, so HR staff can check the audit table to see if the user is an authorized user; if not, they can report the incident accordingly.

Example 8-4   *Trigger Creation—More Details with Email*

```
CREATE OR REPLACE TRIGGER HR_Salary_TableChanges
BEFORE INSERT OR DELETE OR UPDATE ON HR.Salaries
FOR EACH ROW
DECLARE
v_Type VARCHAR(10);
BEGIN


--  v_Type is a variable for the string ' INSERT, 'DELETE' or, ' UPDATE'
IF INSERTING THEN
v_Type := 'INSERT';
ELSIF UPDATING THEN
v_Type := 'UPDATE';
ELSE
v_Type := 'DELETE';
END IF;
-- Once the change is made, insert an entry into Audit table
INSERT INTO HR.Salaries_Audit
(change_type, changed_by, timestamp, new_os_user,
new_empno, new_name, new_job,
new_mgr, new_hiredate, new_sal, new_deptno)
VALUES
(v_Type, USER, SYSDATE, sys_context('userenv','OS_USER'),
:new.empno, :new.name, :new.job,
:new.mgr, :new.hiredate, :new.sal, :new.deptno);
```

```
-- Now send email to the HR staff as before closing
   UTL_MAIL.send_attach_varchar2 (
   sender    => 'DataBaseAlertAdministrator'@ OurOrganization.com',
   recipients  => 'CustomerServiceAtHR@OurOrganization.com',
   cc   => 'Internal_HR_Auditor@ OurOrganization.com',
   bcc    => 'HRSupervisor@ OurOrganization.com',
   subject   => 'Activity on HR.Salaries_Audit_Table',
   message   => 'Note that there was a change in HR.Salaries table. If you do not
recognize the changes made, please report to the database group and your security
office.',
    attachment    => 'A log file is attached.',
    att_filename   => 'HR_Activity_log.txt'
   );
END
```

Note in Example 8-4 the trigger is a "before" trigger. You also can create an "after" trigger for these operations. This example also shows how it can send emails to notify the staff. And the audit file records the username of the person who made the changes with a time stamp at the time the changes are made. For this email section to work in Oracle, UTIL_MAIL must be installed. Per the Oracle documentation, you can use the following command lines to install UTIL_MAIL. Only the DB administrator can do this, for obvious security reasons. The rdbms initialization file init.ora needs to be updated for the SMTP_OUT_SERVER parameter for the email server for the trigger to successfully send email:

```
SQL> @$ORACLE_HOME/rdbms/admin/utlmail.sql
SQL> @$ORACLE_HOME/rdbms/admin/prvtmail.plb
```

As said earlier, creating the triggers and sending emails is only half the work. If the emails are ignored and the logs are never read, any kind of security implementation would be useless because without reading those log files, it is nearly impossible to find what went wrong. For this reason, proactive monitoring is recommended. Again, give users access to what they require as a baseline with roles and privileges. Audit files, tables with personally identifiable information (PII), and other important information should be protected with proper access rights and grants. Grants should be regularly reviewed and revoked when not necessary.

We will end this section by giving two more short examples of triggers for DML and how the integrity of a database can be maintained. Sending email and alerting users can be added as needed, as explained earlier. The trigger shown in Example 8-5 demonstrates how something cannot be changed and will roll back any changes if any attempts are made to change DeptNo with an insert or delete statement.

Example 8-5   *Trigger That Denies a Change*

```
CREATE TRIGGER NotifyHR
ON HR.Salaries
AFTER INSERT, DELETE
AS
    IF EXISTS (SELECT  DeptNo FROM INSERTED WHERE DeptNo = '124')
    BEGIN
        PRINT 'Project Management Dept. (124) cannot be changed'
        ROLLBACK
    END
GO
```

You can test the Example 8-5 script with the insert statement (assuming the table exists) illustrated in Example 8-6.

Example 8-6   *Testing a Trigger Created in Example 8-5 with an Insert Statement*

```
INSERT HR.Salaries
(EmpNo, Name, Job, Mgr, Hiredate, Sal, DeptNo)
VALUES (678923, 'Davidson, Miranda', 'N', '20-Mar-2004', 56432, 124);

This will show an error as follows:

Project Management Dept. (124) cannot be changed
Transaction ended in trigger. The process is aborted
```

Oftentimes, we find that not all table data can be modified by everyone. If a table needs higher privileges to do any data modifications, those can be put as warnings in a trigger as well. This is illustrated in Example 8-7.

Example 8-7   *Trigger to Notify of Higher Privileges*

```
CREATE TRIGGER NotifyHR
ON HR.Salaries
AFTER UPDATE
AS
    IF UPDATE (EmpNo))
    BEGIN
        PRINT 'Not allowed; Employee Number updates need higher privileges'
        ROLLBACK
    END
GO
```

You can test Example 8-7 with the following insert statement (assuming the table exists):

```
UPDATE HR.Salaries   SET
EmpNo=321456
WHERE Name='Davidson, Miranda' AND Hiredate='20-Mar-2004' AND
DeptNo=124;
```

When the update command is not allowed by a user, the following error occurs:

```
Not allowed; Employee Number updates need higher privileges;
Transaction ended in trigger. The process is aborted
```

You might have noticed by now that any SQL statement or a combination of one or more statements with various where clauses and conditions can be inserted inside the triggers to alert the users, create a log file, or just inform the user attempting the transaction. It is the job of the database administrator to constantly be on the alert to change, edit, or create new triggers regularly to protect the data integrity in a database.

Data Structure Monitoring

The second type of changes to track for database structure or integrity consists of various methods. First is to regularly check the data definition language (DDL) commands that are used for creating the data structure and objects. Second is to check how and where to house the data in database objects (allotted memory size, percentage of memory used etc.). Third, if the database needs stored procedures or functions (used in general by all DB users or a privileged few) check how these procedures or functions are created and who has access to them. The following commands are examples of DDL:

- **CREATE:** Creates an object, which can be a database, schema, table, trigger, index, function, stored procedures, and so on.

- **DROP:** Deletes an object. Can be used to delete tables, a database, or views.

- **ALTER:** Alters an existing database or its objects and structures.

- **TRUNCATE:** Removes records from tables, but the tables would remain.

- **RENAME:** Renames existing database objects to a new name. To be used with caution.

Any changes to the database structure need to be considered carefully after the initial creation because renaming or changing the column of a table can have disastrous consequences on the rest of the database due to relations defined earlier. If there is a table column defined as DeptNo as a string and a programmer assumes that they need to change that to a numeric value due to coding difficulties, they need to consider what columns in other tables of the same database or a different database or schema are referencing this particular DeptNo column and in what way. Likewise, some stored procedures of functions that might be using this particular column may need to be examined for changes, if any. This is to say that a knee-jerk reaction to change a table column or to add a new one must be carefully planned, considered, written, and tested. This should involve other HR personnel as well to check whether the changes make any difference to other staff.

For this reason, we create triggers for DDL as well and let them fire if anyone tries to make a change where a change is not expected. In general, DDL triggers respond to server or database events rather than table data modification activities. To store the trigger data log, first create a table where any DDL changes will be recorded. Many more columns can be added as needed, but we will restrict ourselves to these specified columns for brevity in our example. The following script could work for both Oracle and SQL Server with minor changes if any:

```
CREATE TABLE AUDIT_DDL (
curDate date,
OSUser varchar2(100),
curUser varchar2(100),
curHost varchar2(150),
curOwner varchar2(60)
)
```

The trigger that could fire when any DDL attempts are made can look like the following in SQL Server:

```
CREATE TRIGGER HR_Sal_Table_AuditDDL_Trigger
ON HR.Salaries
AFTER UPDATE
AS
  -- Insert data item into the audit_ddl table
INSERT AUDIT_DDL (curDate, OSUser, curUser, curHost, curOwner)
VALUES ('21-Mar-2010', 'davids', 'DavidDBA', '12.136.12.72',
'EndUser');
GO
```

Any attempts made to update the HR.Salaries table will have an entry in the AUDIT_DDL table. SQL Server also has a built-in data structure named EVENTDATA() of type XML and USER of type string that can record all the related items like date, time, and user for an event, which in this case is an insertion of one row of data into the AUDIT_DDL table. We can modify the preceding table and the trigger to accommodate the EVENTDATA():

```
CREATE TABLE AUDIT_DDL (
EvData XML,
curUser varchar2(100)
)
```

The trigger that could fire when any DDL attempts are made can look like the following in SQL Server:

```
CREATE TRIGGER HR_Sal_Table_AuditDDL_Trigger
ON HR.Salaries
AFTER UPDATE
AS
```

```
-- Insert data item into the audit_ddl table
INSERT AUDIT_DDL (EvData, curUser)
VALUES (EVENTDATA(), USER);
GO
```

New entries into the AUDIT_DDL table can be viewed with a single select statement such as the following to see the XML data. Or the table can be opened in SQL Server Management Studio using the GUI and reading each tuple of the table:

```
SELECT EvData FROM AUDIT_DDL WHERE curUser ='DavidsonL'
```

Oracle has a slightly different change in language when creating the same trigger. It can use "after DDL" words for recording the changes in a trigger. Example 8-8 tweaks the earlier trigger for Oracle but with a twist to ignore any changes if the operation is TRUNCATE. We also put in a new IF block to warn users that CREATE is not a general privilege for end users.

Example 8-8   *Trigger That Fires If User Is Not DBA or Privileged User*

```
CREATE OR REPLACE TRIGGER HR_Sal_Table_AuditDDL_Trigger
AFTER DDL ON SCHEMA
-- The above line can also be put as 'AFTER DDL ON DATABASE'
BEGIN
-- If user is not a DBA, rollback transaction
IF (SELECT SYS_CONTEXT('SYS_SESSION_ROLES', 'DBA')   FROM DUAL = 'FALSE')
    ROLLBACK;
END IF;
-- Only if the operation is not TRUNCATE it comes here
-- Insert data item into the audit_ddl table
IF (ora_sysevent != 'TRUNCATE') THEN
INSERT AUDIT_DDL (curDate, OSUser, curUser, curHost, curOwner)
VALUES (SYSDATE, sys_context('USERENV','OS_USER'), sys_context('USERENV',
  'CURRENT_USER'), sys_context('USERENV','HOST'), ora_dict_obj_owner);
END IF;
END;
```

Now that we know about DML and DDL changes and how to track them via triggers, we must be aware that in some circumstances, the triggers need to be disabled briefly. One such situation is when we are exporting or importing data from or into the database tables. If the triggers are not disabled, the data loads will initiate the trigger firing and block further data loading. Disabling and enabling of the triggers is a straightforward process with a SQL Server command as illustrated in the following:

```
DISABLE TRIGGER  HR.HR_Sal_Table_AuditDDL_Trigger
ON HR.Salaries;
ENABLE TRIGGER  HR.HR_Sal_Table_AuditDDL_Trigger
    ON HR.Salaries;
```

In Oracle, it is slightly different, as shown here:

```
ALTER TRIGGER HR.HR_Sal_Table_AuditDDL_Trigger DISABLE;
ALTER TRIGGER HR.HR_Sal_Table_AuditDDL_Trigger ENABLE;
```

There are various other versions, like *ALTER TRIGGER HR.Salaries DISABLE ALL TRIGGERS* to disable all the triggers on a single table.

Third-Party or Internal Audits

Earlier in this chapter, we mentioned the "looking for trouble, expecting trouble to happen" concept and created triggers and other events to record into tables for the system and database administrators to watch. This keeps the database in great shape when the DBA and system administrators regularly attend to the warnings generated and logs created. The question that comes up now is, who will be the responsible party in case of a third-party audit or an internal audit from an independent person or group? The answer is really simple: Each division has to take responsibility for its own actions. No one person can be singled out because security and precautions are the responsibility of everyone. A responsible, accountable, consulted, informed (RACI) matrix should be developed to understand how people should work together and who is responsible for coordinating among groups. The external audit happens for various reasons, such as a regulatory rule, the need to comply with state or federal laws, inquiries into bad practices being implemented, and so on. A third-party external audit is the best way to go because it would not show bias to any person or division in the company, but before an internal or external audit happens, it is necessary to define the scope of the audit.

An auditor usually can look into dozens of areas, pick a problem, and suggest a resolution. Some of the following are included in the scope when we deal with a database audit. Note that this list is not everything. Some of the DBs have specific audit steps that do not belong to another DB. For example, an audit or Oracle database would not necessarily follow the exact steps on an SQL Server DB since both deal with DB structure in different ways and have different filenames and so on.

1. Host identification and authentication mechanisms and access control. This would involve access to the mainframe or a server (Linux, Unix, or Windows) and database files at the operating system level. At the host level, access is restricted to administrators who know what they are doing.

2. Operating system audit—is the DB using a Linux or Windows server as a host? Who is responsible for the operating system and its maintenance? Do they maintain the operating system, patching, updates, and so on regularly and maintain records of their work? And importantly, do those operating system updates align with the database version/updates and do not cause any conflicts?

3. Are the servers that host the database different from servers that have applications?

4. What applications, if any, are using the databases on DB servers? Where are they located, and who maintains those application servers?

5. Check the initialization file (init.ora in Oracle) and review security options.

6. Check the Data Dictionary Views. In Oracle the following tables need to be checked:

- DBA_USERS (database end users, DBAs, and others)

- DBA_ROLES (roles defined in the database and the grants given)

- DBA_ROLE_PRIVS (users to roles privileges)

- ROLE_ROLE_PRIVS (roles to roles privileges)

- DBA_SYS_PRIVS (privileges for roles and users)

- DBA_PROFILES (controls for password, lock date, last logged in, and so on)

7. Check the DBA_USERS in detail. Make sure the users are all valid and currently using the database regularly.

8. Revisit default, anonymous, and generic user IDs provided by the DB software.

9. Are users changing passwords regularly? If unused, are the accounts getting locked properly due to nonuse?

10. Revisit subjects (people or system accounts) to database objects grants for access to make sure that granted privileges are up to date. Excess privileges—either horizontal or vertical escalation—need to be removed immediately.

11. Check how often the backups are being performed on the database, where the backups are stored, and how long they are stored.

12. Who is using the operating system level SQL PLUS? Are the users able to type their passwords to log in? If they can, is the password visible on screen (shoulder surfing problem)?

13. Are there any database links created to other databases? How are they defined (public, private) and maintained, and who is given access to them?

14. Is there enough documentation for the database? Are the DB documents updated regularly?

Audit reports usually address more than these and create a final report and suggest changes if any are required. An external audit may ask for the internal audit report first because the external auditor may want to see if any earlier suggested changes were attended to. Some organizations have a list of security items that are checked regularly for each database. The federal government maintains a check list on its website (https:// public.cyber.mil/stigs/srg-stig-tools/) for public use. We will discuss these things again in Chapter 14, "Follow the Proven Path for Security," in detail. As discussed earlier, www. mitre.org also has all known vulnerabilities listed and updated regularly. It is always best to be prepared and do the proactive monitoring than feel sorry after an incident. It is important to understand that an auditor will not automatically conduct an audit for every micro item of your database. The auditor restricts the audit to what is mentioned in the predefined audit scope. It is advantageous for an organization to prepare a very detailed scope to avoid any problems later. It would be a good idea also to mention to the auditor any federal, state, or other regulatory laws followed by the organization for compliance because these laws change from one state or locale to another.

Software to track logs is available as the Security Information and Event Management (SIEM) product, but SIEM is like buying a membership in a tennis club. Unless the person goes to the club and practices hard, there won't be any results, and also the results are not guaranteed to make one a champion. Likewise, SIEM can be used to look at traffic with a larger lens, and the logs can be directed to appropriate people. The question whether we want all branches to be included in SIEM, the product cost, and maintenance all factor into SIEM. Some may find this cumbersome because not all branches may have many problems or logs to check daily. Some organizations may just allot the additional duties to the administrator to watch logs manually rather than buying an SIEM product.

The following sections cover some examples of the logs created for regular examination by the database team or main administrators.

Excessive Logins

Excessive logins indicate two types of problems. First is a less serious worry, where an end user probably forgot their password and tried to use an expired or wrong password repeatedly. The password policy locks the user after a certain number of attempts (usually between 3 to 8). In the second and more serious case, a hacker guessed a password by social engineering or such methods and tried to log in with a username. Both these cases need to be investigated because in the first case, the user might have moved out of their normal scope of work and was trying to log in, which is considered a violation of the least privilege rule. The resolution method for this process is easy. In Oracle, the audit tables can show details of a return code, such as the following:

```
0 - success
1017 - bad password
28000 - locked account
```

A simple query such as in Example 8-9 can show details of who logged in, the time stamp, the return code, the operating system username, and the hostname as well.

Example 8-9 *Details of Who Logged In, the Return Code from the Audit Table*

```
SELECT TO_CHAR(TIMESTAMP,'MM/DD HH24:MI') TIMESTAMP,
OS_USERNAME, -- this is operating system username
USERNAME, -- database username
TERMINAL,
ACTION_NAME,
RETURNCODE -- will show a valid return code as 0, 1017, 28000 etc.
FROM
SYS.DBA_AUDIT_SESSION
```

```
WHERE
--If we know a username
USERNAME LIKE '%DAVI%'
AND TIMESTAMP BETWEEN SYSDATE-1 AND SYSDATE
ORDER BY
TIMESTAMP DESC;
```

Results would show something like the following:

```
08/22 21:39    USR1    DAVISON    CUSR1-LT    LOGON     28000
08/22 18:37    USR1    DAVISON    CUER1-LT    LOGON     1017
07/22 18:37    USR5    DAVISDF    CUSR5-TC    LOGON     28000
07/22 18:32    USR5    DAVISDF    CUSR5-TC    LOGON     1017
07/22 17:08    USR3    MANDAVI    CUSR3-THK   LOGOFF    0
07/22 17:03    USR3    MANDAVI    CUSR3-THK   LOGOFF    0
```

It's easy to find out which user tried to log in, at what time, and how that process turned out (success, failure, locked out). You can also specify a clause such as **where returncode in ('1017', '28000')** if only those errors are being checked. Notice that the script in Example 8-9 is checking for return codes only for yesterday (**sysdate - 1**) and today (**sysdate**) because **sysdate** is the current date (today or the date when we run the script). Consult the database software you are using to find what tables are used for this audit data. The "terminal" data can show where the user logged in (IP address and so on). These details should be checked against the invited node list (Chapter 7) regularly to make sure that the users are authorized and are connecting from an invited node to use the DB from an approved IP address. See section "IP selection, Proxy, Invited nodes" in Chapter 7, for more details.

In SQL Server, we can see the logs with Object Explorer as shown in Figure 8-2. It is a GUI process in SQL Server Management Studio. The log files are available with a wide variety of search and filter options to get the required data quickly from the log.

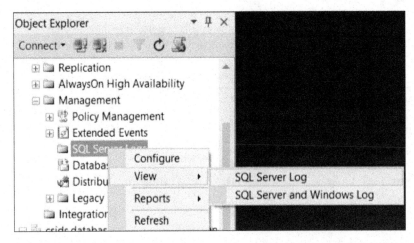

Figure 8-2 *Object Explorer in SQL Server Management Studio*

Failed or Partial Backups

As discussed earlier, backing up the database is important for the integrity of the database. Whether we are using a differential, incremental, or full backup, we must know the outcome (success, failure, and so on) of the backup process. The log that is created by the backup process should be able to show the errors if any. Recall from Chapter 6, "Data Refresh, Backup, and Restore," that we used something like /MyBackUp/15Days/RMAN/ LOGS for storing information in a log. A typical log file will show the errors or success in the log file. Examine the log file closely and regularly to avoid any problems. Likewise, Microsoft SQL Server's log file should be examined for the backup process.

File Size Comparisons by Day/Week/Month

Databases in a corporate setup can grow quickly and exponentially. For example, Facebook's data grows by petabytes every hour, with people posting, liking, commenting, linking to other accounts, and so on. As the DB size goes up, the disk space needs to be increased to accommodate the DB ballooning. The Linux operating system has commands like **df** and **du** to find out the free and used disk spaces. But within the DB itself, Oracle stores the information in tables such as dba_data_files, dba_segments, and dba_temp_files. The following commands can quickly show details of the data size. The data is shown in bytes. Dividing the number by 1024 gives kilobytes; further division by 1024 gives megabytes and gigabytes.

```
select sum(bytes)/1024/1024 size_in_mb from dba_data_files;

select sum(bytes)/1024/1024 size_in_mb from dba_segments;


-- if the segments used by each user are required, group by owner
select owner, sum(bytes)/1024/1024 Size_MB from dba_segments
group  by owner;


select sum(bytes)/1024/1024 from v$datafile;


select sum(bytes)/1024/1024 from dba_free_space;
```

In the case of SQL Server, we can use the tables sys.database_files, sys.partitions, sys. allocation_units, and sys.internal_tables. A variety of commands can be composed by joining these tables to get out data required. First, do a select * from these tables and decide which columns can be joined to obtain the required data. Here is a cryptic example without further explanation. Size displayed can be rounded to MB or GB as explained earlier in this section, with proper formatting for the data.

```
SELECT dbs.NAME, masfile.size
FROM sys.master_files  masfile
INNER JOIN sys.databases dbs ON dbs.database_id = masfile.database_id;
```

Users Escalating Their Privileges as DBA

All DB software has a list of database administrators with higher privileges and end users with lower privileges. If an end user escalates their privileges, the user is trying to go beyond the least privileges policy, which is a security issue. Or if a hacker somehow accessed the database, their first step would be to create a system or DBA account with higher privileges. If you can check the list of authorized DBAs regularly, you can find the list of unauthorized DBAs and remove those privileges.

For this strategy to work, you first need to create a table that has the list of DBAs and their account names with contact information such as email and phone. In the following script, such a table name is ALL_AUTH_DBAS. The script finds out who has the DBA privileges from the DBA_ROLE_PRIVS table, but they're not listed in the ALL_AUTH_DBAS table. Anyone found with this script is violating the policies and needs further investigation.

```
SELECT  GRANTEE, GRANTED_ROLE, ADMIN_OPTION, DEFAULT_ROLE
FROM    DBA_ROLE_PRIVS
WHERE   GRANTED_ROLE = 'DBA'
AND GRANTEE NOT IN (SELECT USERNAME FROM ALL_AUTH_DBAS);
```

User Program Executables and Output Redirection

More often, data operations on a database are automated and run when the DB is expected to be least loaded with logged-in end users—for example, in the hours between 1:00 a.m. to 4:00 a.m. The programs can be anything to load a table, export a table, or refresh the entire DB with an ETL job. If a DB has 40 to 60 tables each with 2 million rows, the process can take a long time, and it is hard to know an error if there is no log when the operation fails. For this purpose, most automated jobs generate a log. In other words, the jobs that run either manually or automatically redirect the output to a file. In Chapter 7, we find a cronjob scheduled as

```
30  05  14  07 * /home/myDatabase/HR/refreshPayScales.ksh
```

Notice that the job would run at 5:30 a.m., but we would not know the results of the job when it actually ran because there was no output saved from this command. Or all running programs may produce an output, but if the output is not saved, it is not automatically put into a file for us. It is our job to save the output to a file that can be monitored for errors. This is especially important when a job is scheduled to run at a preset time on a regular schedule, such as daily or monthly. Modifying the **cron** command that generates a log file would save a lot of trouble and can be done like so:

```
30  05  14  07 * /home/myDatabase/HR/refreshPayScales.ksh > /MyFolder/
Logs/Feb25.log
```

The log file can be emailed immediately after the shell script job was done or can be examined at a later time as needed.

Linux and Unix systems have the convenience of pushing a job to the background by adding 2>&1 at the end of a crontab listing, as shown here:

```
30  05  14  07 * /home/myDatabase/HR/refreshPayScales.ksh > /MyFolder/
Logs/Feb25.log 2>&1
```

These will be further discussed in detail in the section, "LOG File Generation."

Updated Invited Nodes List

A list of excluded nodes in the sqlnet.ora file must generate a log and inform the SA that there was a change. In Chapter 7, we also examined the possibility of including an invited node list and excluded nodes. Linux or system administrators usually have a job created for this process that generates a log when anyone changes the entries in this Oracle system file. The file permissions also can be set to "write" privileges to a select group of people, so not everyone can access the file and make changes. The general setup is to create an administrative account at the operating system level that only has access to this file. If a DBA or Linux system administrator wants to change the content of this sqlnet.ora file, they would have to log in as that administrative account (either with **su** or **sudo su** commands) and make changes. Even then the changes are recorded, and the file date is saved. As a general rule, administrators are taught first to back up the existing sqlnet.ora file and work on a copy of a file when adding or removing contents. If by chance the sqlnet.ora file gets lost or corrupted, you can always restore the configuration from the backed up file.

LOG File Generation

In the previous section, we talk about generating log files automatically. As noted, not all programs generate a log file, but they almost always show some output. Every program that can be run automatically can be run as a crontab in Unix/Linux. In Windows, it can be set up to run in a task scheduler. The beauty of these programs is that they can run with arguments and the output can be redirected to another file. Since a log file is useful to examine in case of errors or in general for daily monitoring, it would be advisable to have as many details as needed in the log file. Let us consider running a simple record count on a table that is updated daily. The first step is to create an SQL command that counts the number of records. The total process contains several steps as described in the following sections for a Unix/Linux environment.

We will assume that we have Table 8-1 in our database with some random data typed for a few rows. We also create a folder named /home/oracle/myScripts to keep our shell and sql files.

Table 8-1 *Employee Table*

Employee_ID	SSN	Date_Created	Date_Modified
678231	777-33-6666	12-Mar-2014	24-Dec-2020
321934	999-44-3333	31-Jul-1999	14-Aug-2018
… … …			
827803	666-88-1111	08-Jan-2017	08-Mar-2023

Creating an SQL File—/home/oracle/myScripts/getcounts.sql

To count the number of rows daily and show the details to the user, we want to have two select statements:

```
Select count(*) from HR.Employee;
Select * from HR.Employee where Date_Modified = sysdate-1;
```

We save this file as **getcounts.sql** and give permissions for anyone to execute. Because this only has two select statements, running the program would not cause any security issues in either the database or the operating system. The first select statement produces a number such as 2135 as the total number of records, and the second select statement would produce all table tuples that were updated yesterday (sysdate − 1).

Creating the Shell File—/home/oracle/myScripts/runsql.ksh

Create a shell file named **runsql.ksh** with any editor and insert the following into the file. Since we are going to run SQL commands, the shell script must know beforehand the Oracle ID with which we want to run the script, the database on which we want to run, and the location of the **sqlplus.exe** command. These are all listed in comments (lines starting with a #) in Example 8-10. It may look like a complicated programming script at first, but on close examination you will find the script is very easy to understand and run.

Example 8-10 *Shell Script to Run an SQL File*

```
#!/bin/bash
# define the Oracle ID
export ORACLE_SID=hrdb
# define the Oracle installed folder
export ORACLE_BASE=/disk1/myDBs/oracle
# define the database on which we will execute sql
export ORACLE_HOME=/disk1/myDBs/oracle /product/21.0.0.0/hr_db
# define the bin folder location where the sqlplus.exe was installed
export PATH=/disk1/myDBs/oracle /product/21.0.0.0/hr_db/bin:.
# define DB user, who is running this shell file and supply password
export uname="DAVIDSONHJ"
export enc_pwd="Once_3191{98$%#}"
# run the sqlplus command and redirect output
sqlplus uname/enc_pwd << EOF > /home/oracle/myScripts/getcounts.log
@/home/oracle/myScripts/getcounts.sql
exit
```

Notice that the @ for running the SQL file as a whole, and we also put the results into getcounts.log file. Once the file is created, it can be run manually or with a crontab. But for safety purposes, Linux and Unix environments take a cautious step in creating shell files. They are not by default executable. So, the next step is to make the file executable:

```
chmod u+x runsql.ksh    or    chmod 600 runsql.ksh (only owner can run
the file)
```

Now our runsql.ksh is executable and can create a log file for us. Note that this log file is the result of the SQL commands in the getcounts.sql file only. Any errors generated by the shell script file are not recorded in the getcounts.log file. We address this topic in the next step when we create the crontab.

Creating the crontab for Running the Shell File in Background

Log in as the administrator who wants to set up the crontab entry for the shell file. To list the existing entries, use crontab -l, and to edit the crontab use crontab -e:

```
15 01 * * * /home/oracle/myScripts/runsql.ksh > /home/oracle/myScripts
/mycron.log 2>&1
```

This schedules the run at 01:15 a.m. and redirects the output to a log file. This mycron.log would now show any and all errors generated by the shell script we created. If the oracle folder is not found, if the line *export ORACLE_SID=brdb* generates an error, it will be recorded in mycron.log. We need both mycron.log and getcounts.log. As we said in an earlier chapter, the more the merrier is always the case with log files because the more information we have, the quicker our problem resolution could be. Also notice that with 2>&1 mentioned at the end of crontab, we pushed the process into the background, so other crontabs or DB processes can run concurrently and without any trouble. Because the job is scheduled to run in the middle of the night, logs are usually examined first thing the next morning.

Examining the Log

Before examining the log files, let us assume that our shell file and SQL file have no errors, and all commands executed well. mycron.log will probably show the following details to the user as text. If the script ran on 09 March 2023 and only one record was updated, that record would be shown (not in tabular format, but just as a text entry as shown in Example 8-11).

Example 8-11 *Partial Listing of Log Generated by a cron Job with Output Redirected to a File*

```
$cat mycron.log
SQL*Plus: Release 21.0.4.0.0 - Production on Sun Mar 23 18:37:21 2022
(c) Copyright 2022 Oracle Corporation. All rights reserved.
Connected to:
...
...
...
Employee_ID

1329
          Employee_ID       SSN              Date_Created        Date_Modified

          827803            666-88-1111      08-Jan-2017         08-Mar-2023
```

If we catenate the getcounts.log from Example 8-10, we will only see the result of SQL commands, which are listed as the last few lines of mycron.log as well, as shown in Example 8-12.

Example 8-12   *The Log Generated by the SQL Script Inside the Shell File Listed in Example 8-10*

```
$cat getcounts.log

Employee_ID

1329
          Employee_ID        SSN              Date_Created      Date_Modified

          827803             666-88-1111      08-Jan-2017       08-Mar-2023
```

In revisiting the shell file, we notice that we did not really "display" any other details to be redirected to the log. Also notice that the file remains in the /home/oracle/myScripts folder and is not emailed or sent to anyone. It is the responsibility of the user to check these log files on a regular basis because the cron job is scheduled to run daily. We now proceed to modify the shell file to echo details and also mail the log files to users immediately after the job is done to alert them. We also have another worry about data being sent to the users on email and the related consequences of exposing PII in the email.

Changing the Shell and SQL Files as Needed

The changes shown in Example 8-13 make the shell file more meaningful and create a better log for reading any bugs as they occur. Notice several **echo** commands and the **date** command.

Example 8-13   *Expanded Version of Shell Script—Running SQL and Sending Email*

```
#!/bin/bash
# show date
date
# define the Oracle ID
export ORACLE_SID=hrdb
# show the oracle_sid
echo "Oracle SID is: $ORACLE_SID"
# define the Oracle installed folder
export ORACLE_BASE=/disk1/myDBs/oracle
# define the database on which we will execute sql
export ORACLE_HOME=/disk1/myDBs/oracle /product/21.0.0.0/hr_db
echo "Oracle database is: $ ORACLE_HOME"
# define the bin folder location where the sqlplus.exe was installed
export PATH=/disk1/myDBs/oracle /product/21.0.0.0/hr_db/bin:.
# define DB user, who is running this shell file and supply password
export uname="DAVIDSONHJ"
```

```
export enc_pwd="Once_3191{98$%#}"
# run the sqlplus command and redirect output
echo "Oracle DB user running the sql script is: $uname"
# look for errors if any in the log at "/home/oracle/myScripts/getcounts.log"
echo "Starting SQL plus. Look for errors if any in: /home/oracle/myScripts/
  getcounts.log"
sqlplus uname/enc_pwd << EOF > /home/oracle/myScripts/getcounts.log
@/home/oracle/myScripts/getcounts.sql
# give a few seconds time for the SQL to finish (not necessary but helps)
Sleep 15
echo "Successfully completed running of the getcounts.sql. Emailing results…."
#email log file to users
mail -s "Daily Morning Crontab Log" username@UserOrganization.com < /home/oracle/
  myScripts/mycron.log
exit
```

The email that arrives to the user contains the log file (mycron.log) copy, which is also available on the host folder at /home/oracle/myScripts/mycron.log. A typical log file shows the details in Example 8-14.

Example 8-14 *Log Generated by the Mail Command in the Script from Example 8-13*

```
Sun Mar 26  11:22:08 EDT 2023

Oracle SID is: hr_db

Oracle database is: /disk1/myDBs/oracle /product/21.0.0.0/hr_db

Oracle DB user running the sql script is: DAVIDSONHJ

Starting SQL plus. Look for errors if any in: /home/oracle/myScripts/getcounts.log

SQL*Plus: Release 21.0.4.0.0 - Production on Sun Mar 23 18:37:21 2022
(c) Copyright 2022 Oracle Corporation. All rights reserved.
Connected to:
…
…
…
Employee_ID

1329


           Employee_ID        SSN           Date_Created      Date_Modified


           827803          666-88-1111      08-Jan-2017       08-Mar-2023
Successfully completed running of the getcounts.sql. Emailing results…."
```

Doesn't this log file look better? Yes and no. Yes because it tells us what is happening from beginning to the end and gives details of who is running, where the files are located, and what step is being done next. No because it is showing the Social Security number (SSN), which is personally identifiable data to the email user. If the user receiving this email is not an authorized user (or even if they are authorized), the PII should never be displayed. This display of SSN comes from the second **select** command we issued in the SQL file getcounts.sql. This can be fixed easily in the SQL file by changing the statement, as shown here:

```
Select Employee_ID, XXX-XX-XXXX as SSN, Date_Created, Date_Modified
from HR.Employee
where Date_Modified = sysdate-1;
```

Various other options, such as masking the SSN except the last four digits and so on, can be employed. These data displays and sending of PII on emails depend on the organizational policies that have to be followed strictly to the letter.

On the SQL Server side, setting up a task scheduler is easier, and all the preceding scripts can be put into a PowerShell script. Example 8-15 shows the runsql.ps1 (PowerShell) file.

Example 8-15   *PowerShell Version Running SQL Script*

```
    $Start-Transcript -Path "C:\myScripts\TSQL\myPSCommand.log" - Append
    $date
$mySQLServer = "HRDBServer"
$myDatabase = "HR_DB"
$echo "DB server is: $mySQLServer; Database is: $myDatabase"
$selectdata = "Select Employee_ID, XXX-XX-XXXX as SSN, Date_Created, Date_Modified
from HR.Employee"
    $echo "Invoking sql command to run the getcounts.sql file"
Invoke-Sqlcmd -ServerInstance $mySQLServer -Database $myDatabase -InputFile
  "C:\myScripts \TSQL\getcounts.sql" > C:\myScripts\TSQL\getcounts.log
# this is not required but shown as an example of running a single query
Invoke-Sqlcmd -ServerInstance $SQLServer -Database $db3 -Query $selectdata >>
  C:\myScripts\TSQL\getcounts.log
    $Stop-Transcript
    $echo "SQL command completed. Emailing details with log file…"
$Send-MailMessage
    -From 'CurrentUser <cuser@SomeCompany.com>'
    -To 'someReceiver <someReceiver@SomeCompany.com>',
        'secondReceiver <secReceiver@SomeCompany.com>'
    -Subject 'Daily log with getcounts.log as an attachment'
    -Body "Please read - Daily morning get counts.log"
    -Attachments "C:\myScripts\TSQL\getcounts.log"
    -Priority High
    -DeliveryNotificationOption OnSuccess, OnFailure
    -SmtpServer 'smtp.SomeCompany.com'
```

Since our SQL commands mostly remain the same because they are platform independent, we can use the same (or almost the same) getcounts.sql file. Notice from the PowerShell file that there are two commands, start-transcript and stop-transcript, at the top and bottom. They record everything that happens inside the script, and the results are redirected to the file. The next step is to set up the task scheduler and initiate this ps1 file to run as a task on the required times and dates. This was described earlier in Chapter 7. Note that the password showed in Examples 8-10 and 8-13 is in plaintext for simplicity. As discussed in Chapter 7, the password should be encrypted and used for better security.

We now know how to set up our database for the best confidentiality and integrity of the data we store and proactively monitor the database, "expecting an error or attack to happen" and being prepared. We also know how to set up a log for every change we make on the database, tables, views, and files at both the DB level and the operating system level. Protecting data integrity is the job of everyone in the organization, and the responsibility does not rest on one person. If the operating system administrators are separated from the database administrators, then they work in tandem to take care of the data the organization owns. Both do their jobs of creating logs and checking with each other for possible trouble, if any. In the end, although creating the logs and generating dozens of files and emails is a great thing, it is only half the job done. If the logs and emails are not read or just plain ignored, the entire process fails because proactive monitoring assumes that the administrators are active and proactive themselves and read the emails and logs without fail.

Any troubles—whether they are at the file level or database level—are addressed immediately, and any users exceeding privileges either horizontally or vertically are kept in check. Any new user creations, an account's excessive usage, or accounts not used as intended are monitored closely, and users are advised of their rights and responsibilities. Password policies should be implemented strictly as a mandatory access control, and no person should be given an exception from these policies. It is also to be noted that database versions—depending on the vendor—use special characters such as @, and $ to mean something. If these characters are used in the password, users should be advised to use them with an escape sequence such as \@ and \$ when required. At the command level, many editing programs, such as PowerShell editor and the Linux command-line interface (CLI), show the password in plaintext. A shoulder-surfing attack can easily expose this password in a plain view. Therefore, this process of typing the password directly with the username should be discouraged for the users and alternative methods of using them with encryption are advised. As technology advances, we adapt with the new rules and protect our data to our best ability. Thus, the protection we provide to the data is good for now, and any changes in the future will align with newer technologies and any emerging new attacks. This is the reason why the security posture of an organization never has an ending point. It is always a progressive and ever-evolving effort.

Summary

To protect data, one can opt for two routes: either take an action after some problem occurs or expect a problem and be ready for it. Proactive monitoring is the second way to monitor databases daily/regularly to see if any problems may crop up. In proactive monitoring, we expect a problem to crop up, and we're ready for it. We also have a plan to deal with a problem in a specific way in proactive monitoring.

Logs can be generated with a variety of methods, such as from shell files, SQL scripts, and so on. These logs need to be read regularly to know if there is a possible problem. Products for Security Information and Event Management (SIEM) exist, but not all organizations opt to use them for various reasons. Among those reasons are having no interest in central software to track logs or share them and not having enough branches to implement SIEM. However, it is important to know that logs must be read regularly to know the activities around databases. There is no real point in creating logs and emailing them to people when they are not read. Both Unix/Linux and Windows PowerShell provide ways to create logs and email them to people. These can be implemented with ease at either the SQL or shell/operating system level. When logs are read, any problems noticed are acted upon immediately, and users are checked for their privileges and the actions they take. As technologies change and logs get modified, we must note that security posture has no start or ending point but needs to be continuously monitoring work.

Chapter 8 Questions

1. What is the advantage of proactive monitoring?

2. A company wants to create logs for every automated job they create. Should the log contain success or failure results?

3. What are the data manipulation language commands in a database?

4. What is the main aim of a trigger in a database?

5. What are the data structure commands?

6. Are triggers only for DDL or DML?

7. Why is an audit required, and what type of audit is best?

8. If you hire a third-party auditor, would they check everything and report to the government or regulatory agency?

9. What type of programs should create logs for review?

10. What are some examples of automated logs?

11. Why should the user-executable programs also have logs?

12. What is the best practice for creating and reading logs?

LAB Work

1. Create a DB, DB table with a primary key, and a trigger to check the primary key while inserting. Check that the primary key trigger is firing when inserting a duplicate item into the primary key column.

2. Create an SQL file and a KSH file on the Linux operating system where you have a database running. Create a crontab to run the KSH file on the database. Generate a log when running the shell file. How can you improve the shell file to generate more meaningful output in the log? (Oracle or mySQL is required for this work in a Linux environment.)

3. Create an SQL file to insert a few rows into the database table that has PII (as described in the section, "LOG File Generation") and a PowerShell file on the Windows operating system where you have a database running. Create a Task Scheduler job to run the PowerShell file to run the SQL file created earlier on the database. Generate a log file when running the PowerShell file. How can you improve the PowerShell file to generate more meaningful output in the log? (SQL Server database is required. SQL Server Express is free.)

Answers to Chapter 8 Questions

1. With proactive monitoring, we always know ahead of time what to expect and where to check if anything goes wrong.

2. Logs should contain both success and failure results.

3. INSERT, UPDATE, DELETE, and MERGE are a few examples of DML. They modify the data inside the data structure of a DB.

4. A trigger causes an error or message to be raised/displayed in case of an insert or delete (or such DB commands) when the DB operation does not follow a specific rule or authorization. The trigger can send an email to any administrator if required. The triggers can be "after" or "before" triggers, which means the warning is fired after or before the intended database operation.

5. Create, drop, alter, and truncate are examples of data structure commands. They modify the database object structure.

6. No. Triggers can be created for both data structure and data modification.

7. A regular database audit can give details of who is doing what, whether any privileges are getting escalated, and in general whether the rules are followed per organizational policies. A third-party auditor is the best one to do the audit because they do not show any bias.

8. Auditors are bound to the "scope" of the audit signed by the organization. Any problems related to the functions mentioned in the audit scope are suggested with resolutions to be implemented. Serious and known violations may be reported by the auditor if they are not remedied.

9. Every automated or manually run program must create a log for review; so we always know what generates a success or failure message.

10. Excessive logins, disk usage, failed and successful backups, file size comparisons, and new users as DBAs are examples of automated logs.

11. It is a good idea to create logs for user executables because we will know easily what goes wrong inside those scripts and data commands.

12. Always create logs (the more the merrier) for every process. Creating logs or emailing the logs to appropriate users is the job only half done. Make sure users read the logs regularly, monitor for trouble, and resolve problems, if any, immediately.

Risks, Monitoring, and Encryption

Security Terms

In this chapter, we discuss the details of keeping everything clean, neat, and without a lot of risk; so, we can monitor, proactively discover, and be prepared for attack or breach. Before that, we first talk about the security terms once again (we also discuss them briefly in Chapter 3, "Goals of Security"). There is a difference between an event and an incident. An "event" is any observable (either by a system or by a human) occurrence. It means something has happened, and we do not know if that something contributed positively or negatively toward our organization. NIST defines an incident as "An occurrence that actually or potentially jeopardizes the confidentiality, integrity, or availability of an information system or the information the system processes, stores, or transmits or that constitutes a violation or imminent threat of violation of security policies, security procedures, or acceptable use policies." Yes, events can be positive, or at least drive us toward some growth. An "incident," on the other hand, is a negative event. A data breach need not necessarily cause any damage and can be termed as an event if no damage were done. But since hackers who steal the data through a breach may cause damage many more weeks later, an event at any given time can become an incident after a few weeks. Those who cause an event might be just curious onlooking attackers and may just go away and may not cause harm. But that would be hardly the case since most of these attackers work for political, power, or financial gains. A person or a system who is trying to attack is the *threat agent*, and the program or avenue that is introduced for the attack is the *threat vector*. A *vulnerability* is a weakness in the system, and a *threat* is something that materializes out of the vulnerability. A *risk* is something that we have with a vulnerability when the threat agent exploits the vulnerability. We might not be aware of the existing vulnerability until it is exploited.

Risk in general is defined as a product of likelihood and impact as shown in the following.

```
Risk = Likelihood (or probability) * Impact
```

NIST has a risk matrix defined for general purpose as shown in Figure 9-1.

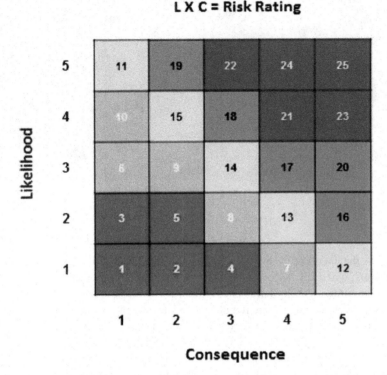

Figure 9-1   *Risk Matrix Shows the Rating as a Product of Likelihood (L) and Consequence (C)*

The horizontal axis shows consequence as numbers 1 to 5, which mean negligible (1), minor (2), moderate (3), critical (4), and severe (5). The vertical axis is the likelihood of a risk happening, which also is in the order of 1 to 5 as minimum (1), low (2), medium (3), high (4), and very high (5). The risk rating (or more simply just risk) is a product from 1 to 25 as shown in the colored boxes. The green zones are acceptable risks in the lower-left corner, and the red zones are obviously high risk and dangerous.

This general formula, though agreeable, does not satisfy varying conditions of information technology where we have aspects of CIA, architecture, ownership, severity, criticality, and many other unknowns. If an incident occurs, there may not be a readily available solution in IT because the incident can be a zero-day attack. A zero-day attack is an incident that has no known fix yet, and one can happen on a system even 15 years after it was introduced into the market. A zero-day attack on a very old IT system may not cause severe loss or even not be worth the effort of a fix if the IT system was already decommissioned. The formula for risk defined previously, therefore, may not fit well for IT. With this in mind, the Information Systems Audit and Control Association (ISACA) now recommends a new and enhanced formula to compute risk. The enhanced formula uses the following:

```
Risk = Criticality * Impact
```

Criticality itself is defined separately as

```
Criticality = Probability (Likelihood) * Severity
```

The common vulnerability scoring system (CVSS) is a scoring system introduced by the National Vulnerability Database (NVD) that indicates the severity of an incident. CVSS scores indicate how severe an incident is. In general, the higher the CVSS, the higher is the severity. Therefore, the risk formula now becomes

```
Risk = Criticality (Likelihood × Vulnerability Scores [CVSS]) *
Impact
```

Let's apply this to a database environment. We have our HR database on a standalone Windows server (DBServer), protected by a firewall and proper authentication techniques. Our applications are on a different server (AppServer). The applications work with Internet Information Server (IIS) web server. We can use the CVSS calculator at https://nvd.nist.gov/vuln-metrics/cvss/v3-calculator to find the CVSS for these events and calculate the risk easily. The scores depend on the following assumptions in our scenario.

1. Database on the server is available 24/7.

2. Application servers have a firewall on the demilitarized zone with inbound and outbound rules properly set/defined.

3. Internal threats are none or negligible.

4. Database access is well controlled and authenticated for database users.

5. Application server access is authenticated for users and system accounts.

6. Database aligns with high CIA rules.

7. Both database and application software packages have no known vulnerabilities, and all patches applied are up to date to these software packages.

8. PII data and healthcare data are well protected with encryption algorithms.

Note that as DB security caretakers, we do not have to know the CVSS calculations and formulas used in the process to calculate risk, but suffice it to know that we can separate our CVSS items that are vulnerable and be able to find their CVSS from the NIST score sheet.

Risk, Mitigation, Transfer, Avoidance, and Ignoring

At this point, for our database, we know what the risks are and where the vulnerabilities or the threats possibly exist. We try to remediate the problems as much as we can to the best of our abilities; for unknown threats or anything new, we will have to accept the risk. The reason is that, in IT as in real life, risk can never be zero. Despite being the best car drivers, we often carry insurance for liability, collision, and comprehensive coverage because we know that an accident can happen. Risk can be dealt with in more than one way. These are discussed in detail later. Note that these are applied to databases and data, and we do not delve into risk calculations and the loss estimates. Data losses are usually very severe and hard to estimate or pinpoint to a specific dollar figure because a flurry of lawsuits and damages can be claimed and dragged into the courts of law for years.

Mitigation

When risk is high, we always look for getting around the risk with a countermeasure. Countermeasures are simple acts by which we try to minimize the damage should a threat actor exploit the vulnerability. Per NIST 800-160, mitigation is a decision, action, or practice intended to reduce the level of risk associated with one or more threat events, threat scenarios, or vulnerabilities. Mitigation methods vary and start from a simple physical barrier installation to high-level software with hardware. For example, to protect against the nuisance of stray animals in the backyard of your house, you install a fence. The fence may not completely eliminate the risk but minimizes it greatly. Likewise, encrypting the database allowing only known IP addresses (allowed IP and excluded IP), authenticating DB users with a strict access card, and physically separating the database from the application servers are all steps that would mitigate a risk of a data breach. However, mitigation might not always work. What if your mitigation methods cost more than you can afford or what the DB itself is worth? It is common knowledge that a countermeasure should be relatively cheap compared to the cost of assets we plan to protect. In the case of databases, the organizational policy decides which data to protect and what the value of such data is. Business and financial policies dictate how much an organization is willing to spend on these countermeasures as well.

Data losses can be greatly mitigated with backup copies, and we may even avoid the losses in the first place if we have a good authentication mechanism for people who log in and deal with confidential data. A credit card company dealing with customer Social Security numbers and credit records has greater responsibility, as does a hospital that deals with patient health records. Their backup methods and authentication methods must be stronger and incorporate multifactor authentication to protect the data. Some of these organizations also have regulatory laws to deal with and are expected to be fined in case of a data breach. What if the organization incurred a data loss due to an error and is fined heavily? Would the organization pay the fines or close the business? That is a subject covered in the next section.

Transfer

Risk can be transferred because we do not know the frequency of a risk materializing. Even if the frequency is known, it is often erratic and cannot be trusted. For this reason, we transfer the risk to a third party in the name of insurance. Not all risk can be transferred to insurance because insurance companies themselves stipulate rules of operation for data and hardware. They also usually have investigators who thoroughly check everything before the insurance company pays any money. Any fraud or disallowed claims will just complicate the situation.

Are there any insurance companies that protect an organization from lawsuits or any damages caused by loss of data? Yes, companies like Amtrust Financial cover some ransom payments, data and system recovery, business interruption, reputational harm, media liability, cyberincident response, and more. Some insurance also protects 1099 contract workers against the risks that come with operating a business. Insurance policies can be drafted to include several types of small-business insurance, including things like general liability insurance and errors and omissions in code. Again, these require due diligence on the side of a contractor or organization. Various items covered in the small print can simply deny a claim citing lack of proper diligence. Due diligence on the DBAs and organization depends on how serious the operations are done on a daily basis, keeping logs, backing up data, protecting the DB servers, regularly patching, watching for attacks, taking the best care of data, and watching the internal threats that might arise due to events or people. Reading the logs, taking actions promptly, and recording the details also count.

Avoiding

The simplest form of having zero risk in any operation is not indulging in that operation. It's like not buying a car when you already know that the maintenance of that particular car would be more expensive in the long run. This is an option when some data collection can be completely stopped. But in the modern days of computer operations, data collection cannot be completely stopped. Any organization that uses credit card operations has a regulation to follow about the data even if the organization denies collecting the data. It also indirectly means data collection cannot just be stopped. Some applications collect it automatically. There is very little leeway to avoid data collection and saying that the organization would not collect any data or has nothing to do with data protection. But organizations that do not collect any personally identifiable information (PII), health information, or credit card data have to still maintain records to prove that they are following the rules of IT security. Any lack of such records can lead to troubles later.

In database security, it is next to impossible to avoid risk because data itself is a changing entity, and data collected can change over time. An organization catering to the customers may not initially collect any personal data, but as time goes by, policies and business operations can change, and avoidance of risk is nearly impossible. It is best to go with local and federal regulations and maintain records and the data safety than argue that the organization has no data to protect. Even the simple usernames and passwords will be considered to be personal data and can be argued in the courts of law for misuse and not protecting customer interests.

Ignoring

Ignoring the risk happens when the actual risk is mitigated to a large extent, transferred to another party, and remaining risks are allowed to happen. This remaining risk is also known as *residual risk* and can fall under risk one has to accept. It can also mean the risk is still existent and maybe dormant, but the chance may be small. One example is to ignore the data loss from a physical tornado that could destroy a data center in full or in part and bring the office building to ruins. Ignoring risk needs to take bold steps and financial backing from the organization itself. For example, in the states of Kansas, Missouri, Indiana, Kentucky, and some others, the chance of a tornado striking an organization in a year is high. Yet an organization can still ignore that risk and move on with day-to-day operations.

Should the data center ignore any physical, technical, or environmental risks? It depends on the organization, the financial backing, and again the type of data. If an organization has good backups stored at different locations that are all not affected by the same threat or stationed in different cities (separated by several miles), a risk can be ignored, but again it depends on the type of business and the organizational policy. For a company like Amazon or Netflix that has dozens of content servers with backups the risk ignorance may work out, but for normal server organizations, ignoring the risk might not be an ideal choice.

Acceptance

Risk acceptance is the last of the choices when risk is mitigated, transferred, and ignored. Notice that ignoring risk is different from accepting the risk. If data is protected very well with antivirus software, regular patches, and physical and environmental controls, it can still be exploited in various ways by internal employees, trusted contractors, zero-day attacks, or other unknown, inexplicable attacks. In accepting that risk, an organization knows beforehand that such attacks can happen but cannot do anything because the organization has already implemented every possible control. The risk that remains—also known as *residual risk* or *leftover risk*—is the risk an organization must accept.

Many organizations accept the residual risks from physical, environmental, and technical threats and threat actors. After implementing every possible control, since there is no such thing as zero risk, any risk that remains has to be accepted and dealt with if a situation arises. And when an attack takes place, the organizations have an option of informing the customers and taking actions to correct the attack. One example of such an instance is an organization letting the customers know in writing that there was a data breach, despite the best efforts already implemented, and customers are offered some data protection with a cybersecurity firm for a period of few months to track any unwanted use of their credit card data or other PII.

Risk mitigation in general is not a one-time fix. Risk mitigation is an ongoing process and should be monitored continuously. The NIST publication has a neat diagram that shows the details of the risk framework, as shown in Figure 9-2. Note that each step has a different publication and/or standard that talks in depth about that area. For example, selecting controls is described in SP 800-53.

Figure 9-2 *Risk Management Framework—Organizational Preparation*

Organized Database Monitoring

Database security in general should follow the defense-in-depth strategy. Data needs to be monitored, logs checked regularly, patches applied to the database software immediately when they are available, due diligence applied with user accounts and passwords, account changes and privilege escalations monitored, unused accounts deleted, and data file sizes monitored. These are some basic skeletal steps that need to be taken care of. Then come the operations and controls of regulatory rules and local and federal laws. Audits usually discover items that an organization forgot to regularly check or had an oversight. An internal audit usually brings out the discrepancies before a third-party external auditor finds out more problems. In some cases, an external auditor finds serious problems that can be reported to various authorities. For example, a stock trading company can be reported to the Securities and Exchange Commission if an auditor finds serious and inconsistent data protection practices.

Though organized monitoring and proactive monitoring are initially hard to maintain, training a few employees, rotating the work among employees, and dual controls can create "trained eyes" for locating problems quickly. Let's examine a single case of error a trained person can spot and quickly discover the problem and apply a fix.

From our earlier discussion, we had this cron job created. It also emails the log to the database administrator when there is a change:

```
30  05  14  07 * /home/myDatabase/HR/refreshPayScales.ksh > /
MyFolder/Logs/Feb25.log
```

When operations on pay scales happen for a reason, such as yearly salary adjustments, usually the DB group is informed earlier that such operations are going to happen. When the DB administrator receives the log, the following items should strike them quickly (not necessarily in the same order), but an experienced and trained eye can check these quickly:

- Was there an earlier note/email about the upcoming changes?

- How big were the changes made? Did the changes happen throughout the organization or just for one single person?

- How consistent is the database after the change? Were there any reports of DB downtime?

- Who was the person authorized to make the change?

- What IP address or terminal did the authorized person use for the change?

- Is the authorized person's IP address or terminal name in the "allowed nodes list" of the database set up?

- How much if any did the database size change after the data updates as compared to the size prior to the updates?

- Were there any reports of wrong data appearing in the salaries updated from end users? This should be continued for several more days (at least 2 or 3 pay periods) to monitor the problems if any arise.

- Was the DB backup affected in any way (size, time, tables, views, or other database objects) due to the change?

- Were there any format problems in data (alphanumeric data for numeric data, data insert or update errors, etc.)?

- If approved and authorized personnel made changes, did they inform the database group of the changes both before and after changes were made?

- Did the log file deliver correctly after the change? If yes, did that log file sent to the DB administrator show any errors?

- If the updates worked but the database server (where the updates were done) crashed or had problems in sending the log file, did the change cause the crash?

- What is the exact time of cron job execution, and how long did it take to complete? Were there any hang-ups or disruptions during the updates? If so, what might have caused those disruptions?

- If the first person reading the log missed some important steps, did anyone else catch an error in the log or receive an email from an end user complaining about the changes?

- If all changes were done correctly, is anyone going to continuously monitor the same job for the next few days to uncover errors if any exist?

- If updates did not go well, who will roll back changes, and how quickly can the rollback happen to avoid further errors? Who is the point of contact for reporting?

Many more problems and fixes can be checked, and most are minor and would not take much time. A trained person can also compare an earlier day's log to the current day's log to see differences and report them quickly. If the DB administrator is checking the log, they may be able to fix the problem quickly without much further ado.

Encrypting the DB: Algorithm Choices

As mentioned repeatedly, the most valuable asset for an organization is its data. How best the organization can protect its data shows how great the organization is and the reputation it has and can build upon. Depending on the database software used, one can pick an encryption method. Simply put, encryption is a way to jumble up data; so, anyone who attempts to steal the data would not be able to use it. There have been dozens of algorithms used for decades for encrypting data, but here we only discuss the latest methods rather than worrying about every single algorithm that was ever created. Also, we must be aware that the encryption methods used currently are dependent on the research that is "good for now" and can change as technology evolves.

SQL Server encryption no longer uses older algorithms but uses AES (128, 192, and 256 versions); the rest of the earlier ones are deprecated. As Microsoft mentions on their websites, the following rules apply to data encryption:

- Strong encryption algorithm obviously consumes more CPU resources (time, effort, resources) than weak encryption.

- Long and complex keys chosen for encryption often yield stronger encryption than short keys due to the key complexity.

- Asymmetric encryption that uses two keys (private/public or one for encryption and the other for decryption) is slower than symmetric encryption.

- Lengthy, complex passwords with various combinations are stronger than short passwords.

- Symmetric encryption that uses the same key for encryption and decryption is recommended when the key is only stored locally and when keys need to be shared across the wire among a few people in the group.

■ A combination of symmetric and asymmetric keys offers better security if you are encrypting lots of data. You should encrypt the data using a symmetric key, and encrypt the symmetric key with an asymmetric key.

■ It is important to note that encrypted data cannot be compressed, but compressed data can be encrypted. If you use compression, you should compress data before encrypting it.

Creating encryption in SQL Server is easy with a GUI, as shown in Figure 9-3. Once an encryption option is chosen for a table, a series of windows guides the user to create a master key and related items. These can be pulled out as metadata from the system tables. Key data is stored in a system catalog view in various tables. Another alternative is to see all columns that are encrypted or not encrypted as the script line shows:

```
SELECT * FROM sys.column_master_keys;
SELECT * FROM sys.column_encryption_keys
SELECT * FROM sys.column_encryption_key_values

-- Remove the "NOT" word for columns that are not encrypted
SELECT * FROM sys.columns WHERE [encryption_type] IS NOT NULL;
```

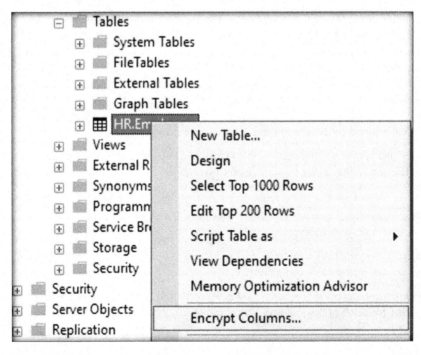

Figure 9-3 *Encrypting a Few Columns of a Table in SQL Server*

Oracle has an elaborate system to set up the encryption that we touch upon briefly here since it needs a wallet, master key creation, and a variety of set up before we can encrypt. The following commands are helpful. To encrypt, the two options available are encrypting the entire tablespace or encrypting a column of transparent data. Both Oracle and SQL Server call this transparent data encryption (TDE). Creating an encrypted tablespace can be as follows:

```
Create tablespace myTableSpace datafile '/../../myTbs.dbf' size 100M
autoextend on maxsize unlimited encryption using 'AES256' encrypt;
```

Oracle applies the default algorithm as AES128 but needs a patch (30398099) to fix the default to AES256. Once patched, the following can work to change the default algorithm:

```
alter system set "_TABLESPACE_ENCRYPTION_DEFAULT_ALGORITHM" = 'AES256'
scope = both sid = '*';
```

Whether a tablespace is encrypted can be checked with two system tables v$tablespace and v$encrypted_tablespaces as shown in the following. The (+) in the following script is for the outer join of table *V$ENCRYPTED_TABLESPACES* noted with a synonym as e.

```
select t.name, t.bigfile, e.ENCRYPTIONALG as ealg, e.ENCRYPTEDTS as
ets, e.STATUS from V$ENCRYPTED_TABLESPACES e, v$tablespace t where
t.ts#=e.ts#(+);
    NAME                 BIGFILE         EALG        ETS        STATUS
    --------------------------------------------------------------------
    First_TableSpace     NO              AES256      YES        NORMAL
    Sec_TableSpace       NO              AES128      YES        NORMAL
    SYSAUX               NO
    TEMP                 NO
```

The other commands that are useful change the associated filenames and give the option of always encrypting the tablespaces as follows:

```
alter tablespace First_TableSpace encryption online using 'AES256'
encrypt  file_name_convert = ('myTbs.dbf', 'myTbs_Encrypted.dbf');


alter system set encrypt_new_tablespaces='ALWAYS';
```

As always, check with the Oracle version and the patches required before the changes can work. Oracle updates the DB patches quarterly and needs to be installed under proper license to get the complete and strengthened package.

Automated Alerts

As explained in Chapter 8, "Proactive Monitoring," the main gist of creating a safe and secure database is to do everything possible to protect data, apply defense-in-depth, and proactively monitor the logs on a regular basis (if daily). Every operation that results in a DDL, DML, user credentials, and database changes (mass inserts, deletes, updates, and so on) can be monitored with task scheduling or cron jobs to generate hands-free jobs that create log files and email them to the database administrators. But recognize that despite the best proactive database administration and defense-in-depth, attacks are still possible because although you monitor the database proactively, hackers are using the new technologies to come up with new attacks. This is the reason we talked about remaining or residual risk that we need to feel comfortable with because it can't just be removed. As we said earlier, these methods help protect the data and the databases according to the current research. When things change, you have to be ready to adapt to the newer methods and continue to learn new ways to protect the data.

Summary

Events are an observable occurrence. Incidents are events that have some negativity associated with them. Incidents need immediate intervention to correct any negative action. Vulnerabilities are weaknesses in a system or software. A threat actor causes a threat when they take advantage of the vulnerability. Risk is associated with a vulnerability and can be measured in more than one way. Risk can be addressed in four ways as mitigation, transfer, avoidance, and ignoring. Acceptance of a risk happens when every step is taken to avoid a threat on a vulnerability but still there is a possibility of some minor damage. The minor damage is something an organization can tolerate. Per NIST, organizational preparation of risk management framework steps includes a circular method of categorizing a system, selecting controls, implementing controls, accessing controls, authorizing a system, and monitoring the controls. Database encryption helps protect data, and there is more than one algorithm that can be used to encrypt. Automated alerts can be used to create logs and monitor the database activity proactively, even if the database is encrypted.

Chapter 9 Questions

1. What is the difference between an event and an incident?

2. Define a threat agent and a threat vector.

3. How can an attacker become a threat after finding a vulnerability?

4. What factors are plotted on a graph to find risk rating?

5. What is a better formula defined by the common vulnerability scoring system (CVSS) for risk?

6. What methods or avenues are available for treating a risk?

7. After all the steps are taken, would risk become zero? What is the name of the risk that remains?

8. What are the steps in the risk management framework defined by NIST?

9. Why is it important to regularly read the logs in monitoring safety?

10. What is the disadvantage of choosing a very strong encryption algorithm to protect the data in a database?

11. What is the importance of compression and encryption for data?

12. When using symmetric or asymmetric encryption, what is the best option to choose?

13. What system tables in Oracle help the DB administrator find the implemented encryption for tables in a database?

14. What is the default encryption algorithm in Oracle?

15. Does encryption of a database mean the DB is impregnably safe?

Answers to Chapter 9 Questions

1. An event is an observable activity and can be either a positive or negative activity. An incident is a negative activity that causes some damage.

2. A person who exploits a vulnerability is a threat agent. A program or a venue that is implemented in the attack is known as a threat vector.

3. An attacker who finds a vulnerability can exploit it for financial or other gain, thereby becoming a threat to the safety of the system or software (database).

4. In a risk rating graph, consequence and likelihood are plotted to arrive at a rating as a numerical number. Risk = Likelihood * Consequence.

5. Risk = Criticality (Likelihood × Vulnerability Scores [CVSS]) * Impact. Criticality itself is defined as Criticality = Probability (Likelihood) * Severity.

6. Risk can be treated in four ways: mitigate, transfer, avoid, and ignore.

7. When all the risk is addressed, there is always some risk left because risk can never be zero; the remaining risk is known as residual risk.

8. NIST's risk management framework has the following steps: 1) categorize the system, 2) select controls, 3) implement controls, 4) assess controls, 5) authorize the system, and 6) monitor the controls. Once the last step is reached, it should revisit the cycle continuously from step 1 again.

9. Regular monitoring minimizes errors, and a trained eye can watch for errors quickly and fix them before a situation escalates to an incident.

10. A strong encryption algorithm has overhead on the CPU and resources due to the work required and needs to keep the keys secret.

11. Encrypted data cannot be compressed, but compressed data can be encrypted.

12. A combination of symmetric and asymmetric keys offers better security if you are encrypting lots of data. You should encrypt the data using a symmetric key, and encrypt the symmetric key with an asymmetric key.

13. Oracle uses V$Encrypted_TableSpaces and V$tablespace system tables to store data of algorithms used and the status.

14. AES128 is the default algorithm in Oracle.

15. No, we follow the defense-in-depth (DiD) rule to protect data, and even with the DiD strategy, a database can be hacked into. That is the main reason security is a continuous process and never has an ending.

Chapter 10

Application Security Fundamentals

There is a well-known saying in programming circles that two things in life are very easy: walking on water and creating an application quickly if the water and the requirements to the application are frozen. As funny as it sounds, the reality is such that the requirements given to an application always keep changing throughout the process, causing endless frustrations to all the stakeholders.

The reason is not hard to understand. An option box can be designed either as a radio button or a checkbox, and until the end user sees the code in action, it is impossible to say which option looks better. Likewise, dropdown windows that show a list of countries or states, text boxes, and many more standard GUI controls can be adjusted to suit the fancies of customers. With free text editing text boxes, differences exist both in terms of language and security. When the programmer is writing code and inserting a text box, they should question whether the free text box is worth the effort because how long the typed text will be is difficult to predict. Limiting the text to a few sentences, words, or characters can frustrate the end user, though it may help the programmer and the application owners. That does not mean every text box should allow endless lengths of characters since storing such data in a back-end database can spell trouble in the database itself. And what if the end user types an abusive word in the text? Would that be granted or meet the professional policies of the application owner?

As if these troubles are not enough with existing standard controls a software package such as Visual Studio provides, there are countless application controls available for free or purchase, and the coders can create their own as well. With those third-party controls, more problems and security threats can be associated and can derail everything in a project. What is addressed so far is a basic skeleton of the application, but there are more inherent troubles.

How we overcome these problems is addressed by two important processes: coding standards and software development. Each of these is described in detail in the following sections. For starters, these processes may look like a waste of time, but as we progress in coding, we will realize that these are mandatory processes for an application to become successful. For a mom-and-pop start-up that develops software and sells it quickly, these steps may sound excessive, but large organizations that develop professional software take these steps very seriously due to regulatory and audit controls.

Coding Standards

Coding standards are rules and policies an organization develops for their own use; they might align with other organizations' standards, but it's not necessary that they do. Horror stories always come out when we read basic code written by programmers who didn't include sufficient documentation of the comments inside the code.

Software errors generally are one of two types: syntax errors and semantic errors. Syntax errors are those that a compiler can spot and would stop an executable from building unless corrected. When the compiler spots syntax errors, it supplies a line number that needs fixing. Semantic errors are those that occur during run time (thus, also known as run-time errors) and are hard to spot. The program would crash but might not give a clue what line of code or library crashed and why. A successful software package must overcome both these errors before it can be deployed or marketed. Look at Example 10-1. This is a Java or C# language type script depicting how hard it is to read the code and understand.

Example 10-1 *Program with a Syntax Error*

```
// Can you find error in the following code?
double [] myArray = new double [100];
for (count=1; count<100; count++)
myArray[count]=2.83628;
```

For an experienced and trained programmer, the error is easy to spot, and software packages even show this kind of error in the code editor (with red underlines or something similar). But to an untrained eye, it is hard to find the error. If you look closely, you will find that the count variable inside the for loop was not defined. It should be spelled out as int count because count is an integer variable that goes from 1 to less than 100. Notice that even after correcting the syntax error, the script will ignore the initial value of myArray (myArray[0]) because the variable count is starting from value 1. The normal default for an array index is zero. If the output is expected to display the initial value, the code should be corrected with count=0 in the loop.

Now look at semantic errors (run-time errors), which are more dangerous. Example 10-2 shows a Java/C# style program segment that poses a run-time error. When compiled, this program goes through the compiler without bugs, but it would crash when it runs.

Example 10-2 *Program with a Semantic/Run-Time Error*

```
// Is there an error in the following code?
double [] myArray = new double [100];
for (int count=0; count<200; count++)
myArray[count]=2.83628;
```

It creates run-time exception because the defined size of the array myArray is 100, but the for loop tries to assign 200 values to the array. After assigning the first 100 values, an exception is raised. There is an inherent security risk in displaying the semantic errors by the compiler. Suppose the semantic error comes from an exception thrown by the program when connecting to a database. The compiler can possibly display the database connection and show an error as shown in Example 10-3.

Example 10-3 *Hypothetical Semantic/Run-Time Error Giving Away Too Much Information*

```
Could not connect to server: Connection timed out. Is the server running on host
  "122.161.219.31" and accepting TCP/IP connections on port 1556?
Request Method: GET
Request URL: http://140.15.112.167:4250/
Exception Type: Operational Error
Exception Value: Could not connect to server: Username, password incorrect
Python Executable: C:/python-project/dbConnection/Scripts/python.exe
Python Version: 3.8.0
Python File: DbConnect.py; line 289.
Server time: Fri. 23 Dec 2022
```

A first look at Example 10-3 would make us think that the information is useful to fix an error because it displays what line of code caused the error (line 289) and in what file (DbConnect.py). It also displays that the database connection is not successful due to the fact that the user entered a bad password and username combination. A bad username and password combination can be due to an expired password or a really badly typed password. The error also shows where the Python package was installed on the machine. Worst of it all, the error shows the URL and the database IP along with the port where an attempt was made to connect to the database. There is really no reason to give away the back-end database details to either legitimate or illegitimate users. End users know the application but never the back-end database, connection, or program type and programming language details used for and in the application. Let us assume that this happens for only a few users who can successfully log in but have not correctly entered the database password. Many users might not get this error. But when a hacker tries this, they may create a username and password for the application but fail to connect to the database and can get this error displayed.

Then starts our horror story of freely giving away the information to a hacker about what program we're using, where it is located, what database it was trying to connect, the database socket address, and when we tried the program (Friday, Dec 23, 2022). From this seemingly gibberish display, a hacker can find all the information and use other attempts to hack the database, server, URL, and more. This is the reason semantic errors pose a very big security threat to the applications. To fix the semantic errors, and show only necessary errors required, many programming languages now come with a try-catch-finally loop that can be customized. Example 10-4 shows how the earlier example can be fixed with a loop that uses try-catch. In other words, to take care of semantic errors is to catch bugs during runtime, showing only required minimal information to the user.

Example 10-4   *Program with try-catch-finally Loop*

```
int n=300;
int [] myArray = new int [100];
try {
            for (int count=0; count<n; count++)
                if (count%2 == 0) myArray[count] = count;
}
catch (Exception e) {
            if (e.toString() !="")
                        System.out.println("Error from assignment");
}
finally {
            System.out.println("The 'try catch' is finished.");
}

// Write code here to assign n<=100 and go back to try-catch
```

Notice that with try-catch-finally we have two distinct advantages. First, we can display whatever message we want after catching the error, and we don't have to show everything to the end user. Second, it would not interrupt program flow and crash. After the code completes the finally section and gets out, it is possible to "dynamically reassign" the value of variable n and go back to run the for loop again.

Now let us look at the programmer side of the coin and ask if the code they write is readable and understandable by the programmers. Understandable code is important because once a programmer leaves the application project and starts working on another, it doesn't take long before they forget what they did in the earlier code and can't recall everything. Also, a newly assigned programmer can't understand the existing code if it is not well documented. Look at Example 10-5 to see if you understand what the code does. Can you find any bugs in the code? How easy is it to understand the purpose of the code itself? Are there any security-related problems in the following script?

Example 10-5   *Problems with "Dry" or Reckless Code*

```
// program by John Doe

import java.lang.Math;
            public class hB{
                    int age, e, m;
                    double c;
                    public void gSize(){
                        c=Math.sqrt(e/m);
                        System.out.println (c);
                    }}
```

Look closely at the code. Although it may work very well and perform to the functional requirements, you can find the following problems:

- It's hard to read or comprehend what the class and method are designed for.

- It's hard to fix bugs if any are found.

- It makes meaningless, dry, and primitive variables, functions, and classes for others to understand.

- It's bad coding practice—for example, the age variable is not used.

- The class name and function name do not sound right and meaningful.

- The class and method are public—meaning that anyone can reuse them. This can be a security-related threat if the class accidentally contains any information that should not be disclosed without authorization.

- The code is not well formatted with parentheses.

Now let us modify the code and make it read better with comments and explanation. Example 10-6 shows a better way to write code with comments starting with //.

Example 10-6   *Well-Written Working Code*

```
// Definition for spaceTravel class that provides a function for
calculating the speed
// light, given mass 'm,' and energy 'e'  - from Einstein's rule E=m*c^2.
// Originally written: Johnson, Katie, Nov 2019. Last modified: Sam
Billings July 2021
// Changes made:  Converted class and its function to protected for
security.

// Include the math function library for space travel calculations
import java.lang.Math;
```

```
// Class spaceTravel has a function for calculating speed of light
protected class spaceTravel {

// define variables
double energy, mass, LiteSpeed;

// This method calculates speed of light and returns it as a double
protected double speedOfLight() {

        LiteSpeed=Math.sqrt(energy/mass);
        return (LiteSpeed);

} // end of method speedOfLight

} // end of class spaceTravel
```

Note the working code in Example 10-5 is different from the well-written working code in Example 10-6, and although both work, the well-written working code saves effort, time, and money in the long run. Lack of time or other excuses are useless in claiming insanity to write better code.

With these two topics discussed, we now come to the point of defining coding standards. Coding standards are recommendations for writing better working code in an organization, and each organization has its own standards. In other words, standards tell the programmers, "This is what we do while coding here, and you should follow that too." If anyone is resistant to following the rules because commenting may take more time, the response is that if writing working code takes 2 hours, writing well-written working code takes 2 hours and 10 minutes. With practice, writing well-commented code becomes a habit that saves several hours, money, and other resources in the long run.

What happens if you don't write comments or better readable code?

■ After a few months, you or others won't understand what you wrote.

■ You will not be able to help others correct/improve the code if you quit the project or company.

■ You never develop a better idea or mind map of coding life and ease of coding.

■ It is impossible to find what changes were made in the last release(s) to know what was improved, what was inserted, or what was deleted.

■ Well-written working code can help close any security vulnerabilities.

■ Many unnecessary loops, goto statements, and so on can continue to cause trouble because they pose both programming and security vulnerabilities.

■ Superfluous code blocks and unused code files continue to occupy the memory and waste resources when running an executable.

The Software Development Process

Software development follows a lifecycle from collecting requirements at step zero to final deployment to decommissioning and throwing out the package when it gets old. This process is called the software development life cycle (SDLC). SDLC consists of several steps, groups of people, and different machines that develop, test, and then deploy the software. The code is also saved on a library or source code repository such as Visual Source Safe. Source code repositories not only show the final working version of the source code but they also have the source code stored at various stages of the SDLC and proper documentation on how the code started, changes made, and the versions created. SDLC follows these detailed steps:

- **Requirements collection:** Before a software package is even thought of and designed, the basic step is to collect requirements for the software. Requirements indicate what the software is supposed to deliver, what inputs it would take, what operating system it will operate on, and other details. The requirements are further divided into functional requirements, user requirements, system requirements, and so on. Requirements are documented and approved before initiating an attempt to design the software. Also note that requirements documentation specifies individual requirements separately rather than combining more than one into a statement or creating vague statements.

- An example of creating vague or complex requirement is as follows.

  "The website allows end users to register with a username and password, checks usernames with existing usernames, rejects duplicates, hits for new names and lengthy passwords, and allows the user to search through the already-registered names."

  Notice that the statement is complex and can easily confuse a software designer. Instead, the sentence must be broken into different requirements.

- New users must be able to register with a username and password.

- Both usernames and passwords must have alphanumeric letters and numbers.

- Usernames must not start with a number or a symbol.

- If a requested username already exists, alternatives should be suggested.

- Usernames cannot have duplicates in the registered usernames database.

- Password lengths must be checked to have a minimum of eight characters.

- Passwords must follow the organizational password policy. See the password policy document for more details on password complexity.

Requirements are usually documented as shown in Table 10-1, and many types of software programs exist to record requirements; Jama, Codebeamer, and Caliber are some examples. Requirements can even be in a simple Notepad file, but the document must clearly identify each requirement without any ambiguity. Most software packages also allow a complex requirement to be broken into subitems like the work development section items shown in Table 10-1.

Table 10-1   *Example of Breaking a Complex Requirement into Individual and Simple Requirements*

Requirement	Specification
New end users must be able to register on the website	Registration rules follow with each subitem as the following.
1.1 Usernames and passwords	Usernames and passwords must have alphanumeric letters and numbers.
1.1.1 Usernames	Usernames must not start with a number or symbol.
1.1.1.1 Check with existing usernames	New usernames must be unique and cannot be used if the username was previously registered by another user.
1.1.2 Passwords	Passwords must follow the organizational password policy.
1.1.2.1 Check password length	Passwords should be 12 characters in length at minimum.
1.1.2.2 Check password age	Passwords should be changed every 60 days, or they will be locked out.
1.1.2.3 Check password characters	Password characters allowed are A–Z, a–z, 0–9, $, #, !, &, %, and underscore only.

At the time of requirement collection, the security aspect must be addressed, and the aspect should be continuously kept in mind as the project progresses because any mistakes done from this stage onward will multiply into a gigantic demon that would overwhelm the project later. Some of the security items to keep in mind are checking for SQL injection in the username text box, password textboxes, thwarting attacks by automatic programs, using CAPTCHA to check for human interface, requiring longer passwords for complexity, initiating two-factor or multi-factor authentication, checking for Unicode input with regular expression validation, and masking passwords to avoid the possibility of shoulder surfing.

■ **Initiation:** Once requirements are collected and finalized, the project is initiated. In the project initiation, people are hired and assigned to do some specific job, time slots are allotted, and project deadlines are designated. In other words, documents are finalized and signed and the project gets a review and a go-ahead at this stage. Budgets are finalized, and people move into their offices or cubes to start the next phase. This is also a stage where Internet connections, VPNs, and the safety of the network are discussed in detail, plans are implemented, and the service level agreements (if any) are signed for the security posture of the project.

Note that some people refer to the initiation as a starting phase and requirements as a second phase.

- **Design:** The design phase involves selecting a flow diagram, creating the documentation, and getting the required details to the coding team, testing team, and the GUI designers. From this stage, it might be possible to go back and forth with the initiation stage to fine-tune details to get clarification. Algorithms created here show what the flow of software should be and satisfies the system, functional, and user requirements collected earlier and distributed across the project teams to achieve the needs of the project. The design team also discusses security at length because every stage of the design must address the vulnerabilities and possible threats and risks associated with each item in the project. For example, the design phase can decide if coders can pick an already available GUI control in the code programming suite such as Visual Studio or create their own control for better security. Creating new controls might also lead to reuses of those controls and possibly new business opportunities. In general, the design phase creates the blueprints for the software and how it should feel, look, and work.

- **Development:** This is the phase where the code goes live and coders use their skills to complete coding per the designed blueprints from the previous phase. Coding in this phase must follow the coding standards discussed in the previous section of this chapter. Coding should be efficient and straightforward with no unnecessary loops and unused variables, classes, or methods. Unused objects should be destroyed before exiting the program. In the design phase when code is complete, the coders also do their own testing of the code, which is known as unit testing. In unit testing, coders check whether the code they developed works in units as required without high coupling and with low cohesion (discussed in the next few sections). When the code passes the unit testing, the developer might write a test document to help the next phase of people who actually test the developed software. This stage also presents opportunities to question how the original requirement was drafted and whether the design suited that particular requirement. Back-and-forth discussions are possible to change the design and the code.

- **Test:** The testing phase, like the requirements phase, tests the software for various requirements. Smooth operation of software does not necessarily mean it meets all requirements of the customer, which were collected earlier. Each test must aim to check whether a particular requirement was satisfied. Testing is usually done manually by a knowledgeable person or with software that creates testing modules automatically. Repeating the tests is important because if a repeat test reveals a situation that creates a problem, it should be recorded and documented for a fix. About 90% of the software packages from the test phase go back to the design phase for bug fixes and removal. A software package like Track Record is used to keep track of and document the found bugs. Once a bug is found and sent back to the design team, a fix needs to be retested against the earlier failure as well as the documented functional requirement. The main test at this repeat procedure is to see if there are regression errors. Regression errors are those that are newly introduced when a bug found earlier is fixed. Whereas developers use their own machines and platform—known as development—the testing team makes use of the quality analysis (QA) platform to test.

Note also that the testing team does not have access to the source code that developers used to write the software. The code is compiled, and testers will only check the executable to find any errors. After the software passes the testing phase, it usually is ready for deployment. Testers must know the importance of the safety and security of the software and test the code and think like hackers. They can go out of their zone to crash the program or find vulnerabilities to make sure that the software aligns with the security posture of the organization. Importantly, a tester is an independent entity who would not yield to any pressure from the developer or the organization.

- **Deployment:** In this phase, the code that passed all the design and testing is ready for end users. End users are usually asked to check this version as a beta version. The end users can be a select group of personnel or people who have volunteered to help test the software. At this beta stage, it is possible find a few more bugs and go back to the design and testing phase. Some organizations release the software first, and if any end users find bugs, they are fixed and a service pack or patch is released to fix those problems. This is the stage where zero-day attacks, known and unknown problems, and a generally chaotic situation can emerge. If the design and testing phases were not completed properly, this stage will reveal those problems, and the project and organization can suffer immensely due to bad reviews and a bad security posture. For example, if at this stage the software collects credit cards and an attacker can steal those easily, the entire customer base will disappear quickly and spell doom for the organization. Deployment does not mean the software is done and dusted. New bugs arise, new attacks can materialize, and the organization continuously monitors what is happening to record any bugs or improper items that make the software slow and create problems. Those are addressed quickly, and a patch is released to correct those errors. If these errors are too many, a larger service pack usually is released.

- **Decommission:** Many times after the software is deployed, newer versions arrive or the application's purpose is no longer required due to new rules, laws, and regulations. In such situations, the older software may not be needed or updating that older software would be expensive (for example, software created on Windows 98 may not work on Windows 11) and would waste resources. Think of it like fixing a car worth $3600 that's been in an accident and repairs would cost $7800. In these cases, the original software is decommissioned or removed from the servers. Removing software needs a specific process because it might be using a particular database, some special files, and libraries. When an application is decommissioned, the entire application, software, related databases, tables, files, libraries, and any socketing software such as third-party data access components need to be removed before the application is removed. The general rule is to keep a backup of all these for a few months, if not years. Usually after the application is removed, it's not re-installed on any machine or website. Any data lost will need to be dealt with through data-loss policies that are in place for the organization.

Models and Selection

SDLC follows a few types of models. Here, we discuss only the security portion for some of these important models and how we will implement security for software. Various models that are still in use are as follows. As mentioned earlier, each model follows the same route from initiation to decommission but with a different rule set.

■ Waterfall model

■ Rapid application development (RAD) model

■ Spiral model

■ V-model

■ Incremental model

■ Agile model

■ Iterative model

■ Big bang model

In the waterfall model, the steps follow just like the falling water. The flow is always forward; there is no going back. The security portion of the software is well-thought-out, and each section builds upon the security built in the previous section. Some institutions say the waterfall model, though very popular, limits the software development capability because you can't go back to earlier sections to fix anything. It also means the software that was being coded must adhere to strict rules of passing the tests in the next section. And during the design, coding, or test phases, the original software requirements submitted cannot be reviewed or modified. If a review or change is needed, then the process repeats again from the first phase or goes through a change management process as established by the organizational policies. The waterfall model is strict with rules of not going back and forth and has no flexibility, but it's well-suited for quick changes and offers a quick one-way route to software development. Waterfall has the advantage of starting the security posture from the beginning and building slowly toward the end. For example, the software being developed may have various built-in controls available (text boxes, username, password controls, radio button, or dropdown list), and the design phase can specify what security needs to go with those (SQL injection check, character length check, and so on). But during the design stage, if the existing controls are not sufficient and if the coding team decides to create their own controls, then the security posture will build on the security posture indicated in the design phase and go with more security functions that align with the newly created controls. Between the coding and test phases, the waterfall model may not go entirely forward because any bugs found in the test phase need to be fixed by the coding team. But the model itself follows the rules that original requirements—system or functional—cannot be modified during design, coding, or test phases. Fixing any problems found in the test phase is fine because those problems indicate that the requirements were not addressed correctly in the coding phase.

RAD has one main idea: get the software out to users as quickly as possible. It does not matter how hard it is or what tools are used; the goal is to get the package to users and test the waters—and do it quickly without bugs. If any bugs are found in the deployed version, the cycle is repeated. From a security standpoint, this is a lot of work because making changes to the software at any stage means the entire security posture may need to be redesigned or addressed again. The organizational policies of a company determine whether this model is implemented. When the need is urgent and end users cannot wait for a very long time, the RAD model is probably the best option, but do keep in mind that security cannot be ignored even if the urgency is great.

Agile development is an adaptive model in which each project needs to be handled differently, and the processes of each project can differ greatly. It also assumes that any existing methods or processes in use for current projects may not serve new projects and the processes need to be adjusted or re-created. The Agile methodology divides a project into tasks. Each task has its own set of planning, requirement collection and analysis, design, coding, and test processes and a fixed time frame. Once a task or iteration is complete, the next task is taken up and repeated with the same set or processes. Each task works on security for that iteration. In other words when each task is completed, that part of completed work is delivered, and when the second iteration is complete, the delivered software will have iterations 1 and 2. When the Nth iteration is delivered, it contains earlier iterations of 1 to N-1. Figure 10-1 shows details.

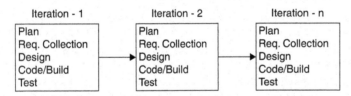

Figure 10-1   *Iterations in the Agile Development Model*

Notice that Agile development takes into consideration the fact that requirements are difficult to keep stable, particularly in IT systems, and customer needs can change quickly. Agile development depends on the following rules or principles:

- **Individuals and interactions:** In the Agile model of software development, self-organization, co-location, pair programming, and motivation are considered very important. Staff interacts with each other regularly and in a dynamic fashion.

- **Working software:** When dealing with customers to understand their requirements, a demonstration of working software is the best means of communication because looking at the software helps a customer know firsthand what the final product can look like.

- **Customer collaboration:** Requirements are difficult to remain fixed and might change, making the collection process hard, at least in the beginning of the project.

Therefore, continuous customer interaction greatly helps get proper requirements at each stage or iteration. The staff is very well aware of the changing requirements and is ready to adapt.

■ **Responding to change:** Agile responds very quickly to changes introduced and banks on the ability to do continuous development.

Traditional SDLCs like waterfall models are predictive because they know in advance what the final product would look like—or at least have an idea of it. On the other hand, Agile is ready to adapt to quick changes. The final product is not known until the project nears completion because every stage/iteration can change and the project script can be modified as the iterations progress. Some of Agile's important advantages are a) it does not follow a fixed set of rules to develop software and is ready for quick change, b) it is customer service oriented, c) it promises to deliver quick demonstratable product, and d) feedback is welcome because new changes can be quickly implemented. From a security point of view, Agile does a great job because it builds security from one layer (or iteration) to the next. Because it is ready to adapt to changes, any new threats are addressed as they are known and adjusted to the new version of software. In short, when the customer requests new changes, the security team can work with those changes, double-check the vulnerabilities that might come up, and introduce fixes for that iteration. It may also be easy to work with piece-by-piece security solutions for each iteration that would help address all the possible vulnerabilities.

Cohesion and Coupling

Two important concepts in security of modules (a library or a simple class) are cohesion and coupling. Cohesion dictates the relationships INSIDE a module. If the class uses its own resources and works well within the constraints defined in that class, it is said to be highly cohesive. The class uses its own resources as desired and is less dependent on other classes. Coupling is how a class or module depends on other classes OUTSIDE its own constraints. A high level of coupling indicates that a class is dependent on other classes. Any change to the other classes can easily derail a highly coupled class.

This raises the question of security considerations for software that has several modules. Are the modules working well within their own constraints and class limits? If the classes are dependent on other classes and methods or functions of other classes, modules, or programs, then we have more vulnerabilities to address that are related to other modules and classes. Highly cohesive modules with low coupling in software provide good functional strength to the software overall. High coupling in software modules is an indication of several troubles, both for the software and security, because external dependence can go wrong if other modules change or the vulnerabilities mount in the other modules. The golden law of good software therefore is high cohesion and low coupling.

Figure 10-2 shows a pictorial representation of cohesion and coupling.

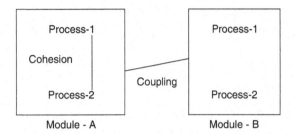

Figure 10-2 *Cohesion (INSIDE, Highly Desired) and Coupling (OUTSIDE, Not Favored) Between Modules in Software*

Development, Test, and Production

Recall from the database security chapters earlier in this book that we wanted databases deployed on separate standalone servers rather than on the servers that host the applications. In this chapter, we discuss more about where to keep the applications.

Applications need three distinct environments, so to speak. All these environments are independent and are connected to respective databases:

- **Development environment (D):** In-house software development needs a development environment where the coders can write their code and do their own unit testing. In short, the development environment is the playing field of the coders where they can write code, remove, rewrite, and edit. Syntax errors that would not allow the coder to compile a successful package happen in the development stage.

- **Test environment (T):** The test environment is where the coder, after finishing writing the code, deploys the executable package (without the source code) for the tester as a release version. The tester may request the coder provide a test document about what changes were made and what the software is about. Testers also have a functional requirements list to compare that the software is working per those requirements. The software package may make several back-and-forth trips from development to test to make sure that the requirements are met correctly and any bugs are fixed. Once those errors are fixed, the test stage can bring out the semantic errors (run-time errors). One example of a run-time error is assigning a tenth value to an array that was declared to contain only eight values. The syntax would not know if this is an error, but when running the program, the error would happen when the tenth value is assigned since the array can technically contain only eight values. These errors are documented by the tester and passed back to the coders. After fixing those errors, the software is recompiled and sent back to the testing group. When the tester documents that the software is free of bugs, it can go to production or be deployed for end users.

It is important to note that a tester can use any tools available to them besides the testing plan provided by the developer. Passing the testing phase does not mean the program or package is free of errors. Errors and security vulnerabilities can happen again when the software is on the production server, and those bugs are fixed later and released as a service pack (fixing several errors in one or more packages) or patches. Organizations like Microsoft name the releases with a specific version like Windows 8, Vista, or 11, and the releases are numbered like 20H2. As long as versions keep coming, older versions of software are saved on the software reserves, known as repositories, by version. Coders who work with software such as Visual Studio have the advantage of using the software repository named Visual Source Safe that saves the entire code by version.

While they write code, developers use the debug option to check/edit/correct their code and do their own unit testing. Even if the testing phase is skipped, developers must do their unit testing, which states that each unit developed is working as desired. This testing is mandatory and happens on the development machine so the syntax and other possible semantic errors can be fixed. But when the code runs to thousands of lines, it is hard to find all the errors due to biased testing by the coder on the code they wrote. When complete, the code is saved on the repository with a version number, subversion number, date, and other details. The code is documented inside the script with proper coding standards as discussed earlier. The testing group maintains separate documentation on what was tested, what was found, and what report was given to the coding group. Some call this testing phase quality assurance because the testers do a rigorous check on the quality of the software being released.

- **Production environment (P):** The released software is deployed to the production server with the help of a system administrator and is considered the "best possible" version. This is known as the D -> T -> P (Development to Test to Production) process. But attackers can still find vulnerabilities the coding team did not anticipate on this best possible released version. When such attacks take place, the system administrator can provide details of the vulnerabilities exploited and remove the software from production servers until the bugs are fixed. The software then goes through the D -> T -> P process once more and is re-released. The D -> T -> P process is a rinse-and-repeat process until the software is completely decommissioned.

- **Rules of the game:** Now let's talk about the rules to protect the application and server security. As said earlier, the applications and software are hosted on a server that might also host some other applications but not the databases. The reason mainly is to avoid a single point of failure. If the server crashes or is attacked, we do not want to expose the database or have the database and applications go down at the same time. Also, software uses development, test, and production application servers separately. If these application servers need access to, say, an SQL Server database, a client for that database is installed on the application servers. The SQL Server client, in tandem with the application, will connect to the database server where the SQL Server database is actually deployed. In other words, an application on the application development server connects to the database on the database development server only; an application on the application test server connects to a database on the database test server only; and an application on an application production server connects to a database on the database production server only. Cross connections of applications and databases are not allowed. Note that the application developers may not have access to the database servers (running on Linux or Windows) to log in directly but have to use their development credentials to access the database via the client installed for that purpose.

Refer to Figure 7-2 in Chapter 7, "Host Security," to see how the application servers and database servers are deployed separately to avoid single point failures. Application developers work in tandem with the development database administrators to access the data whereas the testers have different credentials to access the test database to test the software. So, who ensures that the development database is transferred to the test database for the tester to access and successfully test the software? It is the job of the developer to request the DB administrator for the correct data syncing between the development DB server and the test DB server. Also, a developer should not have access to the test database, and the tester should not have access to the development database or the source code on the development server.

On the test and production application servers, the software deployed is the compact release version of the software that does not have debugging files. It should be known by now that the debug version software exists only on the developer's machine. The team of testers, developers, database administrators, and system administrators work in tandem to plan ahead and release the software in a timely manner. If the organization follows strict change management policies, then we have more work to do because everyone works with the principles of least privilege and separation of duties. These will be discussed in detail in Chapters 13 and 14 of this book.

Client and Server

As we discuss in Chapter 7 and illustrate in Figure 7-1, when an end user is working on an organization's website, an instance of the site is shown on the user's browser. What is on the user's browser is the client instance. This is connected via the Internet to the company's content server, which is the server component. Any data that is sent and received makes a round-trip from client to server regularly. In this set up, there are security risks on both the client and server ends. For simple websites, such as those that show sports news or political information (for example, ESPN and CNN), the end user may not have to log in to the website, but if some business transaction is being conducted on the website (such as Amazon or Netflix) and personally identifiable information (PII) is involved, we need credential protection on either end of the service.

For the time being, let's assume that the website we created has username and password boxes for the end user to log in:

- **Client:** Refer to Figure 5-2 and Table 5-5 in Chapter 5, "Access Control of Data," to recollect the password policies and what can be set up for a good password maintenance. We expect the user to type the registered username and a password that complies with the website and organizational policies, so the website login goes smoothly, and the user can buy or sell something on the website. But a hacker who comes to the website to exploit has other ideas. A hacker can enter something like the following:

```
'; delete *.* from system.dba_users where 1=1;'
```

Notice that this is a combination of database SQL commands. The first semicolon terminates any existing SQL statement, and the next delete statement creates a new one. An interesting thing to note here is the use of the clause where1=1. This where clause tells the DB that the condition is always true.

Assume we have simple username and password boxes and a button to log in to a web application that connects to an Oracle or SQL Server on the back end, as shown in Figure 10-3. We will assume that a generic good user enters their username in the username textbox and the password in the password textbox. The password textbox has a mask with the * character to hide the password. The script associated with the **OK** button in the login window would first get the text strings entered in the username and password boxes, creates and sends an SQL statement as shown in Example 10-7 to the back-end database.

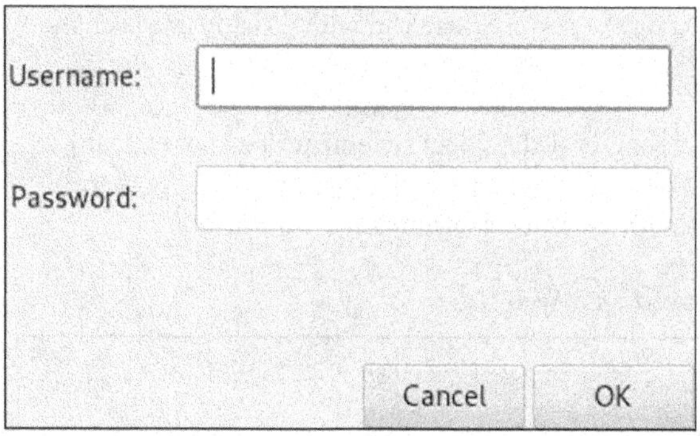

Figure 10-3 *Simple Username and Password Control*

The code is fairly simple.

Example 10-7 *Code for Button Click Event*

```
onLogin_ButtonClick()
{
        String uname = username.text.trim();
        String pwd = password.text.trim();
        String sqlText = "SELECT  SSN, Address, City, Phone FROM HR.Users
                        WHERE Name=' " + uname + " ' and pwd in (SELECT password
    FROM
                        HR.UserPrivateInfo WHERE user=' " + uname + " ');"
                        ...
```

```
                          ...

                          ...
         (Some more processing here on the backend database)
}
```

We will also assume that the user is registered on this site and has valid credentials per the password rules. Looking at the script shown in Example 10-7, if the user were to enter the username as "HotColdBurger," and password as "h0TP@$$_(789=&!@)," the sqlText will transform as the following:

```
               sqlText = SELECT  SSN, Address, City, State, Zip, Phone
FROM HR.Users
                          WHERE Name='HotColdBurger' and pwd in
(SELECT password FROM
                          HR.UserPrivateInfo WHERE
user='HotColdBurger');
```

On clicking the **OK** button, the SQL statement is passed to the back-end database for processing to run this SQL command on the server. It can run with a single line such as

```
SQLExec (sqlText);
```

If the connection to the database is wrong or if the select statement does not execute due to syntax or semantic errors, the website can show something like the hypothetical Example 10-8 for an application in the .NET web environment:

Example 10-8   *Error Message Displayed on a Web Page*

```
System.Data. SqlClient. Sq|Exception: Conversion failed when converting from a
  character
string to uniqueidentifier.


System.Web. HttpUnhandledException: Exception of type
'System.Web. HttpUnhandledException'
....
....
System.Data.SqlClient.SqlDataReader.HasMoreRows()
System.Data.SqlClient.SqlDataReader.ReadInternal(BooleansetTimeout)
at System.Data.SqlClient.SqlDataReader.Read()
```

For a normal user, Example 10-8 does not make much sense, but for a hacker, these lines of data give as much information as they want, such as

- The database table has been accessed correctly (but failed to return data).

- The DB table has more rows.

- The connection is timing out for some reason.

Also, depending on the error lines produced and displayed, the hacker can find the following details: the type of database (for example, Oracle or SQL Server), the server type (for example, .NET and therefore the Windows operating system or Apache Tomcat and therefore the language is Java), the language used to code the front-end application, and much more. With this information, a hacker with experience and imagination will now try a second way to log in as follows:

He can now enter the username as " SmithSon' Or State = 'CA'; -- "

Notice the single quotes, the semicolon, and the two dashes the hacker used cleverly. With this username and any password, he enters the following SQL statement:

```
sqlText = SELECT  SSN, Address, City, State, Zip, Phone FROM HR.Users
            WHERE Name='Smithson' OR  State ='CA'; -- and pwd in
(SELECT password   FROM
            HR.UserPrivateInfo WHERE user='HotColdBurger');
```

The first single quote for Smithson is in the SQL text coined by the programmer. But the hacker used an ending single quote for the word Smithson and added OR State-'CA' to the SQL statement. They also terminated the SQL command with a semicolon and added -- to make the rest of the SQL statement useless as a comment because anything after -- in SQL is a comment and is ignored. In this case, whatever the password entered, it makes no sense because the second part of validating the password is useless as a comment. Also notice that the username can be useless given the OR option. If there is no username such as "Smithson," the SQL statement will still run and produce a large list of records of people who are in the state of California and their SSN, Address, City, State, Zip, and Phone data from the HR.Users table. So, the hacker can steal the PII quickly and even modify some records later.

As a second example, we can see the following:

```
// A simple statement is in SQL and how to run


String sqlText = "SELECT SName, SPwd FROM staff";
ResultSet results = Statement.executeQuery(sqlText); // run it on
backend DB


//To Check user SQL can change like this (NOTICE single quotes)


String queryString = "SELECT * FROM HR.users,
            WHERE   Uname = ' " + UserTextBox.Text + " ' AND
            Userpwd = ' " + pwdTextBox.Text + " ' ;" ; // is
in SQL
```

> **NOTE**   One semicolon in quotes is for the SQL statement. The semicolon outside quotes is the programming language's statement-ending symbol.

```
// if you enter username=JohnWorry12_324 and Password as myCredit_354 the

//SQL statement to run on DB side becomes

SELECT * FROM HR.users
WHERE Uname = 'JohnWorry12_324' AND Userpwd = 'myCredit_354';
```

Running the preceding code brings ALL the table data out to the programmer (since it is select *).

Enter the hacker—SQL injection:

```
// Hacker inputs the following information into boxes

userTextbox:      " '; select * from system.user_info where 1=1; -- "
pwdTextbox:       "abcedrfe"

//SQL statement to run on DB side effectively becomes

SELECT * FROM HR.users WHERE Uname= ' '; select * from system.user_
info where 1=1; --' AND Userpwd='abcedrfe';

SELECT * FROM HR.users WHERE Uname= ' ';
select * from system.user_info where 1=1;
--' AND Userpwd='abcedrfe';
```

Observing this statement closely, the hacker is now able to create three separate SQL statements (terminating each statement with ;) from user input. The program will show results of the second statement to the hacker. System.user_info may contain all names, emails, and so on of users in the database.

Effectively, the entire SQL statement becomes three different statements as

```
SELECT * FROM HR.users WHERE Uname= ' ';
select * from system.user_info where 1=1;
--' AND Userpwd='abcedrfe';
```

First, the SQL statement may not show any data because of a blank username. The hacker knows these details and that's why they terminated the statement with ; (semi-colon). Second, one shows all data of all the DB users because the condition in the where clause is always true. Third, the SQL statement becomes a comment in SQL (-- is a comment in SQL) and has no effect, therefore rendering the entered password text completely useless.

We first discuss how to resolve the entered input for accuracy to avoid SQL commands and how to stop hackers from entering "whatever strings" into the text boxes provided for input on an application. Regular expression validators (REV) are controls that can be applied on another control or a group of controls that accepts data input. Most languages provide these features or they can be written easily with a simple function. For example, a phone number in the United States has a format of XXX-XXX-XXXX and Social Security numbers have a format of XXX-XX-XXXX. The value of X cannot be anything but numerals 0 to 9. A text box asking for this type of data must limit the input to numerals and to a length of 10 characters for phone number and 9 characters for an SSN (and two optional hyphens in between). The total length can be either 12 or 11, depending on whether it's a phone number or SSN. REV's are client-side controls that filter data quickly on the user's screen before sending it to the server. Recall that for security, the input data must be validated at both the client and server sides. Client-side validation has an advantage in that it does not have to send the data to the server, thereby avoiding the round-trip time from the client to the server and back.

A typical REV control in .NET for an application looks as shown in Example 10-9. The following definition also takes into account the international code of one or two digits. The d in the entire validation expression dictates that the data entered inside the text box is only numeric. If anyone tries to enter alphabetic data or any symbols, the data is rejected at the client side. In Example 10-9, there is a text box for phone number, a validator that validates data in the phone number text box, and a button that takes the user to the server.

Example 10-9 *Regular Validator in an aspx Page*

```
<asp:TextBox id="PhoneNumberTextBox" runat="server"/>
    ...
    ...
<asp:RegularExpressionValidator id="RegularExpressionValidator1"
     ControlToValidate="PhoneNumberTextBox"
     ValidationExpression="^(\+\d{1,2}\s)?\(?\d{3}\)?[\s.-]?\d{3}[\s.-]?\d{4}$");
     Display="Static"
     ErrorMessage="Phone number must be in xx-xxx-xxx-xxxx format"
      EnableClientScript="True"
    ...
    ...
</asp:RegularExpressionValidator>

<asp:Button id="LoginButton" onClick="LoginButton_Click" runat="server"/>
```

The event for the button can be auto-generated in .NET or can be manually entered. The C#-like code in Example 10-10 helps validate the data at the server. Note that when the server is validating the data in the phone number textbox, it can validate with different formats, which can be easily customized to suit the user, country, or a required format. The following C#/Java-like script can validate the numeric data with various formats on the server.

Server

In the client-side code, we gave a fixed format for validation of input strings. But on the server side, the LoginButton_Click() event can do more. This is illustrated in Example 10-10.

Example 10-10   *Server-Side Script for Validating Numerical Input*

```
protected void LoginButton_Click (object sender, EventArgs e)
{
//validate phone numbers of format "1234567890"
if (phoneNo.matches("\\d{10}"))
                return true;
//validating phone number with -, . or spaces
else if(phoneNo.matches("\\d{3}[-\\.\\s]\\d{3}[-\\.\\s]\\d{4}"))
                return true;
//validating phone number with extension length from 3 to 5
else if(phoneNo.matches("\\d{3}-\\d{3}-\\d{4}\\s(x|(ext))\\d{3,5}"))
                return true;
//validating phone number where area code is in braces ()
else if(phoneNo.matches("\\(\\d{3}\\)-\\d{3}-\\d{4}"))
return true;
//return false if nothing matches the input
else return false;
}
```

Remember for each textbox that accepts data, there should be a separate REV, but on the server side, several input data can be combined into one method/function to validate to accept or reject data. For example, if the website is restricting users to use a password with a maximum of 15 characters and various complexity rules, they can be incorporated easily on the server side. Client-side REVs also have several built-in formats for phone, SSN, and other common data.

Now consider a case that involves SQL and modifying a website address in the URL. For the purpose of this example, suppose that we have the URL https://myWesbite. Salespoint.com/index.aspx?item=725, which provides some information about product number 725, after a user logs in with credentials. Also, we assume now that this website is reprogrammed and protects our interface on the screen with proper validation with REV as discussed previously, and everything with login and validation was carefully taken care of. If the user enters something like https://myWesbite.Salespoint.com/order-Final.aspx instead of the main login page, they might get an error redirecting users to index.aspx page. This redirection is deemed correct in that a user should not be allowed to go to the final orders page. But what if a hacker enters https://myWesbite.Salespoint.com/index.aspx?item=26725' or where 1=1;'? Notice the single quote and extension of the text with SQL-like script in the URL. This could throw an error with an unusual message such as

```
Syntax error in SQL statement. Item number 26725 not found or invalid
in the Oracle database table "SaleItems."
```

For a hacker, this kind of error statement provides a lot of valuable information:

- It indicates the back-end database used is Oracle.

- The item mentioned is in the SaleItems table.

- The number 26725 doesn't exist in the table. These details imply that the company may not have an item with the specified number but may accept another number.

Notice that the hacker has not even logged in to try the URL with a new item number. So, with this error, the hacker will try another item with a higher or lower number. Hackers can also modify the URL with more advanced queries, as shown in the following, because now they know details of the DB and the table name.

```
https://myWesbite.Salespoint.com/orderFinal.aspx?item=26725||UTL_
INADDR.GET_HOST_NAME in ( SELECT user FROM DUAL );
```

Again, we find that the query combines two different SQL clauses. The first one is for item 26725, and the second one is a binary OR variation for the where clause. The back-end SQL statement may now read them as

```
Select * from SomeTable where item=26725||UTL_INADDR.GET_HOST_NAME in
( SELECT user FROM DUAL );
```

With the above modified SQL statement, results can be returned by SQL if the item 26725 is found or simply gets all other information from the DB. Both DUAL and the UTL_INADDR are Oracle specific, and the hacker knows the details of Oracle structure. The UTL_INADDR.GET_HOST_NAME() function returns the hostname where the Oracle database was installed. It may be a Linux server. But this statement may return an error, as shown in the following, because the hostname usually would not exist in the DUAL table:

```
ORA-XXXXX: Host WEBAPP_SALES unknown or not found
```

This gives more information to the user that the account using the website is a system account by name WEBAPP_SALES. The hacker now will continue passing different values names, and so on to all well-known reserved tables of Oracle to get more and more details. This would finally lead to finding the names of users, maybe their passwords both in plaintext and as a hash, or data from other tables.

Some errors in the web applications may show even more details, like the following in a .NET application, as shown in Example 10-11. Hackers can extract much more information and then keep trying a number or page in the URL that eventually might lead them to valuable information.

Example 10-11   *Error Shown in a .NET Application*

```
Server Error in / Application


A network-related or instance-specific error occurred while establishing a connec-
    tion to SQL Server. The server was not found or was not accessible. Verify that
    the instance name is correct and that SQL Server is configured to allow remote
    connections. (provider: Named Pipes Provider, error: 40 - Could not open a connec-
    tion to SQL Server)


Description: An unhandled exception occurred during the execution of the current web
    request. Please review the stack trace for more information about the error and
    where it originated in the code.


Exception Details: System.Data.SqlClient.SqlException: A network-related or
    instance-specific error occurred while establishing a connection to SQL Server.
    The server was not found or was not accessible. Verify that the instance name is
correct and that SQL Server is configured to allow remote connections. (provider:
    Named Pipes Provider, error: 40 - Could not open a connection to SQL Server)
Source Error:


Line 12: conn. Open()
Line 13: conn = MyProject.System.Data.sqlclient.sqlConnection(curConnection)
Line 14:


    Error: cannot access data with failed connection index.aspx.cs
```

The errors in Example 10-11 even give the line numbers in the code, the code file, and the project name where the code file resides.

Notice from the previous discussion that we were talking about a URL that looks like this:

> https://myWesbite.Salespoint.com/orderFinal.aspx?item=26725.

The string starting with ? and the characters item=26725 after the aspx is known as a query string. Query strings are helpful in passing information from one web page to the next (either forward or backward) but must be used cautiously because they can be exploited as discussed in the previous section. The first query string in the URL is passed with a ?, and further query strings can be passed with & symbol, as shown in the following URL. The programmer can pass many query strings from one web form to another. The following URL has four query strings:

> https://myWesbite.Salespoint.com/orderFinal.aspx?item=26725&warranty=10&type=new&shipping=priority

Passing sensitive information, PII, passwords, or usernames as query strings may offer an easy way to transfer data between different web forms and pages, but they are not recommended because the query strings are visible in the URL field of the browser.

Side Effects of Bad Security in Software

Once the hacker is able to get information from the database about login and or passwords, there are many things they can exploit:

- Copy unauthorized data and threaten the company for a ransom

- Delete/modify existing data, either for fun or for destroying the company

- Introduce random useless data into the database that corrupts reports

- Permanently destroy past data/backups and change scripts to stop automatic backups

- Create a system or administrative account for themselves for exploiting repeatedly

- Monitor a system long term to observe trends and financial data

- Infect systems with viruses or malware and track financial transactions

- Alter security to allow/disallow access as deemed fit by the hacker

- Encrypt/steal/alter the system, database, and programs to demand a ransom

- Purposefully shame an organization via a web or social media hack

- Use current or corrupted data to penetrate an organization and disrupt its regular business operations to cause a loss

Fixing the SQL Injection Attacks

There are simple and easy ways to fix these kind of errors, as explained here:

- The first thing a programmer can do is fix the length of the username or password. This is one reason most credential-seeking websites limit the usernames to 8 to 10 characters or to a valid email address. Passwords are also limited by the length and complexity and what characters can be used (cannot use ;, - -, and so on).

- Validate the text entered in the data on the client side before passing it to the server. Client-side validation can be done easily with a Java script or VB scripts; it can also be done with built-in validators. Regular expression validators are extensively used.

- Do not assume that validated data on the client will go to the server in a clean fashion. Revalidate all the strings the client sends to the server on the server side. This helps eliminate any changes or hacks while the data travels from the client to server.

- Validate the email entered by sending an email to the user with some random data and asking the user to enter that random data on the website.

- Limit the number of login attempts (3, 5, or whatever number suits the organization) and lock the account if the attempts exceed this number.

- Validate both password and username boxes for special characters, such as single quotes, dashes, semicolons, and other SQL reserved characters.

- On the server side, do not use database connection strings, passwords, and SQL commands in plaintext. Rather, they can be set up with data sets, encrypted passwords, and hidden strings with the given language (C#, C++, Perl, Java, and so on). These languages can be combined as well to run as scripts in many environments.

- Put all the SQL commands as stored procedures on the back-end database and follow the database security principles explained in earlier chapters.

- If possible, separate the username and password fields into separate screens or windows. If the username is not found, there is no need to ask for password. These are new techniques implemented by companies such as Google and Microsoft.

- Do not allow automatic password resets on the website. Send a secure link to the email contact and ask the users to follow that link.

- User a two- or three-factor authentication for logging in and more security.

- Do not show to the reader any more information than required. This means the error checking is done correctly to show a simple message such as "The username and password combination is not correct." Showing more information can give hackers more than they ask for. Do not inform users if the username should be an email or a specific string. The hacker may learn and modify input if you give those details. Do not tell the users specifics if the username or password is wrong. Just show a generic message such as "username and password entered do not match."

- Use the database's abilities or functions to suppress errors from being shown to the user. A registered user on an e-commerce website does not need to know what is SQL or to bother about the nuts and bolts behind the Login button.

- Use programming language capabilities such as try-catch-finally to suppress errors and from crashing the programs on the front end. These loops can also be used to dynamically alter the path of a program and provide better interface to the users.

- New technologies and programming logic (Gmail and Microsoft email) also incorporate two validations separately to avoid hacks and for better security—one for username and one for password. The second validation occurs only when the first validation is successful.

Evaluate User Input

User input should be validated on an application. The following are some steps to validate user input:

- Check validity of usernames, emails, and other information. Limit the length and do a regular expression validator to avoid unwanted characters.

- Avoid attacks on the server by not giving too much information about errors and suppress showing unwanted messages and excessive information to the users.

- Avoid silly and wrong ways of programming—use classes, methods, and modules to work independently (high cohesion and low coupling) and efficiently to accept and return data efficiently.

- Do not use connection strings, passwords, and usernames in the code directly. Instead, create a data source with the given DB connection and use that connection information in code to access tables or stored procedures.

- Encrypt the passwords if any are stored in the configuration files.

- Do not leave DB connections open in the code and do not leave any code parenthesis open. Code should compile cleanly without any errors or warnings.

Do Back-End Database Checks

The following are some steps to check for security vulnerabilities on the back-end database:

- Suppress back-end DB information from leaking out when an error occurs. Use the efficiency provided by the try-catch-finally blocks to avoid errors and exit gracefully.

- Use the stored procedures and packages of the database for required DB operations and evaluate input again at the DB level.

- Block attackers from even trying to reach the server (client- and server-side evaluation).

- Evaluate user input and credentials with better identification and authentication every time the DB is accessed.

- Terminate the connection to the DB once a transaction is complete.

- Use all known multipronged methods to avoid giving more information to the user.

- Track the database logins for excessive changes, more transactions, wrong user data, new account creations, and the system accounts that are being used. These should be done automatically on any observed changes.

- Track the database backups, account deletions, creations, and errors on a regular basis (daily, weekly, monthly).

Change Management—Speaking the Same Language

In a corporation where software development follows a model, change management is usually in place to track changes to software, whether it's developed in-house or acquired from a third party. Third-party software needs to be approved by the change management group before it can be installed on the corporate network or computers. Change management has other duties as well to track the users, check the new users with security verification, and approve or revoke the users. Only approved users can get accounts from the corporation. The process usually works as shown in the following steps:

1. Onboard the new user as an employee after a successful interview, security and background checks, and a solid job offer.

2. Employees complete any mandatory security training and apply for access to the computers, network, and database by signing proper forms.

3. Forms signed by employees are checked by the information security officer (ISO) for accuracy in the employee details, their training dates, and so on.

4. The ISO sends the forms to the employee's supervisor for signature. The supervisor's signature indicates that the supervisor sponsors the employee to access the systems.

5. These forms are now sent to change management for review and approval.

6. Change management double-checks the forms and employee details and, if everything is in order, grants approval by signing the form and sending it back to the supervisor/employee.

7. The completed and signed forms are sent to various branches that give access to the employee.

8. Mandatory access such as a picture ID card with a PIN, basic computer network, and email are given first by the general access branches where they create an account and send it to the employee. These details are only good for basic access such as operating system and email read/write.

9. Any database, system, network, mainframe, or other accounts are created as DAC by respective branches and sent separately to the employee.

10. With each account creation, these branches also send details to the employee about the password policies that are in place and how the employee can align themselves to the existing policies.

Software to be acquired from a third party also goes through a similar process, but with a twist. The software is first tested on a standalone machine for all known problems, using the security guidelines an organization follows. Once the software passes the tests per the security guidelines, it is given to the users via either a downloadable option or on request. Again, those users who request the software need to reiterate the change management that the software is required for the users to work (least privilege), and the supervisor needs to approve as well. Software developed in house follows the same rules on who develops, who tests, and who is involved in deployment. Once the in-house software is deployed, any changes to that software cannot be done by the programmer because changes must again go through the change management process, and the reason for the change must be valid for approval.

It might look like the steps take forever, but in an efficient organization, they're quick, and approvals are given in one or two days after the basic steps of security clearance and changes to be approved are genuine. It is important to note that change management is a written process, and a record of change always must be retained by the organization for audits. Usually, some kind of software (either free or paid) is used for the change management process of submitting a request, approval, fixing a date for change, and completing the change and closing the request. Because the changes requested maybe completed successfully or may land the request in hot water for whatever reasons, the original change request must also include a rollback option of putting the software back into the condition it was found before the change was applied. One of the biggest problems with the change requests is that a change requested may be successfully made, but may introduce regression errors. It also means the team of programmers and testers must make sure that a successful change does not create new bugs to be fixed with another change request. The change management process is smooth and works effortlessly when all the parties involved work in tandem. In other words, all those working with a change in an organization have access to the change management software and speak the same language to make a change in an orderly and smooth manner.

In some cases, the change management group also looks after the password creations, system account creation, and removals, reminding users when their passwords are expiring, and other functions. Here is an example of how the change management looks into passwords of system accounts when they are about to expire: The programmer or the DBA who uses the passwords of a particular system account requests new passwords (usually once every 3, 6, or 9 months or year) via a form. The form needs to be signed by the users who all use the account, and it must be countersigned by the supervisor as well. The passwords are then generated by the change management team after proper checks on the forms are completed. There is a reason for change management to get involved in these accounts. For example, if the user is given the full authority to change the passwords, they may create a password like p@55WOrd_(1234567), which usually can pass the password policies but is easy for any hacker to guess. A change management–assisted password would use software to generate a complex password such as g23Q8#s@3y81NPq, which is more secure and yet follows all the password policies and the corporate rules.

Secure Logging In to Applications, Access to Users

Many software packages, websites, and online business processing need a user to log in to do secure transactions. Even desktop applications used in banks and financial institutions or in schools need security with some kind of logging. About 90% of these institutions use the password and username combinations despite the fact that this kind of authentication has the lowest level of security. When the software package uses security, there are two possibilities for logging the users—use the existing credentials or let the users create their own new credentials. Each one has its own problems, of course, and they are discussed in the following sections.

Creating New Credentials

There are dozens of options possible in this area for a username and password. Do we want to allow an email as the username, or do we plan to allow the users to create a unique username? In either case, when the user chooses an option, the username or the email must be checked in the back-end database to make sure it does not already exist. Also, how do we contact the user in case of trouble with the account? Can the problem be easily resolved with an autogenerated email, or do we plan to ask them to call a customer service number to have the username or password manually reset? There is a subtle danger in employing someone who will manually set or reset the passwords or usernames. That employee may steal the data of users and cause harm. This shows yet again that security considerations must start right from the beginning of creating an application.

For these reasons, corporations employ hashing algorithms (discussed in Chapter 5) in storing passwords on a system. If a password is forgotten, a live customer service person or an automated program cannot even provide the user with the forgotten password because it is stored as a hash, but they can create a new temporary password and let the user change it on their own end within a fixed timeframe. If the user fails to change the password in that given timeframe, the account will be locked again.

Additional features of the lock or access are created with multi-factor authentication, such as providing a PIN via text message to the user's registered phone or email address. Authentication on mobile devices is also done with fingerprints or face recognition. It must be remembered that these are not the absolute best ways to avoid an attack because someone can bypass or mimic those once they have the devices in their possession. New applications have an app on the app stores for private browsing for users on their own phone. The assumption in this case is that the phone and app are not shared by anyone else. At best, we can say that these solutions are the best at this time, and we continue to evolve toward better security because it's a continuous process of learning and adapting rather than a method with an end point.

Some corporate applications that need better security use access cards for various purposes. Since issuing many access cards is a problem, one access card should be able to do most functions, and it's useful if that card is programmable for adding or deleting various functions/duties. These organizations usually issue a card to the users and can be programmed for a gate entry, database room entry, office entry, computer logging, and locking and unlocking a storage area or entering a break room. This brings up the question of whether we really need a break room entry door to be locked. Observe that some universities, public offices, or libraries have general entry for anyone to enter and exit the common areas. In one instance, a panhandler entered the break room of a particular department at a university and stole a few lunch boxes when everyone was at a meeting. The access cards have an expiry date and need to be renewed or reprogrammed depending on the duties of the employee, their promotion or demotion, and addition or deletion of responsibilities. Also, in a large corporation, employees move around a lot, which requires reprogramming the cards. Access cards have private and public certificates valid for a few years that can be used for various purposes.

Logging In to Applications

Applications that are used only among staff (around the world) of a corporation can implement the access cards to log in because the access cards have all the data of the user and the valid certificates. Certificates can be easily read by the built-in classes, such as using the .NET framework's System.Security.Cryptography.X509Certificates that are built in to the security and cryptographic classes. These classes can quickly read the certificates on the access cards or those stored in the computer and ask for the PIN from user to validate. Therefore, access cards work as picture ID, credential validation, and multi-factor authentication—card plus PIN. The PIN can be four, six, eight, or any number of digits. However, a longer PIN will be a pain for regular users. Example 10-12 shows a sample Java/C#-like program for reading an X.509 certificate. The results (true or false) are read into string variables that can be used in various ways. Note the inclusion of X.509 certificate built-in library at the top of the listing.

Example 10-12   *C# Code to Read an X.509 Certificate*

```
using System.Security.Cryptography.X509Certificates;

public class X509CertReading
{
    public static void Main()
    {
        // Locate the path to the certificate.
        string CurCertificate = "Certificate.cer";

        // Read certificate into an X509Certificate object.
        X509Certificate myCert = new X509Certificate(CurCertificate);

        // Get the value.
        string resultsTrue = myCert.ToString(true);

        // Get the value.
        string resultsFalse = myCert.ToString(false);
    }
}
```

The important advantage of access cards and certificates is their use in email applications. Corporate email such as Outlook and Lotus Mail can read the user's credentials from the access cards and allow the user to log in to the mail program to receive and send emails from their corporate accounts. Private emails can set up certificates or an additional factor as a PIN that will be received on the user's personal phone. Note that a private user can create their own certificates on the Internet to be used for document signatures and logging in. DocuSign is one free application that can be used for certificate creation.

The access cards are regularly used for logging in to a corporate computer. The computer's keyboard or the laptop has a built-in smart card reader. Inexpensive USB-connected readers are available as well. Many programs—such as ActivClient, EntryProtect, and MIMEsweeper—are installed on a corporate computer that keeps checking the access card validity. Once a stipulated timeframe (usually 10 or 15 minutes) has elapsed without any activity on the system, these programs ask for the PIN (the second authentication factor) for the card and certificate to work on the system. A wrong PIN entry (usually limited to three times) locks the system for good. If an application uses the access card or simple username password combination to log in, the application should be coded to automatically log out in case of inactivity after a specified timeframe. Note that this application logout is different from the access card's inactivity and logout. Access card logout locks the entire computer system, but the application logout only logs out of the application. Thus, if a user has logged in to the application with their access card and switches to another application (say Outlook to read email) for more than 20 minutes, the computer and Outlook would continue to work, but the application that was opened by the user would log the user out of that application. This also means the access card's stipulated time of inactivity can be used differently by different applications and programs. In the previous example, the access was inactive on the application, whereas it is active enough on the system to keep the user logged in.

The access can also be used for digital signatures on documents like Adobe PDF or Microsoft Word in the corporate world. A digital signature has the added advantage of non-repudiation for a receiver and has possible repercussions for the sender. If allowed, the private certificates for digital signatures can also be stored on a corporate computer to be used for one's private documents. But many corporations may not allow private certificates and would probably insist on using the corporate-issued certificates for signatures and email for obvious reasons. These cards can also be used as picture identification on demand.

Using the Databases

Obviously databases have a different credential for users to remember. The usernames and passwords on databases in a corporation would have the same or different policies to follow for users. Recall from the earlier section about databases that databases also have roles for users. Any user who logs in to a database does not automatically get the privilege of "doing anything" on the database. Database logging can also use the access card certificates or use their own separate passwords. Assuming that the DB allows access card authentication with the same PIN that is used to log into a system, there is a subtle problem. Because the card is used for logging in and certificates are used centrally, the database would assume that the card is valid enough for users to log in. Therefore, the database may allow the user to log in without further ado and would not ask for reauthentication. This could be a problem because users may log in to a database that they do not intend to or are required to and see the information they are not entitled to, thereby invalidating the least privilege principle. For this reason, databases have separate logging credentials that can be used with caution (closely observed by the database administrators for misuse). Programmers can use the DB credentials in their code with connection string parameters and access only those DB objects they are entitled to read/write.

As great as an access card sounds as "one card of all functions," a lost card can expose the problems. Shoulder surfing on the employee's keyboard (by other colleagues) can easily give away the PIN entered (associated with the card) by a user. Therefore the use of the access card itself for various uses demands regular training. Since the card has a validity period, an expired card needs to be reissued and certificates renewed or recreated. Older certificates on expired cards need to be imported back to the system and should be reinstalled to work with the newly issued cards.

These are some issues that can irk or frustrate employees, but in light of corporate security, these items are minor and can be adjusted among staff with proper policies. For example, if a policy states that the employees can use the card to enter a building, they should be trained to discourage piggybacking even if the piggybacking employee is a very close friend. In fact, employees are trained not to ask even their closest friends and colleagues for help if they forget their own access cards. They must call their supervisor or go to a central office that can issue a new card in case of loss. Issuing access cards is also done by a different office and needs proper investment to staff the office and issue cards.

Monitoring the card usage (times of use) is the job of back-end administrators, whereas the users themselves have the responsibility of proper use, protecting information, creating and maintaining passwords per policies, reporting suspicious activities, logging out when not present at the work station, locking the system both physically and electronically, and so on. Users must be trained to avoid social engineering attacks on email, via phone, or in person. And when working from home, which has become a regular corporate feature after COVID-19, employing the virtual private network (VPN) when logging in to the corporate network is mandatory, and the corporation should maintain that VPN security at the highest level. Good software can also easily limit the Internet access of users to avoid malware and autodownloading of *any* software (also known as drive-by downloading) that may cause a breach. Continuous monitoring of the corporate software, network, users, and physical building is a process a corporation must adapt to avoid any security breaches. All these need good investment, training, and retraining to provide better long-term security. In the long term, these investments in security will prove more rewarding than letting a data breach occur and suffering the losses.

Summary

Application security starts with good planning from step zero and remains in place as a continuous monitoring event. Coders have the responsibility of using a good coding standard that makes the code efficient and readable. Error messages should not give any inside information to the users. To minimize errors in code, many languages offer a try-catch-finally structure to try a code, catch an error, and fix the error found. Well-written code also helps fix errors easily.

Software development follows a lifecycle (SDLC) and has several steps, starting with requirements collection. Requirements should be simple and follow one requirement per one sentence rather than creating an ambiguous sentence with many requirements combined. Various SDLC models are used for in-house software development.

Cohesion is a concept that tells a module how well it works with relationships INSIDE the module. Coupling is a term used when one module depends on the other module or has OUTSIDE relationships. For software to work well, it is desired to have high cohesion and low coupling.

In-house software follows a set process of development, test, and deployment on production. Checking for errors on both the client and server is important because each can pose a problem. Regular expression validators filter out user input to a required format to minimize SQL injection attacks. Evaluating user input and checking the back-end database are important to avoid any problems in software. For all these to work in tandem, change management is generally used.

Logging into applications can be more secure with X.509 certificates, and many language packages now provide those secure classes to read the digital certificates inside the program/software.

Chapter 10 Questions

1. What are the two types of errors in coding?

2. What errors can a compiler successfully catch before building an executable version of software?

3. When a website crashes due to a semantic error, it shows the database IP, port, username, and what went wrong in the connection. The programmer says this information helps the user fix the details. Is the programmer right?

4. What time of looping helps avoid crashing programs?

5. What are coding standards, and why are they required?

6. The process of software development is known as what?

7. When writing complex requirements, what is the best way to create a requirement in SDLC?

8. At what stage of software development lifecycle does the security posture need consideration?

9. What are the three kinds of machines on which the software development process is dependent?

10. What is cohesion?

11. What is coupling?

12. If the testing phase is planned to be bypassed, what test does a programmer still need to do?

13. What is the exact process of developing software in an organization that has production, test, and development environments?

14. What characters are important to be watched for when a free text box is provided with unlimited length for text entry to avoid SQL injection attacks?

15. What is the easiest way to check the SQL injection attack?

16. What are the query strings in the following URL:

    https://myWesbite.Salespoint.com/item=26725&warranty=10&type=new&shipping=priority

17. Why is change management important?

18. How can an access card be used in a corporate environment that has worldwide offices and has enough funding to support security?

19. At what stage of software development must security be considered?

20. When can a corporation stop worrying about security in software development?

Answer to Chapter 10 Questions

1. Syntax errors (bad declarations and missing script lines) and semantic errors (run-time errors).

2. Syntax errors can be easily caught by compilers.

3. No, the programmer is wrong because we cannot expect the URL to be used only by valid authenticated users. Any hacker can use and try the error details to log in to the database and corrupt the URL, DB, and so on. With zero trust, it is only advised to provide required details to the user—no more and no less.

4. When written correctly, a try-catch-finally usually helps catch errors before the entire program crashes.

5. Coding standards set a programming benchmark for coders to follow consistently. Writing a good and well-documented program per the company policies gives a clear way forward to write concise but accurate code with excellent description for others to follow to fix errors if any come up or update the code easily. It also helps avoid dry and meaningless code.

6. Software development life cycle (SDLC).

7. Break down the requirement to subitems to make sure each subitem is a single requirement.

8. At every stage from ground zero to the final product and until it is decommissioned.

9. It is dependent on development, test (quality assurance), and production machines.

10. Cohesion tells how each object is related to others within the same module. High cohesion happens inside the module. High cohesion is desired.

11. Coupling is how a module interacts with other modules. Coupling happens outside the module. Low coupling is a desired feature.

12. Unit testing is a mandatory testing process the programmer has to complete before compiling the final executable code.

13. Develop, test, and deploy on production (D->T->P).

14. ; (semi-colon), - - (comment), single quotes ('), and all other DB reserved words and letters such as @, !, and others that vary with each DB package.

15. User input validation at both the client and server sides. Regular expression validators help avoid the unnecessary data that is being input and also helps genuine users.

16. The first URL query string must start with a ?, and further query strings must begin with &. The URL provided doesn't have the first query string; therefore, any strings attached to the URL are NOT query strings.

17. It keeps written track of changes to the software either developed in house or purchased from a vendor.

18. Access can be used for various purposes, such as building entry, logging into the computer, entering a secure room, logging into another application program that needs a certificate, checking email, non-repudiation, and electronic signatures. Other functions can be programmed or deleted as required from time to time. It can be used for both MAC and DAC.

19. Security is paramount right from the beginning to the end of the software development life cycle.

20. Never. Security is a process rather than a one-time do-and-forget task. A corporation must continuously learn and adapt to the new attacks and hacking attempts and update their software with a continuous monitoring process.

The Unseen Back End

From the viewpoint of a programmer or hacker, the most interesting aspect of a software package or working website is the back-end infrastructure where the actual processing goes on. For the programmer building a package or business website, accuracy of data and smooth flow of iterations are important, but the hacker looks for vulnerabilities to get into the back end and steal or corrupt data. In other words, the back end is the real structure where everything is positioned and steers the users correctly.

We almost always have a database connected on the back end to store and retrieve data. Invariably the data contains personally identifiable information (PII) such as email addresses, credit card numbers, and other data like medical data. In Chapter 10, "Application Security Fundamentals," we discuss the vulnerabilities that might arise from text boxes and URL addresses and the use of second or third authentication. In this chapter, we examine how the front-end user connects to the database on the back end.

For a website business like Amazon, Netflix, or Google, there are millions of customers who log in at a given time to order or browse the available products. Any loss of connections or data corruption results in millions of dollars in lost business. Therefore, these sites have content servers stationed around the country for a reliable connection, geographically closest to an end user's location. When the closest server fails to connect, the next closest is tried. This ensures content is always delivered quickly and smoothly. A hacker's intent is to access these servers on the back end to get the data or the "content," possibly find usernames and passwords, and even create an administrative account to return to later.

The database connections are initiated with a given connection string when an end user sends a query to inquire for a product or buy or return a product. That poses the question of whether every end user should know the database's connection details. If we assume that each end user is granted a database account to access the entire product database in an online company like Amazon, it is possible that the company will need a billion database accounts to access the product database. With that number of database accounts, one stolen username/password combination is sufficient for a hacker to access the database and possibly crash the entire Amazon business. From a security point of view, it would be a huge vulnerability in the infrastructure.

Understand that users have user accounts, whereas separate system accounts are used to access the database. These database or system accounts working in the background act as a mediator between an end user and the database. There is no need for any end user to know where the database is stationed geographically or what system account acts as a mediator between them and the database. Everything happens on the back end. For better security, the user data is stored in a separate user database, but when a particular user wants to access the product database, the hidden database or system account works as a handler between the end user account and the database. The same system account can easily deal with more than one end user because ACID database transactions occur concurrently, as discussed in Chapter 4, "Database Security Introduction." Figure 11-1 is a simplified illustration of how an application handles various user accounts with other corporate back-end databases. Notice that the end users cannot directly access a database when using a particular application, even if the users are part of the database group. The application handles the details among various databases and user requests as required.

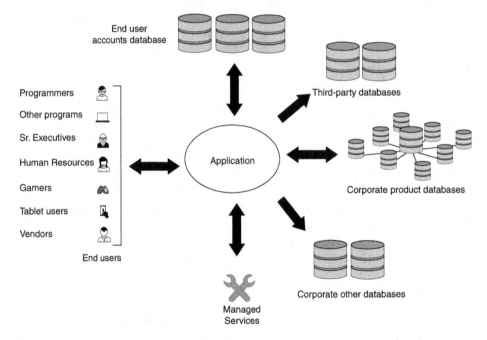

Figure 11-1 *Interaction Among End Users and Application and Databases*

Assuming that the application is well designed for an end user to register for username and password credentials, the end user data is stored separately in the end user database. Recall from the earlier chapters that to protect data in databases, applications and databases are stored on separate servers. Assuming this application is developed for a corporation that sells a few thousand products, once an end user enters their credentials, the following steps can be expected by the application (a desktop, a mobile app, or a LAN application or a website):

1. Evaluate user input for accuracy of username and passwords.

2. Check with the user database for an existing account and either log in, use second authentication, or prompt for creating a new user for people who do not have an account.

3. Depending on the user's next few inquiries, fetch data from and to the corporate product database, other corporate databases, and third-party databases available for the application.

4. Optionally use or send information to other managed services on the network that are required for the application to run.

5. Keep a constant vigil on a logged-in user's actions and login and idle times to update the user databases and other databases or services.

6. Update orders and inquiries (even if the user did not order any items to buy) to keep a history for the user's browsing habits to suggest other products for sale.

Notice that the application is the ringleader to keep everything going between the end user and the databases or the managed services. Therefore, the application has to be highly scalable, accessible, available, and confidential; maintain integrity; and use a limited number of accounts to access databases and services. These database accounts and service details are stored in the application. For example, for .NET web applications, the database details are stored in a standard XML file known as web.config. The file typically looks like that shown in Example 11-1.

Example 11-1 *Example of web.config File from .NET Web Application*

```
<?xml version="1.0"?>
<!--
For more information on how to configure your ASP.NET application, please visit
https://go.microsoft.com/fwlink/?LinkId=169433
-->
<configuration>


    <connectionStrings>
<add name="myDBConn" connectionString="Data Source=DBID;Persist Security
Info=True;User ID=myIDName;Password=somesecPwd;Unicode=True" providerName="System.
Data.OracleClient"/>
    </connectionStrings>


<system.web>
    <compilation debug="true" targetFramework="4.0"/>
    <httpRuntime/>
```

```
        <pages controlRenderingCompatibilityVersion="3.5" clientIDMode="AutoID"/>
    </system.web>

    <system.codedom>
        <compilers>
        <compiler language="c#;cs;csharp" extension=".cs"
    ...

    ...

    ...

            <providerOption name="CompilerVersion" value="v4.0"/>
        </compiler>
        <compiler language="vb;vbs;visualbasic;vbscript" extension=".vb"
    ...

    ...

    ...

            <providerOption name="CompilerVersion" value="v4.0"/>
        </compiler>
        </compilers>
    </system.codedom>

</configuration>
```

When the application creates the web.config file, it stores the database connection information inside the configuration file. Notice that this information is stored in plain text and gives all possible information. When the application is deployed on the server, web.config is also deployed. If a hacker gets hold of this file and other settings files, they are opening an invitation for the hackers to attack. In this case, the first step is to block access for the file. This can be done easily with Internet Information Server (IIS) on Windows by 1) blocking directory access, 2) encrypting the web.config file's settings, and 3) moving the connection settings to another file stored under a different location. Yet another option is to provide an encryption routine that routinely encrypts and decrypts the passwords and usernames when using the database(s).

The first option is straightforward and easy. Open the IIS console and click the **Directory Browsing** icon, as shown in Figure 11-2.

Opening Directory Browsing displays the dialog box shown in Figure 11-3. In the Actions area on the left side is a Disable option. Use it to disable the all browsing or part of it (specifying time, size, extension, and/or date). It is also possible to set up a custom error page.

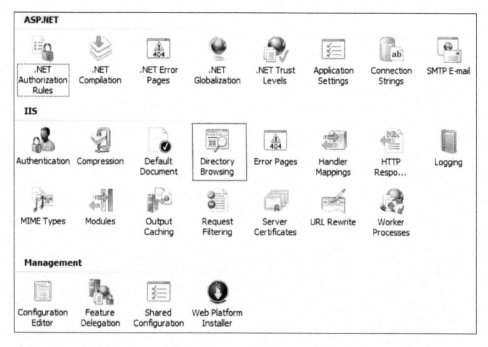

Figure 11-2 *Directory Browsing Option in Internet Information Server (IIS)*

The same details are also stored in web.config (or you can directly use web.config) when this feature is set up.

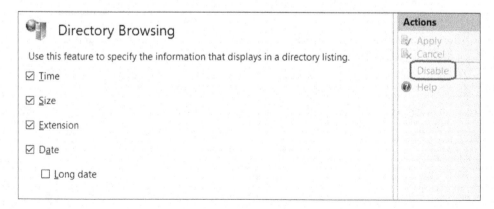

Figure 11-3 *Directory Browsing Options*

The web.config file then has an entry for enabling and disabling, such as what's shown in the following listing. Clicking the IIS icon and changing the web.config file to insert the Enabled=false option have the same result.

```
<system.webServer>
    <directoryBrowse enabled="true" showFlags="Date,Time,Extension,
Size" />
</system.webServer>
```

For disabling, change the enabled attribute like so:

```
<system.webServer>
    <directoryBrowse enabled="false" />
</system.webServer>
```

The second choice of encrypting the password and connection string in the web.config file needs slightly different work. In ASP.NET, Microsoft provides a utility named aspnet_regiis.exe with various options. This can be used to register dynamic link libraries (DLLs) and do a variety of things with an ASP.NET application. The following command (at the administrator prompt from within Visual Studio's command prompt) converts the plain text web.config file's connection strings to encrypted long text in the node Encrypted data — Cypher data. The aspnet_regiis.exe tool is located in the %windows%\Microsoft. NET\Framework\versionNumber folder.

```
C:\Users\...\source>aspnet_regiis.exe -pef "connectionStrings"
"C:\Users\ ...\source\repos\TestOracleCon\TestOracleCon" -prov
"DataProtectionConfigurationProvider"
```

After running this command from the command prompt, the following data is displayed in the DOS window after a few seconds. Note the ending line message that says "succeeded." It also lists the version of the utility that installs and uninstalls ASP.NET on the local machine. This is the same utility that can be used to register DLLs.

```
Microsoft (R) ASP.NET RegIIS version 4.0.30319.0
Administration utility to install and uninstall ASP.NET on the local
machine.
Copyright (C) Microsoft Corporation.  All rights reserved.
Encrypting configuration section...
Succeeded!
```

Let's briefly consider the provider (-prov) option details. Per Microsoft documentation, we can encrypt and decrypt sections of a web.config file using a ProtectedConfiguration-Provider class. The following list describes the protected configuration providers included in the .NET Framework:

- DpapiProtectedConfigurationProvider uses the Windows Data Protection API (DPAPI) to encrypt and decrypt data.

- RsaProtectedConfigurationProvider uses the RSA encryption algorithm to encrypt and decrypt data.

Both providers offer strong encryption of data. However, if you are planning on using the same encrypted configuration file on multiple servers, such as a web farm, only the RsaProtectedConfigurationProvider enables you to export the encryption keys and import them on another server. The DpapiProtectedConfigurationProvider uses the Windows built-in cryptographic services and can be configured for either machine-specific or user-account-specific protection. Machine-specific protection is useful for anonymous services but provides less security. User-account-specific protection can be used with services that run with a specific user identity.

Note also that the -prov option can have a default value of RsaProtectedConfigurationProvider (if the -prov option is not mentioned).

Notice that the command **aspnet_regiis.exe** takes arguments for what node of XML file you want to encrypt (in our case, the connectionStrings node from Example 11-1), the directory or the location of web.config file in the application (C:\Users\ ...\source\repos\TestOracleCon\TestOracleCon), and the type of provider (DataProtectionConfigurationProvider). The option pef indicates the following details per Microsoft's documentation. Notice the provider option in the following and compare it to the details used for a provider as DataProtectionConfigurationProvider in the command used previously.

```
-pef section web-app-physical-dir


Encrypt the configuration section. Optional arguments: [-prov
provider]. Use this provider to encrypt.

.NET also provides the following option for machine.config file.



[-pkm] Encrypt/decrypt the machine.config instead of web.config.
```

Once the web.config file is encrypted, reopen it in a text editor as shown in Example 11-2. Notice the <CipherData> node with the encrypted connection string. Because the .NET environment knows the keys and encryption options, datasets built with this connection string are automatically decrypted while establishing the connection between the application and the database or service.

Example 11-2   *Example of Partially Encrypted web.config File from .NET Web Application*

```
<?xml version="1.0"?>
<!--

For more information on how to configure your ASP.NET application, please visit
https://go.microsoft.com/fwlink/?LinkId=169433
```

```
-->
<configuration>

<connectionStrings configProtectionProvider="DataProtectionConfigurationProvider">
    <EncryptedData>
    <CipherData>
<CipherValue>
```

```
AQAAANCMnd8BFdERjHoAwE/Cl+sBAAAAUUFyZEv2MkuUegi5WUskqQQAAAACAAAAAADZgAAwAAAABAAAAA
omTMbSz0bJL5mneFS3LSDAAAAAASAAACgAAAAEAAAAPn2KtNszEs0qIEfc4O/riTYAQAAnmvBtj43gtRNm+
Sn8xuZnWS5kVEOGMgdOg2p7fKnlrP8kq/7yw5NKklH5eA86aVVazI4Z6qM/Ap9SiW+DxZyHdl5GLzwjccJg
ReodpXCaxMjDDtALXkriYrXelpQxMf1XdQMS6Ah38bGbFSdIUFLG/DQlLSzifyy0Kes+RcuMtktIAeg0eI
kzYYGwpZ99D16S8t4sI61/nJ12YFji797E/wYVV8nR2vypC7bAtpPZHDoA80sos0BxFyHoaHSopFivv8s-
48sA9Fd9PzPEEWYlItToBgPzO6VlF9twQfqS5hlhD/4rQ8vDQzb+cBIIkL9wTbQMbGAww3eAnHD8pBH+G
OaIOh4fTECNH36uZfIem3fIDQRzYu94+iX89BD5uhVYXHI3OQlnlNu0qYSiUM8ZaOTHcDHyISpDt/2A7tYk
PZqtoP50dMxsAcBdokbdJ4EsYJQnUwc4gOGbLktH5QJnWzjtu+ba+NJawmlR6C+XyguesMQqiDKBQxdQwN
4YwmOIBIkPabbuV3OM4tzh5c5IOb0DDytZIStxdvFt9INX9MeYFUL2BGD0To4aSlIAJm1f0gRIfbnYBdwWXH
zk0m45qzwCndbXqlYnElC/2VDZbW2bNwfxCQR3ChQAAABFe5v6LbE2TPH/uzlJWsp+HByYLQ==
```

```
</CipherValue>
    </CipherData>
    </EncryptedData>
</connectionStrings>
<system.web>
    <compilation debug="true" targetFramework="4.0"/>
    <httpRuntime/>
    <pages controlRenderingCompatibilityVersion="3.5" clientIDMode="AutoID"/>
</system.web>

<system.codedom>
    <compilers>
    <compiler language="c#;cs;csharp" extension=".cs"
…
…

        <providerOption name="CompilerVersion" value="v4.0"/>
    </compiler>
    <compiler language="vb;vbs;visualbasic;vbscript" extension=".vb"
…
…

        <providerOption name="CompilerVersion" value="v4.0"/>
    </compiler>
    </compilers>
</system.codedom>
</configuration>
```

With RSA encryption the configuration will look slightly different as below

```
<configuration>
  <connectionStrings configProtectionProvider="RsaProtectedConfigurationProvider">
    <EncryptedData Type=http://www.w3.org/2001/04/xmlenc#Element
        xmlns=http://www.w3.org/2001/04/xmlenc#>
    <EncryptionMethod Algorithm=http://www.w3.org/2001/04/xmlenc#aes256-cbc />
    <KeyInfo xmlns=http://www.w3.org/2000/09/xmldsig#>
    <EncryptedKey xmlns=http://www.w3.org/2001/04/xmlenc#>
    <EncryptionMethod Algorithm=http://www.w3.org/2001/04/xmlenc#rsa-1_5 />
        <KeyInfo xmlns=http://www.w3.org/2000/09/xmldsig#>
        <KeyName>Rsa Key</KeyName>
        </KeyInfo>
        <CipherData>
            <CipherValue>HJUB1JnAUpskZY0gSiYRyUMj174+CacBiKfQL6O134BSh+bUNEOnQkTRzYf
louPvsuZ4vLl55JO4F3cDmfReATbzvggwgs0Pa7kTwKHR3Uw+VE8tcrdhBR27IxIxrtJETl5fNZLxvrHHNK-
bqeYNIhkqZvRfMGG1zPRtw3jx4szaBR/fAd4JW6IOqNxY+4T7GtDjHIc0NTXjEeZOeUbr02OX9SuRGi7haxh
YZGv/SqEmMJQwJSFi/KOwF2Mx63xxXpo3B5LSL0CsKfDEvcSjJFvnjE3EoYjv9PqhATMFzxRH+oJ5U7hXScZ
mIXLo7KdI6j8q+zI41T0oLEkFQKwaUsA==</CipherValue>
        </CipherData>
    </EncryptedKey>
    </KeyInfo>
    <CipherData>
        <CipherValue>mOY+g09vyckjDF+XNigCBNqXcB6HUb9hWqcpNifvPslKe01K9/W2KMjqFO2H-
6CoGf+2pTyZ8xqfRsvO4bRKLwF25nPrl+ecqWF8shIZgRXwhhk79byWbNdlo4k1RgMBEwCuibGc+LV8ThtJ
u9icYJ6DOKbtMorUCH5X3hvZcJ2hObiRTXgqML4QG5EEy98LrmSG64muZPVIg5+yKlIeZZgtEWdw1xONPZf-
hwa5LbxFfIbMLEFduRNdB3UZnCf+w0s8V4lxWreTBo1EmGn4F9TPiyzCZYoqFU8PBoLd3mlGqNeTFoeMixYp
rehCODvJv9b4Ww+inkF/BNa+LsmjCaiA==</CipherValue>
    </CipherData>
    </EncryptedData>
  </connectionStrings>
  <system.web>
    <compilation debug="true" targetFramework="4.0"/>
    <httpRuntime/>
    <pages controlRenderingCompatibilityVersion="3.5" clientIDMode="AutoID"/>
  </system.web>
  <system.codedom>
    <compilers>
        <compiler language="c#;cs;csharp" extension=".cs" type="Microsoft.CSharp.
CSharpCodeProvider, System, Version=4.0.0.0, Culture=neutral, PublicKeyToke
n=b77a5c561934e089" warningLevel="4" compilerOptions="/langversion:default/
nowarn:1659;1699;1701">
            <providerOption name="CompilerVersion" value="v4.0"/>
        </compiler>
```

```
        <compiler language="vb;vbs;visualbasic;vbscript" extension=".
vb" type="Microsoft.VisualBasic.VBCodeProvider, System, Version=4.0.0.0,
Culture=neutral, PublicKeyToken=b77a5c561934e089" warningLevel="4" compilerOp-
tions="/langversion:default/nowarn:41008 /define:_MYTYPE=\&quot;Web\&quot; /option-
Infer+">
        <providerOption name="CompilerVersion" value="v4.0"/>
      </compiler>
    </compilers>
  </system.codedom>
</configuration>
```

Did we solve our problem yet? Maybe. The system accounts for an application's uses and has a set password that is supplied only to the programmers to implement after properly vetting those programmers and network administrators. What if the programmer or network administrator becomes a disgruntled employee or leaves the organization and tries to attack the network either as an internal employee or external hacker? For that reason, passwords need to change every once in a while. The password duration depends on the organization and its policies. Some set the time as one year, some set it every four months, and so on. When we change the passwords, it is cumbersome to change the web. config and keep repeating this every time. For that reason, we can include all application settings in a file, and all we do is keep the web.config file intact but change the settings in a separate file. That option looks Example 11-3 in the web.config file and the application settings element in the XML file in Example 11-4.

Example 11-3   *Specifying AppSettings as a File for .NET Web Application*

```
</connectionStrings>
    <appSettings file="..\..\AppSettingsSecrets.config">
    <add key="webpages:Version" value="3.0.0.0" />
    <add key="webpages:Enabled" value="false" />
    <add key="ClientValidationEnabled" value="true" />
    <add key="UnobtrusiveJavaScriptEnabled" value="true" />
  ...
...
    </appSettings>
    <system.web>
```

Example 11-4   *Contents of the AppSettingsSecrets.config File for a .NET Web Application*

```
The connection strings and all the secret data etc., are now in a separate markup
file, "AppSettingsSecrets.config." This file is also an XML markup identical to the
web.config file and is listed below.

<appSettings>
```

```
  <!-- SendGrid-->
  <add key="mailAccount" value="My Gmail account." />
  <add key="mailPassword" value="PA$$&*02=12%&37." />
  <!-- Twilio-->
 <connectionStrings>
<add name="myDBConn" connectionString="Data Source=DBID;Persist Security
Info=True;User ID=myIDName;Password=somesecPwd;Unicode=True" providerName="System.
Data.OracleClient"/>
 </connectionStrings>
</appSettings>
```

Three important things need to be mentioned:

- The ASP.NET runtime merges the contents of the external file (in this case, AppSettingsSecrets.config) with the markup mentioned in the <appSettings> element of the web.config file. If the specified file is not found, run time environment ignores the element. This makes it easy to change passwords once in a while.

- Notice the path for the AppSettingsSecrets.config file in the appsettings element of XML in the web.config file in Example 11-3. It is two levels above the solution and is not part of the solution folder being built. ASP.NET will not add this file to a repository. The programmer should not add the AppSettingsSecrets.config file to the project while building the application.

- The file AppSettingsSecrets.config can have any extension instead of "config," but keeping it as a configuration file has an added advantage. IIS will not serve any configuration files to the end users and keeps them secret.

Earlier we talked about blocking the directory access. When such a feature is enabled, if anyone tries to browse the directory level contents on a web application, it will show an error message such as those shown in Figure 11-4.

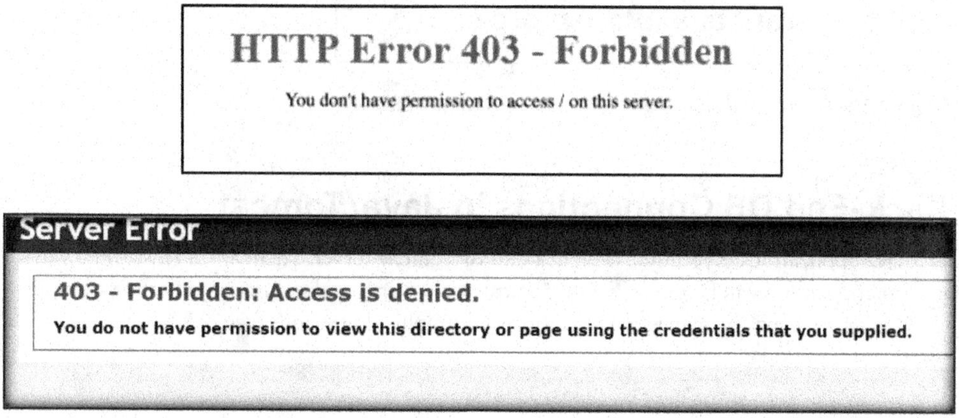

Figure 11-4 *Directory Browsing Error Examples*

This is a standard error produced and displayed by IIS. But what if we want to show a somewhat more friendly and yet secure message to redirect the end user to another page? That kind of redirection helps avoid telling the user that they tried to access a directory (for security purposes) and that the directory browsing was blocked. In the IIS, the option is to go to the **Error Pages** section of the IIS shown in Figure 11-5.

Status Code	Path	Type	Entry Type
401	%SystemDrive%\inetpub\custerr\<LANGUAGE-TAG>\401.htm	File	Inherited
403	%SystemDrive%\inetpub\custerr\<LANGUAGE-TAG>\403.htm	File	Inherited
404	%SystemDrive%\inetpub\custerr\<LANGUAGE-TAG>\404.htm	File	Inherited
405	%SystemDrive%\inetpub\custerr\<LANGUAGE-TAG>\405.htm	File	Inherited
406	%SystemDrive%\inetpub\custerr\<LANGUAGE-TAG>\406.htm	File	Inherited
412	%SystemDrive%\inetpub\custerr\<LANGUAGE-TAG>\412.htm	File	Inherited
500	%SystemDrive%\inetpub\custerr\<LANGUAGE-TAG>\500.htm	File	Inherited
501	%SystemDrive%\inetpub\custerr\<LANGUAGE-TAG>\501.htm	File	Inherited
502	%SystemDrive%\inetpub\custerr\<LANGUAGE-TAG>\502.htm	File	Inherited

Figure 11-5   *Standard Error Pages Shown by IIS*

Double-click the 403 status code page (which is 403.htm) and remove anything you do not want an end user to see. A custom page will then be created to show for error 403. For example, PayPal's custom page looks like Figure 11-6. Other error pages numbered 401 to 502 can be edited similarly to show custom messages to the end user. Some applications send the end user to a login page, and some just prevent the end user from moving further by using various techniques that are easily programmable.

This page couldn't be found.

Want to explore more?

Figure 11-6   *PayPal's Custom Error Page (Partial Listing)*

Back-End DB Connections in Java/Tomcat

Java applications typically use a back end of Tomcat server. There are at least three ways an application can be deployed on Tomcat: via a war file, directly copying the files to a folder, or using the manager application as a graphical user interface (GUI).

A typical application folder in Tomcat looks like the one shown in Figure 11-7. Tomcat would take care of the security in the connection strings and passwords. However, it is also possible to use encryption and decryption with code in Java (as well as in C#, VB, and so on) if the connection strings are used in the script directly.

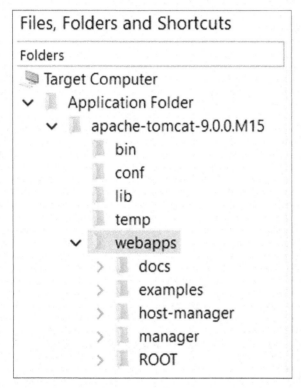

Figure 11-7 *Tomcat Server Showing the Directory Structure for Web Applications*

Each web application will have files and folders as shown in Figure 11-8. ContextRoot is the name of an application (for example, MyJavaApplication).

Folders META-INF and WEB-INF can contain the details for connections, secure data, and anything that should not be shown to an end user. These are protected folders and are never visible to any end users for security purposes. But usually, the connection strings can be stored in the configuration folder conf under the server. Examples 11-5 and 11-6 show the details (for Oracle and SQL Server as examples for DB connections, respectively). Note that the IP and port numbers were randomly picked in these examples and should be replaced with correct IP and port numbers.

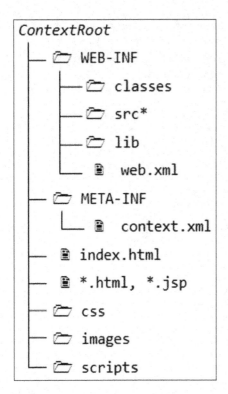

Figure 11-8 *Tomcat Server Showing a File Structure for Web Applications*

Example 11-5 *Partial Contents of server.xml File for Oracle DB in a Java Web Application in Tomcat*

```
<Resource name="jdbc/NewConnDS"
        auth="Container"
        type="javax.sql.DataSource"
              driverClassName="oracle.jdbc.driver.OracleDriver"
              url="jdbc:oracle:thin:@(DESCRIPTION=(LOAD_BALANCE=on)
        (ADDRESS_LIST=
            (ADDRESS=(PROTOCOL=TCP)(HOST=182.23.75.232) (PORT=1521))
            (ADDRESS=(PROTOCOL=TCP)(HOST=182.23.85.233)(PORT=1530)))
            (CONNECT_DATA=(SERVICE_NAME=myDatabase)))"
                                     username="System_web_account"
                                     password="P@$$word^%$#=123"
   />
```

Example 11-6 *Partial Contents of server.xml File for SQL Server in a Java Web Application in Tomcat*

```
        <Resource name="jdbc/confluence" auth="Container" type="javax.sql.Data-
Source"
                  username="System_web_account"
                  password="P@$$word^%$#=123"
                  driverClassName="net.sourceforge.jtds.jdbc.Driver
                  url="jdbc:jtds:sqlserver: :@(DESCRIPTION=(LOAD_BALANCE=on)
                                    (ADDRESS_LIST=
                                    (ADDRESS=(PROTOCOL=TCP)(HOST=182.23.75.232)
  (PORT=4521))
                                    (ADDRESS=(PROTOCOL=TCP)(HOST=182.23.85.233)
  (PORT=5510)))

                                    (CONNECT_DATA=(SERVICE_NAME=myDatabase)) )"
                                  validationQuery="select 1" />
```

Connection Strings and Passwords in Code

There is an older method of using connection strings directly in the code that is cumbersome, painful, and not well protected because all information about a database is written in the code when it's compiled and deployed. Even the basic database statements are written in SQL and executed from the application. In fact, the connection variable myConn uses the same configuration specified in Example 11-6, but now the entire connection string is hard-coded into the script file rather than using a configuration file on server.

We first discuss how this connection can be used to get data from the database and work out why this is not a reliable method that can be improved or even discarded due to security vulnerabilities. Look closely at the myConn object defined as follows.

```
    Connection myConn = DriverManager.getConnection(
                                        " jdbc:jtds:sqlserver: :@
(DESCRIPTION=(LOAD_BALANCE=on)
                                    (ADDRESS_LIST= (ADDRESS=(PROTOCOL=TCP)
(HOST=182.23.75.232) (PORT=4521))
                                    (ADDRESS=(PROTOCOL=TCP)
(HOST=182.23.85.233)(PORT=5510)))
                                    (CONNECT_DATA=(SERVICE_NAME=myDatabase))
                                    'System_web_account, 'P@$$word^%$#=123')";
```

Since we decided to put the entire connection string into a string variable, it also carries the username and password. Once the connection is defined, it can now be used in opening the DB and reading data. First create a statement for connection. Running the statement with executeQuery returns a class named ResultSet:

```
myStatement = myConn.createStatement();
    String sqlToRun = "select fName, lName from HR.Employee";
ResultSet myData=myStatement.executeQuery (sqlToRun);
```

Once the statement runs, we have the dataset in myData. The dataset can now be read as follows:

```
while(myData.next()){
MessageBox (myData.getString (1) + " " + myData.getString(2));
}
```

This way of coding is straightforward and gives results quickly, but there are many problems with this script. First, the script is all plaintext and exposes the database connection details, password, and even the username. Second, the SQL statements must not have any bugs and should work or be tested first. Any additional quotation marks or misspelled SQL statements, table names, column names, or usernames and passwords would pose trouble for the script and need to be corrected and recompiled. Third, the programmer must know the database tables, schemas, and complete details before even creating the statement (in the string variable sqlToRun). Coders must also know what kind of data is returned on successful execution of the statement to convert the data to a string or integer. If anyone who has access to this code wants to get information from other tables, they can try the schema name mentioned in the statement and get access to other tables, views, and much more information. These are some of the reasons why front-end SQL code is a bad idea from a security and DB point of view. These can be better done with stored procedures, which we discuss in the next section.

Stored Procedures and Functions

All databases provide functionality to create stored procedures and functions on the back end. These are like methods written in Java or C#, but they're written in Structured Query Language (SQL) and work on the back-end database. All the front-end application has to do is call the stored procedure with required parameters to accomplish a task. Stored procedures can be embedded into datasets created by the .NET environment IDE or with other languages. Recall from the earlier discussion that we used a very simple SQL statement:

```
select fName, lName from HR.Employee
```

What if the statement is complicated, has many things to do, or has more than one schema or table/view or other objects? For example, the SQL script shown in Example 11-7 inside the code pulls data out of a single schema and a single table and checks the row count and takes some action.

Example 11-7   *Sample Stored Procedure in SQL Server*

```
DECLARE @uName VARCHAR(50) -- User name
DECLARE @filePath VARCHAR(100) -- path for file
DECLARE @fileName VARCHAR(256) -- name for file


SELECT FName, LName, ID from [master].[dbo].[PersonTable]


DECLARE myCursor CURSOR FOR
SELECT LName
FROM [master].[dbo].[PersonTable]
WHERE LName NOT IN ('Samson','Jefferson', 'Williamson')


SET @myCount = (SELECT COUNT(*) FROM [master].[dbo].[PersonTable])


IF myCount > 0 THEN


BEGIN

                -- Remove the temp table
                TRUNCATE TABLE [master].[dbo].[PersonTable_TMP]

                -- Process each row
                OPEN myCursor
                FETCH NEXT FROM myCursor INTO @uName

                WHILE @@FETCH_STATUS = 0
                BEGIN

                            SET @fileName = @filePath + @uName
                            -- do something with the filename
                            ...

                            ...


                            FETCH NEXT FROM myCursor INTO @uName
                END
END
                CLOSE myCursor
                DEALLOCATE myCursor
END IF
```

The entire SQL script shown in Example 11-7 is hard to type and can easily have many missing characters or typing mistakes that could lead to errors in the script. Although script errors of C# and Java are checked quickly by compilers, a SQL command is usually created as a string and run from within the scripts of other languages. Thus, errors are difficult to handle. For this reason, all database systems provide stored procedures for programmability. For security purposes, using stored procedures is a straightforward and easy option. Stored procedures also hide behind the back-end database and are not visible to the front-end users. If worse comes to worst and the code is exposed to hackers, only the name of the stored procedure is exposed, and the hackers will not know exactly what the procedure does. This is a better protection for the data, front-end code, and the database itself.

Modern language IDEs such as Visual Studio allow the programmers to embed stored procedures easily into the project and compile them quickly. Figures 11-9 through 11-13 show an example of creating a dataset in Visual Studio and adding a table adapter and the stored procedure.

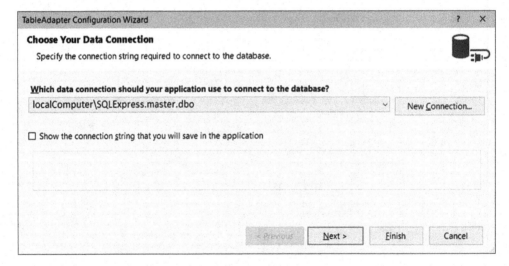

Figure 11-9   *Adding an Existing DB Stored Procedure to a Database in Visual Studio (1)*

The connection can start by clicking the **New Connection** button to create a DB connection or by using an existing connection by selecting it from the dropdown window. The next step is to name the connection to be able to use it later, if required. Clicking the **Next** button progresses to the steps shown in Figures 11-10 and 11-11.

In Figure 11-11, notice that instead of creating statements for SQL, we are picking up an already-created back-end stored procedure. If a proper matching driver is used in Visual Studio, it can connect to an Oracle DB or any other DB and accurately pick up the stored procedures. The advantage with stored procedures is also that we can pass parameters to the procedures back and forth for data manipulation.

Note that the **Select** dropdown shown in Figure 11-12 allows you to automatically pick up the existing stored procedures from a database. The programmer just has to choose which stored procedure to use. Once it is picked up, the parameters required for that stored procedure are shown on the right side. Optionally, for each of the select, insert, update, and delete options of the SQL commands, a separate stored procedure can be used, or the SQL statements can be autogenerated by the IDE.

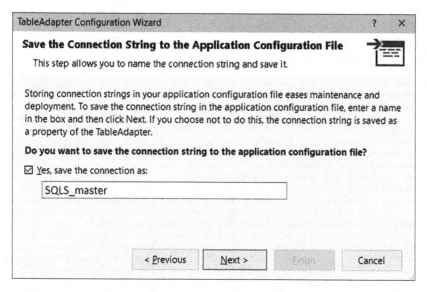

Figure 11-10 *Adding an Existing DB Stored Procedure to a Database in Visual Studio (2)*

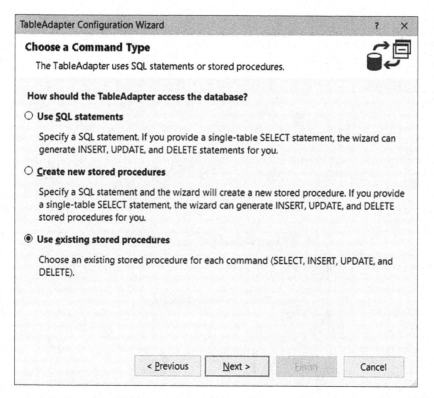

Figure 11-11 *Adding an Existing DB Stored Procedure to a Database in Visual Studio (3)*

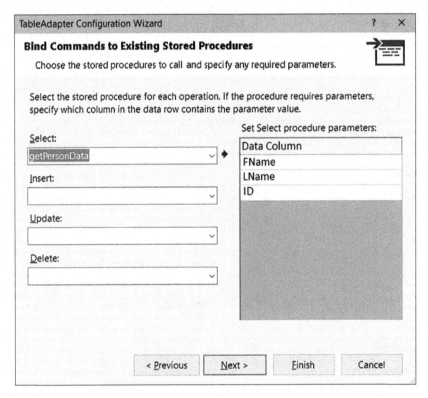

Figure 11-12 *Adding an Existing DB Stored Procedure to a Database in Visual Studio (4)*

Once created, this can be saved to show the dataset, as shown in Figure 11-13.

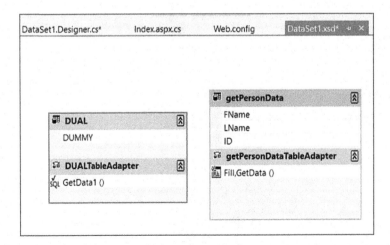

Figure 11-13 *Adding an Existing DB Stored Procedure to a Database in Visual Studio (5)*

In the previous example depicted in Figures 11-9 through 11-13, we have added a stored procedure named getPersonData, which returns three columns of data by name FName, LName, and ID. We also know that the stored procedure that is returning these values is a data table. To run the stored procedure and read data to a table, we can quickly do a few lines of code as shown:

```
DataSet1. getPersonDataTable  myTable = new DataSet1.getPersonDataTable();
string firstName = (string) myTable.row[0] ["FName"];
```

The string variable firstName now will contain the FName column of the table (as generated by the stored procedure) from row 0. Other data can be easily read this way. Stored procedures can be written to not return any output or can be written to generate a single scalar value as output. By looking at the dataset or the script, a hacker may not know many details from the database because the connection strings are encoded in the web. config file, and the database details are hidden. We can even have more security by encrypting the files and creating a new file association to protect data. This is a method some businesses incorporate to protect data of their customers and corporation.

File Encryption, Types, and Association

In Chapter 6, "Data Refresh, Backup, and Restore," in the "Security in Invoking ETL Job," we talk about encrypting passwords and decrypting when required in the Linux/Unix environment with a single-line Perl script. For security purposes, any application using data files or files with protected information should consider encrypting the files or creating a new file format that is not readable by general applications. For example, an application named Universal Coffee Flavor may want to keep its files encrypted and create a new file format extension named ucf. The ucf files are then decrypted in the application when read. The files with the ucf extension are therefore unreadable by Notepad, Word, video playing software, and other common applications. Fortunately, many programming languages in environments such as .NET and Java provide a crypto class that has built-in functions for encrypting and decrypting files or simple strings. Example 11-8 shows a simple example of encrypting a file with the AES cryptographic algorithm.

For the sake of discussion, we will assume that these are defined in a class named CryptoExample in which we included a crypto package and the other necessary libraries. A great many varieties of cryptographic algorithms are included in the Java libraries, but we use the AES algorithm in the example. The justCrypt method is the same for both encryption and decryption except for the parameters. Note that for the catch{} loop, many exceptions can be added with an or (or ‖ symbols) to avoid a crash in the code. It is left for the user to decide what other exceptions to add. We will use the same ucf extension for the encrypted file for demonstration and the .dat file as input and readable text file. The output file after decryption is a plaintext file. Also note that the other libraries for files and input and output streams such as java.io.FileInputStream and java. io.FileOutputStream need to be included in the script to run without any syntax errors.

Example 11-8   *Sample Java Script to Encrypt or Decrypt a File*

```java
// Include the required libraries

import java.security.KeyPair;
import java.security.KeyPairGenerator;
import java.security.Signature;
import  java.security.SecureRandom;
import javax.crypto.BadPaddingException;
import javax.crypto.Cipher;
import javax.crypto.spec.SecretKeySpec;
import java.io.File;
import java.io.*;

public class CryptoExample{

    private static final String AES_ALGORITHM = "AES/CTR/NoPadding";

    public static void main(String args[]){
        // This is the 16-byte (128 bits) key used to encrypt the file. Use rand
function if needed
        // Should be multiples of 16 bytes
        String secKey = "7890246781043279";

        // This is the actual text file
        File inFile = new File("PlainText.dat");

        // Encrypted file with given key
        File encFile = new File("myCompanyDataEnc.ucf");

        // The same key will be used to decrypt as well
        File decFile = new File("myCompanyDataDec.txt");

        try {
        // use  ENCRYPT_MODE for encryption.
            CryptoExample.justCrypt(Cipher.ENCRYPT_MODE, secKey, inFile, enc-
    File);

            // use  DECRYPT_MODE for decryption. Uncomment this after encryption
works
            // CryptoExample.justCrypt(Cipher.DECRYPT_MODE, secKey, encFile,
decFile);
        }
        catch (Exception er) {
            System.out.println(er.getMessage());
        }
```

```
    } // main


    public static void justCrypt (int cipherMode, String myKey, File inputFile,
File outputFile)
    {
        try {
                // define the key, cipher types and initiate the cipher

            // define the key, cipher types and initiate the cipher
            SecretKeySpec encdecKey = new SecretKeySpec(myKey.getBytes(), "AES");
            Cipher myCipher = Cipher.getInstance(AES_ALGORITHM);
            myCipher.init(cipherMode, encdecKey);

            FileInputStream inComingFileStream = new FileInputStream(inputFile);
            byte[] inFileBytes = new byte[(int) inputFile.length()];
            inComingFileStream.read(inFileBytes);

            // doFinal is the encrypting or decrypting method
            byte[] outFileBytes = myCipher.doFinal(inFileBytes);

            FileOutputStream outFileStream = new FileOutputStream(outputFile);
            outFileStream.write(outFileBytes);
            inComingFileStream.close();
            outFileStream.close();
        }
        // Add as many exceptions as required
        catch (Exception  ex)
        {
            System.out.println(ex.getMessage());
        }

    } // end justCrypt

} // CryptoExample
```

Note that the secKey defined in the code is for AES algorithm, which uses a key of length in multiples of 16 bytes. If you provide a key shorter than 16-byte multiples—say, for example, 19 bytes—the error would be Invalid AES key length: 19 bytes. See question 8 at the end of the chapter for working on this example as an exercise.

In cybersecurity, we often hear a law named Kerckhoff's principle. It states that a system should be designed to be secure if everything about the system, except for the key, is public knowledge. It also means "enemy knows the system" but *not* the key. So, keeping the key is of paramount importance when security is important even if everything else is hacked and becomes public.

If we go back to Example 11-8, we note that the key is embedded into the code and anyone can read it—especially the programmers or internal employees who have access to the Java file. Once any of these employees leave the organization or plot an internal attack while being employed, we have a difficult situation to overcome. For that reason, the key is usually put in a file that's encrypted with another key known only to a few vetted employees who have proven themselves as reliable. The longer the key, the better the security, but again, there is no such thing as a "reliable employee" when it comes to security because we follow the rules of zero trust. Considering the zero-trust policy, the key is changed as often as required or at least with every version of software and/or at least once a year.

In Windows and other operating systems, files can be encrypted and archived. Files can also be associated with a particular program to open automatically. Therefore, it is important to make sure that the association is removed when files need to be secure and contain confidential information. Encryption, archiving, and association can be easily done with the GUI of the operating system and the software itself.

At this point, we have taken good care of our file system, saved in a good manner, not allowed the software programmers to use hard-coded connection strings for data, and so on, but the basic question of initial login with username and password remains the weakest link because social engineering hacks and enticing people to disclose details of a program remain rampant in getting a system down or in stealing data. To overcome this, we can add yet another security layer to the software by implementing smart card login.

Implementing Public Key Infrastructure and Smart Card

PKI was discussed in Chapter 10 about using X.509 certificates (public and private) with the help of certificate stores and issuing and revoking certificates. In general software programs, where allowed, can make use of the smart card logging. But with many general applications on the Internet that offer services, it is hard to implement smart card with certificates. Smart card usage can be best implemented for internal corporate applications that are only accessible for users who have a smart card. Also note that the smart card is not issued to everyone. There is a background check and an elaborate vetting process involved before a card is issued. Once issued, the card is also governed by the corporate policies that deal with least privilege, non-repudiation, and so on.

If a corporation wants to implement smart card access to an application, they also have two options for allowing members access. One way is to use Active Directory, where every smart card holder is registered and let everyone have access. The second way is to deal with an internal small table on the back-end database that stores the names and IDs of smart card users who are allowed to use it. The second option further vets the smart card holders or allows only a few approved users who hold the smart card. In other words, an HR person may not be able to use a project management application, and a programmer may not be able to use an HR payroll program—even if they have a smart card.

The problem with PKI or certificates is that there should be a separate entity to issue, renew, or revoke the certificates on a regular basis. Smart cards also have an expiry date. Lost cards, users forgetting their PIN for the smart card, and users on a long absence (for medical reasons, for example) need maintenance for the smart card. All these involve human, office, time, and financial resources to make it work. Security is a multipronged and a long-standing policy and cannot adapt something like a "one-time done and closed" posture. This is the main reason most web applications implement a not-so-perfect username and password method to log in with other security policies, like multi-factor authentication (or at least two-factor authentication) as a PIN on the user's personal phone or email address. Interestingly, some of these methods have been in place for a long time for phone calls with credit card companies. When someone called their credit card company, the representative who came on the line always asked for the name, Social Security number, some kind of secret code, and the address of the user to confirm that the caller is the true credit card holder. This kind of vetting on the phone is a multi-pronged process to filter fake users. The Internet implements another way of recalling a secret question and a preset answer.

Examples of Key Pairs on Java and Linux

PKI consists of two keys or a key pair—one public key and one private key—for each user. A signature object can also be created in Java and other languages for digital signature and non-repudiation. Verification of signature is also easy with simple built-in methods and processes available in the KeyPair, Signature, and other libraries readily available. Example 11-9 is the listing from a Java script that generates a key pair and signature objects. The script also uses the public key to encrypt a string. It is easy to extend the same code to a file stream instead of a single string to encrypt the files as required.

Example 11-9 *Sample Java Script to Create a Key Pair and Use It in a Signature*

```
import java.security.KeyPair;
import java.security.KeyPairGenerator;
import java.security.Signature;
import java.security.SecureRandom;
import javax.crypto.BadPaddingException;
import javax.crypto.Cipher;

public class CipherSample {
    private static final String AES_ALGORITHM = "AES/CTR/NoPadding";
    //private static final String PROVIDER = BouncyCastleProvider.PROVIDER_NAME;
```

```java
public static void main(String args[]) throws Exception{
//Creating KeyPair generator object
KeyPairGenerator keyPairGen = KeyPairGenerator.getInstance("RSA");

//Initializing the KeyPairGenerator
keyPairGen.initialize(4096);

//Generating the pair of keys
KeyPair pair = keyPairGen.generateKeyPair();

//Getting the private key from the key pair
PrivateKey privKey = pair.getPrivate();

//Getting the public key from the key pair
PublicKey publicKey = pair.getPublic();
System.out.println("Keys generated");

//Creating a Cipher object
Cipher cipher = Cipher.getInstance("RSA/ECB/PKCS1Padding");

//Initializing a Cipher object
cipher.init(Cipher.ENCRYPT_MODE, pair.getPublic());

//Adding data to the cipher
    byte[] input = "My personally identifiable information is now well protected".
getBytes();
    cipher.update(input);

//encrypting the data
    byte[] cipherText = cipher.doFinal();

System.out.println(new String(cipherText, "UTF8"));
System.out.println("The public key is...");
System.out.println(pair.getPublic());
System.out.println("The private key is...");
System.out.println(pair.getPrivate());


Signature mySign = Signature.getInstance("SHA256withRSA");
mySign.initSign(pair.getPrivate());
```

```
        mySign.update(input);
        byte[] digitalSignature = mySign.sign();


        //Verify signature with public key
        Signature yourSign = Signature.getInstance("SHA256withRSA");
        yourSign.initVerify(publicKey);
        byte[] messageBytes = "My personally identifiable information is now well
protected".getBytes();
        yourSign.update(messageBytes);
        boolean isCorrect = yourSign.verify(digitalSignature);
        if (isCorrect==true)
                System.out.println("Signature correctly verified...");
        else
                System.out.println("Sign verification error..");
        } //
}
```

One tests the code shown in Example 11-9 by changing the Java script line for the messagesBytes variable as "My personally identifiable information is NOT well protected." This message would not be the same as the input variable defined to sign the message. Even adding a single space to the messageBytes variable results in an error. Thus, any change in message indicates that the message is not authentic. A similar function or method can be adapted to file encryption and signatures as well.

Linux has a much easier way to create keys and encrypt files. OpenSSL, which we discuss in Chapter 2, "Security Details," can help in a variety of ways. Here are some refreshers. OpenSSL can do both symmetric and asymmetric encryption and decryption as well. For the sake of discussion, assume that we have a file named hello.dat in our folder. If not, create one as a dummy.

Symmetric Encryption

Note the following details before running any commands on Linux:

- We use the same key for encrypting and decrypting in a symmetric system.

- The -p option prints the output with SALT. (SALT is a numeric number of variable length used to encrypt the file or text for a better encryption.)

- aes-256-cbc is the algorithm type used.

- rsa is Rivest-Shamir-Adleman, the inventors of Advanced Encryption Standard aka AES. It can be used with 128, 256 bits. The more the better.

- cbc is cipher block chaining (a method used in the algorithm).

Now run the following commands one by one using **openssl**:

```
openssl enc -aes-256-cbc  -p -in hello.dat  -out hello.enc


Enter password:  The system will ask for password (enter any string
and remember it)
```

To decrypt, use the same **openssl** command with the **-d** option:

```
openssl aes-256-cbc -d  -in hello.enc -out newFile.txt


Enter password:   (Enter a wrong password and check first. Then enter
the correct password)
```

If you entered the correct password, newFile.txt will have readable text that is the same as hello.dat.

Instead of typing the password every time, we can store the key in a file and repeat the openssl.

Store the password (or key) in a file and use it as shown:

```
Openssl rand 128 > mykey.txt                    .... (generate a random
key)
```

or use some user-typed password (any strong password as text in single quotes):

```
echo 'myp@55wo_rd' > mykey.txt
```

Now use the key generated to encrypt the file:

```
openssl enc -aes-256-cbc  -p -in hello.dat  -out hello.enc -k  myKey.
txt
```

Since you used a key as an argument, it will *not* ask for a password anymore.

To decrypt the file, use the same **openssl** command with the **-d** option:

```
openssl aes-256-cbc -d  -in hello.enc -out newFile.txt -k myKey.txt
```

Asymmetric Encryption

Here we use one key for encrypting and a different key for decrypting.

Generate a private key first (with optional bit length):

```
openssl genpkey -algorithm RSA -out myprivatekey.pem -pkeyopt rsa_
keygen_bits:2048
```

-pkeyopt is the option given for number of bits. From the private key, generate the public key:

```
openssl rsa   -in myprivatekey.pem -out mypublickey.pem
```

Using the rsautl utility for the RSA algorithm and the public key, we can encrypt a file:

```
openssl rsautl -encrypt -inkey mypublickey.pem  -in hello.dat  -out hello.enc
```

Now use the private key to decrypt the encrypted file:

```
openssl rsautl -decrypt -inkey myprivatekey.pem  -in  hello.enc  -out newFile.txt
```

You can open newFile.txt with the **cat** command and see the contents, which should be the same as that of the original hello.dat file. Signatures can be added to Linux files with the gpg utility.

Vulnerabilities, Threats, and Web Security

Computer and Internet or web security depends on one thing: YOU. You are always the first line of defense. Simply because a reputable company or an organization releases software doesn't make it automatically immune to attackers. Hackers are smart and always have time to put effort into breaking software. For that reason, many of the software giants have regular updates to their software and send free security patches to fix vulnerabilities.

Applying security patches is one thing, but being aware of a hacking attempt is another. Educating and training employees helps the users recognize a hacking, malware, or a phishing attempt and avoid falling into the trap. Constant awareness is the key in recognizing a threat attempt. Whether the software—either on the front end or back end— was designed by a reputable company or a newbie, vulnerabilities exist, and a threat can materialize.

Junk mail and phishing remain major problems. Phishing encompasses a variety of methods, such as offers of free samples for COVID-19 testing, offers for zero-percent interest on credit cards forever, free distribution of a million dollars from an African nation, tax fraud emails from the Internal Revenue Service (IRS), and many others. Hackers and phishing email senders continue to find new methods to send emails for users to click a link that resembles an authentic website but collects user information. Vulnerabilities exist in the form of free text in website text boxes, SQL injection, man-in-the-middle attacks, website duplication, drive-by downloading, and free software offers that collect personal data of users. In one instance, users were sent friend links on Facebook and received pictures of a woman. After the pictures were received, they were morphed with software into pornographic photos, and the so-called Facebook friends demanded money. Dozens of cases were filed on an Asian nation that had a call center to call U.S. taxpayers about their unpaid taxes and demanded payment with a card. The following remain the top security threats on the Internet:

- Phishing, spear phishing, and whaling

- Ransomware

- SQL injection

- Cross-site scripting

- Denial of service (DoS) and distributed denial of service (DDoS)

- Viruses

- Worms

- Spyware

- Offers for free goods and software

- Internal threats (employees or contractors)

Attack Types and Mitigations

Each organization issues a global threat intelligence report regularly to warn users of impending and current dangers. Because most of the older methods—such as SQL injection, spyware, adware, viruses, and worms—are well known, in this section, we talk about the threats described in the Blackberry annual report from November 2022. To paraphrase the entire report in one sentence, no operating system, framework, software, smartphone, or computer is 100% safe.

Here, we outline some examples of the problems in each operating system. The problems indicated in the following sections should be considered to be additional basic problems that might occur along with website logging, SQL injection, cross-site scripting attacks, and viruses. Some of these attacks, such as ransomware, can happen on any operating system but may be more prevalent on one than another.

Windows

Common attacks in Windows include

- Downloaders, ransomware, infostealers

- File infectors

- Remote access Trojans

Among many problems, Qakbot remains active with Windows. Qakbot is a program that entices users to click a link (usually provided via email) that runs a Java script to initiate installation of a malicious DLL with an ISO file. The DLL has an extension of DAT to fool the user into thinking a data file has been delivered. The links provided and the address the email is sent from look authentic to the users. Regular training of employees, avoiding delivery of emails with strong filters, and explaining to users to be aware of emails that ask users to click a link are some solutions to the problem.

Ransomware is delivered via phishing, whaling, and spear phishing attempts where the user is enticed to download or give information via phone or email. Like software as a service (SaaS) and platform as a service (PaaS), hackers now have ransomware as a service (RaaS) that keeps evolving. The newer versions of ransomware can escape the search of the search programs implemented by the systems administrators, due to the string encryption the ransomware programs implement.

Infostealers work in a variety of ways with programs and ports to steal data. For example, FTP uses port 20 and has a long-known vulnerability. Infostealers are programmed to read VPN credentials, browsers, and so on. Since COVID-19, remote working has become a new norm, and thus many employees use a VPN to connect to the corporate network. A username and password would be required to run the VPN, but a physical smart card and the associated PIN would be a better way to log in to the VPN to avoid information being stolen. Malware as a service (MaaS) is available for hackers to buy and deploy. They use key loggers, screenshots, or other ways to steal data and other credentials such as usernames, passwords, and PINs. Remote access Trojans can detect web cameras and http URLs and read the keystrokes of users to steal the data. File infectors are well-known or new viruses or worms.

However, least privilege and other policies that are set as mandatory access control (MAC) work best. In such cases, an end user receiving an email may be able to click but cannot download or install the ISO file because the user is least privileged and not allowed to download or install any programs. Any new installation needs the system administrator's intervention. Of course, the system administrator should be well aware of the problems with current-day viruses and attacks and refuse to install any programs other than those required for a user to perform their daily functions. If any program is required, it is released and delivered via the software center on Windows and a corporatewide announcement is made about the release. User education, training, and extensive awareness are the keys to avoiding ransomware.

Remember that no one solution will cater to all the problems, and a zero-trust policy that's continually improving and a multipronged security posture are the only way to prevent attacks. Even for home users, the best option is to use a normal account for reading email and accessing the Internet, thereby avoiding automatic installation of software without asking the user for credentials. This is so because of two reasons. One, most operating systems only allow new programs or updates to be installed by only administrative users and, two, programs that install themselves look if the user logged in as an administrator and can assume automatic permissions to force the installation.

macOS/OSX

Common attacks in macOS/OSX include

- Adware/spyware

- Browser hijackers

- Proxy malware and agents

The Mac operating system is less vulnerable to attacks because these systems are not well incorporated in a corporate network for reasons such as price and ease of use of the operating system, but it still has problems with browsers, adware, and other malware. Adware lures users to click a link, which takes the user to a request to install free software to prevent or gain something (also for free, of course). Once that software is installed, the user has virtually opened doors for information to pass back and forth.

Linux

Common attacks in Linux include

- Bots and botnets

- Malware and tooling

- Crypto miners and cryptojacking

Linux is a free and powerful environment for hosting web servers, databases, and more, and many types of software, DBs, and Java back ends depend on Linux for deployment. Cloud services are hosted by Linux as well. In system administrators' circles, the joke goes, "Clouds in the sky are nothing but a bunch of Linux servers."

Botnets—individual bots sending brute force attacks to cause Denial of Service (DoS) or Distributed Denial of Service (DDoS)—are the primary problems in the Linux operating system. Limiting user logins, increasing awareness, and employing least privilege are some methods to prevent attacks on Linux. Not allowing the users to log in directly to system accounts with authentication and implementing **sudo** for high-level commands are other ways.

Mobile Devices

Common attacks on mobile devices include

- Android

- iOS

- Data stealing with apps

As technology is evolving, hackers are going full pace with it and creating their own services and attempts to explore more ways to hack, and smart devices are no exception. Hackers now can create apps and entice users to download them. Numerous apps are known to be stealing data and exploiting end users. In recent times, TikTok and even Facebook have been accused of stealing user data without permission. Europe has dealt with this kind of data stealing with General Data Protection Regulation (GDPR), a European law that established protections for privacy and security of personal data of individuals in European Economic Area (EEA)–based operations and certain non-EEA organizations that process personal data of individuals in the EEA. With GDPR in place, organizations cannot disclose or share data with other organizations. Google and other companies have been fined after being found to have violated GDPR. The United States has similar rules for personal data protection.

Automobile industries, banks, financial institutions, healthcare facilities (nursing homes and hospitals), multinational companies such as oil companies, energy companies such as gas and electric are at the top of the list for hackers for many reasons. The main reason is that these companies are rich and yet poorly protect their networks due to lack of understanding or laziness to upgrade and follow strict security postures. Also, most of the people who work for these facilities are not computer savvy other than using the computers for their minimal daily functioning. Those who are using older systems notice that the companies that sold the equipment or software are no longer in business or have not released any patches for known vulnerabilities. Other than those seeking to hack, none of the people who work for these facilities have time or interest to find the existing vulnerabilities, report them, and fix them. Replacing older systems is expensive and takes time, effort, and retraining of staff. Hacking attacks continue to happen all over the world. Thanks to the Internet and new technologies, the hackers can operate from their own facilities from any country in the world.

The financial industry continues to suffer from attacks as well. Banks, ATMs, and individual users are targeted daily with phishing and free offers that all spell doom at the end. Groups of system administrators continually scan the system logs and new account creations for any undesired activity to try to prevent attacks or malware. Hacking attempts cause two main problems besides financial trouble. The origin of the hacker is usually hidden or compromised—meaning that they may reside in Europe but the logs may show the attacker lives in the United States. Also, the hackers are financed by groups or political stalwarts with command control centers stationed in their own countries to intentionally cause trouble among nations.

As said earlier, the only way to avoid an attack is complete awareness, education, and retraining to help users continuously watch and keep their eyes open. And to remember that the first line of defense—to data, software, front end, back end, cloud, and operating system—always starts with YOU. Feigning ignorance about cross-platform languages, different operating system compatibility, and so on, are not valid excuses when suffering through a painful cyberattack because the attackers now use programming languages that are cross-platform compatible (such as GoLang) and may increase their efforts on Linux and Mac OS as well.

Summary

End users interact with an application that uses different and protected accounts for database transactions. The accounts that connect to DBs use a connection string in the configuration files. If not encrypted, the connection strings are open in plaintext mode and pose a vulnerability.

Both IIS and Tomcat offer security tools for applications. Among them is blocking directory browsing, encrypting the connections strings, and displaying an appropriately coded message rather than using the default provided by IIS. Stored procedures offer a great way of protecting the SQL scripts. Stored procedures can be embedded into most of the language frameworks, such as .NET language packages. Stored procedures also offer a way to debug SQL easily on the DB side for both syntax and semantic mistakes.

File encryptions can also be done using built-in security algorithm classes in most of the language packages and frameworks. OpenSSL in Linux can be used for encryption and decryption with various options on files and messages.

There are various vulnerabilities in each operating system, and some of the vulnerabilities, like ransomware, are common for all operating systems. Each system needs a separate set of checks and mitigations to thwart an attack to keep the system safe.

Chapter 11 Questions

1. Why is it necessary to encrypt a connection string of a database in high-level language programs when deploying the application on a web server?

2. In how many possible ways can we protect the connection string data in high-level language coding?

3. Which is the default configuration protection provider for iisreg.ext in Windows and .NET framework?

4. Is there a way to modify the default errors provided by IIS to end users?

5. On Java Tomcat servers where do the connection strings reside for confidentiality?

6. What is a stored procedure and how does it provide security?

7. How can files be encrypted in Java or Linux with PKI?

8. Modify Example 11-8 and create a long key for the secKey variable with a 32-byte length key from a file instead of typing the key in the code. Run the program and encrypt the file first and then decrypt the file back to a text file. Compare the PlainText.dat file with the decrypted myCompanyDataDec.txt file to make sure they are the same. What happens if you provide a secKey as 7890246781043279MYPASSWORD and compile?

9. Copy the listing from Example 11-9 and create the input variable from a file named ExernalMsg.txt. Create keys and a signature for that file (you can read the bytes from that file to a plaintext message). Verify that signature again and print a message if the signature is correctly verified.

10. What command can do symmetric and asymmetric key generation, encrypting, and decrypting functions in Linux?

Answers to Chapter 11 Questions

1. If the code or configuration file is exposed at all, database connection strings that contain the DB details, IP addresses, and port numbers will be protected if the connection string is encrypted.

2. In more than one way, we can protect the connection data of a database. Some of these methods are hiding the connection string in a separate file, encrypting the connection string with various built-in algorithms, disabling the directory browsing with Internet Information Server (IIS), and encrypting the files.

3. The default value provided for protection is RsaProtectedConfigurationProvider.

4. Yes, IIS provides an Error Pages option for various errors such as 401, 405, 500, and so on. These are simple html files residing on the server. They can be modified to suit one's requirements.

5. The WEB-INF and META-INF folders can hold confidential information and are protected by the server.

6. Stored procedures provide database back-end programmability. Instead of writing SQL statements on the front-end program (which is hard to debug and even to write), coding staff are often encouraged to use stored procedures for confidentiality and for easy error checking on the DB server. Stored procedures are developed first and debugged for errors and are connected easily to datasets in the front end. Several stored procedures can be connected to a dataset or to a table adapter directly in .NET framework. Since all the database operations happen on the back end with stored procedures, they provide better security from hackers or attackers.

7. Java and Linux provide built-in libraries for generating keys—both public and private—and also digital signatures for non-repudiation. Several of the following libraries are helpful:

```
import java.security.KeyPair;
import java.security.KeyPairGenerator;
import java.security.Signature;
import java.security.SecureRandom;
import javax.crypto.BadPaddingException;
import javax.crypto.Cipher;
import javax.crypto.spec.SecretKeySpec;
```

8. Complete this work on your own.

9. Complete this work on your own.

10. The **openssl** command in Linux can do all these functions.

Securing Software—In-House and Vendor

Depending on its resources, requirements, and, of course, finances, an organization can choose to develop software on their own or buy it commercially, if one is available. Commercial off-the-shelf (COTS) software may fit most people's needs, but when it is not sufficient, the only way forward is to create one. Usually word processing, spreadsheet, and presentation software is best purchased or downloaded as an open-source option, like OpenOffice. If you look at the Notepad software that's free with Windows as an accessory, it has very limited functions besides just editing text, but it's still useful for many people. It's a skeleton program that works for basic necessities. Commercial office documents require more than these basic necessities.

When we think of software, as discussed in the earlier chapters, security should come to mind as the very first step. Simply being created by a reputable firm does not mean software has no vulnerabilities and can be installed on the spot. In reality, most purchased software needs to be tested before it can be put on corporate network computers. This is for two reasons: the zero-trust policy and lack of knowledge of what the software does when we install. Does the software have a backdoor Trojan? Does it transmit user data somewhere where it is sold and redistributed to another company? Does the software steal personal data of users? If it is collecting some data, what kind of data does it gather? Since not everything is connected to the Internet, does it also download some packages from other locations? Does it use a third-party library that may or may not be stable and comply with the corporate security policies? How stable is the program when it is used in extreme conditions (running 24 hours a day nonstop for 7 days a week and 365 days a year)? Does it interfere with other programs and libraries of the operating system? Until we know these details and more, we cannot simply get some software and install it.

Internal Development Versus Vendors

When COTS software isn't available, applications should be developed or given contract to develop in house. Software development follows a process, as we discuss in earlier chapters. The process must also follow a lifecycle from start to end. When possible, software development, testing, and deployment should be on independent servers.

Let's consider the vendor or COTS software first and then examine the in-house development with a proper software development lifecycle (SDLC). Each has a different problem and different security challenges. Again, even if our internal staff are excellently vetted and have been working for years and established credibility, our policy must remain the same—zero trust.

Vendor or COTS Software

When we talk about COTS software, we aren't discussing generally available Word, Excel, and other such programs; we're considering an application for banking, sending and receiving utility bills, or a car dealer advertising the available cars and accepting online payments. Better yet, think about software for a scientific application for an organization like NASA. The following considerations apply to this type of software acquisition:

- **Operating system:** Does the software work on any operating system like Linux, Windows, or Mac? Is there a compatibility or test report available?

- **Framework:** What framework does the software need on the background? Once installed, does the software automatically download the latest packages or libraries of the framework or version DLLs? If so, what are the advantages and disadvantages of downloading? Additional loading and installation of third-party tools may not be safe and need added checks on those products.

- **Credentials:** Does the software need special or additional login credentials, or can it be made to work with the existing corporate smart cards without additional log in? Consider this to be a very important factor because additional login credentials are a pain to users as well as less secure. Using an existing smart card makes sure that the software is not used outside the corporate network and conforms to the policies.

- **Space required for the program:** Does the software need a lot of hard disk space, external USB drives, or other memory areas? Does it have a separate database of users? If it has its own data, how is the data and user information stored and protected? Does the software take some backup on a daily or other regular basis?

- **Background processes:** If the software is running any background processes, what are they, and what do they send or receive in and outside the corporate network? What ports or IP addresses does it need to open? If any ports are open, are ports shared with other services that may interfere with the overall functioning of the software?

- **Data transmission:** Does the software use any encryption of data for data at rest and data in transit? If so, what encryption standards does it follow? Where does the data transmission start and end? What channels are used for data transmission?

- **Information or file collection:** What information (user, corporate, or third party— PII or otherwise) and files does the software collect and save for the future? If the software uses some surveys for ratings, where are they sent, and how are they used?

- **Logs:** This is very important to consider for audits. Does the software create logs for users and usage and keep them for audits? Where are the logs stored, and what information is available in the logs? If the logs are easily accessible to all, is there some trouble with log files if a hacker inserts some kind of code into the logs, like the well-known log4j bug?

- **Patches:** All software supplied by a third party (or developed in house) contains some vulnerabilities that will be found sooner or later. How easy or hard is patch management, and how often are the patches released? Does patch management need training and change from one version to the next, or does it remain a standard procedure for all patches released currently and in the future?

- **Versions and contract:** What kind of contract does the software need? Is it a buy-once-own-forever product, or is it a product that is licensed for a fixed number of months/years and will automatically deactivate? During the contract period, if there is a new version released, would it be installed without additional cost? Also, would a new version require a new approval process even if the changes from existing version to new version are minimal?

- **Ease of use:** How easy is the software for normal end users to use? Does it assume a special background (for example, in the engineering or medical field) and training? Is it targeted for a special community only?

- **Breach:** In the case of a data breach by the software or an attacker due to a vulnerability in the software, how does the vendor support or reimburse the customer?

- **Support:** What kind of helpdesk support is available for users, and what are the times the help desk person is available? Is there an additional cost involved?

- **Additional components:** Does the software have additional components sold separately for additional features? For example, software may run very well, but producing reports may require a report server and additional fees.

- **Price and users:** How expensive is the software to buy and maintain? If software is for general use, how many users does it support at one time? Also, is there an additional price for additional users?

Action Plan

The list in the preceding section is not exhaustive, but we can appropriately guess how good the software will be if we know these basic terms. And finally, once we have these items checked out, we need to turn the checklist into an action plan to test the software.

Turning the checklist into an action plan poses several questions, including the following: Where do we test the software if we decided to acquire it? Can we install the software on our network and go ahead? But remember we have a policy of zero trust. If we plan to install the software directly on the network, the entire purpose of the action plan and checklist is defeated. We need an independent machine that would give us ample opportunities to observe the results of testing the software and check the reports we are provided. Once we are happy with the results, the software is then "approved" for deployment and given to end users on development, test, and, finally, production networks.

This is a tedious process, but with good resources (both human and financial), this process becomes easier when various people work simultaneously on the software. Software that meets the corporate policies and other guidelines will then be put on a common area—the software center of Windows or a common shared drive—for people to download and install. By "install," we mean a click-and-done process for end users because not all users are tech savvy and can do a rigorous step-by-step process of choosing components and installing them. Notice also that any software, even if it is approved, is not downloadable on the end user machines because these machines follow the mandatory access control (MAC) and discretionary access control (DAC) rules indicated earlier and would not allow a normal end user to download or install anything. But users can download an approved version of a new software from a software center. However, if the software requires special features, it is only installable by the system administrators. For this, an additional step of the end user requesting the software, the supervisor approving it based on need, and then the software being installed has to happen. A record of these requests must be saved for audits.

We must remember that when the software releases a new version, the new version is not automatically approved but still must go through the entire approval process once more. This all sounds like a pain and a complete waste of time, but it's necessary for security because we must always adhere to zero trust.

In-House Software Development

Let us now turn our attention to in-house software development, which requires an elaborate plan, starting with requirements collection, moving through selecting a SDLC model, and finishing with decommissioning the software. In-house software development also assumes that you have enough financial, time, and human resources as well and have considered all possible constraints. The following are considerations regarding security and how to proceed:

- Which language(s) do you use for coding?

- Is the project manager or team lead aware that the programming language selection is not assigned to a programmer but to a team lead who can envision the final product?

- Are all the coding personnel aware of security considerations, such as input validation and averting an SQL injection attack?

- For what platform(s) or framework(s) is the software going to be developed and used?

- What SDLC would development follow? If a waterfall model (or the like) is selected, how would the organization guarantee the requirements will not be changed?

- Is there a separate environment for development, test, and production?

- Are there any DBs involved in the back end? How much DB space is required at minimum?

- If the DB and front-end coding development environment are not from the same company (for example, Microsoft's Visual Studio for front-end coding and PostgreSQL as the DB on back-end storage/coding), does either the front end or back end (or both) need a third-party component to be installed? If so, how secure and reliable is the third-party component?

- What security, if any, needs to be considered if a third-party bridge/component is required?

- Does the DB need to be encrypted and/or contain personally identifiable information (PII)?

- After the code is complete, who reviews the code?

- Who creates a test plan to see the software in action and test it?

- From a security point of view, how are any login credentials maintained?

- Does the corporation know about the Open Web Application Security Project (OWASP) security procedures and follow a code check step before deploying?

- What tools are used for static application security testing (SAST) or code review?

- Does the written code compile well with built-in tools and pass the code review of the IDE (Visual Studio, Eclipse, NetBeans, and so on)?

- With future patch releases and fixes, will the code successfully follow the continuous testing process with good results?

- What kind of dynamic code testing would it need, and how are the results evaluated?

The list can go on and on. OWASP is a nonprofit organization with a goal of helping website owners and security experts protect web applications from various cyberattacks. Some of the techniques employed by the OWASP can also be applied to desktop applications.

Initial Considerations for In-House Software

Assuming that the project is fixed for in-house software development and the requirements collection was complete, *the* first consideration is to pick a platform, framework, and language for the code. If an organization has various coding languages and many software people who can accomplish the work, the manager has to decide the language, platform, and the framework. Asking a programmer to decide is a bad idea because the programmer may have their own limitations and preferences. A website or an Internet application can be developed both in Java and C#, and the languages look similar in syntax. But does the project involve needs that can be better served by one language or the other? At this point, security depends on the language capabilities and vulnerabilities found or existing in the IDE, operating system, framework, third-party, or any other back-end libraries that may be required, and so on.

Second, what different environments are available for secure development and testing of the application? It's best if the application being considered can be developed on a development server where all the coding, database, and repository are stationed. But do note that this option takes up human, time, and financial resources due to staging, network connections, maintenance, and so on. Security for the second step depends on the back-end database chosen, the environment's abilities to transfer files back and forth to a test machine, safe Internet/intranet connections, and stability when logged in for long hours via remote or network connection.

A third consideration is the type of SDLC model. Usually, programmers or managers do not decide the software model but corporate policies do.

Once these are considered and chosen, a design document is the fourth consideration. Usually the design document has the algorithms and programming like loops, and it explains how each library or module is developed and where it is stored for the team lead to compile the entire project seamlessly to deploy on the test server for a tester. Every method, library, or module must specifically mention security in the design document.

The fifth consideration is the allocation of funds and work and the creation of a schedule with deadlines and the work breakdown structure. The work breakdown structure (WBS) resembles Figure 12-1. The illustration considers a high-level project and divides the hardware and software sections into successive steps and possible security problems. Each step further divides into subtasks, which are allotted to personnel with a timeframe to develop them. At every stage of a task or subtask, security is considered and best attention is given to each aspect of a vulnerability.

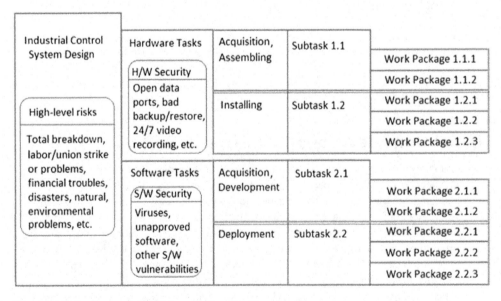

Figure 12-1 *Example WBS in a Project for Two Levels*

The sixth consideration is the coding stage itself. While coding, every stage of the development and tested versions of the software and the milestones accomplished are saved on the code repository such as Visual Source Safe by month, day, and year. In Chapter 10, we discussed software coding practices and standards. These practices are checked and followed at every stage and any "dry code" is rejected and sent back to be rewritten per the organizational policies. It also means the code being written by one person is checked by another person on a regular basis as a quick high-level review. A high-level review does not consider everything about syntax or semantics but does include the coding practices and how the code is written (rudimentary versus professional).

When the code is ready but before it's passed for professional testing, there are two more steps on the development side, which together are a seventh step. These two steps can be done in any order. First is the review of code by another professional who has experience writing and reviewing code per the organizational policies. The code is reviewed line by line and compared against the original user requirements. The code is also pitted against the strict coding standards, readability, and other policies. Note that the code review here is both by manual methods and by using software tools. The second step is the unit testing. Unit testing is done on the programmer's end even if the entire project wants to skip the testing phase later. Unit testing is what the coder performs to check their own code against bugs—both existing and regression varieties. At this stage, most syntax errors have been eliminated, but semantic errors might still remain. Both unit testing and code review also check the security aspects closely to identify any possible vulnerabilities such as buffer overflow, unused variables, arrays, classes, superfluous code, dead code, DB connections that were opened but not closed, passwords and usernames from the front end that aren't validated, and so on. This stage makes sure that the code is well written, well read, and professional, and it works with optimal sources.

In the eighth stage, the code is ready for putting on a testing environment for a tester to check the running code against the functional requirements. The tester at this point would not have access to the source code, IDE, or tools used by the programmer. Instead, the tester gets a release version of the code's executable and required libraries (without any debug information), the original functional requirements of how the code should perform, and a testing document with inputs to supply and outputs to observe. Testers perform code testing without any bias and try to crash the code with unusual inputs and database connections and report in writing with any problems found. From this stage it is normal to go back and forth to the sixth stage of coding. Occasionally, as the code evolves, if the SDLC model chosen allows, this stage may even revert to the first stage for modification of the original user and functional requirements and some changes to the design.

Code Security Check

After the code is ready, it's time for running a security check—a harder version of it actually since all the earlier stages have checked security at every stage. Why do we have to even do this since we already checked the security? It is because we have the zero-trust policy. Maybe the programmer inadvertently made a mistake, but the problem actually might have passed the review and syntax checks. We never know. Now we adopt a different approach for code testing—known as source code analysis tool for static application security testing (SAST) tools. The first example is a simple tool available in most programming languages. Figure 12-2 shows the embedded tool in Visual Studio. We discuss each item in Figure 12-2 one by one.

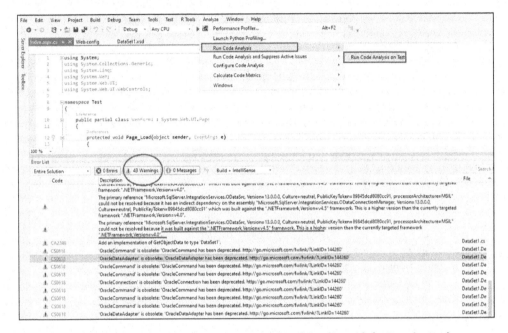

Figure 12-2 *Code Analysis Tool in Microsoft Visual Studio and the Results in the Bottom Window*

1. The code is analyzed on a website application that has one page (index.aspx) and one dataset named Dataset1.xsd. The web.config file is auto included in the project. The code analysis shows several warnings (43).

2. A programmer may have started coding with what is given to them in the Visual Studio installation, and it didn't show any syntax or semantic errors in the compilation or manual review. Notice the red underlines of the message in the bottom window; the code built in a higher version of the .NET framework than it is targeted. This mismatch needs to be corrected.

3. There is no GetObjectData() in Dataset1. If the programmer thinks this basic option is not required, it can be ignored.

4. It appears that the project was using Oracle DB on the back end but uses an OracleDataAdapter that's obsolete (old or deprecated). It shows that the programmer did not implement a better version of the Oracle driver for connections. This could be a problem if the system administrator of the server already installed a new version

of Oracle drivers for the database. This code has no bugs or semantic errors on the development or test servers, but may fail on the production server.

5. Clicking each warning link provided (CS0618, for example) takes us to more details of the warning and how it can be avoided. For CS0618, Microsoft provides the information in Example 12-1 for how it is generated and how it can be avoided.

Example 12-1   *Microsoft's Example of Producing a CS0618 Error in Code and How to Avoid It*

```
// CS0618.cs
Using System;

public class C
{
       // warn if referenced
       [Obsolete("Use newMethod instead", false)]
       public static void m2()
       {
       }

       public static void newMethod()
       {
       }
}

class MyClass
{
    public static void Main()
    {
       C.m2();  // This call will result in "CS0618"
    }
}
```

6. The code analysis in Visual Studio does not fix the code but can only point out possible errors that may occur. Fixing or ignoring those is the team's responsibility.

Fixing the Final Product—SAST Tools

Dozens of SAST tools are available in many varieties, forms, prices, and colors. Choosing a tool is not easy because not all tools are built for a quick fix-it frizzle. OWASP recommends picking a tool that could cater to the well-known and documented top ten vulnerabilities, which are shown in Figure 12-3.

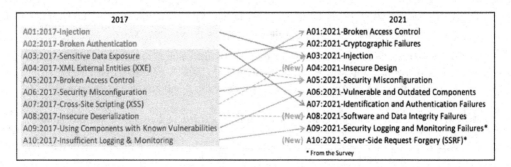

Figure 12-3 *OWASP's Top Ten Vulnerabilities Listed as Three Classes*

The list shown in Figure 12-3 is "as viewed or known now" and is not the absolute final list. The list also has changed from the previous list of 2017 because, given the conditions, hackers continue to evolve their methods and use faster technology for their attacks. OWASP has done the benchmark testing of the available products and indicates the following point to keep in mind when selecting a SAST tool. Of course, the very first item to check is the compatibility of the tool to the programming language used.

■ Accuracy of the tool to point out a vulnerability

■ False positive/false negative rates

■ Ability to understand the libraries/frameworks implemented

■ Requirement for buildable source code

■ Ability to run against binaries such as DLL and EXE files (instead of source)

■ Availability as a plugin into preferred developer IDEs

■ Ease of setup/use/maintenance/upgrade

■ Ability to include in continuous integration/deployment tools or run independently

■ License cost (might vary by user, organization, app, or lines of code)

■ Interoperability of output (type of file, ease of reading and reporting)

Many of the SAST tools have what is known as a rules pack that changes regularly and needs updating by the user or administrator. The SAST tools can also be easily embedded into the IDE, so the programming staff can run the tool from within the development environment. A sample run may show a pie graph similar to the one depicted in Figure 12-4. It's important to notice that the majority of problems is caused by database access control (usernames, passwords, open connection strings, bad scripts). The list of problems is also categorized in a table in Figure 12-5.

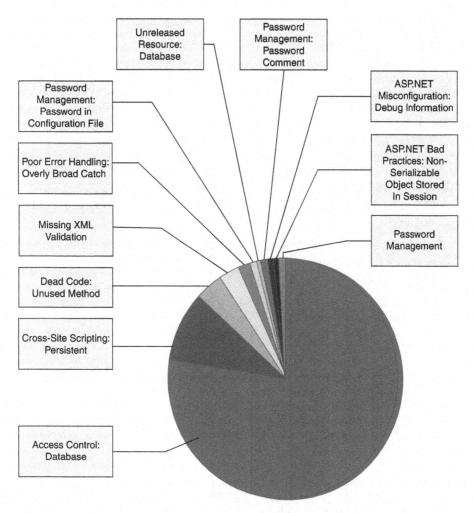

Figure 12-4   *SAST Tool Showing Possible Concerns as a Pie Graph*

Issues by Category	
Access Control: Database	9
Cross-Site Scripting: Persistent	2
Dead Code: Unused Method	5
Missing XML Validation	4
Poor Error Handling: Overly Broad Catch	2
Password Management: Password in Configuration File	1
Unreleased Resource: Database	1
Password Management: Password in Comment	1
ASP.NET Misconfiguration: Debug Information	1
ASP.NET Bad Practices: Non-Serializable Object Stored in Session	1
Password Management	1

Figure 12-5   *List of Concerns by Category*

In Figure 12-5, notice the error of poor error handling: Overly Broad Catch. This indicates the code has a try-catch-finally script but uses something like

```
catch (exception ex)
{
}
```

In this instance, the catch statement is trying to look for an exception. But if the exception arises from file handling, bad input, bad DB connection, or something similar, it will not point to the exact error. In other words, a generic catch will just catch a bug, and the coding personnel will have a hard time trying to find out where the error is coming from to determine how to fix it. The basic logic of using try-catch is to catch a specific error, correct it, and rerun the failed script to avoid a crash, but this overly broad catch defeats that basic purpose of try-catch.

Let's look at another item reported in the SAST tool—Password Management: Password in Configuration File. Upon looking into the configuration file, we find the following listing for a database connection:

```
</connectionStrings>
    <add name="myConnString"
            connectionString="DATA SOURCE=(DESCRIPTION=(ADDRESS =
            (PROTOCOL = TCP)(HOST = 11.12.21.22)(PORT = 1588))
            (connect_data = (sid =
            myDBID)(SERVER = DEDICATED)));PASSWORD=mysecpa55word
            ;PERSIST SECURITY
            INFO=True;USER ID=Ap_dev_user; Validate
            Connection=true"
            providerName="Oracle.DataAccess.Client" />
</connectionStrings>
```

Because the password is exposed in the connection string, we will encrypt it with some tool (as discussed in earlier chapters). We will then be more secure. But what if you find the following listing in the configuration file? Is the password encrypted, or are the hexadecimal characters actually the correct password? To find that, we will have to dig into code to look for any decryption method written or the password:

```
<configuration>
    ...
    <appSettings>
        <add key="pwd" value="0xAcD82k834301AF" />
    </appSettings>
    ...
</configuration>
```

Now, looking at the configuration file, the coder and reviewer may not have any doubt or feel something is wrong about the script. But a SAST tool can show something like the following warning for the programmer to double-check.

If the configuration file has a default password, be sure to obscure or mask it in the configuration file. For example, the configuration listed may have an encrypted password with the hexadecimal value *0xAcD82k834301AF* as follows.

```
<configuration>
    ...
    <appSettings>
        <add key="pwd" value="0xAcD82k834301AF " />
    </appSettings>
    ...
</configuration>
```

But verify and locate where the password is used in the entire code and check that a decryption algorithm was deployed. If no decryption algorithm exists in the code, then probably the password has hexadecimal characters (to make it hard for users to remember). Note that the application still has not overcome the vulnerability because the password is stored in plaintext, although it was actually hexadecimal characters.

As another example from a JSP file, consider the error pointed out by the SAST tool shown in Example 12-2.

Example 12-2   *Validating the Returned Value of a Function*

```
Problem: Bad or No Input Validation
Details:  A method in index.jsp may be sending unvalidated data to a web browser on
  line 24, and may lead to browser executing malicious code.
Page Source: myJavaPage.jsp:13  getParameter()
11 adminString = adminString.replaceAll("[^A-Za-z0-9_/.&?=-]", "");
12 }
13 String myID = request.getParameter("WindowsSA");
14 if(myID!=null){
15 myID = myID.replaceAll("[^A-Za-z0-9_/.&?=-]", "");
...
...
23
24 <FRAME>
```

The code seems harmless, but the SAST tool is asking the user to double-check if the returned valued from getParameter() needs to be validated because it may contain some SQL script or something that might expose data to a hacker.

Let's look at another example reported by the SAST tool, as shown in Example 12-3, and how easily a programmer can forget this kind of error.

Example 12-3   *Bad Assignments of Variables Might Show an Error*

```
Problem: Improper code
Details: getInformation() in myFile.java can crash the program by dereferencing a
  null-pointer on line 14. myFile.java:14 Dereferenced : attributeObject()


getInformation()
{
...
12 catch (ClassCastException castex) {
13 /* The attribute had the wrong class. */
14 String myName = attributeObject.getClass().getName();
15 LogUtility.log.debug("In getBoardId(): Session attribute \"cpdProcessForm\" has
unexpected type: " + myName);
...

...

}
```

The string myName was initiated on the same line, and the value might be either null or valid depending on the attributeObject(). It was not set to any value in the first case. And there is no check for the myName variable, such as (if(myName==null)...). This is a bad programming practice that may result in hard-to-catch errors.

In the last example produced by the SAST tool, we can see a concern raised on the Java server page, as shown in Example 12-4.

Example 12-4   *Print Statement Might Expose Some Information*

```
Details: A function in myJavaPage.jsp might expose system data or debugging
  information by calling print() on line 27. The information exposed by print()
  may help an attacker in creating a novel attack.

Where: myJavaPage.jsp:Line 11 System.getProperty()
9
10 <%
11 String subNod = System.getProperty("system.jb.node.name", "----");
12 subNod  =  subNod.substring(subNod.length()-4, subNod.length());
13 %>
Sink: hrcBanner.jsp:27 javax.servlet.jsp.JspWriter.print()
25 <td width="30%"> </td>
26 <td width="15%" align=right valign="bottom">
27 <b><font color=maroon>node:<%= subNod %>  v2.9.22.6</font></b>
28 </td>
```

Each of these problems needs to be addressed before a final executable is deployed. One important thing that needs to be mentioned is the report produced by the SAST tool.

Some tools produce an XML file, some produce a different format file that can be read only by the SAST tool, and some tools have the ability to create a PDF report for distribution. It is important for everyone to know that a generic XML file is more acceptable than a special format file because not all users may have the SAST tool installed on their machine.

Fine-Tuning the Product—Testing and Release

Once the code is ready with all bugs shown by the SAST tool cleared up or fixed, the SAST tool is run again to make sure the concerns shown earlier no longer pose a threat. It is also possible to go through another round of testing with the testing group to make sure that after the SAST tool recommendations were followed, there are no further errors or regression errors. The programming group actually has the errors listed in another software tool for reference. When an error is fixed, a note is made for the fix. After all the known errors are eliminated, executable code can be deployed on the production server or distributed via media, assuming that it also passed the testing phase and did not cause any regression errors (in a second deployment or later). At this stage, can we feel that our code is secure and there is nothing else to fix? That is our next topic of discussion. The code that will be deployed is the release version without any debug files. A final check on all the security details on the software is required as well before sending the code to production servers.

Deploying an application on a production server involves planning, setting up a time, and validating the deployment. Programmers or testers or even project or program managers cannot install and deploy any applications or software on the servers. It is the job of a system administrator (SA). Products are deployed by working in tandem with the SA to set up login credentials (with a smart card, if required), multifactor authentication, tools, frameworks, and libraries required for the application to run and checking the disk sizes on both the production server and the back-end database. These are necessary steps to make sure that the application does not overrun the allotted sizes or quickly overwhelm the servers when a huge number of people try to access the application. If a huge number of people are expected to be using the application, several servers are banded together with a switch, such as F5, and code is deployed on all servers at the same time. Depending on the number of users expected and the load on the database or servers, the SA will likely decide how many servers are required.

Finally, we note a few more things about documentation and accessibility of servers. Programmers have the responsibility to create the documentation, standard operating procedures, user guides, and test documents for software they write. They have access to the development server where they can deploy the application (either as a debug version or as a release version) and test; this server is their playing field. Once they are happy with the code, the application development group may not have access to test servers to deploy the application. The SA will do the release version of code deployment on test servers as well with the help of programmers. There is an important point to consider when deploying a release version of the code. It contains smaller size files, needs less memory space, has a smaller attack surface, and would not reveal any more information than is minimally required. Programmers may be able to test on the test servers independently, but their testing may not reveal important problems. This is the reason why the tester and programmer have to do their jobs with the policies of separation of duties and the least privilege. When the code is deployed on production servers, the coder or tester may or may not have access to the deployed application. It all depends on the corporate policies. Are we done with the software and can we relax and be happy that we did our best to create secure software and protect user and corporate data? We do not know that for sure until one of those nightmares happen because once the software is open to the public or end users, they will operate in a different realm and with a different mental state to cause a crash or create trouble. If a hacker finds a vulnerability, they will even try to hack the server and get the data they need. For this reason, deployed software needs constant vigilance.

Logs needs to be checked daily, databases need to be monitored, user logins (time of login and functions they are doing with the software) are checked, locked accounts (if any) are dealt with, and firewall logs need attention. Corporations releasing their own software call this step continuous monitoring. Audit teams also check the software to make sure the software follows the policies and any deficiencies are corrected immediately.

Patches and Updates

As a part of continuous monitoring, it is the policy of most corporations to check what is wrong with the deployed software, find any bugs, and fix them quickly. Some examples of problems that are both not very serious and are very serious are listed in Table 12-1.

Next comes the question of when does the organization fix these problems. Some corporations fix problems on a daily basis but release the update or a patch on a regular schedule. For example, Microsoft releases updates on every second Tuesday of the month. Oracle releases every quarter, and Red Hat Linux has no fixed agenda but releases whenever they fix something—sometimes daily and sometimes in a few days, weeks, or months. However, they recommend that the patches be applied quickly or within 30 days or so. If a corporation decides to apply patches, we know that the patch has to be first tested on a standalone machine before it can be allowed to be installed on end user machines.

There are also a few other considerations. As an example, for viewing some PDF files in code, Visual Studio programmers may use a PDF library such as Crystal Reports, and for connecting to Oracle with Visual Studio, they may need Oracle Data Access Components. These are libraries provided by respective organizations that can be installed easily. Dozens of these extensions are available free or for purchase on Microsoft stores. There are also NuGet packages that might be tested. Each of these need to be tested before they can be installed. Some database software packages such as PostGreSQL are free and extensively need NuGet packages to read data. If the data is PII and the NuGet package is not validated correctly, we may not know how secure that package is. Like Microsoft and other software companies that release their own software, the NuGet package owners release their own fixes. Every time there is a library or package fix, these need to be evaluated and combined into the software. If we install a package without looking into their background and research, the package may be decommissioned for security reasons, and yet we might continue using it, thereby causing or keeping a vulnerability intentionally open. This is the main reason why every piece of software needs a continuous monitoring process to check what needs to update.

Table 12-1   *Software Problems That Need Attention for Patching*

Serious Problems That Need an Urgent Fix	Problems That Need to Be Fixed but Not Urgent
Newfound vulnerability that can be used to load virus (for example, Log4j problem).	Spelling or grammar mistakes in the help file.
Software shows "illegal option," and crashes when selecting a particular option in the menu.	The user manual says the file can be saved in various formats, including PDF and TXT, but the file saving dialog box does not have these options.
Network administrators found that the software leaves a communication port open even after the software is closed.	A warning message box sounds a ding on speakers and the ding sound is randomly continued while using the software.
The software does not validate input in a text box in a second window after logging in.	For every chosen option, a new message box pops up and frustrates the users.
Software abruptly closes all windows and restarts on choosing the "analyze" option on code review.	There might be broken links for the URL when the software asks users to refer to a link in the given URL.
A displayed error makes no sense to end users and only shows "this operation cannot be completed at this time."	A help file shipped with a patch/service pack is not updated but is still the same help file from older version.
The software allows some users to see the password in plaintext.	Software updated still shows the version number as an older version.
The software doesn't have protection for newly found malware named Covid-19Infection.	The selected option in a given list of options works OK but shows a weird message briefly.
The software allows users to send emails to others freely and anonymously.	A bothersome message box asking to allow or not allow displays every time the software opens (chosen settings not saved).
The software downloaded cannot be verified with the hash provided.	The website error messages to end users are not well-constructed sentences.
The utility company's software prints utility bills for customers showing they owe $50,000 or more every month.	When typing a password correctly per policies, the software displays "this option is not available at this time," but also changes the password correctly.

A **hot fix** needs to be installed immediately, whereas a **cold fix** might need to close the running software, other programs, and operating system, and restart—and it can be done silently at night. A single **patch** (small-size fix for a single problem) or a **service pack** that contains several patches is available for users to download and install. This shows that continuous monitoring is important to learn what needs to be fixed and how soon. Continuous monitoring is done in several ways, among which user input and internal or external hacking attempts are checked regularly. These checks are only possible if someone is vigilant, is trained well, reads logs daily, and checks the front- and back-end details.

Auditing helps check whether the software is following the security and other policies per the organizational rules and recommends changes. Auditors are best chosen as third-party personnel for their unbiased views. Any remediations suggested by the auditors need to be implemented. In any case, as long as the software is for sale, is maintained and functioning, monitoring is mandatory and bug fixes need to be sent regularly. Security holes, however small, are always a problem as vulnerabilities and can be used by attackers at any time to create a threat. Software released with major changes, updates, and more features is usually given a new version number and sold at higher prices. Like everyone does, the software companies have their own learning curve and continue to improve their software features and diversify. Any company that is sold to another company advises their users of the contacts in the new organization, should a problem arise.

Product Retirement/Decommissioning

Everything finally comes to a conclusion and software is no exception. Software that's no longer required or used and is outdated or upgraded to a better version needs to be decommissioned or removed. Decommissioning requires a detailed plan to notify all personnel about the decommissioning, the people involved, the front end and back end that are affected, accounts to be removed, functions that will not be available, and the lack of support (help or technical) once the software is removed. The following personnel are informed in advance and asked for input:

- End users

- System administrators

- Network administrators

- Database users

- Database administrators

- Office or project managers

Retired products might not get updates but might remain in use if the end user requires. Windows XP version is an example of this software before it was removed. Usually, a software product is put into retirement first and then decommissioned after a few months of grace period. The time of a few months is a flexibility for users to upgrade to the next version of software that has better features. Once a software is about to be decommissioned, it is important to address any objections raised by the users or administrators in the grace period. If the users want to continue using the same older version of software, they are given a warning that support will not be available, and any security breaches need to be dealt with on their own; the parent company disowns all the responsibility for a breach. These paper or electronic communications to users are all stored records for the purpose of law, audit, and organizational policies. Software-producing companies might also go bankrupt and abruptly close. In such cases, there is no further warning or support.

End users will migrate to new software or decide their own fate with the help of their managers. Database administrators (DBAs) need to know the details of decommissioning of the database, which are related to the application being decommissioned; DBAs may need to

- Back up data, formatting, and reports
- Back up database objects and user accounts
- Back up any scheduled jobs
- Clean up or drop/purge database objects
- Remove user accounts, if any
- Remove object roles and permissions
- Free the tablespaces and disk space
- Purge DB logs, if any
- Remove allowed IP addresses and port numbers allotted to the software
- Inform their own team of the upcoming decommission and decision not to support
- Cancel any log accumulation in files or emails

Network and system administrators will need to

- Back up the files used for the software
- Back up logs for the future audits, if any
- Remove/close the active IP addresses
- Close ports used by the software if any
- Remove firewall rules created for the software
- Monitor the URLs if any are set up for the software
- Remove the setup from IIS, Tomcat, or other servers
- Redirect any support requests to the helpdesk

If the software works with Active Directory (AD0, smart card login, or other corporate methods), those people who allot permissions to users for using the AD or smart cards are informed as well. When decommissioning, those administrators need to remove these additional permissions given for the software so as not to allow any end user to run the decommissioned software or misuse those permissions in another way.

The grace period is when all these backup jobs are done and on a scheduled date, all the personnel work in tandem to remove the application from servers and general use. Once removed, further requests of any kind are not entertained, and the software is supposed to have died its natural death. The backup data, logs, and other items created by the network and database administrators are kept for a time per data backup policies of an organization. They are destroyed later, again per the data destruction policies of the organization. This kind of care is necessary for preserving the data and security posture of the organization because our basic skeleton item for any of the policies remains "zero trust." Once the scheduled deadline passes, an email is sent to all about the removal of software and support. No further requests of any kind—even for the backed-up data—are entertained.

Summary

Software can be developed in house (internally) or purchased from vendors. Commercial off-the-shelf (COTS) software first must be evaluated for compatibility on the operating system, what credentials are used, what framework it needs, and other details. Software can be a single package or updated on a contract basis. Action plans need to be prepared for the COTS software and be checked regularly.

In-house software has many considerations before the software is developed, along with the third-party libraries and other accessories that may be required for it to function. The software platform, framework, and libraries used need constant updating and patching. Code security for in-house software can be checked with various tools, either from within a package such as Microsoft's Visual Studio or with a third-party tool such as Fortify (or both). The outputs produced by these tools need to be checked and corrected for each concern pointed out by the tool.

Product retirement follows a different rule set. All concerned parties discuss what resources the package uses and decommission each resource to that product one by one without jeopardizing other applications. A retired software product, its software code, and the database are usually backed up and kept for a few years per the organizational policies before they are completely destroyed.

Chapter 12 Questions

1. Microsoft has released a new service pack for Windows computers. How does a corporate system administrator decide when to install the update on the corporate computers?

2. List five reasons why vendor software needs to be tested before it is installed on a corporate network.

3. After a list of checks for vendor-acquired software is created, what is the next step before acquiring the software from the vendor?

4. What are the basic rules for developing software in a corporate environment?

5. At what point of the work breakdown structure (WBS) does security of the software come into consideration?

6. Why are the programmers who create the software not a good choice for testing their own software?

7. How is the code reviewed once it passes the testing phase or unit testing?

8. Why is it necessary to do a code review with a software tool after the software is ready and found to have no syntax errors?

9. What are the top five vulnerabilities created by the OWASP?

10. What are some of the important features required for a good software application security testing (SAST) tool?

11. The following program was pointed out by a SAST tool as a potential error. How would you find the error and fix it if you are the programmer?

```
public findMyString()
{
        /* The attribute may have a wrong value */
        String myName = attributeObject.getClass().getName();
        LogUtility.log.debug("In getBoardId(): Session attribute \
        "getNameForm\" has some
        unknown data: " + myName);
        ...
        ...
        ...
}
```

12. What should database and network administrators do when a software product is decommissioned?

Answers to Chapter 12 Questions

1. After checking and testing the service pack on an independent machine and immediately after the service pack passes the test.

2. The following are some of the several reasons: 1) What background processes does the software run? 2) What data does the software collect and transmit? 3) Does the software support patching for breaches or vulnerabilities if any? 4) What network IPs or ports does the software open and use? 5) What disk space or database space does it require? 6) How easy is the software to use and is there helpdesk support for the end users of the software?

3. Turn the checklist into an action plan and implement. This is also known as thoroughly checking the software against the created checklist.

4. Sticking to an SDLC, selecting a development model, creating documentation, choosing a security posture, selecting resources (coding platform, framework, coding language, human, financial, time), creating software on the development machine, unit testing on the programmer machine and the development server, testing the release version by a different person on the test server, deploying the bug-free software on a production server, continuous monitoring, and optionally decommissioning the software.

5. From the very beginning step to the very end of WBS, security is considered at every level, task, sublevel, and subtask.

6. Due to biased views and the policy of separation of duties, programmers must not be involved in testing the software.

7. Code that runs without syntax errors must be manually reviewed by another programming person who pits the code against the original user requirements and 1) checks code readability, 2) checks compatibility with corporate coding practices and policies, and 3) finds any unchecked issues.

8. Many issues not found by manual code reviewers are usually found with software application security testing (SAST) tools. These issues may include bad libraries, mismatched versions of frameworks or operating system, and deprecated versions of external components.

9. They include broken access control, cryptographic failures (for example, expired certificates), injection (for example, SQL), insecure/bad design, and security misconfiguration (for example, open and plaintext passwords).

10. The following are some important features required for a good software application security testing (SAST) tool:

    - Accuracy of the tool to point out a vulnerability

    - False positive/false negative rates

    - Ability to understand the libraries/frameworks implemented

- Requirement for buildable source code

- Ability to run against binaries such as DLL and EXE files (instead of source)

- Availability as a plugin into preferred developer IDEs

- Ease of setup/use/maintenance/upgrade

- Ability to include in continuous integration/deployment tools or run independently

- License cost (might vary by user, organization, app, or lines of code)

- Interoperability of output (type of file, ease of reading and reporting)

11. The variable myName does not have a check. It is not initialized, and if the getName() method or the getClass() method returns a null or invalid, myName will have a null value. Then the following debug() will show a wrong value for the myName variable. As a programmer, always initialize a variable and check for null. The following could be a better option:

```
String myName = null;
muName = attributeObject.getClass().getName();
if (myName !=null)
LogUtility.log.debug("In getBoardId(): Session attribute \
"getNameForm\" has some unknown data: " + myName);
else
messageBox(myName variable read from getName() is null")
```

12. They first should back up data, files, and settings that are related to the software. They should also remove any allowed IP addresses and close ports that are no longer required, remove firewall monitoring, database objects, user permissions, roles, and inform their own team of the decommissioning and stopping of further support for the software.

Security Administration

Each day, programmers are busy writing code, and technical administrators—such as network, system, or DB administrator—are busy with their respective jobs. The program and project managers are working with their teams to meet deadlines and keep the team on their feet. None of these personnel can actually check background of a new or existing user, new programmer, or any other new employee who wants access to a software program, system, or smart card. In fact, these personnel are simply unfit to do the background checks and other required necessities before access is granted. There must be other employees who are experienced to deal with this kind of administrative work of filling forms, checking credit, doing background investigation, and getting clearance for new employees and keeping in touch with all the current employees. This is a process that requires a significant paper or electronic trail, signatures, and permissions (both permissions requested and granted or revoked).

In this chapter, we first talk about three important steps any employee must go through and why they are necessary. These steps come after a new employee is onboarded or given an offer of employment and enters an office. These also apply to those who are already employed for a while and need additional privileges. Notice the word *need*; privileges or access is provided when there is a need but not when an employee "wants" them.

Least Privilege, Need to Know, and Separation of Duties

Least privilege by its definition allows the minimum required equipment, access, software, and other facilities required for an employee to do their job. It also tells the employee not to poke their nose into matters unnecessary for their regular work. Here is an example: A programmer is hired to code a scientific application for desktop use. He is given access to the Windows operating system, a development machine with Visual Studio, and a back-end database of SQL Server Express. They can log in to the development machine and create, test, and save the work on a code repository whenever they want. If the programmer wants to access the hosting Windows server to check other business transactions on the back-end database, they would be simply told by the administrators, "You do not have to worry about those," for the reason we've mentioned before: zero trust. As far as the programmer is concerned, their job does not require them to get access to the Windows server that will host their application. They also don't need to know what other businesses are conducted on the back-end database. All they have to do is use their given privileges and complete the work allotted. Given this condition, we now know that the programmer needs to know some details without ever needing to know other details that are not required for their job.

"Need to know" depends on the level of clearance an employee is given. No information is disclosed to anyone unless there is a need for the person to know. For example, a human resources person does not need to know the IP address of a database server, the ports used for a networking firewall, or why an employee's manager put a great comment and recommended promotion for a junior employee bypassing all the senior employees in a particular department. It is not the job of HR to decide or know those details. As an employee progresses in a firm, they may be given more responsibilities and higher privileges, thereby forcing the clearance levels to change. With stricter clearance levels given to an employee, the employee may need to know more details of something they have to deal with. Then the need-to-know levels change, privileges are escalated, and more information will be provided. Downward scaling of privileges likewise applies to employees who are not performing well, and the need to know will be restricted further as well.

Separation of duties is the third principle that must be implemented to separate what work each person can perform. This principle states that a person should not do more than one task in a priority activity. Separation of duties helps detect fraud, biased or bigoted comments, security flaws, and more. For example, a programming group may have a few disgruntled people who can write a logic bomb in the code, and the code can compile without syntax and semantic errors. When the code is reviewed by software, it will fail to detect any errors or problems. But when the code is reviewed line by line by a third party, the logic bomb can be detected. Likewise, the programmer should not be doing the job of a DB administrator or that of a network administrator because that would mean the programmer would have access to information that should not be disclosed to anyone or could exploit the information. Separation of duties helps everyone do their jobs independently but in tandem when working together. It also protects the privileges of one user from the others. In a large corporation, teams working together can create a cadence and follow the steps one by one. Note that there is a backup contact for each branch and one branch does not interfere with the work of other branches. Table 13-1 shows details of an example cadence when a new program is being deployed. Teams agree to the cadence in advance and follow the steps for successful deployment.

Table 13-1 *Cadence Prepared to Show Each Member/Team's Responsibility as Separation of Duties*

Date and Time	Details of Work	Main Contact	Backup Contact
21 Aug 2018 0800 AM-0845 AM	Network administrator sets up firewall's inbound and outbound rules for the application.	Charlotte	Bill
21 Aug 2018 0845 AM-0915 AM	Windows system administrator copies files required for the application, enables the Internet Information Server and its ports.	John	Maria
21 Aug 2018 0915 AM-0945 AM	Database administrator keeps the DB ready and open for the application.	Beatrice	Dean
21 Aug 2018 0945 AM-1145 AM	Programming, test, and other groups test the application live.	Programming group	Testing group, security branch
21 Aug 2018 1200 PM-1215 PM	Closure, successful deployment.	All groups	All groups

Note that all the staff and branches agree to revert, roll back, or clean the changes made, if any, in case of a problem with any group that might result in unsuccessful deployment. In such cases, roles remain the same, but a different date is chosen, and a fresh cadence with a new date and time is prepared. It also means that the duties of one group will not be mixed or transferred to another group if problems arise. Each group has to solve their own problems and work in tandem with the other groups. In some cases, when many groups are involved, the cadence can run for more than 48 hours. The times mentioned are also flexible by a few minutes (earlier or later) for unforeseen circumstances and for each group to communicate with other groups about the progress.

Rotation of work is another kind of subpolicy implemented by large organizations for detecting fraud and for supporting one employee when they go on vacation or leave. The logic behind the rotation of work is that if only one employee is assigned to some work, in their absence, a second employee should be trained to complete the work. Also, if only one employee knows how to do a particular task, they may do some kind of mischief or steal some data or information. The second employee can detect those issues when the work is rotated to other employees. In small organizations, this may not work, but in general, rotation of work is also good in places that have people working shifts that cover 24 hours a day. In such cases, people who work during the daytime update those who work at night with what was accomplished during the day, and vice versa.

Who Is Who and Why

The following list describes some of the important roles in the security administration branch. It is important to note, however, that this list of roles may or may not exist in every organization, and in some places, other designations might exist.

- **The chief privacy officer (CPO):** After various problems with dozens of laws around the world and the emergence of GDPR for the European nations, this newly created position protects different types of important data. A CPO has the job to protect data of the customers, company, employees, vendors, and so on.

- **The chief security officer (CSO):** This person is responsible for the security of the physical and digital assets in an organization. The CSO should be able to visualize the security vulnerabilities an organization may possibly face and determine how well the organization's assets (of all types) are protected.

- **CSO and CISO:** The chief information security officer (CISO) usually handles the security of technology—both hardware and software. The CISO also has extensive knowledge of the computer systems, programming, deployment methods, tools used, systems to be acquired, retired, and so on. The role of the CSO is much broader compared to the CISO role. The CSO takes a holistic view of the organization's business risks, physical security, technological risks, and other possible risks. The CISO should usually report directly to the CSO, and they should work together to reduce the attack surface on the organizational exposure to the Internet and general public.

- **Security steering board:** Security is everyone's responsibility and is never a one-person job. Therefore, all security decisions are put to the security steering board/committee, which includes staff from each department who come together to make a good decision collectively. The CEO or a mutually agreeable official in the organization elected by other staff can chair the board. Other C-level managers and department executives and the internal auditor can work with the chair. The security steering board meets regularly to discuss the organizational stance to the security posture and makes modifications as required.

- **Audit committee:** This generally consists of an internal audit followed by an external audit by a third party. Organizations designate an employee familiar with the cybersecurity as an internal auditor. This person should have transparency and accuracy of the organization's security posture and communicates the reports to all stakeholders to instill confidence in how the organization is protecting the data and information systems. The audit committee has more than just one internal auditor and has employees from all departments. Audits are conducted regularly, and reports are generally available to anyone who has a need to know. External auditing should happen at least once a year by a third party who provides an unbiased view of how well the organization is performing their data protection and following the security policies. External auditors may work with the internal auditors and produce a report for the audit committee. Recommendations given by the third-party auditor are considered, discussed, and implemented as soon as possible.

- **Information systems security officer (ISSO):** This person can be appointed for each department or for the entire organization, depending on the size of the organization. ISSO is a point of contact for proper forms to sign for the users, informing users of the training, possible threats arising from known and unknown vulnerabilities, data leaks, breaches, if any, and so on. They work with the network and system administrators to keep the workforce up to date about the ongoing security problems. ISSOs work with the **information systems security manager (ISSM)** to draft a security posture with policies, update the policies, check the clearance for users or labels for the objects, sign forms for allowing authorization, remind users of security training lapses, and keep the workforce up to date about the security rules and regulations. The ISSO may or may not be a technical person but does need some technical knowledge about the ongoing processes in the organization and about cybersecurity. Individual departmental ISSOs work in their realms for providing local security. For example, an ISSO in HR works with the HR staff to complete the required training, letting users know of potential breaches, what data cannot be sent outside the HR department (electronically or via phone or paper), and supports the business processes of HR. Likewise, the programming group's ISSO worries about software breaches and possible data leaks and informs the ISSM. Note that neither the ISSO nor the ISSM takes care of the cybersecurity breach if one happens. The actual technical work is done by the respective departments (network, database, programming, HR). Updates are made to the ISSO, who acts as a liaison for the organization's security posture. The ISSM's duty is more of a policy enforcement for both internal and external security posture.

- **Security administrator (SA):** Security administration can also be done by the system administrators (operating system, database, applications, and so on), but if resources are available, the security administrator can be an additional person who looks at the specific security network devices, applications, hardware, and software components. SAs look at the common security controls such as IDS, IPS, firewalls, antivirus, malware and email protection, security proxies, data loss prevention, breaches, undisclosed or unapproved data transmission, and so on. When a problem is found, SAs inform the ISSO and ISSM, who let the rest of the workforce know of the details. SAs have the job of reading logs; detecting the breaches; stopping an attack, spill, or a breach; and the related technical work.

- **Security analyst:** This is a kind of junior position to the ISSO who may develop or modify new or existing policies, standards, and guidelines and create a baseline for MAC (mandatory access control). For example, the security analyst would work with password policies that need to have a complexity rule and figure out how to enforce any new rules.

Recall the RACI matrix in Chapter 3 "Goals of Security." It is sometimes called RASCI matrix (responsible, accountable, supporting, consulted, and informed). For security purposes, everyone who plays a part can be in the supporting role, even if they are not actively involved in security administration and policies.

Note there's an important difference between privacy and security. **Privacy** is an individual's control of how much information (personal or otherwise) they want to release. **Security** is a mechanism that is implemented to provide that level of control to individuals or systems in the organization. To protect personally identifiable information (PII) and a company's databases, organizations create various privacy and security policies for a stable security posture and implement various digital, analog, email, or paper controls to strictly follow that security posture. Organizations that have policies on cybersecurity and implement them well do not rest easy. They often have to conduct **privacy impact analysis** to check how their security controls are working in response to a possible breach. They also have to conduct **risk assessment** to check how their sensitive data is protected in case of an attack or spill. For the controls to be successful, often an ethical hack attack is initiated to find a report. **Ethical hackers** conduct an organization-wide fake attack to find any holes in security and report on recommended changes.

Scope or User Privilege Creep

When several people work together in an organization, human errors normally happen due to various factors. User privileges may go unchecked when software or hardware changes take place or when people move around due to office space adjustments. If each person has a set of software, hardware, updates, and specific office products, it may be easy to fix everyone's machine with a baseline configuration. However, often this is impossible because different groups need different hardware and software. But we also know that common software, operating systems, email software, and such all can have the same version. For this reason, a companywide MAC is implemented, and everyone's system comes with a baseline configuration. For example, the following can be implemented uniformly to every single user whether the user works for programming, HR, or testing:

- Operating system
  - Microsoft Windows 10 (Enterprise or user edition)
  - Build 10.0.19.xx.xxx (April 2023)
- Hardware
  - Lenovo, Inc.
  - 160 GB hard disk
  - 64 GB RAM
  - Smart card reader built in
  - 2 USBs, one DVD-ROM
  - HDMI external port
- Software
  - Open Office (word processing, spreadsheet, presentations, database)

- Lotus email

- Firefox browser

- OfficeMgr (example software for all office employees)

- Antivirus software package

- Windows Defender security

When MAC is implemented, the baseline discussed earlier could be the same for everyone. But those who need additional software or hardware will have to submit their requests in writing (email or paper) with a proper signature (digital or otherwise). But remember that all the users who have the baseline machines and software can only use the machines as a normal end user and not as a system administrator. There are three important reasons for this. First, if an end user is given the privileges of a system administrator, we're violating the zero-trust policy. Second, when the users unknowingly go to a website, the system may automatically download some malicious software, assuming that permission was given automatically. Third, the end user may download software they think is authentic but in reality is a fake. By giving the system administrator privileges to normal users, the privileges were escalated unknowingly. The scope of work an end user can do with the administrator privileges is nearly limitless. In other words, privileges have creeped for no reason. Human error is the top reason this could happen, but there are other reasons, too.

Note that the users who have received the standard configured machine cannot delete software or enable any USB or such. The reason is office policies deemed that the user should have and use this configuration as required for their work. If a person prefers not to use a program, that is fine, but the programs installed cannot be just removed or uninstalled.

Privileges cannot be exceeded intentionally, but we know accidents happen, and those system administrators who favor some employees may give more privileges to some than others. It also can happen that temporarily an employee is given more privileges to do some job, but the privileges were not revoked after the work was complete. It may be possible that an organization can assume a senior employee who has been with the organization for many years is harmless and gives more privileges. Once privilege escalation happens, the trusted employee could take advantage of it and behave differently. The following are some possible reasons for privilege escalations.

- System administrators forgot to rescind temporarily granted escalated privileges.

- The security administrator trusts an employee blindly and gives more privileges.

- The organization simply does not have a policy for privileges, and everyone has full access.

- Employee(s) and the approving supervisor have formed a team that is planning mischief on systems and request additional privileges.

- Privileges were accidentally increased when new software or a higher version of the same software was installed.

- The organization does not have a skilled person who oversees the privilege creep.

- The ISSO and ISSM are lazy and do not notice the privilege creep.

- The organization has no defined security posture and has a "so what?" attitude.

- The organization has no internal or external audit process in place.

For these and many other reasons, every month or so, a security administrative officer such as an ISSO conducts an internal audit or access reviews to check whether any of the machines and end users have gone over the minimum allotted privileges. This person reads the logs to see what the users are doing in their day-to-day job responsibilities. Local branch ISSOs have the responsibility to check and inform the ISSM as well. These checks can be done easily by reading the logs, emails generated by the privilege creep, and accesses. Keep in mind that one person reading the logs or checking the systems will not do justice because that reporting person can also make mistakes or might not notice privilege creep. This is where job rotation helps among all employees.

Change Management

In Chapter 10, "Application Security Fundamentals," we briefly discuss change management (CM) and how an onboarding employee is granted permissions. But change management has more work than discussed earlier. We must note that any end user who is requesting something from CM is already cleared of all checks, such as background, security, credit, and so on. CM does not get involved in any of those checks again, and it isn't their job to do the background checking. CM is solely for approving or disapproving any requests for software change or privileges. The Change Approval Board (CAB) includes staff trained to do the following:

- Examine and correct the submitted request for accuracy of what is needed, what is available, and proper signatures of the end users and managers

- Act as a central point for the request to send and receive information from various branches

- Inform users of pending dates and updates to applications, software, or hardware

- Help users create an efficient CM process though a centrally available application

- Obtain details, update the change, and record the process if the requested change did not work on the first assumed date (extend dates)

- Close the requests when work is completed after prompting other branches to close their work performed

Consider two examples of the CM process. In the first example, a new employee is hired as a programmer and needs access. The employee has no ID except their driver's license with which they obtained the organization's identification with their picture and an employee number. On the first day, the new employee meets the supervisor, who provides a form to fill for a computer, email, and other software access. The form can be on paper because the employee does not have access to anything yet. All the standard non-disclosure agreements, confidentiality, and so on are included in that form, and the employee affirms that they agree to the conditions and signs the form. The rest of the process goes like this:

1. The signed account and computer access request form is countersigned by the supervisor and forwarded (either physically or electronically) to the CM office.

2. The signatures of the requesting employee and the supervisor are checked by the CM office.

3. If the requesting employee needs any training prior to being granted access, the application remains pending until that training is complete and a valid certificate is produced.

4. After due diligence and due care, the employee is given access to the basic computer, email, and office software that are needed.

5. Permissions on the computer files and drives (installed or mapped) are given at the minimum level per the as-needed basis, based on the least privilege policy.

6. The employee is sent a copy of the form they signed for their records.

7. Locally within the branch, the employee is directed to work with the departmental system administrator (if any) to get access for additional software, permissions to access more files, folders, or physical entrances and exits. CM does not interfere with the local branch work.

8. At this point, if the employee needs software, such as Visual Studio, Java IDE (like Eclipse), NetBeans, or database access, they are asked to submit another valid request for software installation.

9. The software installation forms need a signature from the supervisor to justify the need for additional software.

10. The approved software request goes to a central systems administration branch, where the manager directs the request to one of their employees.

11. The system administrator's employee contacts the requesting employee to set up a time to sit together to install software or installs software remotely.

12. All the requests can be electronically generated, signed, and forwarded. The entire process may seem like it takes years, but in reality, all these tasks are accomplished on the same day or in two days at most.

In the second example, we discuss how a programmer is making a change to existing software. The existing software has a problem that needs to be fixed. The programmer has documented the reported problem and requested the supervisor grant him permission to correct the bug. The process now goes as follows:

1. The employee submits a change request (CR) to the supervisor, giving reasons for the request and enclosing the documentation gathered about the bug.

2. The employee gives a valid reason for the bug fix—the situation of what can go wrong if the bug is not fixed as soon as possible.

3. The employee also has to note in the request who will fix bug, who will test the results, who will double-check regression errors, the dates when the work will start and complete, and whether any other branch is involved in the work (code repository staff, operating system or network administrators, and other people involved). An example of involving other branches is stated as, "Network administrator has to switch off firewall while the code is being tested and deployed."

4. The supervisor accepts the request, countersigns it, and submits it to the CM branch.

5. The CM branch inspects the request and signatures and sends an email to all branches involved telling them that there is a request and it is formally accepted.

6. The programmer receives the OK to start work; they start and complete the work and involve the tester and network or system administrator to test the code on a given date.

7. The tester sends a report of their testing to the programmer and encloses a copy of the CM's original change request.

8. Any problems noticed are reverted to step 6 and tested again.

9. On successful testing, the programmer transfers their files to the system administrator to deploy. These files contain the changes the programmer made to fix the bug.

10. On the stipulated date, the network administrator closes the firewall (if required as in the given example), and the system administrator copies the file to the required area.

11. When all jobs are completed, each of these administrators sends an email to sign off their work on the software and tell the CM that their job is complete.

12. When all jobs are complete, the CM branch staff close the change request and note it as successful. The completed request is saved by the date and a change request number for audit purposes—either internal or external.

Documenting the Process

Since paper use is limited these days, digital signatures, documentation, sending requests and approvals, communicating questions about what is included and not included, delegating who works on what part of a change, and so on can be done with a single electronic station or software process. These software packages are very efficient. An example access request form that can be used by a new employee or someone who wants to renew is shown in Figure 13-1.

Notice that the privilege access forms can have different languages, vocabularies, and technical terms and be different for each organization. They're signed by different people depending on the business a corporation carries out. The forms also evolve as a corporation progresses from year to year due to updated technologies, privileges, and business options available. There is no single form that can fit all businesses because each business deals with a different process and work. For example, those who work in healthcare have certain privileges because they deal with HIPAA regulations, and those in the education field have a different set of rules, as shown in Figure 13-1. Likewise, government organizations have a different form for each branch. Access is also not granted forever. The forms are valid for a year or two, and they must be re-signed due to upgrades, downgrades, or horizontal or vertical privilege creep.

Notice that the form in Figure 13-1 can be used for initial access as well as privilege escalation. For both, a supervisor's signature is mandatory. The form also has a number at the bottom right with a revision date. This tells us that like every end user, the university has a learning curve for creating and maintaining a security posture. This is because we do not know how the future will change with hackers creating innovative attacks. For that reason, the form will have the details known at present and align with the current security posture. As more and more attacks happen, the security posture will change; therefore, the format and language of this form will change as well.

Example University Medical Center

COMPUTER ACCESS, PRIVILEGE REQUEST FORM

Email completed forms to helpdesk@exunimedcenter.com. For questions, call the university Help Desk at 800-123-4567. All fields are mandatory and illegible forms will not be processed.

User Last Name: User MI: User First Name:

User Email Address if any:

Employer Name: University Department:

User contact phone:

Job Classification (MD, RN, etc.):

User Job Title:

User Phone #:

IRB # (if any):

Is this for special access/privilege? If so, explain below (how requester uses this access):

Please read and sign below.

CONFIDENTIALITY / NON-DISCLOSURE AGREEMENT

It is the intent of this User that university corporate or patient information obtained under this Agreement will remain confidential at all times. Confidential information includes, but is not limited to, patient, employee, financial, intellectual property, quality, financially non-public, contractual, and information of a competitive advantage nature, from any source or in any form (i.e., paper, magnetic or optical media, conversations, film, etc.). All information contained within a patient's medical record (hard copy and electronic) is confidential. Aggregate data output (diagnosis, procedure service, specialty, physician, etc.) is also confidential and may only be released by individuals authorized to do so by their position. Passwords to any computer system that processes/stores patient specific clinical data or corporate and employee data are also confidential. This information is protected by state and federal law and by the policies of the Example University Medical Center (EUMC).

I, the undersigned User, understand that EUMC shall take appropriate action to ensure compliance with any and all applicable federal, state and local laws and regulations regarding such a violation including, but not limited to, the Health Insurance Portability and Accountability Act of 1996 (HIPAA) and the Health Information Technology for Economic and Clinical Health (HITECH) Act. The intent of these laws and policies is to ensure that confidential information will remain confidential through its use and as a necessity to accomplish the missions of this organization.

In order to be allowed access to EUMC systems and/or be granted authorization to access any form of confidential information identified above, I, the undersigned, agree to comply with the following terms and conditions:

■ I agree to use my unique user ID and password only in the course and scope of my employment and solely for legitimate application access. Any patient or financial data available to me through access to EUMC computer systems will be treated as confidential information.

■ My computer user account is equivalent to my LEGAL SIGNATURE. I will not disclose this account or password to anyone or allow anyone other than myself to access the system using it and understand that I am responsible and accountable for all entries made and all retrievals accessed under my user account, even if such action was made by me or by another due to my intentional or negligent act or omission.

■ I will not access or attempt to access any EUMC computer system fraudulently by using an account and password other than my own.

■ I agree to comply with the applicable provisions of HIPAA, HITECH and any other federal or state laws or regulations protecting Health Information Privacy and Security and to protect to the fullest extent required by state and federal laws and hospital policy the patient's right to confidentiality of all medical and personal information.

- ■ I will not access or attempt to access for the purpose of inquiry, manipulation, deletion or alteration any data outside the scope of my responsibility, including my own electronic medical record, data regarding family members, or that of friends/associates. In addition, I will not access or attempt to access confidential information, including personnel, billing or private information outside the scope of my employment.

- ■ I agree not to use information obtained from EUMC computer systems in any way that is detrimental to the organization, its members or patients.

- ■ I agree to use care in handling printed reports, report copies, and fax documents and appropriately destroy or dispose of non-permanent paper copies containing patient, workforce, or corporate confidential information.

- ■ I agree that I will not leave any workstation unsecured when logged into an EUMC computer application and agree to log completely off of the system at the end of each workday.

- ■ I will notify EUMC of any change to the information provided on this form, including name, email address, job title or employment arrangement, within 24 hours of the change,

- ■ If I supervise individuals who have been granted access to EUMC systems, I will notify EUMC of any change in employment status on my employees' part within 24 hours of such change.

- ■ I will not intentionally damage, corrupt, or inappropriately delete data or computer programs or copy data or programs to other devices or media without authorization.

- ■ I will not tamper with any EUMC network-connected device without the express written permission of the CIO or designee. Tampering includes loading of any applications.

- ■ I understand a detailed record of user's access to applications is recorded electronically. Access and use will be audited regularly, at any time on a random basis, or for cause. I consent to having all or any part of their use of and access to EUMC's computer systems audited and reviewed at any time to ensure compliance with this agreement.

- ■ Annual recertification is required to maintain this access. If I do not use my account regularly, I acknowledge that it is EUMC corporate policy to disable my access. If I do not use this account for more than six months, I will need to resubmit this form with appropriate authorization.

I understand and acknowledge that improper access to, use or disclosure of EUMC business or patient confidential information, whether verbally or from a paper-based or a computer-based record is a violation of law and/or EUMC corporate policies. I understand and acknowledge that any violation of any part of the above agreement can result in termination of medical record and/or computer access privileges, and may result in regulatory or legal action, fines or civil money penalties. I also understand and acknowledge that disclosure of confidential information is prohibited indefinitely, even after termination of business relationship, expiration or cancellation of this agreement, or unless specifically waived in writing by the authorized party.

User Acknowledgment

I, acknowledge having received, read, been given an opportunity to ask any questions and agree to abide by the terms of this Agreement. I understand that if I violate any part of the agreement, access to EUMC systems can and may be revoked, and I may be subject to legal and or regulatory action, fines or civil money penalties.

X

User [digital] Signature

Date

X

Signature of Supervisor Who's Authorizing Access

Supervisor Name:

Department:

Phone #:

Date:

Form # 432001 / Rev 11-21-2023

Figure 13-1 *Access Form for Requesting Computer/Email Access Privileges*

Not all organizations have forms that are complicated to read or understand for an average end user. Some organizations have a simple format that could apply to a variety of uses. Figure 13-2 shows a simple form that assumes that a requesting user and sanctioning authority both agreed to terms and conditions when the user started working for the organization.

Note that in some cases, organizations insist that the user complete some training before even applying for access. This training is enforced on the users (either online web training or in-class orientation at the start) about the security posture of the organization, and the user must agree to the conditions set forth. It is common for the form also to include a question about the date of the training the user completed and where. And the supervisor or the departmental ISSO must verify that date before endorsing the application on the user's behalf.

Your name *

Today's date

08/01/2023

Your email address *

Type of request (choose all that apply) *

☐ Hardware (computer, printer, etc.)

☐ Networking

☐ Email

☐ Server access

☐ Other

Details *

Submit

Figure 13-2 *Simple Form for a Quick Fix Sent to the Help Desk and Change Management*

Figure 13-3 is from a Google search for an access form for a government entity (the United States Navy). The following items are worth noting. (Page 4 has instructions for completing the form and is therefore not included in Figure 13-3.)

- On the top of the form is the privacy act clearly stated.

- The form can be used for first-time access or to reissue or reactivate an existing user's privileges after initial access has elapsed (typically one to three years).

- Box 10 reiterates to the user that a certain training—information assurance—is to be completed before privilege can be issued. The date of completion is cross-checked with the information assurance training website when the applicant submits the form. The ISSO or ISSM should make sure that the training is up to date.

- Item 11 asks for justification. This box needs to mention why the user needs privileges or access.

- Box 12 specifically asks whether the user needs plain access or privileged access (such as system administration). If privileged access is requested, additional form(s) may need to be signed, as mentioned in box 12a.

- The requester and supervisor sign the forms, followed by Information Assurance Manager (IAM) along with the date, department name, and contact details.

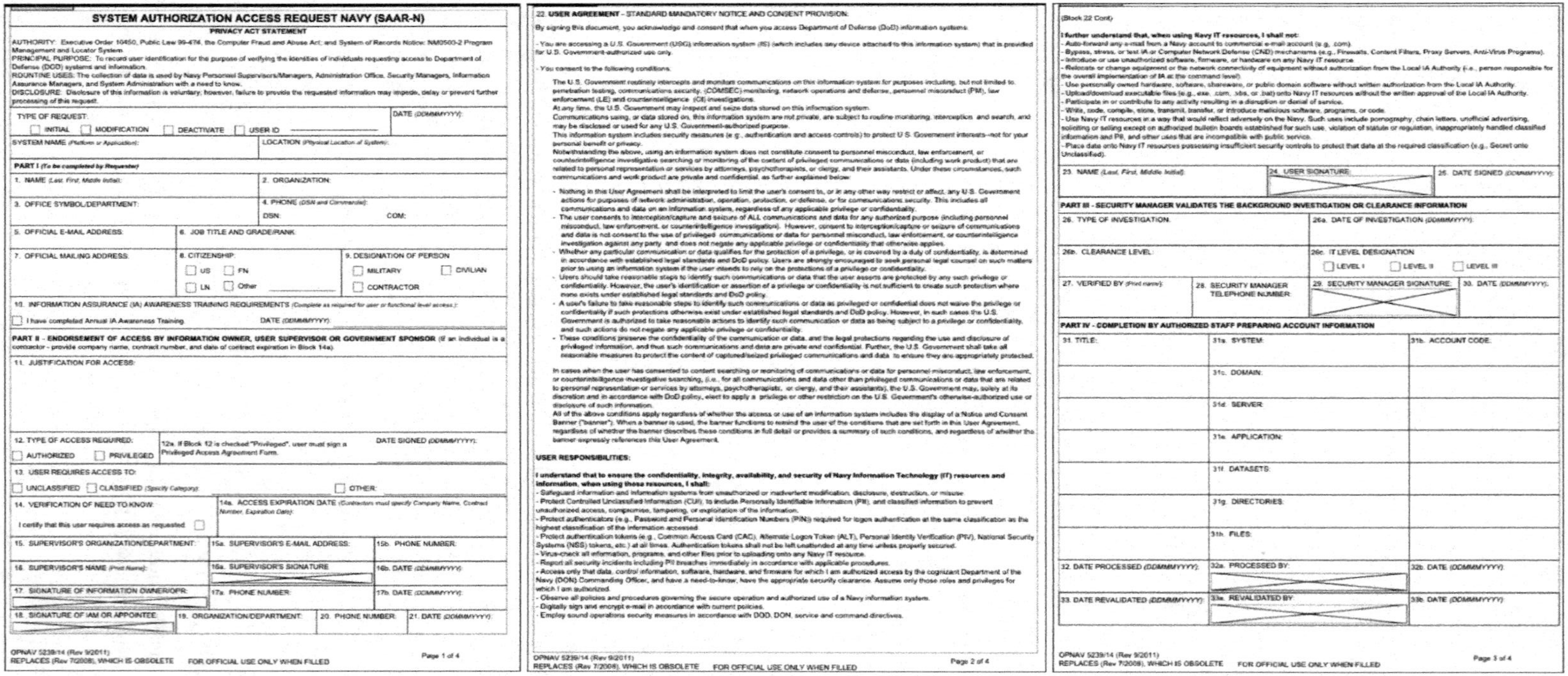

SYSTEM AUTHORIZATION ACCESS REQUEST NAVY (SAAR-N)

PRIVACY ACT STATEMENT

TYPE OF REQUEST: INITIAL / MODIFICATION / DEACTIVATE / USER ID — DATE (DDMMMYYYY)

SYSTEM NAME — LOCATION

PART I

1. NAME — 2. ORGANIZATION
3. OFFICE SYMBOL/DEPARTMENT — 4. PHONE (DSN / COM)
5. OFFICIAL E-MAIL ADDRESS — 6. JOB TITLE AND GRADE/RANK
7. OFFICIAL MAILING ADDRESS — 8. CITIZENSHIP (US, FN, LN, Other) — 9. DESIGNATION OF PERSON (MILITARY, CIVILIAN, CONTRACTOR)
10. INFORMATION ASSURANCE (IA) AWARENESS TRAINING REQUIREMENTS — I have completed Annual IA Awareness Training. DATE

PART II - ENDORSEMENT OF ACCESS BY INFORMATION OWNER, USER SUPERVISOR OR GOVERNMENT SPONSOR

11. JUSTIFICATION FOR ACCESS
12. TYPE OF ACCESS REQUIRED: AUTHORIZED / PRIVILEGED — 12a. If Block 12 is checked "Privileged", user must sign a Privileged Access Agreement Form. — DATE SIGNED
13. USER REQUIRES ACCESS TO: UNCLASSIFIED / CLASSIFIED / OTHER
14. VERIFICATION OF NEED TO KNOW — I certify that this user requires access as requested. — 14a. ACCESS EXPIRATION DATE
15. SUPERVISOR'S ORGANIZATION/DEPARTMENT — 15a. SUPERVISOR'S E-MAIL ADDRESS — 15b. PHONE NUMBER
16. SUPERVISOR'S NAME — 16a. SUPERVISOR'S SIGNATURE — 16b. DATE
17. SIGNATURE OF INFORMATION OWNER/OPR — 17a. PHONE NUMBER — 17b. DATE
18. SIGNATURE OF IAM OR APPOINTEE — 19. ORGANIZATION/DEPARTMENT — 20. PHONE NUMBER — 21. DATE

OPNAV 5239/14 (Rev 9/2011) REPLACES (Rev 7/2008), WHICH IS OBSOLETE — FOR OFFICIAL USE ONLY WHEN FILLED — Page 1 of 4

22. **USER AGREEMENT** - STANDARD MANDATORY NOTICE AND CONSENT PROVISION

USER RESPONSIBILITIES:

I understand that to ensure the confidentiality, integrity, availability, and security of Navy Information Technology (IT) resources and information, when using those resources, I shall:

OPNAV 5239/14 (Rev 9/2011) REPLACES (Rev 7/2008), WHICH IS OBSOLETE — FOR OFFICIAL USE ONLY WHEN FILLED — Page 2 of 4

(Block 22 Cont)

I further understand that, when using Navy IT resources, I shall not:

23. NAME — 24. USER SIGNATURE — 25. DATE SIGNED

PART III - SECURITY MANAGER VALIDATES THE BACKGROUND INVESTIGATION OR CLEARANCE INFORMATION

26. TYPE OF INVESTIGATION — 26a. DATE OF INVESTIGATION
26b. CLEARANCE LEVEL — 26c. IT LEVEL DESIGNATION (LEVEL I, LEVEL II, LEVEL III)
27. VERIFIED BY — 28. SECURITY MANAGER TELEPHONE NUMBER — 29. SECURITY MANAGER SIGNATURE — 30. DATE

PART IV - COMPLETION BY AUTHORIZED STAFF PREPARING ACCOUNT INFORMATION

31. TITLE — 31a. SYSTEM — 31b. ACCOUNT CODE
31c. DOMAIN
31d. SERVER
31e. APPLICATION
31f. DATASETS
31g. DIRECTORIES
31h. FILES
32. DATE PROCESSED — 32a. PROCESSED BY — 32b. DATE
33. DATE REVALIDATED — 33a. REVALIDATED BY — 33b. DATE

OPNAV 5239/14 (Rev 9/2011) REPLACES (Rev 7/2008), WHICH IS OBSOLETE — FOR OFFICIAL USE ONLY WHEN FILLED — Page 3 of 4

Figure 13-3 *The First Three Pages of Form 5239/14 for the United States Navy*

- Box 22 gives exhaustive information about what a user can do, what they cannot do, and what responsibilities they have when access is issued/granted. Since data is very important and may hold classified or other PII, all these instructions are necessary.

- The bottom of the form shows how the form improved over the years, and when the form is filled completely it becomes a "For official user only (FOUO)" document that can't be distributed without proper authorization and needs to follow the basic security rules of confidentiality, integrity, and accountability (CIA).

CM and the CAB allows submission of these forms and closely follows them as they progress. In other words, as shown in Figure 13-4, CM acts as a central point for various things among various departments. All concerned department personnel can access the forms when required and sign, accept, or reject the forms as a need arises. Once completed, the forms are stored on a repository with a case number. Then the approval is forwarded to some administrator who can create an account, grant/extend access, and close the case. For example, a person named David asks for access to a database, and CM tells the database administrator that the form was accepted and access can be granted. The DBA then creates a DB account on the desired database, creates a role, adds permissions, and informs the user what their username and password are and how to connect to the DB.

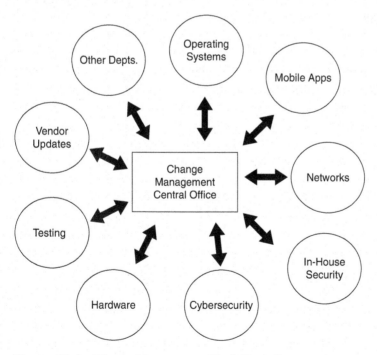

Figure 13-4 *Change Management Used Centrally*

When an organization does these things repeatedly, instead of creating a form for every single user, CM sometimes may have standard templates created for these jobs (like SQL Server report models) by service catalogue or they may use forms with digital signatures and upload them to a private location. All the user has to do is fill the form and forward it to CAB, which copies the signed form to their standard template and forwards it to others. All this is usually accomplished within a day or two, barring any unforeseen circumstances, such as the user did not complete required training, the user is not eligible for access or did not pass a background check, privileges on some systems cannot be escalated for anyone, or signatures or dates indicated were wrong. In such cases, forms are sent back, and the process is repeated. The following are some of the templates and work objectives of CM:

- Onboard a new employee with a form.

- Change requests for new software or in existing software.

- Decommission of deprecated software.

- Break fixes in software, hardware, firmware, or an operating system.

- Emergency requests for access, software, hardware, and so on.

- Report generation for each branch and the organization. These can indicate what is pending, what is going to be done, deadlines met and missed, and so on.

- Classifying a request as an emergency, urgent, normal, standard, and so on.

- Type of work—new, upgrade, change, and so on.

- Impact of the proposed work—corporatewide, limited, minimal, local.

- A list of branches and personnel who will be need to work on the change and can be chosen if known in advance. If the personnel is not known in advance, CM can allocate the work to the branch, and the branch will allocate personnel when approved.

A typical change management form template is shown in Figure 13-5. Note the justification, costs for resources, implications of the change (what happens if the change is implemented or not implemented and how the change affects the business, application, and the organization overall). The date and a unique number are required for each change as well as the change category.

Figure 13-6 shows the details of a change process (working clockwise from the top), from requesting a change to its closure. Simply requesting a change is never sufficient, but a requested change needs to be analyzed for its impact locally or on the whole organization before submitting the request. This is a general diagram of steps defined by Information Technology Infrastructure Library (ITIL).

Change Request		
Project:		**Date:**
Change Requestor:		**Change No:**
Change Category (Check all that apply):		
☐ Schedule ☐ Cost ☐ Scope ☐ Requirements ☐ Testing ☐ Resources		
Does this Change Affect (Check all that apply): ☐ Corrective ☐ Preventative ☐ Defect Repair ☐ Updates ☐ Other		
Describe the Change Being Requested:		
Reson for the Change:		
Technical Changes Required:		
Risks:		
Resources and Costs:		
Describe the Implications to Quality:		
Justification of Approval, Rejection or Deferral:		
Disposition: Approve Reject Defer		
Change Approval:		
Name	**Signature**	**Date**

Figure 13-5   *Change Management Template Example*

CM has several advantages:

- It keeps a central contact with every other department and personnel.

- Any change made to the software, hardware, or system in any manner needs to be approved, and the CAB keeps a record of that change.

- Any privilege escalations found by any system administrator can be reported to CM, which can look into the records and see if the privileges are authorized.

- Some accounts that need special attention (system accounts, application accounts) are protected by CM with a password. It also means these system account passwords cannot be changed at will by others without the permission of CM.

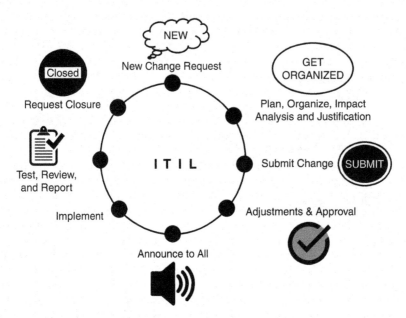

Figure 13-6　*Change Mangement Template as Related to ITIL*

■ The change management staff work closely with the individual branch ISSOs and ISSM and keeps the systems in order. Any upcoming changes are shared with the users before they are made.

■ CM has a software portal where everyone can request a change and modify the dates, and the requested change is communicated to others automatically. Each individual does not have to request other personnel to come and join the work. Rather the branch names are included in the change request. If any branch does not like the time proposed for the request, they can request another date and time.

■ CM has readymade templates for regular changes, such as simple account creations. One can just use the template and does not have to create a lot of details every time a similar request is made.

■ From the change management portal, each branch can create their own reports and check what changes are being done by their own branch, what other branches are asking help from their branch, what changes have been completed, what changes are pending, and so on.

■ Nobody, even the CEO, can force changes to the software, hardware, or systems without letting the CM office know in advance. This prevents unauthorized changes and helps in security of the software, hardware, and components, as well as the security posture of the corporation overall. This is because CM has documentation for every single change made and keeps a record for audit purposes.

Now that you know how CM works centrally with everyone, an important question arises as who can create a request for change on the CM-provided software. If the access form allows a user to access the CM software, the user can create a ticket themselves. If not, they can forward the request to CM or the help desk, and either of those offices will create the request on behalf of the user. A request can be created by a help desk, end users who have access to the CM software, administrators, and CM office personnel. CM personnel can also adjust/change/drop/create requests depending on changes and additional valid requests received from various users.

One final important point needs to be mentioned about CM, ISSO, and ISSM offices. This point is actually from a human activity point of view and the "tendency to control people" by the CM, ISSO, and the cybersecurity staff for no particular reason. Those who are designated as cybersecurity staff tend to believe they ride a higher horse and are more important than others. These staff members try to exercise more control than necessary and find faults to reject the forms—although the forms are already filled and signed by all parties correctly. They may point to a missing comma or word or such. Some forms are flatly rejected when they do not match an already-existing approved form. The process of refilling the forms to suit the style of a particular cybersecurity staff member is a painstaking job. One needs patience to deal with the people because these minor problems are often caused by these staff and have nothing to do with the form or actual security. Neither is it due to how accurately the form is completed.

Another often-talked-about problem is the regular check of privileges by these staff after privileges are granted, although they already checked the forms and access privileges just a few days before. Sometimes it happens that the staff who checked all user privileges earlier did not keep any records, erased those records, or just quit. A repetitive check is forced on all users to confirm the users have proper base or extended privileges. When one branch does this repetitive check, other branches—like network security, server security, and physical security—have to repeat those processes as well to align simultaneously with the newly collected data and records with the same date/month for audit purposes.

This kind of work is more user-created noise than actual cybersecurity. To move forward, the only thing the users can do is to ignore the noise and comply. Any complaints to higher authorities on how wasteful these efforts are will only make the process worse and harder. It is common that the complaining individuals are targeted for future requests as well. The mantra is therefore to comply rather than complain. Nobody is saying the checks are not important. Yes, it is necessary and mandatory to check the users regularly and see the logs and privileges granted and how long they are or should be valid, but an overkill of the same process is really not necessary. Unfortunately, some cybersecurity staff continue to do it, and the users have to just learn to go with the flow rather than fight the process.

Legal Liabilities

At one point, even a senior staff member who has gone through all the CM, access, and privilege approval processes gets frustrated and might question if all the verification is actually necessary even for staff who has worked at an organization for decades. The first reason for the checks is the legal, practical, and regulatory problems that might arise, which can prove to be dangerous and financially debilitating. The second reason is the zero-trust policy and ever-vigilant security posture to avoid any legal problems now or in the future. To deal with the legal problems if any arise, a corporation sets up their own policies for ethical behavior and compliance with various frameworks, regulations, local and federal laws, and such. The policies, typically supported by approved processes and procedures, also include how the organization investigates and what techniques are used to further find information and details to investigate and report if a crime is committed. These processes and procedures effectively help implement or execute the policies. Once those techniques reveal details, evidence is gathered for reporting purposes. Gathering evidence is also known as *forensics*.

When data on a computer or the computer itself is assessed without proper access privileges, it is an illegal action and can be said to be a computer crime. To make a security policy work, it is important to understand the legal problems and laws. The following are some of the considerations for an organization:

- Organizational policies are created and based on the federal, state, county, and city laws and regulations.

- Organizations must create policies and procedures to keep the organization and its employees safe and from violating any of these laws.

- Every one of the organizational staff should be trained to and retrained to keep the policies in mind before taking any action.

- The following list shows how the laws and regulations shape the standards and policies to be followed in that order (1 to 2 to 3 to 3a, 3b, and 3c):

  1. State, federal, county, city laws, industrial and other regulations

  2. Company policies [from previous step #1]

  3. Mandatory functional implementation policies (FIP) [from previous step #2]

     a. Standards (FIPS) based on mandatory FIP

     b. Procedures and processes (instructions, standard operating procedure (SOP), manuals, user guides, FAQ)

     c. Guidelines or recommendations (for example, NIST SP 800-X, STIG, and so on)

Laws come in different types and varieties. A person, an employee, or the whole organization can be sued by a hungry lawyer for one breach with more than one case under different laws and by different statutes. It is important to know the following details to maintain a good security posture:

- Civil laws are usually based on a set of rules and noncriminal rights among legal persons (citizens, immigrants, and residents). Civil laws pertain to injury to an individual or a party (a corporation). Some examples of civil laws include personal injury, aggravating battery, negligence, defamation, medical malpractice, and fraud.

- Administrative laws are usually the regulations that pave the way for standards of performance and conduct. Banking, insurance, and Security Exchange Commission (SEC) regulations are examples of administrative laws.

- Common laws are based on judgments delivered earlier. These are also where the judges look for legal precedence to deliver a verdict.

- Criminal laws pose imprisonment, monetary penalties, and other damages.

- Civil/tort laws provide compensatory damage and monetary restitution but no prison/jail time.

- Customary laws are more complicated and are based on cultural customs, traditions, and common beliefs. For example, some countries like China, India, Iran, and Saudi Arabia follow a set of local laws customary to their own nations.

- Religious law is based on religious practices of a particular area or country.

- A mixed law system is a combination of every possible law that allows one to sue.

- It is important to note that laws are made by the lawmakers but are interpreted by the court and justice system to impose penalties. Laws passed are applicable to a country or a union and within its borders.

Legal problems can arise once we have a data breach or a detected attack, and lawyers will search for every possible loophole to sue under every possible law applicable. The following are some privacy rules that apply to most countries:

- Information privacy dictates how personal information such as medical records and credit information is handled.

- Bodily privacy deals with the physical being of a person and any invasion thereof. Examples are a forced drug test, genetic testing, and so on.

- Territorial privacy is about private property, territorial workspace, or public space.

- Communications privacy is for protecting the entities' communication on media such as email, postal mail, and voice or fax communication.

The following activities can be considered a breach of confidentiality but can be exempted in some rare cases as decided by a judge on a case-by-case basis:

- Disclosure

- Exposure

- Increased accessibility

- Blackmail

- Appropriation

- Distortion

Intellectual property laws can apply to both organizations and to individuals. Intellectual property is mainly divided into two categories:

- Industrial or corporate property

  - Inventions and patents

  - Trademarks

  - Industrial designs and diagrams such as blueprints

  - Geographic indications of source

- Copyright

  - Literary works like books, articles, engineering or architectural designs, plays, and poems

  - Artistic works such as music, songs, films, paintings, photographs, and sculptures

When accessing and abusing privileges, many types of harm are addressed under computer security and crime laws:

- Unauthorized access

- Unauthorized alteration, destruction, or disclosure of information

- Insertion of malicious programming code

- Computer-assisted crime (uses computer/server as a tool)

- Computer-targeted crime (an activity directed at the computer/server)

- Computer is incidental (uses computer data for criminal activities)

Problems with cybercrime or computer crime laws are multifold. Territorial wars, poorly enforced laws, and governments encouraging their hackers on another country's networks remain a problem. Here are some points to keep in mind:

- Some countries have no or poorly defined crime laws for cybercrime.

- Each country's law enforcement technical capabilities are different.

- In cases that involve international attention, governments may not want to assist each other for the fear of losing face.

- Transnational criminal activities are hard to point to a certain geographic location and take the attacks to a court of law.

- Jurisdiction remains a main problem for legal disputes because laws differ for each country.

International groups that deal with computer crimes have some protections in place, but how much they help for a large breach or ransomware attack depends on the situation. The following are helpful organizations that cooperate across the borders to solve a problem:

- The G8 nations all have common international agreements on computer crime.

- Mutual Legal Assistance Treaties (MLAT) allow the U.S. law enforcement agencies such as FBI and Department of State to work in tandem with law enforcement of other nations.

- European Union Border Controls generally involves the International Criminal Police Organization (INTERPOL).

- United Nations (UN) agreements help resolve some cases.

Now that we have a set of rules and how they affect nations and individuals, we need to show evidence of a crime if there is a breach. Not everything can be produced in a court as evidence. There are procedures (collectively known as chain of custody) to follow before a judge can admit something as valid evidence. Handling of computer evidence in a crime or a data breach needs to keep the following in mind:

- Minimize corruption of original data when collecting evidence.

- Keep a detailed log of your actions with the time and date of action.

- Follow all the rules when collecting computer evidence.

- If anything is not clearly known to the evidence collector, seek technical legal advice.

- Strictly follow the organizational security policy and obtain written permission.

- Capture as accurately as possible an image of the system and the corruption.

- If required, be prepared to testify and show the details collected.

- Be aware that the court may ask you to show that data collection activities are repeatable.

- When collecting data, go from volatile to persistent evidence.

- Don't run any additional programs on the affected system.

- Don't switch off, log off, or disconnect the machine from the network.

- Data collection can be handled bit by bit or in another way but must be in good format.

- Maintain a chain of custody for proof of that evidence.

Digital investigation with forensics involves various stages because the crime might have occurred in one location and spread to various other sections or even geographical locations. Thus, it is important to verify each system in all locations.

Software Analysis

Applications, either purchased or built in-house, may have permissions to write data to various locations of a system such as hard disk, USB, and so on. Examples of stored data include:

- A browser storing a user's browsing history, cookies, and temporary files

- Operating systems storing logs, swap files, deleted files, spool files, and temporary files

- Applications can have encrypted files, but files might be used for steganography and so on.

- Viruses and malware such as Trojan horses, logs, unallocated or randomly allocated space (hidden blocks), boot sectors, and slack space.

- Forensic toolkits such as Forensic Toolkit and EnCase help find digital evidence by in-depth analysis of files and software, but still require experience and analytical mind.

Network Analysis

Network is the generic usual route how an attack, virus, or hijacker can make way into a corporate computer system. Internal users can log into a variety of nodes, systems, and sub-networks as well if privileges are granted. Network analysis is complicated and needs in-depth research. The following are important considerations.

- Network data contains full packets of data, and all packets are important to catch a problem.

- Security alert data and logs are stored on the system or a firewall-designated location.

- Use good network data tools for log file collection from the firewall, IPS/IDS, routers, and switches.

- Captured data alone might be unreadable or has no meaning unless we can analyze that data. Analysis of captured network data can be done with tools such as Wireshark or TCPDump.

- Network analysis requires good knowledge of the network topography, how it is structured and used, and what protocols are used.

Hardware or a Device Analysis

Hardware or a physical device analysis is interesting because it needs good knowledge of how a computer works in terms of its architecture, memory, registers, drivers, shell, and so on. A device may contain

- Disk storage (HDD, USB)
- CPU (32- or 64-bit processor)
- Swap space (size and type)
- Arithmetic logic unit (ALU)
- Registers—accumulator and others
- Control unit
- Main memory (RAM)
- Backup memory
- Input
- Output
- Assembler
- Printer or other peripherals

Having discussed the laws and problems with an employee, they can be trained to follow the training schedules and do their best in their day-to-day job. But what an employee actually does despite agreeing to a non-disclosure statement, default other assumptions, and having the least privilege access depends on the ethics of the employee. In one sentence, *ethics dictate what one "should" do*, whereas a *law dictates what one "must" do*. Per agreed rules with a host of experts and committees, the Internet Activities Board (IAB) characterizes the following activities as unethical and unacceptable on the Internet:

- Unauthorized access to the resources of the Internet
- Attempts to disrupt or disrupting the intended use of the Internet
- Wastes resources (HR, capacity, computer) through disruptive actions
- Corrupts or destroys the integrity of computer-based data or information
- Compromises the privacy of users or an organization

And for the users to follow the correct ethics, corporate policies should provide a plan of action and milestones (POAM), which is reviewed every few months:

- Incorporate corporate policy and guidelines to computer ethics for the organization.
- Add the computer ethics policy to the computer security stature and posture.

- From the first orientation day, instruct employees to follow computer ethics guidelines.

- If there is an organizational business ethics policy, include computer ethics in it.

- Continue to train and encourage each employee to learn more about computer ethics and spread what they learned to others.

In the end, any policy, however nicely written, is useless when not enforced. Therefore, corporations must strictly and mandatorily enforce policies or impose penalties such as removing privileges, disabling access to the network or computer system, and regularly informing employees of the impending trouble with laws and regulations when they are not followed to the letter.

Be Proactive—Benefits and Measures

Given the security guidelines and legal problems that might arise, it is always beneficial to be proactive. And being proactive means a corporation takes every possible care they can and accepts the risk they cannot minimize or they can accept. By being proactive, a corporation will try to find vulnerabilities and possible attacks that might happen before a hacker finds those vulnerabilities and creates a breach. Reactive measures take care of breaches after they happen and try to minimize the damage, but by being proactive we can possibly prevent a breach from happening. There are some activities a corporate security posture can address by being proactive. With the rise of social media websites such as Facebook and Twitter, human error remains the biggest cause of attacks. To prevent attacks, some of the proactive measures are discussed in the following list. Remember, these are not the only measures to implement, but they are the current best options, and as time and technology progress, the list will have to be modified to suit the security posture for the day. In other words, we should think like an attacker and stay ahead of the race to protect our security.

- **Know your assets:** It is important to know what systems, software, phones, fax machines, printers, network hardware, databases, authorized cell phones, tablets, backup rooms, server details, and all other assets are. As the systems age and are replaced, it is important to know how to dispose of the older equipment or software and how a new baseline is created for the newer systems. For this reason, corporations conduct a review (at least annually) of their equipment and keep a record of the assets. End users also sign a document about what equipment they have and promise to protect the equipment either at the office or at home if they are authorized to work from home. After COVID-19, remote work has become a new norm; thus, keeping the equipment safe at remote locations is very important as well.

- **Security awareness and training:** As we've mentioned quite a few times, the first line of defense in cybersecurity is *you*. For proactive cybersecurity to work, every employee needs to be trained to recognize an intrusion, a bad email, or how to take care of their own security. Social engineering attacks such as phishing try to exploit people's weaknesses to find more information and steal login credentials by posing as a manager of some other branch or sending an email to lure the employees with a cash reward or some other enticement. Training about security alone will not work unless an employee is constantly aware and able to recognize anything suspicious. Using strong and complex passwords per corporate password policies, not disclosing information to anyone without authorization, locking the system when the user is inactive for more than 30 minutes, and using multifactor authentication are some of the measures that must be implemented. The central security office's ISSM must also keep a close watch on the known and upcoming attacks and inform the users regularly to be aware of new possible attacks and how to be proactive in preventing them (by not opening links sent in email, checking email addresses of the sender on Global Address List (GAL) to make sure it is authentic, and using filters to block junk emails).

- **Continuous monitoring or observation:** Monitoring and observation can be done manually and with automated software. In continuous monitoring, we look for malicious code (logic bombs, viruses), failures in the IAAA steps (discussed in Chapter 1, "The Basics of Cybersecurity"), unusual network traffic, unexpected or unknown database queries, disproportionate login attempts, new account creations that were not authorized or are unknown, connections from unknown IP addresses, attempts to access ports, and so on. Automated jobs can create a log entry alert and email the administrators when they detect these unusual activities. However, a proactive cybersecurity plan will not work if the created logs are not read regularly, and the warning emails are ignored due to repetitive procedures and laziness of the administrators. Audits also check the log files and recommend changes on how or what the logs should contain or not contain for improving the continuous monitoring activities.

- **Look for trouble:** Proactive security teams in a corporate computer network constantly check for malware, viruses, worms, Trojan horses, and other threats. Even if these problems do not exist, security professionals check for programs that were not authorized for installation, running programs that are delaying the network traffic, programs that tie the system in a loop, and so on. These can happen even with an in-house developed program where the programmer made a semantic mistake. Such programs or processes need to be killed or removed, and coders need to be advised to improve the code. It is important to note that this step of looking for trouble needs to be updated regularly because malware and threats keep changing.

- **Database, network, and software firewalls:** When implementing IDS and IPS for hardware, networks, or software, firewalls can track all the traffic. When unwanted traffic is blocked, a firewall should create an entry in the log. Rules are set up for logging the successful traffic and suspected packets of data as well. Network and system administrators should continuously read the firewall logs to detect any breaches before or after they occur. New rules for inbound and outbound traffic can be created as required, and monitoring logs regularly help reduce the threats on the attack surface.

- **Do not assume but do test:** Even after we have created a great security policy, trained everyone to be aware, and have not detected any attacks on the corporate network, there is no guarantee that a corporate network is free from all breaches. The attack surface must be tested to prove that it can withstand an attempt by hackers. Ethical hacking, also known as white hat hacking, helps test system security with penetration testing (PenTesting). PenTesting should be done with written permission granted to access and attack a network just like a hacker does. PenTesting can briefly disable a working network and may reveal vulnerabilities. A report explains the vulnerabilities to be addressed for improving the security.

- **Filter, filter, filter:** Use lots of filters for email, software, spam, and network traffic. Antispam software can remove various kinds of inappropriate incoming email. Antivirus software, such as McAfee, implements known signatures of viruses to block threats, but it needs to be updated regularly with newly found viruses and their signatures. Antimalware software checks traffic for heuristic or investigative trends to see whether the new traffic pattern can be a threat that we did not know earlier (a known signature doesn't already exist).

- **Password protection:** Corporate policies must be very strict with user passwords. Social engineering attacks mainly aim to get passwords from end users and are easy avenues for an attacker to lure an employee. Password complexity rules must be followed to the letter without an exception. Passwords also should have a lifetime (30, 60, 90 days) and history (the last five passwords cannot be reused). Any accounts unused for 30 days or more should be locked, and those accounts that were not used in more than 90 days or so should be removed for good. Forgotten passwords should not be reset by phone or personal requests but must go through a change management process of submitting a request and redirecting it to the appropriate branch to keep records.

- **Implement multi-factor authentication (MFA):** Do not allow users to log in to any system through one factor like username and password. Second or third factors— entering a known PIN or receiving a temporary one-time password (OTP, which is usually a six-digit code) on the phone—should be implemented. OTPs offer the best defense for security and have a lifetime of 30 minutes or less. MFA is hard to hack because a hacker looking to log in must know the OTP and have the login credentials.

- **Assess, mitigate, and accept risk:** A derailed risk assessment gives information about the vulnerabilities that exist, risks that might materialize, and a threat that can happen. Risk assessment, usually best done by a third party without bias, examines the corporate assets in detail for probable vulnerabilities in each asset. A detailed report is then submitted, giving the vulnerabilities found, risks that a corporation faces from the vulnerabilities, and the losses if a threat materializes on the vulnerability. With that report in hand, the security team decides which risks to mitigate, which risks can be accepted, and the risk tolerance of the corporation. This process helps a corporation learn the asset's weaknesses and their own ability to deal with the vulnerabilities. Again, assets and vulnerabilities associated with an asset change and risk assessment should happen at least once a year.

■ **Revise security posture and adapt new plans:** The cybersecurity posture for a corporation changes regularly due to changes in business needs, mergers, procurements, and many other factors. As technology is changing and becoming faster, hackers adapt and invent newer ways to create attacks. One example is ransomware that emerged as a new threat but was not known earlier. Every business and government organization have to adapt to find a solution to the new attacks. This is the reason why the security posture for a company cannot be cast in stone and must change regularly. Many security professionals and the ISC2 recommend the plan be revised at least once a year or whenever required. It means all the proactive policies we've discussed need to be changed at least once a year and new plans adopted. Note that even if there is no known attack, the security plans must be revised regularly.

■ **Reactive measures:** After all the security steps have been put in place and the attack surface is minimized, what if a corporation still suffers from an unexpected and unknown attack? These are also listed in detail in document NIST 800-61, "Computer Security Incident Handling Guide." Generally, the following are the measures that are done to limit loss/damage:

  ■ **Contain breach:** The first thing to do in any breach is to stop the attack or minimize it.

  ■ **Investigate:** Can the staff quickly find out what happened and how the attack came into being? What is the cause or vulnerability that allowed the attack to happen? Reading the logs, firewall rules, and trends in the packet data can reveal details. Each department is put on alert to check their settings and determine the cause.

  ■ **Inform:** Keep the C-level managers informed about the cause and how it happened and what procedures are being followed to find and contain the attack so everyone is aware of the situation and can be alert.

  ■ **Remediate:** If the cause is found, do the staff know how to fix it quickly or can the corporation hire someone to fix it? If so, remediate the problem as soon as possible.

  ■ **Document lessons learned:** With reactive security measures, if we have found a breach, it directly implies that the proactive measures a corporation put in place failed somehow. This is a serious problem and needs to be corrected. The corporation now reconvenes the security team to put a new measure in place for proactive security so that the same attack will not happen again. The lesson learned from the attack is documented for the future.

  ■ **Consider insurance:** It is possible to obtain insurance (risk transfer) for some organizations if they find a breach. Terms for insurance on what is covered and what is not covered vary greatly from one location to another, one insuring company to another, and among different types of businesses. Read the fine print before signing up for insurance.

Summary

Security administration has many steps, among which least privilege, need to know, and separation of duties are very important. Many officers and C-level managers such as CISO, CSO, and CPO work in tandem to maintain the security posture of an organization. To protect security, usually a baseline is created that helps prevent privilege creep or scope change of a user/system. The baseline protects with the principle of mandatory access control (MAC) for all.

Change management is a process whereby everyone works with others to make sure the changes are correctly authorized and implemented. Various forms are used to grant privileges to users and all the forms are usually signed by the employee and supervisor and then go to the change advisory board (CAB), which works to approve or reject the request. The CAB also decides if a software change is required and can be approved or rejected. Proper justification needs to be provided to the CAB for a change to be approved. There are many advantages of the change management process when an organization deals with many software packages and employees from various departments.

Legal liabilities must be kept in mind because company policies align with local and federal laws. Laws can be civil, religious, or criminal and also come in a variety of other ways. They can change from one state to another and from one country to another. Chain of custody is an important process for collecting information from an incident or the collected evidence may be deemed inadmissible. Protection of assets can be proactive or reactive. Proactive methods expect a problem to happen so people are ready to handle them, whereas reactive measures work when an incident actually materializes. NIST's 800-61 has a detailed list of steps to be taken in case of a computer security incident.

Chapter 13 Questions

1. How should a corporation grant privileges to either new or already-employed staff?

2. What is least privilege?

3. What is the difference between a CSO and CISO?

4. What is the difference between privacy and security?

5. What is the advantage of a baseline configuration for a computer system?

6. List five or more ways privilege escalations happen in a corporate environment.

7. Why is change management important?

8. How is a computer crime categorized?

9. How many nations does the international computer crime law apply to?

10. How does a copyright differ from a trade secret?

11. What are some laws that a security professional should be aware of?

12. What are some examples of computer harm that come under crime laws?

13. Why is being proactive helpful in preventing a computer hack?

14. Why is security awareness for users important even after they are well trained?

15. How is PenTesting important for a company's security posture?

16. How often should the security posture be revised and why?

17. What are the reactive steps if there is a breach or an attack?

Answers to Chapter 13 Questions

1. Privileges and grants are given based on the need for an employee to work on a particular system or computer and not because the employee wants access.

2. Least privilege access dictates that the employee be given minimum access privileges that are required for their job to be completed successfully. Least privilege also depends on the level of clearance a subject has.

3. CISO (chief information security officer) usually handles the security of technology—both hardware and software. The CISO also has extensive knowledge of the computer systems, programming, deployment methods, tools used, and systems to be acquired and retired. The role of the CSO is much broader compared to the CISO role. The CSO takes a holistic view of the organization's business risks, physical security, technological risks, and other possible risks.

4. Privacy is an individual's control of how much information (personal or otherwise) they want to release. Security is a mechanism that is implemented to provide that level of control to individuals or systems in the organization.

5. Baseline configuration helps create a uniformly secure system that has required software and hardware for all users and minimizes privilege creep and reduces attack surface. Providing baseline configuration on systems is a part of mandatory access control (MAC).

6. The following are some ways privilege escalations can happen:

   a. System administrators forget to rescind temporarily given escalated privileges.

   b. The security administrator trusts an employee blindly and gives more privileges.

   c. The organization simply does not have a policy for privileges, and everyone has full access.

   d. Employee(s) and the approving supervisor have formed a team that is planning mischief on systems and request additional privileges.

   e. Privileges were accidentally increased by an installing software.

   f. The organization does not have a skilled person who oversees the privilege creep.

   g. The ISSO and ISSM are lazy and do not notice the privilege creep.

   h. The organization has no defined security posture and follows a "so what?" attitude.

   i. The organization has no internal or external audit process in place.

7. Change management keeps track of changes made to software, hardware, or systems and needs authorization. It keeps track of assets and changes to assist with a successful audit. It also helps maintain an organization's integrity in maintaining the systems and software.

8. Computer crimes can be categorized as computer assisted (used a computer as an attack tool), computer targeted (the machine is the target of an attack), and computer incidental (some or all of the information from the computer has been used for an attack).

9. Each country has its own laws, and no one international law fits every nation. Therefore, it is hard to investigate and prosecute international criminals.

10. Copyright applies to written works, books, music, and such original works from authors or a corporation. Trade secret is like a formula for soda or a health drink. Until disclosed, it remains a secret. It's more like proprietary information.

11. Civil law, administrative law, criminal law, religious law, and mixed laws.

12. Examples of computer harm that come under crime laws are

   a. Unauthorized access

   b. Unauthorized alteration, destruction, or disclosure of information

   c. Insertion of malicious programming code

   d. Computer-assisted crime (uses computer/server as a tool)

   e. Computer-targeted crime (an activity directed at the computer/server)

   f. Computer is incidental (uses computer data for criminal activities)

13. By being proactive, a corporation can implement all security measures, thinking like a hacker to create a good security posture. Being proactive also means a corporation will try to find their own vulnerabilities before a hacker does.

14. Training provides education to know where an attack might be coming from. But awareness tells the users what not to do and what to do in case of a suspicious situation.

15. PenTesting helps uncover any vulnerabilities in the security posture and presents a report to the organization about where the possible vulnerabilities are and how to fix them.

16. It is best to revise the security posture at least once a year, but possibly more often as required. Revision is important for including new attacks and modern methods associated with improved, faster technology.

17. Containing the breach, investigation of the attack, informing the upper-level managers, and remediating the problem are important. Lessons learned should be created to document the breach for future help. Cybersecurity insurance, if available, can be another consideration.

Chapter 14

Follow a Proven Path for Security

If a corporate computer network was well planned and protected, has well-trained staff, and has a solid security posture and policy in place, they might have done their due diligence. However, that does not mean all the systems are guaranteed to be safe. We need to test the network regularly to prove that point. Security testing can be done internally by each branch and also by hiring a third-party ethical hacker who can conduct an in-depth penetration test (PenTest). Before a test can be even carried out, you must remember that the testing tools available may not all be free. Plus, who will be the person authorized to say yes to a PenTest, who stands to watch the tests, who takes the reports, and who will implement the improvements suggested in the report? You also know that the testing needs to be done on software, hardware, networks, the security process, and the posture adopted by the organization. In other words, before testing can be carried out, you have homework to do to set the house in order. With these things mind, security administration comes to the fore.

Advantages of Security Administration

To makes security work best, there must be a group of people who can take care of the security posture and who meet regularly to discuss the current state of security and how it can be continuously improved. For the security team to work in a holistic way, it should include a member from each department or branch, who then can discuss their point of view. The security administration should consist of

- Physical security
- Network security
- Software security
- Mobile devices security
- Data and database security

- Human resources
- Test division security
- Reports security
- Documentation security
- Asset repositories security
- Payroll and financial security
- Server room security
- Accounting security
- Hardware security
- Operating system security
- Cloud security
- Personal security
- Perimeter security (not IT related)
- Central change management
- Off premises storage security

The advantage of including each person is to include and have representation from each branch in the organization. Each department then designates their own information system security officer (ISSO). All the individual ISSOs will then report to the information system security manager (ISSM), chief information security officer (CISO), and then the chief security officer (CSO). Once the hierarchy is established, it is easy to go top down if any breach is found. In case of a breach, communication is easier to manage with the hierarchical structure wherein each branch follows its own ISSO who passes information throughout the branch.

As discussed in Chapter 13, "Security Administration," centrally established change management (CM) and the change approval board (CAB) help keep the integrity of the hardware, software, and systems as well as protect the confidentiality of the data and tools used by the corporation. Centrally managed change management helps minimize and conduct confidential and easy communication among all branches about a requested change. Sometimes a requesting employee may not know the names of the personnel who can do the job, and in such cases, CM will auto allocate some needed personnel. It is the job of the IT security committee to designate someone to do the following:

- Conduct or help conduct a PenTest
- Assist the penetration testing on the scheduled day

- Give and obtain proper authorizations and signed papers

- Plan a testing date with each department

- Cooperate during the test with the PenTesting professional

- Receive the report from the test

- Assimilate and discuss details of the report with each branch

- Remediate the problems highlighted in the report

- Create a record of the lessons learned from the whole procedure and be ready for the next round

Testing should also *not* be a one-and-done process but should be continuous monitoring. Since external testing can be expensive, it is possible to do internal testing several times a year. External testing to get an unbiased and independent report is generally recommended at least once a year.

When the security posture is evaluated with PenTesting there are some advantages:

- PenTesting mimics a situation when the tester presents themselves as a malicious external attacker. Their main goal is to see whether they can break the application or website and possibly steal data, create a system account, cause delays, stop processes, or shut down the service (DoS or DDoS).

- PenTesting can be made precise in terms of generating fewer false positives, but it takes a lot of time, permissions, and modifications to the testing strategy from the target company. False positives are mostly a result of tools/controls incorrectly identifying an activity or not detecting the pen testers' pre-set activities and giving a wrong response.

- PenTesting acts as a self-defense tool, whereby an organization can double-check their response plans and reiterate their everyday security policy and posture.

- Automated PenTesting helps in continuous monitoring because it can help identify new vulnerabilities or regression vulnerabilities after a vulnerability was fixed in an environment that changes a lot with people coming in and going out and database or software changing almost every day.

Penetration Testing

PenTesting can and should be used both in manual and automated ways. PenTesting basically follows three fundamental steps.

- **Explore/reconnaissance:** This is the first stage where the attacker tries to glean everything about the target. In this step, the tester finds what operating system the target has, what software is in use, what the latest patches are, and whether any vulnerabilities exist. Some more items—like hidden content, vulnerabilities, open ports, signatures of any viruses—are checked too. This phase gives a picture of the target to the attacker.

- **Break/attack:** In this phase, depending on the actual vulnerabilities found from the exploring stage, commands are sent to break or attack.

- **Generate a report:** A well-written and easily understandable report is prepared, showing the results of testing. The report includes vulnerabilities found, what method/tool was used to exploit those vulnerabilities, how bad the exploits turned out, and the level of severity of the exploitation and possible damage if it were not fixed.

The goal for the tester is to find as many vulnerabilities as possible that may pose a threat for the organization. PenTesting can also check whether an already-known and reported vulnerability has been fixed and test again to see if the fixed defect does not exist anymore. For this reason, PenTesting needs to be conducted repeatedly.

PenTesting comes in a variety of ways and needs a separate tool for each branch depending on what is being tested. Some of the widely used tools are listed in Table 14-1. The free tools offer some level of security testing but not everything. Many also provide training on how to use the basics and the details of particular security (Wi-Fi for example).

Table 14-1   *PenTesting Tools for Various Branches*

Name	Used For	Features
NMAP	Network scanning	Checks network devices, port scanning, and so on.
Metasploit	Vulnerability or weakness detection	More than a thousand types of exploits are available on many platforms with post-exploit code.
Kali Linux	PenTesting tool	Open-source Linux distribution of PenTesting tools (500+).
Burp Suite	Web application scanner, security testing (the basic version, Dastardly, is free)	Recurring scalable and almost everything scanner.
WireShark	Analyze protocols and monitor networks	Network traffic analysis, live data, packet captures, and check protocols.
SQLmap	SQL injection tool	SQL injection attacks/vulnerabilities.
Aircrack-ng	Wi-Fi network security check	Complete suite of tools to crack a Wi-Fi network. Works for Linux, macOS, and Windows.

Name	Used For	Features
BeEF	Browser exploitation framework penetration tool	Attacks web browsers with client-side vectors.
Zed Attack Proxy (ZAP)	Open-source PenTest tool	OWASP open-source tool for Linux, Windows, and macOS. Can be used also as an API.
Rapid7	Vulnerability management, managed detection response tool	Variety of tools for web and application security and also cloud security. Powerful reporting for compliance and remediation.
Intruder	Vulnerability scanner/penetration testing tool.	Internal and external vulnerability scanning and penetration testing.
Nessus	Vulnerability assessment	Tests for thousands of vulnerabilities. Integrates well with other products and is regularly updated with new threats.

Before running any of these tools, the most important thing to know is that one needs a written permission from the application, network, computer, or website owners. Note that written permission needs a valid signature (manual or digital) authorizing the ethical hacker. Without this permission, a hacker—ethical or not—can end up in a jail. For this reason, permission is also known as a "get out of jail free" card.

In this chapter, we discuss the details of PenTesting with three tools in brief.

ZAP

We start with the Zed Attack Proxy tool. The package is free and can be downloaded and run in a variety of ways. It can be run from the command line or as an API. From the command line, several commands can be executed, such as the following:

-quickurl http://example.com/ -quickout /path/to/report.xml

The first item (quickurl) looks at the URL provided to attack (example.com), and quickout is the file where we get the report. Other types or formats of reports are possible instead of XML. Another option, quickprogress, shows the progress on the screen as the URL is attacked. Documentation provides all steps required to attack a URL. For example, Listing 14-1 can be used as an authentication helper (can be added directly to automation framework).

Listing 14-1 *Adding Automatic Authentication in ZAP*

```
env:
  contexts:
  - name: "target"
    urls:
    - https://example.com
    includePaths: []
    excludePaths: []
    authentication:
      method: "browser"
      parameters:
        loginPageUrl: "https://example.com/login"
      verification:
        method: "autodetect"
    sessionManagement:
      method: "autodetect"
    users:
    - name: "test@example.com"
      credentials:
        username: "test@example.com"
        password: "password123"
```

Notice that Listing 14-1 describes an environment for the URL example.com and the username and passwords. These help authenticate the ZAP into the URL and check for errors. This is the reason why PenTesting needs written permission and needs to provide the credentials to pen tester. ZAP can be downloaded as a GUI and run manually. ZAP GUI has the following self-explanatory items, as shown in Figures 14-1 and 14-2:

1. **Menu bar:** Typical functions and setup.

2. **Toolbar:** Shows small icons as buttons for one-click actions for many features.

3. **Tree window:** The left side of the window displays the targets (sites).

4. **Workspace window:** The main area of work for requests, responses, and scripts. All these can be edited, saved, and so on.

5. **Information window:** This where we get information from the tool—the results, errors, and all communication to help an attacker perfect their mechanisms.

6. **Footer:** One-line summary for the user with icons to distinguish messages.

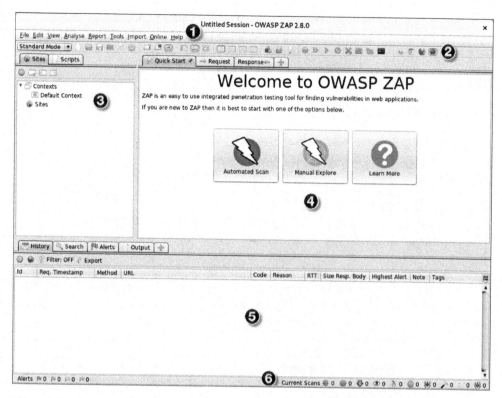

Figure 14-1   *ZAP GUI Interface*

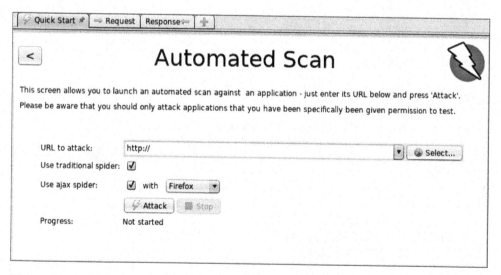

Figure 14-2   *ZAP GUI Interface, Automated Scan*

Like every modern-day application, ZAP GUI has the online help, warnings, and various flags to show the severity of the vulnerabilities. If the tool is integrated as an API, one can use it with Java, as shown in Listing 14-2.

Listing 14-2 *ZAP Java Code in Passive Scan with API*

```java
public class PassiveScan {

    private static final int ZAP_PORT = 8080;
    private static final String ZAP_API_KEY = null;
    private static final String ZAP_ADDRESS = "localhost";

    public static void main(String[] args) {
        ClientApi api = new ClientApi(ZAP_ADDRESS, ZAP_PORT, ZAP_API_KEY);
        int numberOfRecords;

        try {
            // TODO : explore the app (Spider, etc) before using the Passive Scan API,
            // Refer the explore section for details
            // Loop until the passive scan has finished
            while (true) {
                Thread.sleep(2000);
                api.pscan.recordsToScan();
                numberOfRecords = Integer.parseInt(((ApiResponseElement) api.pscan.recordsToScan()).getValue());
                System.out.println("Number of records left for scanning : " + numberOfRecords);
                if (numberOfRecords == 0) {
                    break;
                }
            } // while

            System.out.println("Passive Scan completed");

            // Print Passive scan results/alerts
            System.out.println("Alerts:");
            System.out.println(new String(api.core.xmlreport(), StandardCharsets.UTF_8));

        } // try
        catch (Exception e) {
            System.out.println("Exception : " + e.getMessage());
            e.printStackTrace();
        } // catch
    } // main
} // class
```

From the script it is easy to see the port number, key, and URL used with the clientAPI class. Active scan can similarly be conducted easily with all the built-in classes. The script is mostly self-explanatory for a seasoned Java developer and is as simple as creating a class, calling recordsToScan(), and printing the results in an XML file. Simple-to-understand quick 10-minute videos are available on the ZAP website for anyone to learn this tool. In addition, there are other marketplace tools that integrate with ZAP that you can buy or download for free. All details are available on the ZAP website with useful links to the respective URLs.

Burp Suite

Our second tool is the Burp suite, which is widely used for PenTesting. Burp suite is not free. The free version, Dastardly, has a few features but not much. Dastardly is the dynamic application security testing (DAST) tool that can find seven different vulnerabilities. The DAST tool can also be used with Continuous Integration (CI) and Continuous Development (CD), also known as the CI/CD pipeline. The professional version of the Burp suite is more exhaustive and helpful and works for hundreds of problems. The site where you can download the Burp suite also has a free training portal for web security with dozens of labs to try.

Figures 14-3 and 14-4 show the Burp suite.

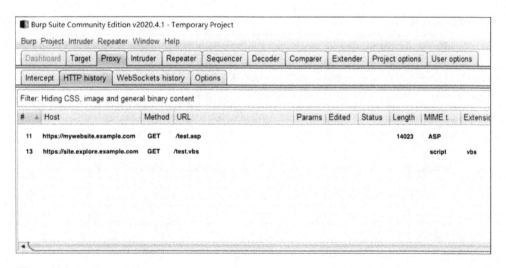

Figure 14-3 *Burp Suite*

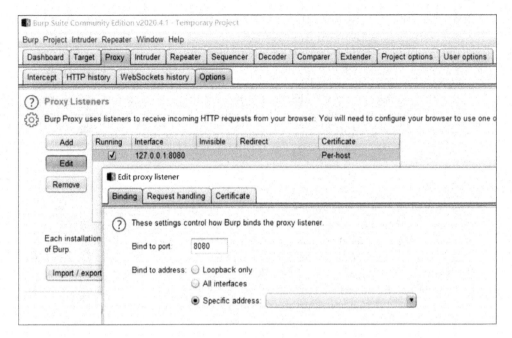

Figure 14-4   *Burp Suite for Proxy Listener Setup*

Aircrack-ng

Lastly, we discuss the Wi-Fi attack tool Aircrack-ng. It has tools for wireless cracking that are heavily scripted command-line tools (you need a lot of knowledge of Linux). The website describes the tool as useful for the following:

- **Monitoring:** Packet capture and data export to text files for further processing

- **Attacking:** Replay attacks, deauthentication, and fake access points via packet injection

- **Testing:** Checking Wi-Fi cards and driver capabilities (capture/injection)

- **Cracking:** WEP and WPA PSK (WPA 1 and 2) protocols

Figures 14-5 through 14-7 (adapted directly from the Aircrack-ng website) show some of the various commands issued. Notice in Figure 14-5 how the key was found and how many keys were tested by the software.

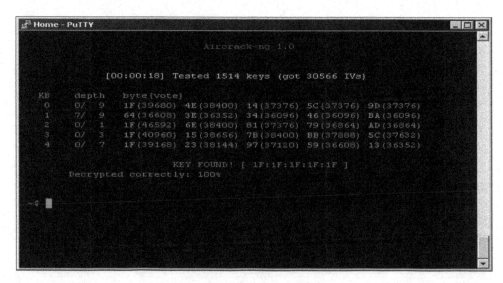

Figure 14-5 *Aircrack-ng Results from the PuTTY Window*

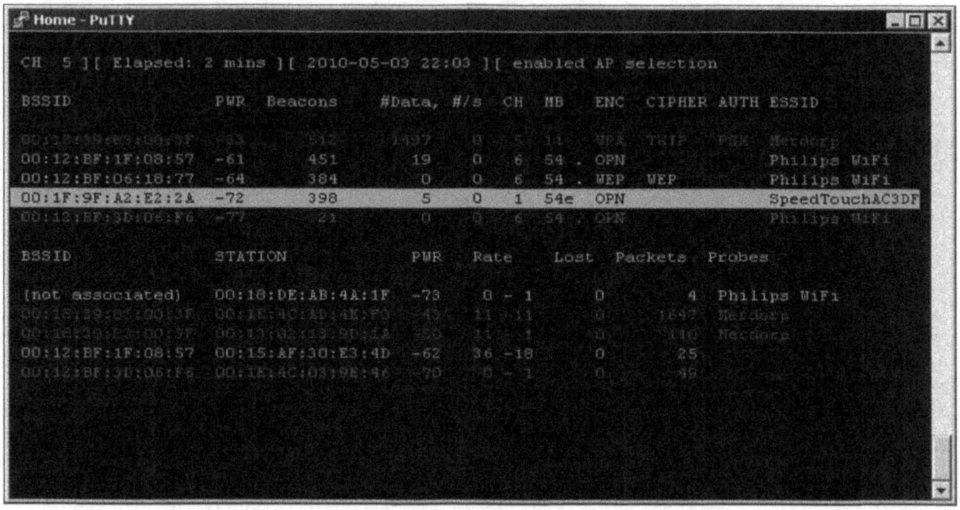

Figure 14-6 *Airodump-ng Results from the PuTTY Window*

```
Home - PuTTY                                                    _ □ ×
root@bt:~# airmon-ng


Interface        Chipset           Driver

wlan0            Atheros           ath5k - [phy0]
wlan1            RTL8187           rtl8187 - [phy2]
wlan2            AR9001U           ar9170usb - [phy4]


root@bt:~# ▮
```

Figure 14-7   *Airmon-ng Results from the PuTTY Window*

It's not simple to master any of the PenTesting tools we've mentioned. Mastery takes time, patience, and effort. For example, the Burp suite needs a lot of inside knowledge of how the websites work, what can be cracked, and how to insert various tags, SQL commands, and so on into the script to run. Some automated testing is available, but the results will not make it any easier for the user if they lack understanding of SQL or HTML and scripting details for the website. Likewise, Aircrack-ng needs details of Linux, Windows, or the chipsets of the Wi-Fi boxes. Aircrack-ng also mentions specifically that not all chipsets are even supported by their PenTesting software, and those supported may or may not work. The knowledge required to probe for the chipset and then deciding if the chipset allows a packet of data to inject are basic requirements and take time to master. In other words, becoming an ethical hacker requires time and effort, but it is really useful to test the websites and applications for the security stature of an organization.

Penetration Test Reports

After the PenTesting is done, the tester should prepare a report for the organization to follow a routine of fixing the vulnerabilities found. NIST's technical guide to information security testing and assessment, special publication 800-115, gives details of how to report what was found in testing. Many other formats are available, but generally, the following details are agreed among all:

A. **Executive summary:** Without giving too many technical details, this section should describe in a few paragraphs (one page at maximum) what was tested, what was found, the biggest risks and vulnerabilities, and the urgent fixes recommended. It can also give a risk rating (such as 1 to 5, with 5 being the maximum risk score or whatever rating the tester follows generally) to indicate a worst-case scenario. This summary is generally directed at busy C-level managers who will filter the report to their staff to take appropriate actions.

B. **Dates of test and permissions:** This is where the tester or their company is identified, dates of testing are mentioned, who-is-who in the testing is explained, and the written permissions are obtained. A copy of the permissions can be attached to the report to prove that the testing was done by invitation and was an ethical task rather than something a hacker attempted. It would be nice to share the qualifications, certifications, and experience of the pen tester (or their organization) in this area as well.

C. **Test scope and method:** Since not everything can be tested or needs to be tested, this section provides what is tested: hardware, network, software, applications, physical security, or anything else that an organization hired the pen tester to check. Note that this is required even for internal PenTesting or for an external ethical hacker. How the testing was conducted also needs to be mentioned. It is also necessary to mention whether the testing is limited to internal networks and intranet applications or websites or both internal and external attacks were carried out for testing. The report can also mention the type of data found (PII, PHI, and so on).

D. **Tools used:** This section must include what software for automated testing was used, how the manual testing was conducted, what parameters and command lines were used, and how/why those parameters were chosen for testing, along with any screenshots or listing of the commands (which can be repeated if necessary for a demonstration).

E. **Internal testing:** Results for each test—one section per test giving the common vulnerabilities and exposure (CVE; see Chapter 4, "Database Security Introduction," and https://cve.mitre.org)—details of parameters, outcomes of what was input to the testing tool, software or system, and what the output was (expected, unexpected). If any of the tests yielded or exposed a vulnerability, the seriousness of the vulnerability is indicated with a color code (for example, dark red for a serious problem and green for a test that passed).

F. **External testing:** This is identical to the internal testing and reporting except that the tests here are conducted from outside the network. The same details as in section E will be mentioned for each test.

G. **Conclusion and recommendations:** This is the most read part of the report. It should reflect what the ethical hacker found, the seriousness of vulnerabilities, where they exist, and the chance of getting the organization's security hacked. For each vulnerability, the pen tester should give a recommendation on how to remediate the problem to overcome the vulnerability. If this testing is a repeated one, it should also mention what was found in the earlier report, what was remediated, and what was not, along with any regression vulnerabilities found.

Make sure to reread, spell check, double-check, and revise. Reports should be prepared with good caution and in a professional manner. The report must be checked for bad spelling and technical correctness because the organization can ask for a demonstration with a repeat test being done in person. Any bugs should be eliminated and the report presented in a timely manner.

Some reports also include references for URLs, tools, and books, but it is the choice of the testing person or the organization. An example of vulnerabilities found and their risk is shown in Table 14-2.

Table 14-2 *Vulnerabilities Found and Their Risk, Impact, and Remediation*

Vulnerability	Risk	Impact	Remediation
CVE-2022-23305	Remote exploit without authorization	High	Apply latest patch available from Oracle, Inc.
CVE-2023-21779	Visual Studio remote code execution vulnerability	Medium	Apply available patch from Microsoft, Inc.

Another example of the report is shown here: The pen tester went to check the folder and found files on a Windows server as follows.

```
07/22/2023   10:23 AM          <DIR>                    .
07/22/2023   10:23 AM          <DIR>                    . .
07/25/2023   11:43 AM          143876              screenshot.png
07/25/2023   11:43 AM          1,321,917           CustomerData.xlsx
...
...
08/12/2023   09:20 PM          4,296               SecCert2022.pfx
```

Looking at these details, we know that there may be two important files: customer data in Excel sheet form and the security certificate in the pfx form. Both the files can be breached with other tools. If the hacker can actually access the root folders, their intention will be to first create a system account so that they can come back and reattack anytime they want. The following is a command a hacker can try:

```
C:\>net user / add PeaceDove pa$$<dro>
```

At this point, if the password policies are set to good complexity, the server will respond with an error; otherwise, the hacker has successfully created the username "PeaceDove" with the password. If the policy for passwords is well set, then the error can be still corrected by the hacker, as shown here:

```
C:\>net user / add PeaceDove pa$$<dro>?>@*$
```

The hacker can still create the account and come back anytime. This is a serious vulnerability. The report now should mention all these details and the remediation for the problem found—close directory-level access, move the customer data and certificate files to another location, encrypt those files (if not already encrypted), and then repeat the test to make sure the vulnerability is remediated.

Audits—Internal and External and STIG Checking

Security testing can be done with various tools for penetration, and yet the security posture can be attacked by a hacker. The main reasons for these are human error and laziness of the organization to implement remedies suggested by the pen tester. Other contributors to final doom are probably a "yeah-so-what" attitude and recklessness that an attack might not happen to the organization, or the chance of it happening is very low. For these reasons, continuous monitoring and regular checks of what was done, is being done, and will be done should take precedence for security.

The U.S. Department of Defense (DoD) has designed a guide called Security Technical Implementation Guide (STIG), which gives various causes of errors and vulnerabilities along with a rank and the corresponding CVE. The STIG testing is *not* a PenTesting software but lists the vulnerabilities known in a vendor-sold software package and how to find them along with a recommendation of how to fix the found weaknesses. In other words, STIGs are templates for secure computing. The STIG checklists are primarily for the government, but the public can use them at their own effort. The STIGs are categorized as I, II, or III or by vulnerability ID, and there is also a STIG viewer program that can be downloaded. STIGs are separately enclosed in a zip file that is read by the viewer. STIGs are classified by the software vendor (Microsoft, Linux, Oracle, and so on) and by version of the software. For someone testing the Linux-related STIGs, they can start the STIG viewer, which loads the zip file with all STIGs, and choose the Linux subject. Then the viewer will show all the STIGs known by their category. This can be used to do internal testing for the particular vulnerability. Figure 14-8 shows the STIG viewer. The loaded STIGs are in the STIG Library provided by DoD and are shown in the bottom of the figure. Figure 14-9 shows the search for string "SQL" with a list of vendors whose STIGs are available.

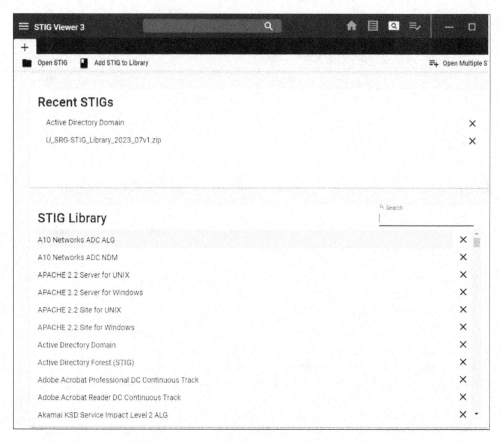

Figure 14-8   *DoD's STIG Viewer Available for the Public*

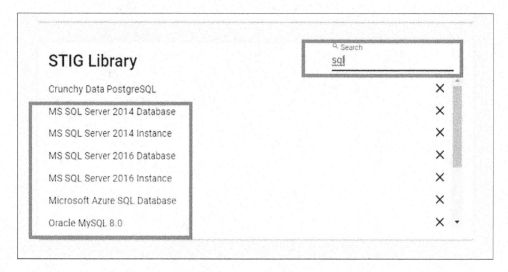

Figure 14-9   *STIGs for "sql" Search String*

In Figure 14-8, note that the STIGs are listed by the software vendor. Even if the software you've purchased has remediated all the known problems at the time of shipping the software to you (or when you downloaded it), there could be some problems in setup or some newly discovered vulnerabilities. These are listed in the STIG and need to be corrected. Internally, the branch that has the software can do this in cooperation with the other branches. For example, if you are using SQL Server software on Windows servers, you can run these STIG checks one by one with the help of a systems administrator who helped host the software on the servers. Also, each server needs to be checked for the same STIG separately and the recommended remediation applied. Software like Fortify can check coding errors and any loopholes but would not be able to check STIG noted or well known. All the checks done on a piece of software can be noted with comments and a checklist file (*.ckl) saved for audit purposes.

Let's look into how a STIG item is checked and remediated. In Figure 14-10, a STIG by group ID V-213933 was selected, and the right side of window shows all the details of that STIG. The STIG has a category, classification, and rule. If we move further down the right side panel, details of the findings, how the accounts should not be shared, and all other information are shown in text form. Where applicable, a remediation is suggested for correcting this finding. While correcting a finding or when a finding is not applicable, you can type notes like "Not applicable, this was corrected on 8/22/2019" or something similar and save the file as a checklist file.

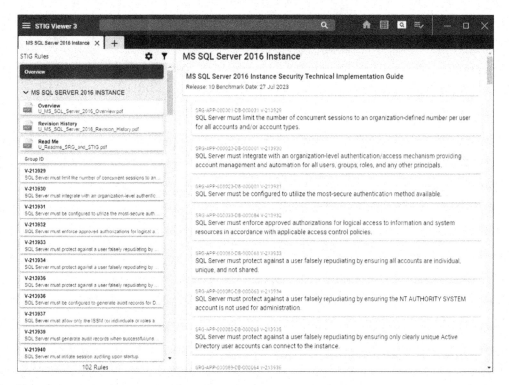

Figure 14-10 *STIGs Noticed in a Microsoft SQL Server 2016 Instance*

Figure 14-11 shows details of the V-213933 for MS SQL Server instance. It also gives the severity category and classification and explains how to fix that vulnerability, along with other details.

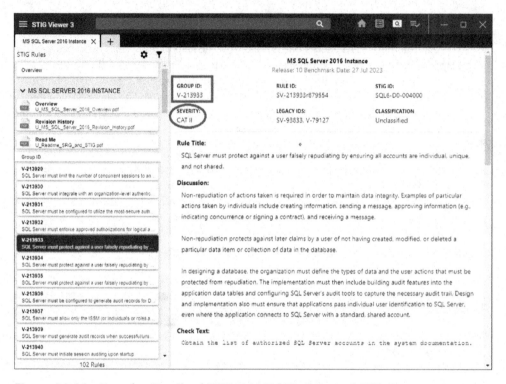

Figure 14-11   *Complete Details of STIG V-213933 in Microsoft SQL Server*

Look at the description given on the right side of Figure 14-11 for another STIG by ID for Microsoft Office 365 Plus, a product that provides Access, Excel, and others. Excel and Access can run macros written in Visual Basic script, but running those can be a security threat in a corporate environment because a disgruntled employee can run any macro that might cause a security incident.

If you haven't already noticed, it is worth noticing now that the STIG check for this item is not something Microsoft Corporation can fix because the system where the Office 365 product is installed needs to be maintained for security by the local administrator. Some offices may allow running macros, but some may not. This is not a security flaw in the product per se, but it is a route a hacker can adapt to write script in the macro to hack a product. This is where a STIG check comes handy—to check for vulnerabilities that can be controlled on the client side.

The text in Figure 14-12 shows how to check for the error in the first case under the Check Text subheading and when it is a finding. The Fix Text area informs the user how to fix the vulnerability by disabling macros. The text also says "the policy setting," implying that the policies need to kick in from the organization. At the bottom of the description is the reference list with the NIST document list and other details.

```
                        Microsoft Office 365 ProPlus
                    Release: 9 Benchmark Date: 27 Apr 2023

GROUP ID: V-223280       RULE ID: SV-223280r879616      STIG ID: O365-AC-000001
SEVERITY: CAT II         LEGACY IDS: SV-108737, V-99633  CLASSIFICATION: Unclassified

Rule Title:
      Macros must be blocked from running in Access files from the Internet.
Discussion:
      This policy setting allows you to block macros from running in Office files that come from the Internet.

      If you enable this policy setting, macros are blocked from running, even if "Enable all macros" is selected
      in the Macro Settings section of the Trust Center. Also, instead of having the choice to "Enable Content",
      users will receive a notification that macros are blocked from running. If the Office file is saved to a trusted
      location or was previously trusted by the user, macros will be allowed to run.

      If you disable or do not configure this policy setting, the settings configured in the Macro Settings section
      of the Trust Center determine whether macros run in Office files that come from the Internet.
Check Text:
      Verify the policy value for User Configuration >> Administrative Templates >> Microsoft Access 2016 >>
      Application Settings >> Security >> Trust Center "Block macros from running in Office files from the
      Internet" is set to "Enabled".

      Use the Windows Registry Editor to navigate to the following key:

      HKCU\Software\Policies\Microsoft\Office\16.0\access\security

      If the value blockcontentexecutionfrominternet is REG_DWORD = 1, this is not a finding.
Fix Text:
      Set the policy value for User Configuration >> Administrative Templates >> Microsoft Access 2016 >>
      Application Settings >> Security >> Trust Center "Block macros from running in Office files from the
      Internet" to "Enabled".
                                    References
CCI-001170
Prevents the automatic execution of mobile code in organization-defined software applications.
NIST SP 800-53 Revision 4 :: SC-18 (4)
NIST SP 800-53A :: SC-18 (4).1 (iii) (iv)
NIST SP 800-53 :: SC-18 (4)
NIST SP 800-53 Revision 5 :: SC-18 (4)
```

Figure 14-12 *Recommended STIG Detail on the Rule Discussion, Checking and Fixing the Vulnerability*

There is a small problem with STIGs and checklists. The STIGs are updated regularly, but they may not match the exact software version you might be using. If we are using SQL Server version 2022, the STIG lists downloaded may only be available for SQL Server version 2019 but not for the exact SQL Server 2022 version. But the STIG checks—whatever version they are—help maintain quality for the vendor software. STIG checks can also be added by vendors or whoever notices problems and has a solution they can recommend. For this, there is a vendor process to follow on the DoD website at https://public.cyber.mil/stigs/vendor-process/. There is a quarterly release of STIG lists that can be checked from the same website.

Instead of buying some software and then looking for a STIG checklist for that software, what if there is an approved list of vendor software? The DoD cyber.mil website also has an approved products list (APL). Figure 14-13 shows a list of products that can be searched. From the **Device Type**, **Vendor**, or **Key Words** dropdown menus, you can choose a product and look for the results. For the approved list of Wireless Access Bridge, Figure 14-13 shows three choices. (Look for "results returned" in the bottom-left side.) The first one is a CommScope Ruckus Smart Zone 100, 300, and virtual smart zone (vSZ). It also lists three buttons for **APL Memo**, **IO Certification**, and the **Request CAP**. Clicking **IO Certification** shows the certifications by date. For this particular model, the latest certification was in January 2023. The product list can be exported for distribution in Excel or PDF formats for further use.

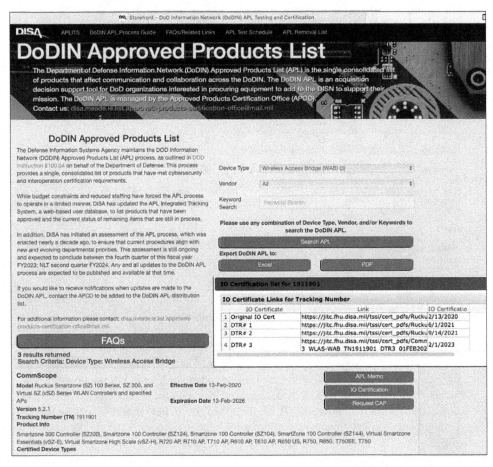

Figure 14-13 *List of Approved Products for Wireless Access Bridge*

Interestingly, the website also lists to-be-removed products, as shown in Figure 14-14. The website specifically says the following:

The solutions listed below are no longer approved for purchase for new installation by any components of the DoD as set forth in DoDI 8100.04. However, products procured prior to DoDIN APL removal may be eligible for continued operation in DoD networks provided applicable security requirements are met (IAVA, STIG, etc.).

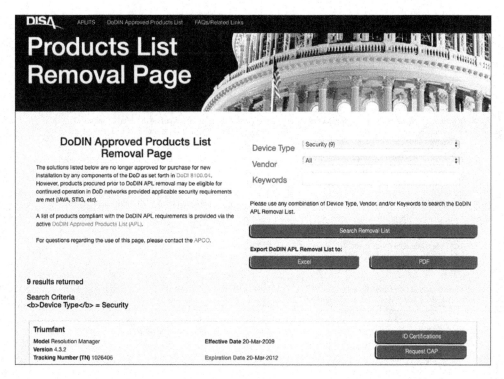

Figure 14-14   *DoD/DISA Products List Removal Page*

Besides the DISA unclassified checklists for STIG discussed previously, there exist some other standards and general checks per NIST and DoD 8500 directives. These can be found on the internet. For example, Figure 14-15 is an item from the DoD-8500 list.

NIST standards tell what can be implemented, but they are not any policies per se. They are recommendations for use. Policies need to be created depending on the NIST standards and directives. DISA STIG lists are similar recommendations to fix vulnerabilities. The STIG list doesn't find vulnerabilities; it lists them as per the software version and release dates and provides recommendations for remediation. Also, STIGs help to build gold disc images. It would be wise to follow all these directives to create an organizational policy for a better security posture.

DCPP-1 Ports, Protocols, and Services

Overview

DoD information systems comply with DoD ports, protocols, and services guidance. AIS applications, outsourced IT-based processes and platform IT identify the network ports, protocols, and services they plan to use as early in the life cycle as possible and notify hosting enclaves. Enclaves register all active ports, protocols, and services in accordance with DoD and DoD Component guidance.

MAC / CONF	Impact	Subject Area
MACI MACII MACIII	Medium	Security Design and Configuration

Details
Threat
Open, undocumented, and unnecessary ports, protocols, and services increase the risk of data compromise and system unavailability. Adhering to DoD guidance minimizes the inherent risk associated with ports, protocols, and services.

Guidance
1. DoD information systems shall comply with DoD ports, protocols, and services guidance.
2. A port, protocol, or service that does not explicitly support a business function shall be disabled or removed.
3. A list of ports, protocols, and services shall be documented and regularly updated and maintained through the CCB.

4. Organizations shall identify the network ports, protocols, and services they plan to use within AIS applications, outsourced IT-based processes and platform IT as early in the life cycle as possible and notify hosting enclaves.
5. Enclaves shall register all active ports, protocols, and services in accordance with DoD and DoD Component guidance.
6. Components shall monitor emerging threats and vulnerabilities to the ports, protocols, and services they use.

References
JTF-GNO PNP Update Message, 14 March 2003
ASD/C3I Memorandum DoD Ports, Protocols and Services, 28 January 2003
DoD Ports, Protocols and Services Security Technical Guidance, 05 November 2005
Firewall Guidance Message. September 2002
DoDI 8551.1, Ports, Protocols, and Services Management (PPSM), 13 August 2004
http://iase.disa.mil/ports/index.html
DoDD O-8530.1, Computer Network Defense (CND), 08 January 2001

Figure 14-15   *Example of an Item from the DoD-8500 List Showing a Threat and Guidance on How to Fix the Threat*

OPSEC—The Operational Security

After we have created a application or a website and gone through every possible security step we can and created proper policies, we may be able to assume that the security stature is good enough. But is it? You really do not know, so now you also do continuous monitoring and update your hardware and software to make sure you are in sync with the up-to-date security to patch vulnerabilities and watch the risk. Then the process of operational security (OPSEC) kicks in.

NIST defines OPSEC as a

systematic and proven process by which potential adversaries can be denied information about capabilities and intentions by identifying, controlling, and protecting generally unclassified evidence of the planning and execution of sensitive activities. The process involves five steps: identification of critical information, analysis of threats, analysis of vulnerabilities, assessment of risks, and application of appropriate countermeasures.

OPSEC is a team process where everyone has a role. These five steps are described in detail in the following list. In an indirect way, what we have done so far is OPSEC; we have followed the processes of the five steps one by one. It's important to notice that the process is a continuous cycle and does not have a start or end point. It needs to be repeated and goes on for a good security posture, as shown in Figure 14-16.

Figure 14-16   *OPSEC Cycle as Illustrated by the Director of National Intelligence*

1. **Identification of critical information:** Before any action can be done, the first step is to identify what to protect. For this reason, critical information or assets must be identified and the data classified per organizational policies. Examples of critical information are PII, PHI, financial and accounting information, audit data, and patented and private information.

2. **Analysis of threats:** Threat analysis for the identified assets or critical information is the second step where we proceed to find out what threats may exist or materialize, who can cause the threats, how bad the effect of a threat can be, and so on. Can threats (the actions) be caused by external or internal agents? These vectors or threat agents are either people or items such as viruses and malware. In this step, a detailed analysis is created to get ready for possible trouble before it actually happens.

3. **Analysis of vulnerabilities:** In this step, you want to know what weaknesses your systems, hardware, or software have, address those vulnerabilities, and, if possible, remediate them as soon as possible. For this step, you use software such as Fortify, STIG checks, and manual code checks. If you know of a patch being available from a reputable firm, you want to know about it as well. Note that all vulnerabilities may not apply to all systems.

4. **Assessment of risks:** Once you know the assets, their values, their vulnerabilities, and how these vulnerabilities pose a problem if a threat materializes, you want to know how much risk you have from that threat. You create a threat and risk matrix to see what you can do for that particular risk. A risk can be mitigated, transferred, ignored, or accepted depending on the level and the damage it might cause.

5. **Application of appropriate countermeasures:** In this step, you address the risk. A risk can be accepted if the countermeasure is more expensive than the damage the risk would cause. But for mitigating a risk, some countermeasures are mandatory and advised. For example, buying a firewall is very important for the computer network even though a particular risk might not materialize in the near future. Having a firewall is important because it protects against multiple vulnerabilities, not just one virus or malware. For instance, for someone living in the state of California, earthquakes pose more than normal risk, and companies in that state need earthquake insurance (risk transfer). But for someone in New York, buying earthquake insurance may not be necessary; they would accept the risk because earthquakes are less likely in their state. For data, encryption and protection of the PII or PHI are some steps of countermeasures. Training and awareness of employees also fall under this step because they enable the employees to be aware and know threats before they materialize.

An optional sixth step of continuous and periodic monitoring is recommended by the Director of National Intelligence (DNI). In general, this step should be done regularly or at least once a year:

Assess periodically (continuous monitoring): This is the process where you learn about new problems, new security patches available, any new threats materializing, possible countermeasures available and how or if those threats and countermeasures apply to your organization in facing those threats. In this step, you also find what you learned and document what happened, how it happened, and how to be ready if it happens again.

Digital Forensics—Software Tools

Even when we have all the problems addressed, if a threat materializes, what should you do? We discussed this in the earlier chapters: how to collect information, how to stop the damage, and so on. But not all the information you collect may be useful in presenting it to a court of law or to the authorities. Digital forensics, per the International Council of E-Commerce Consultants (EC-Council), is defined as a process of identifying, preserving, analyzing, and documenting digital evidence. These are further detailed as nine different phases:

Phase 1. **First response:** In this phase, the first occurrence of a security incident such as a data breach is known or noticed. If a new account creation, file copy, or file locks were noticed, immediately the system administrator or the data owners are notified of a breach or leak of data. Depending on the type of security incident, actions in this phase are different for each instance.

Phase 2. **Search and seizure:** Once an incident is noticed, searching for the details of how and where it happened and getting control of those devices to get more information follow. Search and seizure does not mean a hijacked router or network device is just switched off by pulling the plug. On the contrary, it involves controlling the device, getting the logs, and finding more information while the device is functioning.

Phase 3. **Collect evidence:** Collecting the evidence in a systematic manner is important or the information that was collected may be deemed useless. Proper forensic methods should be followed for handling the evidence, which include e-discovery methods.

Phase 4. **Secure the evidence:** The collected data must be accurate, authentic, and accessible for it to be presented to a court of law or authorities.

Phase 5. **Data acquisition:** This step, also known as data collection, involves the process of retrieving the electronically stored information (ESI). When such retrieval is done correctly, it can show the difference between the data before and after a security incident. Note that this information also must have details of who collected the data, what time, and the digital signature of the collector.

Phase 6. **Data analysis:** Collected data is analyzed to show that there was a breach or modification and that the evidence can be presented to the court. Data analysis involves various methods such as examination, modeling, conversion, and diverse statistical methods.

Phase 7. **Evidence assessment:** Once the data is analyzed, the investigator creates provable evidence of the assessment. The evidence depends on what can be proved and the scope of the case presented in a court of law. Not all evidence may be allowed or applies to a particular security incidence.

Phase 8. **Document and report:** Creating documentation in a proper format is necessary for all findings. Adequate and acceptable evidence should be mentioned with pictures, text, and anything else necessary for a court of law. It should be noted that each court (federal or state) may have a different format and details for what is allowed and what can be presented.

Phase 9. **Testify as an expert witness:** In this case, the professional who investigated the security incident and accurately retrieved evidence per the forensic procedures can testify as a witness when required and explain the processes followed and what was found.

A number of software packages are available for digital forensics. The sleuth kit, OSForensics, FTK manager, Hex Editor Neo, Autopsy, and Bulk Extractor are some of the tools that help in digital forensics. Autopsy is a free downloadable end-to-end open-source tool. Autopsy uses cases and data sources as starting points. These can be a disk image or USB drive. From the left side menu, a case and data source can be added before a scan can begin. The rest of the results are self-explanatory to most users. Figure 14-17 shows an example window. Clicking **Recent Documents** shows there are 24 files. Selecting the Hacking into computer systems.lnk file shows its details in Hex, strings, file metadata, and so on. Autopsy also has reporting features. A final report can be generated with all analysis results using the **Generate Report** toolbar button. Reports can be generated in HTML, XLS, KML, and other formats.

Add-on modules can be written or requested from Autopsy for a price. These modules differ from one organization to the next depending on the investigative case and are not generally provided free. Neither are they useful for all. But examples and some generic modules for law enforcement and help on how to write your own modules are provided for individual requests.

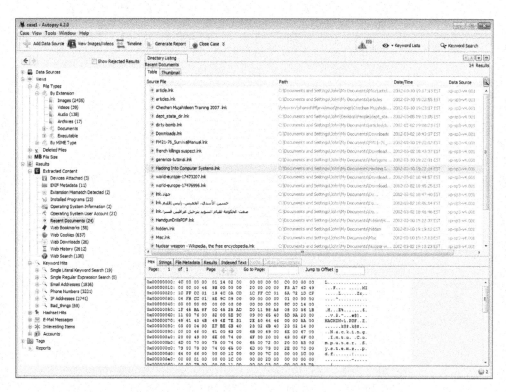

Figure 14-17 *Example of Autopsy Digital Forensics Case Window*

Lessons Learned/Continuous Improvement

The last—but still an important—part of maintaining a great security posture is to create the lessons learned document and write what the organization has learned as well as how these lessons help in the future in training employees and avoiding a repetition of a security incident. In this process, you need to do the following:

- **List the items or important tasks:** Since security is everyone's job, the process of taking care is well documented, staff is trained, and made aware first. Even with all the care and due diligence, things can still go wrong. Thus, we create a list of important tasks for security and watch them on a regular basis.

- **Create a table of successes/failures:** A sample table is created to check what went wrong, what could improve, and maybe even what was missing. A responsible party already allocated will need to read it. If no one has been allocated, a new responsibility needs to be assigned. This table can look like a list of vulnerabilities, such as Table 14-3, which shows the effect of a countermeasure on an incident if any, and what remediation is available or recommended. It also has a point of contact who should know about the results. Other details like the date when the vulnerability was noticed first, who noticed, and so on, can go into the table to provide more information.

Table 14-3 *Lessons Learned Table for an Incident (CM – Countermeasure, POC – Point of Contact)*

Vulnerability/ Task/Item	CM Was NOT in Place	CM Worked Well	CM Failed	CM Worked Partly	Remediation
"WetPaint" virus			X		Update firewall with new signature from vendor. (POC: network administrator)
CVE-2023-38169 (MS SQL Server's ODBC problem)	X				Newly discovered CVE. Install patch from Microsoft immediately. (POC: database administrator)
End user input eight characters or less in a new password creation attempt		Password policy did not allow the user to create eight-character password			None, but keep watching this CM for effectiveness. (POC: system administrators of all Windows, Unix, and Linux systems)

Vulnerability/ Task/Item	CM Was NOT in Place	CM Worked Well	CM Failed	CM Worked Partly	Remediation
File downloads by end users with least privileges				X	Large files are failing to download but files up to 27 MB are downloading fine. This should not happen. Modify the policy and file download rules. (POC: system administrators of all Windows, Mac, Unix, Linux, and mobile operating systems)

- **Share with staff and ask feedback:** Once the table is created and the document is done, it should be circulated to the points of contact, staff, and all other concerned persons. It is very important to seek feedback and involve staff in the process to know what they think of the process and how it can be improved. When the staff feels they are being heard, productivity naturally improves and the process gets better. We also know that feedback from different levels of staff would be different, and everyone's opinion should be considered in detail.

- **Incorporate feedback into the document:** Once feedback is received, corrections should be made to the lessons learned document or a "discussion" part is added with proper answers to each concern raised by the staff and all employees.

- **Reevaluate the lessons:** With the feedback given, reevaluate the process and improvise it for what should be done next time, should the same incident arise.

- **Recirculate and store for the future:** The last step is to circulate the document once more with added features and feedback and store the document on a repository for everyone's use. A repository is important because it is a well-known fact that people may quickly forget where they saved the document when they need it most. It is also possible that their certificates and smart card might have changed or renewed, and any files saved earlier on email or disk may not be accessible with the new certificates. And everyone should be aware of the repository location in case they need to access the lessons learned document.

Summary

It is usually best to create and follow a set policy depending on NIST and other recommendations for a better security posture of an organization. Security does not just include information technology; it can be and is spawned over a wide range of branches, departments, and areas. Change management and CAB can help form a better security posture as well.

PenTesting can be either done in house or by an external third party. There are many PenTesting tools available for free and purchase. Reporting results of a PenTest follows a standard template where the pen tester gives a report and suggests a solution. A repeated PenTest should normally look at any earlier PenTest reports and make sure the earlier bugs identified, if any, are corrected.

STIG checking helps check vulnerabilities in commercial off-the-shelf software such as Oracle, MS SQL Server, or Office 365. A STIG viewer helps track all related STIGs into a file named check list file. The Department of Defense also has approved a list of products that one can check before actually buying a product if it is approved. DoD also provides a list of retired products that are no longer supported with new IT security stature.

After following all security measures, we also need to monitor security regularly. This is called Operational Security (OPSEC). OPSEC is a systematic and proven process by which potential adversaries can be denied information. If information security is hacked at all, there are proper methods to collect and report information. These are grouped into digital forensics.

Lessons learned is a step of security posture as well where we collect all the information from a breach; analyze what happened, why it happened, and what damages were done and evaluate how we fixed the problem. This lessons learned document helps avoid future attacks. These documents need to be checked for correctness and saved for the future.

Chapter 14 Questions

1. Which departments or branches in an organization should be included or excluded to represent it's security administration?

2. What is the advantage of PenTesting?

3. What are the steps in penetration attack testing?

4. What is the OWASP's ZAP tool?

5. What is Dastardly?

6. What functions can Aircrack-ng accomplish?

7. What is the last item described in a well-prepared penetration test report?

8. Is STIG checking the same as PenTesting?

9. How are the STIGs described on the DoD military website?

10. Where can one find the approved product list and the removal lists?

11. What are the basic steps of OPSEC?

12. What is digital forensics, and what are the correct steps in digital forensics?

13. Why should the lessons learned document seek feedback from staff?

Answers to Chapter 14 Questions

1. Security administration must consist of people from each department without exception.

2. Penetration testing is helpful in testing the security posture of an organization to find vulnerabilities before they are found by an attacker. In other words, penetration testing is an allowed, invited, and accepted external or internal attack to fortify the organization's security.

3. Explore or reconnaissance, break/attack, and generate a report are the three steps in a PenTest.

4. ZAP is an easy-to-use integrated PenTesting tool for finding vulnerabilities in web applications.

5. Dastardly is the dynamic application security testing (DAST) tool (from Burp suite) that can find seven different vulnerabilities. The DAST tool can also be used with Continuous Integration (CI) and Continuous Development (CD), also known as the CI/CD pipeline.

6. Aircrack-ng can do the following:

   Monitoring: Packet capture and data export to text files for further processing

   Attacking: Replay attacks, de-authentication, fake access points, and so on via packet injection

   Testing: Checking Wi-Fi cards and driver capabilities (capture/injection)

   Cracking: WEP and WPA PSK (WPA 1 and 2) protocols

7. Conclusions on what was found and recommendations on how to fix problems.

8. No, STIG checking is a recommendation to fix a vulnerability in a vendor software whereas PenTesting tries to crack the network, system, or software to see if any vulnerabilities exist and, if they do, demonstrate how a hacker can exploit them.

9. STIGs are given a group ID, severity (CAT I, II, or III), STIG ID, rule ID, and related legacy IDs. Each rule is described in detail. Discussion of the finding is given as well with a list of references.

10. The Department of Defense Information network (DoDIN) website lists both approved product lists and a removal list.

11. Operational security or OPSEC is a lifecycle with the following six steps:

    ■ Identification of critical information

    ■ Analysis of threats

    ■ Analysis of vulnerabilities

- Assessment of risks

- Applying appropriate countermeasures

- Continuous monitoring

12. Digital forensics is defined as a process of identifying, preserving, analyzing, and documenting digital evidence. The steps involved are

- First response

- Search and seizure

- Collecting evidence

- Securing evidence

- Data acquisition

- Data analysis

- Evidence assessment

- Document and report

- Testify as a witness

13. It is very important to seek feedback because when the staff feels they are being heard, productivity naturally improves, and the process gets better. We also know that feedback from different levels of staff would be different, and everyone's opinion should be considered in detail.

Mobile Devices and Application Security

After discussing everything in detail about databases and applications, it's now time to consider mobile devices and security. A mobile device can be a smart phone, a tablet, a gadget in the car, or anything similar. These devices interact with back-end security, back-end databases, wireless networks, memory on the device itself, the front-end interface, programming languages, ever-changing frameworks, and more. As we look through these, mobile application security poses an enhanced threat that is beyond databases and applications. When we design the mobile applications, we need to have three-pronged security: one for databases, one for applications, and one for the mobile device itself.

The testing for mobile devices also varies with all these factors involved because hackers have their own way of attacking mobile devices from public places offering free Wi-Fi and Internet connections. Note also that the applications for mobile devices are developed either in specific languages (native to apple or Android) or a common variant like Xamarin. Native applications, as their name implies, belong or are native to one type of device only. In an environment like Xamarin, the same code base can be compiled for iOS or Android. Again, another factor to consider is the system/standard/software development kits (SDKs) the application uses, and the vulnerabilities that can crop up from the SDKs or publicly downloaded free SDKs.

Apple and Android devices have different languages, different security features and memory, and so on, although the behind-the-scene security posture is generally the same where data storage, code quality, authentication, network, related application programming interfaces (APIs), and the SDKs are concerned. We discuss these in the following sections. These details are also discussed in the Open Worldwide Application Security Project (OWASP) mobile applications security testing guide (MASTG) and mobile applications security verification standard (MASVS).

Authentication

In Chapter 1, "The Basics of Cybersecurity," we discussed at length the IAAA steps and how authentication takes place. Authentication with mobile devices needs a different approach because it needs a check on the device end point. New devices such as iPhone and Samsung's Android phone have biometric authentication with face recognition and fingerprint recognition. On the other end is the authentication for database, servers, and other libraries and applications. Does the application use any additional security? If so, how is that implemented, and how is the end user's personally identifiable information (PII) protected? Because a personal phone now can carry fingerprints, photos, health applications with protected health information (PHI), or payment applications with credit card data (PCI-DSS rules apply), and other personal data, how does the application keep the data private? In other words, is the PII, PHI, or other such data available to the application directly? If the application can actually access the data, does it share with other applications or just transfer all this to their main servers? If authentication is done with parameters in query strings (Chapter 10, "Application Security Fundamentals"), are they checked at both ends correctly?

Authentication rules that were discussed in Chapter 2, "Security Details," apply here as well. To recall them quickly, the following list describes the K-H-A factors:

- **What the users know (K):** A PIN, password, or a pass phrase
- **What the users have (H):** A smart card, a credit card, an identification card
- **What the users are (A):** A fingerprint, palm print, retina scan, or other biometric parameter

Applications that handle any personal data or health data need to have second-factor authentication, also known as multifactor authentication. An example of second-factor authentication is a one-time password (OTP) of a PIN generated and sent to the user's mobile device, which will be used to validate the first factor. Many applications like Gmail and Hotmail use these factors. Another idea is to link a website login to the mobile application login and ask for the second factor. Figure 15-1 shows an example of such an application.

When a user tries to log in to a website (myWebsite.com in Figure 15-1), they're asked for the PIN generated on the OKTA app on their phone. Both the website asking for the PIN and the OKTA application are connected on the server and have encrypted communication from end to end. There is also another verification the OKTA application does on the mobile phone before it provides the OTP—verifying the user via a built-in face recognition or some other software on the iPhone or Android phone. This is a real multifactor authentication where a website needs a username and OTP, and OKTA needs face recognition to supply the OTP (123345 in Figure 15-1); then the generated OTP needs to be entered on the website. Instead of a website, this can be used for other applications as well as for authenticating users. Additional security and policy standards apply if any data is related to credit cards (PCI-DSS), financial data, or such. But if passwords are used instead of a PIN, the typical password policies discussed in Chapter 5, "Access Control Data," apply about length, history, and complexity.

Figure 15-1 *Authentication with OKTA Verify Application: Logging in on a Website on the Left. OTP Generation with Face Recognition on the Phone on the Right*

Authentication follows the earlier step of identification and may be either stateless or stateful. In a stateful version of authentication, a unique session ID is generated for keeping continuous communication with the user. When a user logs in, a unique ID is generated to serve as a reference for the time and session the user keeps the connection active or until they log off. The session ID details are stored on the server's logs for reference and later auditing. The session ID doesn't contain any user data or PII. This is an older method of authentication that has been replaced by almost everyone. The vulnerability here is that if the session can be hijacked, the user details can be stolen, and a hacker can mimic the original user. The stateless authentication keeps all the user information as a client-side token. This token is passed to any server when communicating. It also means the server will not hold any information on the server. Of course, the token and such details need to be encrypted for security, thereby warranting an authentication server for this purpose. It is easier to use a framework's built-in SDK for authentication than to create one from step zero. HTTPS is stateless, and newer versions of all mobile access are done with HTTPS, which is recommended for encryption and security. HTTPS is better, makes a website work faster, and gives access to better features of the browser. Search engines also keep the HTTPS sites on top in their rankings for quicker search. Importantly, as security becomes more significant, implementing HTTPS is always a better idea.

OAuth 2.0 or a later version is another way to implement security. The protocol in Figure 15-2 shows the flow of user authentication.

Abstract Protocol Flow

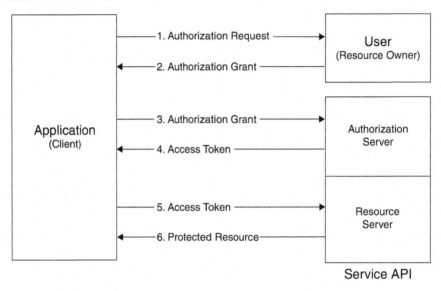

Figure 15-2   *OAuth2.0 Flow of Information for Authenticating*

Notice that the authentication details have three different steps (1-2, 3-4, 5-6), with each step having to send something and receive something. When the client receives an authorization grant (2 in Figure 15-2), they have to send the authorization grant along with their own credentials for the ID to get an access token (4 in Figure 15-2). The access token alone will work for accessing the resource in the third step. The advantage in this is that neither session ID nor credentials of the client are ever sent to the resource server. The resource basically relies on the access token alone, thereby protecting the client and other information details on either side.

If authentication is important security, then logging out or terminating a session is also very important because an open session can be a vulnerability for a hack. Often a mobile user would not log off an application (such as Facebook or Twitter) because it is a pain to log in and log out every single time. But the application can terminate an open session and remove any cookies or data stored. Programming languages have built-in commands and libraries to destroy an unattended session with session_destroy(), session_get_cookie_params(), and other calls that can help remove the session. Other security details, like locking an account, blocking a user after several unsuccessful attempts, emailing the user to reset passwords, and having password policies are all important and should go hand in hand with the aforementioned methods.

Cryptography

In Chapter 2, we discuss the symmetric and asymmetric algorithms for cryptography. The following are the currently recommended algorithms. If any other algorithms are used, they should be remediated and advised as a security flaw.

- **Confidentiality:** AES-GCM-256 or ChaCha20-Poly1305

- **Integrity:** SHA-256, SHA-384, SHA-512, BLAKE3, the SHA-3 family

- **Digital signature:** RSA (3072 bits and higher), ECDSA with NIST P-384

- **Key establishment:** RSA (>=3072 bits), DH (>=3072 bits), ECDH with NIST P-384

Shorter key lengths (for convenience or laziness), bad/weak random number generation techniques, padding of numbers, salt generation, and the mode chosen for the cipher blocks are all considerations for good security. Keys should be protected as we have seen in Chapter 5 and with Kerchoff's law. Key protection should be considered at rest and in transit.

Keys at rest can be on a server or the local machine. The following details are important to note for protecting keys at rest:

- **Remote key vaults** (for example, Amazon KMS and Azure Key Vault): A better way to keep them secure.

- **Keys in storage:** All keys and their cryptographic actions should happen in a trusted execution environment (TEC) (for example, Android Keystore and Secure Enclave) or encrypt data encryption keys with key encryption keys.

- **Keys in memory:** Should be in the memory for the shortest time and should be nullified or cleaned from memory after cryptographic operations are complete or in case of error.

- **Sharing:** As explained in Chapter 5, one should never share the same key with accounts or devices with the exception of the public keys that are used for signature or encryption with PKI and GAL. Private keys are never shared with anyone.

Keys in transit can be protected with end-to-end encryption, with a combination of symmetric and asymmetric keys. For example, a symmetric key is encrypted with a public key from the asymmetric key pair and transported. The receiver can decrypt and get the information but has to use the private key of the asymmetric key pair to get the information. Linux, Apple, Android, and almost all operating systems already have cryptographic functions in their libraries or SDKs. These should be used for mobile security in accordance with the cryptographic policies of the organization. Also, there are industrial regulations for the cryptographic policies created by various countries.

Code Quality and Injection Attacks

The general injection attacks we discuss in Chapter 10, such as SQL injection and XML injection, all exist even in mobile applications. In addition, dump collection, memory management, and clearing up used memory with variables should be considered. All the inputs, data, and certificate data such as X.509 information should be verified against a format for unusual characters, scripts, and any unwanted input. These can be done with regular expression validators at entry points and also on servers as discussed earlier. In addition, mobile applications have another vulnerability in that they can receive information from QR codes, files, or pictures sent by messages that might include a virus or other malware applications. Some of these security checks have to be manual, though some can be automatic. The following are some typical red flags in code:

■ If integer variables are used for arrays, indexing, or calculations, make sure that unsigned integer types are used to prevent any errors.

■ Functions like strcpy, strncat, strlcat, strncpy, strlcpy, sprint, snprintf, and gets or other functions that deal with strings need specific attention as they are deemed unsafe.

■ When using C++, it is recommended that you use ANSI C++ string classes.

■ Functions that copy memory (such as memcpy) must make sure before copying that the target size can accommodate the source data.

■ While copying data, make sure that the source and target memories are not overlapping.

■ Any untrusted data is not allowed to be inserted, created, or concatenated to format strings.

User Privacy on the Device

One argument is that the mobile application on one's smart phone is safer than the website accessed from a computer. The other argument is the price we pay for using a mobile application whose security we do not know, at least not until it is hacked. Two important considerations are in this section—the responsibility of the application-creating organization or person and the responsibility of the users who use the application.

Both Google and Apple started a labeling process for their applications and ask the developers to comply with the rules in accordance with the National Institute of Standards and Technology's (NIST's) consumer software security labeling. Per this recommendation, the technical criteria for the mobile software app are a series of *claims* about the software. Claims can be as follows:

■ **Descriptive claims:** This category describes information about the label itself. It identifies who is making claims about information within the label, what the label applies to, when the claims were made, and how a consumer can obtain other supporting information required by the label.

- **Secure software development claims:** This category describes how the software provider claims to adhere to accepted secure software development practices throughout the software development life cycle (SDLC). By addressing these criteria, the consumer is informed that secure software development best practices were employed.

The following details are required for each claim.

Descriptive Claims

A descriptive claim includes and demonstrates the following:

- Claimant
- Label scope
- Software identifiers
- Claim date
- Security update status
- Minimum duration of security update support
- Security update method

Secure Software Development Claims

A secure software development claim should include and demonstrate the following:

- Implements a secure software development process
- Practices secure design and vulnerability remediation
- Practices responsible vulnerability reporting disclosure
- Uses multifactor authentication (if applicable)
- Free from hard-coded secrets and logic bombs
- Uses strong cryptography (if applicable)
- User data is identified and secured

Developers and organizations releasing software to the Google and Apple stores remain completely and solely responsible for the application security, patching, descriptions, and declarations made on these storefronts. In accordance with their own security policies, these stores also reserve the right to remove any application if a security breach or vulnerability is found either by them or by hackers. Despite these precautions, an application is not guaranteed to be safe because new attacks can materialize, and what has been a safe application can be declared as vulnerable to the new attacks. It is also equally possible that the application developers do not declare how the data collected will be used or what data is being collected. It is not illegal to collect data (but dissemination without agreement may be illegal), and any information might not be provided by the developer. For this reason, end user education and responsibility are more important. End users have to exercise their own rights and wisdom to decide if they can install or not install a mobile application. As said in earlier chapters more than once, the first line of defense in cybersecurity is *you*.

The following are some considerations users need to keep in mind while using an application.

- What biometric data does the application collect (face recognition, fingerprint, and so on)? Does the application inform you first about this data being collected or sent to other applications from the same organization? (For example, Facebook may use the same credentials for WhatsApp and other applications.)

- Does the application inform the user before using the camera, GPS data, scanner, personal data, or other such information or credentials stored on the mobile device?

- Where does the application come from or is downloaded from? Is the location where the application is available and safe and follows the NIST guidelines described previously?

- Does the application disclose all the rules, regulations, end user agreements, and so on?

- If the application does something beyond security, does it inform the user that such an action can result in jail breaking or such?

These questions should be able to put the end user at ease and make it easy for them to decide if an application is safe. Because the smart phone or mobile device belongs to the owner, it is at the discretion of the owner to install and allow an application access to their device. Per recently published papers, due to COVID-19 and data protection goals, here are simple data protection goals that are being considered:

- **Unlinkability:** PII data should never be linked to any other data outside the domain. This includes data minimization, anonymization, and pseudonymization in any format.

- **Transparency:** Per various data regulations and rules, users can ask for any or all information that the application has or uses. Users must also have clear and lucid instructions on how to request this information. The information might include privacy policies, user education, proper logging and auditing mechanisms, and so on.

■ **Intervenability:** If the users discover their information is wrong on the application, they should be able to make corrections to their personal information, request its deletion, withdraw any consents given previously, and receive instructions on how to do so. All these are not "either/or" features; they must be "and" features. It means the user has complete rights to their own data. This includes privacy settings in the application, points of contact, and so on.

Sandboxing

In mobile applications or general cybersecurity, sandboxing is a mechanism to separate all running programs from each other, so each program runs in isolation or with little coupling. This helps prevent software vulnerabilities such as viruses and malware from extending to other programs. A sandboxing memory area helps execute unknown code from untrusted programs without a risk to the host machine. A sandbox is a tightly controlled set of resources (ports, memory, disk space, and so on) for an application to run. When an application is running in the sandbox, a lot of functions such as full network access, finding details about the host system, and reading from more than the required input devices are restricted or not allowed.

In iOS access control technology, sandboxing is enforced at the kernel level. Its purpose is limiting system and user data damage that may occur if an app is compromised in some way. Android applications have a similar technology for a process sandbox. Any application running in the sandbox must explicitly request access to resources and data that are outside their individual sandbox. A request to access resources is made by informing the user what permissions the app needs to use system data/features. The system will then examine the permissions asked for, and depending on how sensitive the data or feature is, it may grant the permission, deny the permission, or make the request of the user. If user intervention is required for such access, the operating system will ask the user to grant permission. This is the reason we see, "The application you want to install needs permission from …." or a similar message box as a pop-up on the mobile device. Application developers and content providers can access the underlying file system, which might share files automatically. Most operating system sandbox's default permissions prevent this kind of automatic sharing.

Apple's iOS sandbox is a mandatory access control (MAC) mechanism, which tells what resources an app can and can't access. Compared to Android systems, iOS offers very few inter-process communication (IPC) options, thereby minimizing the attack surface. Figure 15-3 shows the security architecture of iOS. A similar or comparable architecture exists for Android as well.

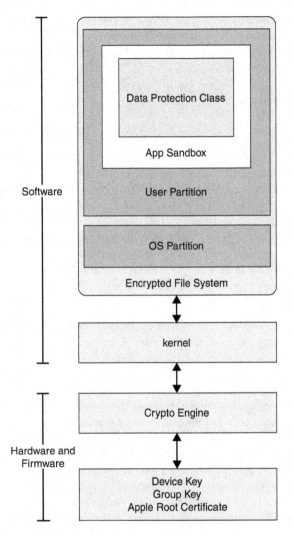

Figure 15-3 *iOS Security Architecture*

Mobile Applications Security Testing

Testing applications on mobile devices is quite similar to testing software applications to find vulnerabilities and fix them before a hacker does. There are three ways testing can be performed. These are

- **Black-box testing (blind testing):** The tester is not provided with any information, or the tester has zero knowledge about the system being tested. This is similar to ethical hacking where the tester is acting like a real hacker to find what can be discovered. Notice that the black-box testing might jail break or completely destroy a device. For that reason, the tester will ask for a written and signed agreement.

- **White-box testing:** This testing is quite the opposite of black-box testing. The tester is provided with "full details" of the network, resources, and everything before they can start testing. The advantage is that because the tester knows everything beforehand, they can test it faster. With the provided knowledge or with the results of the test, a tester can improve their testing in a sophisticated way and build better test cases. But the disadvantage is that the tester may be biased and do testing only with known cases and miss some potential vulnerability since information provided to the tester may be subject to human errors.

- **Gray-box testing:** This approach that falls between white- and black-box testing. In this case, the tester is provided with some information and is asked to find what they can discover. Since black-box testing may jail break, and white-box testing may not find all vulnerabilities, gray-box testing is somewhat a compromise for the number of test cases, the cost incurred, and so on.

The features to test in mobile devices include but aren't limited to the following:

- Vulnerability analysis

- Manual and automated code review

- Penetration testing (Chapter 14, "Follow a Proven Path for Security") and reports

- Data identification (at rest, in use, and in transit)

- Architecture identification (network, OS, the application)

- Security test during application development process (type of SDLC)

- What tests the developers used (unit, regression, and so on)

- Testing against functional and user requirements

- Regularity of a test and corrections made

- Patch history

- Possibility of reverse-engineering an application

- Encrypting techniques and protocols used

- Data and code obfuscation

- PII and PHI data protection

- Type of executable (release or debug version)

NIST's Directions for Mobile Device Security

OWASP's mobile applications security verification standard (MASVS) provides a template for mobile security that can be utilized. Mobile device security — Corporate Owned, Personally Enabled (COPE) NIST 1800-21B is a NIST special publication that explains specific cybersecurity challenges and talks at length about security for 1) corporate-owned personally enabled devices that are ideal at work spaces and lists a series of problems and solutions on how to install software that keeps the devices safe. A similar document exists (1800-22b) for bring your own device (BYOD) to work models. Both documents explain the problems and possible solutions tested by the NIST. But as mentioned earlier, these are the problems and suggested solutions at present. As technology evolves, you need to keep up the pace and adapt. Table 15-1 provides a problems list on the COPE devices as listed by the NIST.

Table 15-1   *Possible List of Vulnerabilities and Threats on COPE Devices*

Threat Event #	Details
1	Unauthorized access to sensitive information via a malicious or privacy-intrusive application
2	Theft of credentials through a short message service (SMS) or email phishing campaign
3	Malicious applications installed via URLs in SMS or email messages
4	Confidentiality and integrity loss due to exploitation of known vulnerability in the operating system or firmware
5	Violation of privacy via misuse of device sensors
6	Compromise of the integrity of the device or its network communications via installation of malicious EMM/mobile device management, network, virtual private network (VPN) profiles, or certificates
7	Loss of confidentiality of sensitive information via eavesdropping on unencrypted device communications
8	Compromise of device integrity via observed, inferred, or brute-forced device unlock code
9	Unauthorized access to back-end services via authentication or credential storage vulnerabilities in internally developed applications
10	Unauthorized access of enterprise resources from an unmanaged and potentially compromised device

Threat Event #	Details
11	Loss of organizational data due to a lost or stolen device
12	Loss of confidentiality of organizational data due to its unauthorized storage in nonorganizationally managed services

NIST has documented the tools shown in Table 15-2 in protecting mobile devices from the threats listed in Table 15-1.

Table 15-2 *Technologies Tested by NIST That Help Avoid an Attack on Mobile Devices*

Technology Partner/ Collaborator	Build Involvement
Appthority	Appthority Cloud Service, Mobile Threat Intelligence
Kryptowire	Kryptowire Cloud Service, Application Vetting
Lookout	Lookout Cloud Service/Lookout Agent Version 5.10.0.142 (iOS), 5.9.0.420 (Android), Mobile Threat Defense
MobileIron	MobileIron Core Version 9.7.0.1, MobileIron Agent Version 11.0.1A (iOS), 10.2.1.1.3R (Android), Enterprise Mobility Management
Palo Alto Networks	Palo Alto Networks PA-220
Qualcomm	Qualcomm Trusted Execution Environment (version is device dependent)

For the BYOD version, the threat events are different and are listed in Table 15-3 in NIST's SP 1800-22B document.

Table 15-3 *Threats and Vulnerabilities in Mobile Devices for BYOD*

Threat Event #	Details
1	Privacy intrusive applications
2	Account credential theft through phishing (SMS, email, and so on)
3	Outdated phones
4	Sensitive data transmissions
5	Brute-force attacks to unlock a phone
6	Application credential storage vulnerability
7	Unmanaged device protection
8	Lost or stolen data protection
9	Protecting enterprise data from being inadvertently backed up to a cloud service

The following list describes insights into the mobile device (BYOD) when using with corporate data and information processing:

- **Separate organization and personal information:** When traveling outside corporate networks and systems, an unprotected personal device poses a risk. BYODs also risk personal data of users because applications may be able to capture PII from user devices. To mitigate these problems, organizational and personal information should be separated by restricting data flow between organization-managed applications and other applications not related to organizational business.

- **Encrypt data in transit:** BYODs might connect to nonsecure networks, putting both PII and organizational data at risk. To avoid this problem, mobile devices should connect to the organization only over a trusted and recommended corporate-installed VPN or encrypt all incoming and outgoing data. A user should not be able to access corporate network or data without the recommended VPN connection and required certificates.

- **Identify vulnerable applications:** BYODs might already have or the users might install applications that may have unknown security vulnerabilities. When such applications are identified, an organization should advise the BYOD owner to remove the employee's corporate credentials or configuration files from the device. Uninstalling such applications may give rise to conflict between the employee and the organization.

- **Prevent or detect malware:** BYOD applications may increase the risk of installing malware or unknown viruses. An organization that allows BYOD must ask users to deploy a corporate-recommended malware detection tool to identify malicious applications. Security features built into the OS could also help prevent or detect such applications and the presence of malware.

- **Trusted device access:** Despite the training and awareness given to the end users, BYODs may try to connect to the corporate network from any trusted or untrusted location. Thus, BYODs should have software in a way that an employee would not be able to access the organization's resources without the required and valid certificates.

- **Restrict information collection:** Mobile device management tools can sometimes track what applications are installed on the device, location information such as physical address, geographic coordinates, location history, Internet protocol (IP) address, and service set identifier (SSID) usernames and passwords. Most mobile device management tools can be configured to exclude application and location information. This is also very useful when device and application data is shared outside the organization.

NIST's Cybersecurity Practice Guide demonstrates how organizations can use standards based, commercially available products to help with mobile device security.

The following details are important to note in protecting the devices, whether they are COPE or BYOD.

- **Trusted execution environment (TEE):** A controlled and separate environment that allows trusted applications to run to provide enhanced security.

- **Enterprise mobility management (EMM):** Usually has two components: a back-end service to set up policies and configurations and an application that integrates the device to the back-end service. Both Apple and Android have mobile device management (MDM) solutions that alert the user.

- **Virtual private network (VPN):** A VPN gateway increases the security and protects against breaches on confidentiality, integrity, and authentication. VPNs also can provide encryption.

- **Application vetting service (AVS):** We discussed this earlier on how the storefronts hosted by Google and Apple verify and reject applications that are not secure. AVS may check/vet the corporate applications only or all applications on the device.

- **Mobile threat defense (MTD):** These are usually applications that continually track the device. They may analyze other applications, OS versions, updates, and network traffic (encrypted or not). They can be used mixing with the EMMs and provide analysis of threats and vulnerabilities found on the device.

- **Operating system capabilities (OSC):** Each OS has its own capabilities that can be checked from the manufacturer's website or information. Some are less prone to hacking than others.

- **Device attestation (DA):** This is a process of telling the users that their BYOD is free of unauthorized applications and modifications. The attestation process requires certificates and a trusted execution environment, which guarantee the integrity of the device and data used in transmission. DA also checks for secure boot and the attestation process itself.

- **Application programming interface (API):** This should be managed by the corporation on how the APIs are digitally signed, if the APIs are required, and so on. In case of dangerous APIs, the device should be wiped clean. These features can be available from EMM or MDM services.

- **Application sandboxing:** This was discussed earlier in details on how each application runs in its own sandbox and does not interfere with other applications.

Table 15-4 gives possible solutions with commercially available products for BYOD. Notice that some of the features are already built into the devices and do not need any installation, but regular patching and updating of the OS are necessary to fix any vulnerabilities.

Table 15-4   *Commercial Products for BYOD*

Product	Details
IBM MaaS360 Mobile Device Management Agent (various versions)	Mobile device management
Kryptowire Cloud Service	Application vetting
Palo Alto Networks PA-VM-100s (various versions)	Firewall Virtual private network (VPN)
Qualcomm mobile version	Trusted execution environment
Zimperium Defense Suite (various versions)	Mobile threat defense
Apple iOS Version 13 or later Google Android Version 10 (or later)	Mobile device operating system

NIST also has a third and important document for addressing the cloud environment: Mobile device security - Cloud and hybrid builds, SP 1800-4. The problems listed in this area are similar to the COPE and BYOD. The following are some possible threats:

- Mobile malware
- Social engineering
- Stolen data due to loss, theft, or disposal
- Unauthorized access
- Electronic eavesdropping
- Electronic tracking
- Access to data by third-party applications

Sections B and C of the document give details of the problems and how to set up a mobile device for cloud applications such as Office 365, email, and so on. While the cloud provider takes care of the services on their end, it is the responsibility of the end user to manage their own mobile device.

Summary

Mobile device security depends on various factors and is different from other IT devices because these mobile devices can be carried freely and can be connected to Wi-Fi networks anywhere. Free Wi-Fi networks and even some password-protected networks cannot be easily trusted. Authentication on the mobile devices varies in many ways from normal PIN, password, or biometric/fingerprint recognition. The mobile devices also use cryptography defined in NIST publications.

Stores (such as Google and Apple) that provide applications follow a standard labeling process with a claim. A claim can be either descriptive or a secure software development claim. In addition, according to new research and publications, data protection goals have three more suggested factors of unlinkability, transparency, and intervenability.

The sandboxing mechanism in mobile devices is helpful in separating the running programs from each other and avoiding any adverse reaction among applications. Mobile apps can be tested with black-, white-, or gray-box testing methods.

NIST 1800-21B special publication explains various specific cybersecurity challenges. This publication is useful in creating a policy for mobile security stature.

Chapter 15 Questions

1. What are the three authentication rules?

2. What are the six steps in OAuth 2.0?

3. What is the advantage in OAuth 2.0?

4. What are some problems in cryptography on mobile devices even if a good and correctly recommended algorithm is used?

5. How should the keys be protected in cryptography?

6. What are some problems to be checked in code review?

7. What should a secure software development claim include?

8. Who is responsible for a vulnerability after the application is loaded to a storefront (Apple or Android)?

9. If any application is using other resources on the mobile device, what is the best an end user can do?

10. What are the three goals for data protection?

11. What is sandboxing?

12. What are different kinds of testing?

13. Which kind of testing is cost-effective?

14. What types of mobile devices are considered for security?

15. What are the problems with SMS and phishing on mobile devices?

16. Why should mobile device communications be encrypted?

17. What are the best ways to protect a BYOD that can connect to a corporate environment?

18. What are the possible threats for mobile devices used with cloud and hybrid environments as identified by the NIST?

Answers to Chapter 15 Questions

1. What you know (K), what you have (H), and what you are (A).

2. i.   The client sends an authorization request to the resource owner.

ii. The client receives an authorization grant from the resource owner.

iii. The client sends an authorization grant to the authorization server.

iv. The client receives an access token from the authorization server.

v.   The client sends an access token to the resource server.

vi. The client receives access to the protected resource from the resource server.

3. No session ID or credentials are sent to the resource server. Only the granted access token is used.

4. Shorter key length, bad or weak random number generation, padding numbers, and the mode chosen for cipher blocks.

5. Keys can be protected with remote vaults or in storage with a trusted execution environment. Keys in memory should be removed or nullified. Keys should never be shared if they are private. Symmetric and asymmetric methods should be combined while transmitting keys and private keys should not be disclosed to anyone.

6. Variable types (unsigned or signed), bounds, indexes, and size of the memory while copying a source to a target area are some of the problems.

7. i.   Implements a secure software development process

ii. Practices secure design and vulnerability remediation

iii. Practices responsible vulnerability reporting disclosure

iv. Uses multifactor authentication (if applicable)

v.   Free from hard-coded secrets and logic bombs

vi. Uses strong cryptography (if applicable)

vii. User data is identified and secured

8. The developer or the organization that created the application is solely responsible.

9. Check all the following and make sure the application is safe:

i.   What biometric data does the application collect (face recognition, fingerprint, and so on)? Does the application inform first about this data being collected or sent to other applications from the same organization? (For example, Facebook may use the same credentials for WhatsApp and other applications.)

ii. Does the application inform the user before using the camera, GPS data, scanner, personal data, or other such information or credentials stored on the mobile device?

iii. Where does the application come from or downloaded from? Is the location where the application is available safe and follows NIST guidelines described previously?

iv. Does the application disclose all the rules, regulations, and end user agreements?

v. If the application does something beyond security, does it inform the user that such an action can result in jail breaking or such?

10. i. Unlinkability

ii. Transparency

iii. Intervenability

11. Sandboxing is a mechanism to separate all running programs from each other so that each program runs in isolation or with least coupling.

12. Black-box testing, white-box testing, and gray-box testing.

13. Gray-box testing is cost-effective since the tester will know some information first and then find what they can discover with their own tools.

14. Corporate-owned, personally enabled (COPE), bring your own device (BYOD), and mobile devices for cloud and hybrid builds.

15. Theft of credentials, email scams, and installation of malicious applications with QR codes and bad URLs are some examples of problems.

16. To prevent loss of confidentiality and sensitive information encryption.

17. Separation of organizational and personal information, sandboxing, using secure certificates, using an approved VPN, and encrypting both inbound and outbound data.

18. Mobile malware, Social engineering, Stolen data due to loss, theft, or disposal, Unauthorized access, Electronic eavesdropping, Electronic tracking, Access to data by third-party applications

Corporate Security in Practice

After discussing at length all the possible attacks and how to mitigate those attacks and how to apply due diligence to avoid an attack or transfer it to insurance, we know that security must be considered right from step zero for anything in a corporate setting. If not, worrying late is better than never worrying at all about security. Feigning ignorance does not work, and it is not helpful. We also know that employee training and increasing awareness among staff are mandatory to recognize an attack or attempt to breach. Everyone in the corporate setting has the responsibility of taking care of security and working in tandem to reach out and cooperate with each other.

Figure 16-1 shows an example of corporate security for a fictitious organization named Total Gold Security Inc., where each branch works with cooperation from other branches, and almost all branches are centrally connected to change management (CM). Recall that the CM process and the change approval board (CAB) has to work with everyone and keep records of the changes to track who is requesting the change, if the change can be authorized, the time frame required for the change, and what happens if the changes are not implemented.

The following points are also worth noting from the figure:

1. All branches are connected to the change management (CM) office and request, obtain, and receive permissions as required after signing proper documents either on paper or digitally.

2. All requests and receipts are processed, and records are maintained for these by the CM office.

3. Each branch has its staff (see the box named Staff in top-right corner) in various capacities and may have an information system security officer (ISSO). Not all branches may have all the staff mentioned. For example, the human resources branch may decide not to hire any contractors.

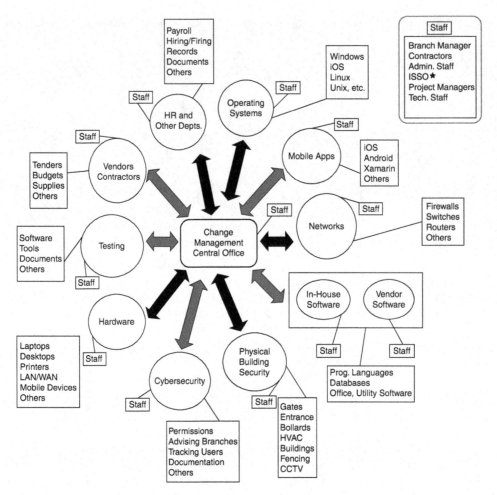

Figure 16-1 *Centrally Managed Corporate Secure Environment in Total Gold Security Inc.*

4. ISSOs can share work with more than one branch or one ISSO can be the security officer for more than one branch.

5. Applications can be developed in house or they can be purchased. For example, buying payroll software might be cheaper than hiring programmers to do the payroll software from ground zero. Whether software is developed in house or purchased from a vendor, it is tested and goes through vetting before it's installed on the corporate network.

6. If one department creates something new or needs other branches to know of an update, they can directly email the other branches.

7. Any changes to general software, hardware, configurations, and so on must go through the CM office, which approves, disapproves, or asks for more information.

8. If any new breaches or attacks are known to occur in any corporate setting, the cybersecurity branch would notice them first and inform all the users in other branches. The cybersecurity branch also keeps employees in check for privilege escalations and unauthorized access.

9. The cybersecurity branch checks, issues, activates, cancels, suspends, or deactivates permissions, access, physical smart cards, and so on.

10. The cybersecurity office works with the physical security branch to allow access, issue smart cards, program smart cards for privileges, and also advise users when their cards need a renewal or are about to expire.

11. If there is a new version of an operating system update, service pack, or a patch, the operating systems branch works with the cybersecurity branch to update the baseline architecture. Then the cybersecurity branch will inform all users to update their machines in a given time frame (typically 30 to 60 days).

12. The network branch continues to track the firewall logs, switches, LAN, WAN, and all other equipment along with the individual computers (laptops, desktops, printers, and so on) for vulnerabilities. This tracking is done regularly (typically once a month or so). The network branch also advises the users how to fix found vulnerabilities and might direct users to get fixes from the software center (Windows) or might send patches directly to users via encrypted and digitally signed email.

13. Physical security staff take care of who is entering and leaving the facility; does physical checks with a human guard stationed at the gate to watch traffic; handles entrance gate locking and unlocking with smart cards or other biometric sensors; protects the building with bollards, fences, and so on; installs warning signs for property; and manages the physical design of driveways, parking lots, HVAC systems, closed-circuit TVs (CCTV), and so on.

14. Any kind of intrusion or breach occurring anywhere in Total Gold Security Inc. must be immediately shared with every other branch so they can take precautions and further steps.

15. Each branch is equipped with tools and software to address their own concerns and continue to work smoothly. Some software may be common for all branches (for example, Office and email).

16. Each branch and its staff only get the bare minimum required privileges and mandatory access control (MAC)–approved baseline software necessary for their work. Any additional software needs to go through a ticket to CM, which reviews and approves the software. The software requested then is installed by the desktop or laptop maintenance hardware staff or other branch responsible for software maintenance.

17. When an employee is fired or is leaving, their credentials are immediately backed up and removed from all branches. All accounts and access usernames, and passwords related to that employee are deactivated/deleted, and the computer or other hardware issued is recovered from the employee quickly to be examined and wiped later.

18. An audit for each branch happens internally and externally. Each branch has its own list of Secure Technical Implementation Guides (STIGs) to follow, and any mismatches are resolved quickly. Auditors are certified and have authority to recommend changes to the configuration and/or settings of hardware, software, or anything else required for that branch.

19. All branches' ISSOs report to the information system security manager (ISSM), who in turn reports to the chief information security officer (CISO) and chief executive officer (CEO).

20. Total Gold Security Inc. has a press release branch that shares details of any breaches or attacks via an experienced person. Not every employee speaks to the press and shares details of a breach. This is to avoid any unnecessary trouble with law and order.

21. While following least privilege and separation of duties, each branch trusts the other branches to do their job to accomplish the bigger project to meet the corporate mission and its goals. The gray arrows indicate the scope of the book—databases, software, security administration, and mobile applications.

Let's consider a few different cases for this scenario. In all cases, remember our motto is zero-trust security, which means we trust nobody in security-related matters, even if they are CEO of our own organization or the top-notch officer from another organization. We must also keep it in mind that not all organizations follow these rules. Depending on resources (human, budgetary, etc.), these steps differ from one organization to another.

Case # 1: A Person Is Joining an Organization as a New Employee

New employees, before they start working, have a few steps to go through:

Step 1. They have to sign forms to give consent to the company hiring them for a background check, credit check, and possibly a security clearance. Some organizations also collect biometrics such as a picture of the employee's face, fingerprints, or palm prints. The same biometrics can be used to issue an authentication card or for giving/escalating/de-escalating/removing privileges. The second step is to make a solid job offer.

Step 2. An ID card is issued as either one smart card with a PIN or a general identification card and a special access smart card. A computer with a structured computer baseline configuration with the minimum required software is issued to the user. The official email is accessible to the user from the day the card was issued onward but only with the smart card of a verifiable authentication system. Authentication can be one factor or two or more factors.

Step 3.   The employee is asked to take the required short-term training (in person or online) about company policies, conduct, and security. At this time, the employee owns a mandatory access controlled (MAC) base configuration computer. Onboarding is complete, and the employee starts working with the others.

Step 4.   After a few days, the branch supervisor and the team may decide to grant discretionary access controls (DAC) with additional forms, signatures, and approvals. Any access given via DAC is mostly likely to be role based because the employee works for a particular branch, and full access to everything is never given immediately or even after several years of working in the same job or in different jobs or capacities. DACs are given, removed, or updated regularly.

Step 5.   The employee gets audited regularly (as does everyone else) to check that there are no privilege escalations, unnecessary data transfers, or other issues. Any security breaches are reported, and action should be taken. Training shortfalls are addressed, and the employee is advised to be up to date with their training. This process goes on as long as the employee is actively working for the organization.

Table 16-1 shows four new employees who are in different groups or branches and how they are given the MAC baseline configuration systems, privileges for their work, and other details. Notice each employee's work is different, so the privileges vary.

Table 16-1   *Details of Checks for Each Type of Employee for Ensuring Security*

Steps	Human Resources Employee	Programmer or IT Employee	Perimeter Station Guard	Accounting Manager
1	Interview, background and credit checks, EOE/AA violations in previous HR jobs, references and clearance (if any).	Interview, background and credit checks and code violations, references and fraud (if any).	Interview, background and credit checks, references, police records (if any).	Interview, background and credit checks, references and fraud, cooking account books (altering account details dishonestly), and so on.
2	Issue ID card and create multifactor authentication for the main office building entrance and physical HR office.	Issue ID card and create multifactor authentication for the main office building entrance and programming office block.	Issue ID card and create multifactor authentication for the main office building entrance and perimeter station kiosks.	Issue ID card and create a multifactor authentication for the main office building entrance and physical accounting office.

Steps	Human Resources Employee	Programmer or IT Employee	Perimeter Station Guard	Accounting Manager
3 (MAC)	Obtain signatures on mandatory forms such as NDA, workplace violations, penalties for fraud, and so on. Provide office space to sit and work with a computer of baseline configuration. Complete HR software, payrolls, and so on.	Obtain signatures on mandatory forms such as NDA, code violations, penalties for fraud, and so on. Provide office space to sit and work with a computer of baseline configuration, software tools like Visual Studio, Java, and databases.	Obtain signatures on mandatory forms such as NDA, negligence in work, penalties for fraud, and so on. Provide access to kiosk, computer inside kiosk, and employee and visitor scanning tools. May provide a uniform to wear.	Obtain signatures on mandatory forms such as NDA, accounting violations, penalties for cooking account books, and fraud. Provide computer with baseline configuration and accounting software.
4 (MAC)	Provide online links or in-class registration details required for HR training, SHARP, EOE/AA, customer service, active shooter, computer security and awareness to complete training as soon as possible.	Provide online links or in-class registration details for all required training, SHARP, EOE/AA, active shooter, computer security and awareness, and coding standards to complete training as soon as possible.	Provide online links or in-class registration details for all required training, SHARP, EOE/AA, active shooter, customer service, computer security and awareness to complete training as soon as possible.	Provide online links or in-class registration details for all required training, SHARP, EOE/AA, active shooter, customer service, computer security and awareness, and accounting rules and regulations to complete training as soon as possible.
5	Validate required minimum training completed and provide access to HR systems.	Validate required minimum training completed and jump start on coding projects.	Validate required minimum training completed and provide access to perimeter gate and kiosk controls, scanners, phone, and software.	Validate required minimum training completed and provide full access to accounting systems, audits, and managed staff records.

Steps	Human Resources Employee	Programmer or IT Employee	Perimeter Station Guard	Accounting Manager
6 (DAC)	Add user to common group email boxes of HR such as hr and hr_payroll on the company portal of @example.com.	Add user to common group email boxes of coding or databases such as coders_mail and dba_group on company portal of @example.com.	Add user to common phone messaging system, announcements, security groups. May use email per company policies.	Add user to common group email boxes of accounting such as audit_acc and acct_group on company portal of @example.com.
7 (DAC)	Consider giving more privileges if required for work; signatures required on forms.	Consider giving more privileges if required for work; honor requests for more software packages if required by the project. Proper signatures required on all forms.	Privileges may increase after a few months of reliable work and proof of good conduct.	Privileges remain in place and possibly deescalate some privileges if the manager thinks they can transfer some work to subordinates.
8 (MAC)	Audit employee activity at least once a year for training shortfalls, violations, customer service, and so on.	Audit employee activity at least once a year for training shortfalls, code violations, quality, documentation, and so on.	Audit employee activity at least once a month for violations, customer service, laxity, and other issues, and yearly for required minimum training shortfalls.	Audit employee activity at least once a year for things like training shortfalls, performance, employee treatment, and accounting frauds.
9 (Optional)	Provide regular updates to employee about new tools, software, rules, and regulations in HR. Encourage employee in self-improvement.	Provide regular updates to employee about things like new tools, projects, languages, and databases. Encourage employee for self-improvement.	Updated training with new tools as physical security tools update.	Provide regular updates to employee about new tools, software, rules and regulations in accounting. Encourage employee in self-improvement, poll subordinates about manager's performance and rating.

Activities 3, 4, and 8 are mandatory controls that apply to anyone—whether the employee is a C-level manager or a security guard. Nobody can escape these steps. DAC steps in 6 and 7 happen at the branch level and depend on what the employee and employee's manager agree to do in their day-to-day work. DAC steps also need proper signatures on forms both by the employee and the manager. As explained earlier in Chapter 13, "Security Administration," these forms go through change management and then to cybersecurity branches that grant, edit, or ask for more information before granting the privileges. Again, the rules of least privilege, separation of duties, and dual control per organizational policies apply at every stage. As the policies change, the privileges have to be adjusted. Steps 6 to 9 are continuously monitored as an employee moves or is moved around the branches and departments for different work or responsibilities.

Case # 2: An Employee Is Fired or Is Voluntarily Leaving the Organization

From a security point of view, an employee (permanent, temporary, or contractor) leaving an organization is always a concern because they carry credentials with them and may know some internal organizational data, connections, IP addresses, and have access cards. The following minimum steps are usually required to avoid any security issues:

Step 1.   The employee's credentials on computers, the network, and databases are cancelled before the employee's departure date. In the case of firing, the access to these systems is cancelled before the supervisor informs the employee of the firing with a printed letter.

Step 2.   Required exit forms are signed by both the employee and the supervisor.

Step 3.   The laptop or desktop issued to the employee is recovered along with the identity card or smart card.

Step 4.   The employee is escorted out of the building cordially, either by another employee or the supervisor, to make sure that the fired or quitting employee does not carry any company-provided items (for example, files on USB drives, paper records, company patents) with them.

Step 5.   Any DAC credentials, such as database accounts and privileges given for accessing other software, are cancelled immediately.

Step 6.   (Optional) If the job required a certain level of clearance, the corresponding authorities are informed that the particular employee's clearance is no longer valid for the organization. The last step that might happen in a few weeks is to clear up all accounts of the employee by paying the dues if any, transferring any retirement accounts, and closing records on the employee for good. Of course, the records will remain with the organization for future audits and references per company policies. In all these steps, the cybersecurity branch keeps a tab on the employee activities and watches for any troubles.

Case # 3: An Existing Employee Wants to Renew Their Credentials

As discussed earlier, an employee's credentials are valid for only a few years—usually three to five. At the end of this period, the employee has to renew the credentials with the organization. The reason is that in three to five years, many changes can happen with technology, the way identity information is issued, smart cards, and the security posture of a company or the company can be sold or acquire other organizations or businesses. The following minimum steps are required:

Step 1.   Before the credentials expire (ID card and the PIN or biometric authentication), inform the supervisor and team leads about a possible delay (even if it is brief) in renewing or reorganizing the card and credentials back to the systems.

Step 2.   Fill out forms for the new credentials and get the supervisor to approve them.

Step 3.   With the newly signed forms, go to the credentials-issuing office and obtain new details (ID card, PIN, scan fingerprints, handprints, facial features for face recognition, and so on).

Step 4.   Test the credentials with the company's main gate entrance(s) and building entrances where the older card previously worked.

Step 5.   If the ID card has digital certificates, use them to register the card with email programs and the global directory. Publish your public keys.

Step 6.   Save your old digital certificates per organizational policies and use them to read older email. Without these older certificates, the older email will not be accessible.

Step 7.   Check all applications, software, and databases where the employee used their credentials to register credentials associated with the newly issued ID.

Step 8.   Report any problems to the cybersecurity and ID card–issuing offices.

Case # 4: An Existing Employee's Privileges Are Increased/Decreased

Employees get promoted, demoted, or moved to another branch. In a large organization, it's normal for people to move around a lot. It's also possible that people move from one physical office building to another either in the same city or between two cities or countries. The following are some minimum steps required:

Step 1.   Assess the employee's new responsibilities and current privileges.

Step 2.   Keep or remove privileges required for the new responsibilities.

Step 3.   Employee fills out new forms with the new branch unit and its supervisor for any privileges required for that branch and forwards the forms to cybersecurity through change management.

Step 4.   Reimage the employee's computer to the new baseline configuration if the employee carries the same machine to the new job.

Step 5.   In the new job, request required software with new forms signed both by the employee and the supervisor and forward the forms to the software installation people.

Step 6.   If the employee is demoted in the same branch, adjust privileges and remove the software that should not be used. The request to adjust privileges and remove software is submitted by the supervisor to the software installation and maintenance branch.

Step 7.   The software branch may optionally reimage the computer to the baseline configuration instead of removing software and individual privileges. The same applies for increasing privileges.

Step 8.   If the employee needs to get more privileges in the same job, new forms are filed describing why those privileges are required and how they will be used. The supervisor has to certify those and forward them to the cybersecurity team.

Step 9.   In some cases (for example, when an existing employee is given access to check closed-circuit camera recordings in the network server rooms daily), new secondary ID cards are issued to access special rooms or an existing ID card can be reprogrammed for additional access.

Step 10.   In all cases, justification, clearance levels, and required access need to be mentioned in the forms and certified by the supervisor before the cybersecurity or physical security teams (ISSO) can endorse the application and provide the required privileges.

Case # 5: A Visitor/Vendor to the Organizational Facility

In any organization, visitors, customers, or vendors might need to meet with people. Per the zero-trust policy, no one can be admitted to the facility to roam freely. The following are the minimum required rules:

- Make sure vendors and visitors are setting up their appointments in advance (whenever possible) with one employee or a group in the organization.

- Visitors or vendors report to the front desk where they might be issued a temporary badge.

- A temporary badge is not a free pass; the person wearing a temporary badge must always be accompanied by a company employee wearing the company badge.

- Visitors or vendors must be first met at the entrance with an employee who invites them into the premises after proper introductions.

- Visitors or vendors are not allowed—even with a company employee accompanying them—to areas such as server rooms and secure areas where restrictions apply.

- Any person wearing a temporary badge and moving around the company premises is reported promptly to the main office.

- Visitors or vendors cannot access computer systems, printers, cabinets, or any documents and should be checked upon exit to make sure that they are not carrying any of these.

- If company policies require, visitors or vendors should be prepared to leave items such as their cell phones, car keys, electronic equipment, and USB drives in a secure locker.

- Visitors or vendors should not carry any firearms or unauthorized equipment (for example, laptops).

- Visitors or vendors cannot connect any equipment to the company's network or phone lines.

- Visitors or vendors can only use voice phones with permission.

- When exiting, an employee must accompany the visitors or vendors to the exit doors of the building where the visitors or vendors surrender their temporary badges.

Physical Security of DB and Applications

Some physical security is associated with database and application security because both these involve stationing them into a physical building. An organization can be spread over a large area with several buildings, or it can be housed in a single building occupying one or more suites of several thousand square feet of real estate space. Physical security for the databases concerns storage (including primary and secondary backups) and server areas (rooms and buildings). For applications it can be repositories stored on servers, files on shared drives, their locations, and so on. The following are the minimum required physical security controls an organization has to deal with:

- Company premises are protected by fences, warning signs, or an entrance gate that might be controlled by a physical guard or electronic access.

- Bollards protect the building from vehicle-ramming attacks if someone tries to drive a truck or such into the building to cause damages. Entrances to the building are usually double-door systems referred to as a "man trap." The first door closes, and the user has to use their card or biometrics to open the second door to enter the facility. As usual, anyone arriving at the man trap without a proper ID has to go to the help center or call their supervisor for further directions.

- Employees who forget their access cards are trained *not to ask others* to let them enter the facility, even if they are C-level managers.

- HVAC systems and the plenum spaces where the wiring and tubes run are well protected and hidden from public view.

- Fire hazard warnings and lights are installed throughout the facilities. It is possible to link the fire and other warning systems (such as for tornados or floods) to the user emails for alerts.

- Emergency lights are required to switch on automatically when there is a power failure.

- If resources are available, the corporation should explore and invest in alternative power generators and sources for uninterrupted power supply (UPS) to keep the databases and applications running.

- The chain of command is established from top-level managers to bottom-level employees to pass along information about any hazards or dangers in the company facilities.

- Databases and servers hosting the databases are placed in separate rooms (if resources are available) that are accessible only to the administrators with proper privileges after vetting and clearances.

- Databases are encrypted and backed up regularly to prevent any losses or ransomware attacks.

- Physical disks where the databases are stored are out of sight for anyone, including the administrators. The size of physical disks and the databases are monitored daily.

- Physical security for the buildings and company premises is 24x7x365 with either a guard stationed at the entrances or CCTV cameras placed with proper pan and zoom lenses.

- CCTV recordings are created for data rooms inside the buildings.

- All the inside and outside CCTV recordings are monitored daily for any suspicious activities, noting the time of the activity and why it was required or suspicious.

- Applications developed are always stored by version on a repository such as Visual Source Safe. Each version of the software is stored separately on these repositories. It is important to know that the stored software is readable at any time and not corrupted.

- Application files are also backed up on a secondary area such as a shared drive with proper privileges, just in case the primary repository is not available for any reason.

- Any data, for either applications or DBs, that are on the cloud also need a backup. This backup can be worked out with the cloud providers, whereby the provider takes care of the backup and provides a warranty. But for small-scale applications and DBs hosted with a less-known cloud provider, it might be useful to have a local backup as well.

- Both the primary and secondary application storage areas require credentials (username and password or role-based authentication) to access the application code files.

- Exit signs, warnings, and escape routes in case of an emergency are displayed prominently for everyone to see and follow.

- Employees are well trained, and a table-top exercise is conducted regularly (at least once a year) to educate the staff to be aware of the necessities of physical security.

- Optionally, an organization can follow automatic switching off of the lights to save electricity and automatic door locking mechanisms as required.

- In case of a fire, water sprinklers need to be activated. These need to be designed in consultation with the local fire departments.

- The data center and its rooms would not use water because it could be a hazard for the servers and data itself. Therefore, inert gas suppression systems are advised.

- Damages due to high winds, downed power lines, hurricanes, and tornadoes need to be kept in mind and mitigating activities designed with proper organizational policies.

- Organizations should regularly check the physical space of each employee to see if any unapproved devices (for example, coffee machines, kettles, and microwave ovens) are connected to the electric outlets. Unapproved devices must be disconnected and removed from the individual offices/cubes. Employees are encouraged to use general break room appliances instead of installing their own appliances in their allotted physical office space.

- Applications or databases are only accessible physically with proper MAC and DAC privileges and two-factor authentications.

- For organizations allowing remote work and telework schedules, new rules kick in. Employees must use only allowed VPNs to connect to the organizational network to access resources.

- Access to the VPN is still controlled by two-factor authentication.

- A user opting to telework must sign a document that their telework environment (typically a room in their home) serves as an office room and has no fire or chemical hazards. The rooms must also have fire alarms and adequate ventilation. Any changes to these circumstances must be reported to the supervisor.

- Teleworking professionals must also provide written information with details about their secure and stable Internet connections and the name of the Internet service provider, the speed of Internet connection, and other details required by the organization.

■ At least one latest backup copy of databases or the application must be stored at the secondary site in case the primary site is destroyed by fire or other natural or environmental disaster.

■ Some organizations outsource their databases and applications to a second source protected by another party or company.

■ All the computers, printers, tablets, phones, and other electronic equipment prominently display warnings to users not to misuse the company resources. Employees agree to the terms by clicking a button or typing their name in a text box before proceeding further. Violations are taken seriously, and privileges are removed without any warnings.

■ Proper insurance is required for data losses and applications to transfer risk. Contractors and third-party developers must provide liability insurance, professional indemnity, and insurance against fraud, stealing, and so on.

Business Continuity and Disaster Recovery

NIST publication 800-34 Rev 1 describes contingency plans for federal information systems. With all the protections in place, you can still have a disaster strike that puts the data center and applications out of commission. How soon you can get back to work and normalcy depends on how prepared you are and what plans you have in place before a disaster strikes.

The contingency plan has the following suggested steps:

Step 1.   Create a business continuity plan policy statement and get it approved by the organization.

Step 2.   Determine the business assets and processes and their criticality.

Step 3.   Identify all resources and their requirements.

Step 4.   Identify the resources' priority—what should be restored first, second, and so on.

Step 5.   Determine if you have a backup and recovery in place. If so, do they actually work?

Step 6.   Determine the costs for assets that are lost or irreplaceable.

Step 7.   Who are the personnel involved for continuity and recovery, and what are their responsibilities?

Step 8.   Does the organization have an alternate site for quick business operations?

Step 9.   Test the business continuity plan at least once a year (though it is recommended to do the testing more than once a year).

Step 10.   Test the plan in real time to make sure it works as intended.

Step 11.   Understand the following important terms in business continuity:

- **Maximum Tolerable Downtime (MTD):** The MTD represents the total amount of time the organization is willing to accept for a business process outage or disruption. MTD includes all impact considerations. Determining MTD is very important because it could leave contingency planners with imprecise direction on (1) selection of an appropriate recovery method, and (2) the depth of detail that will be required when developing recovery procedures, including their scope and content.

- **Recovery Time Objective (RTO):** RTO defines the maximum amount of time that a system resource can remain unavailable. After the RTO has elapsed, there is an unacceptable impact on other system resources, supported mission/business processes, and the MTD. Determining the RTO is important for selecting appropriate technologies that are best suited for meeting the MTD. When it is not feasible to immediately meet the RTO and the MTD is inflexible, a Plan of Action and Milestone (POA&M) should be initiated to document the situation and plan for its mitigation.

- **Recovery Point Objective (RPO):** The RPO represents the point in time prior to a disruption or system outage to which mission/business process data can be recovered (given the most recent backup copy of the data). Unlike RTO, RPO is not considered to be part of MTD. Rather, it is a factor of how much data loss the mission or business process can tolerate during the recovery process.

Because the RTO must ensure that the MTD is not exceeded, the RTO must normally be shorter than the MTD.

Disaster recovery procedures should be assigned to the appropriate recovery team and typically address the following actions:

1. Obtaining authorization to access damaged facilities and/or geographic area

2. Notifying internal and external business partners associated with the system

3. Obtaining necessary office supplies and work space

4. Obtaining and installing necessary hardware components

5. Obtaining and loading backup media

6. Restoring critical operating system and application software

7. Restoring system data to a known state

8. Testing system functionality including security controls

9. Connecting the system to a network or other external systems and operating alternate equipment successfully

10. Notifying internal and external business partners about successful recovery

It is important to note that recovery procedures should be written in a straightforward, clear step-by-step style. To prevent difficulty or confusion in an emergency, no procedural steps should be assumed or omitted. A checklist format is useful for documenting the sequential recovery procedures and for troubleshooting problems if the system cannot be recovered properly. Note that each team should have their own recovery procedures and yet work in tandem with a cadence created earlier.

Attacks and Loss—Recognizing and Remediating

Data is the backbone of every business because it contains customer contacts, financial or personal records, service orders, trouble tickets, backups, and more. With regulations like GDPR, the data is owned by customers, and permissions need to be obtained before it can be shared. Despite attempts to create a secure stature, due care, and due diligence, attacks can happen, and data loss can occur. The following are some indications that might give a clue to the breach, hack, or attack:

- Devices and systems seem to work slowly, despite the fact that the network is working perfectly.

- Windows Task Manager doesn't work, programs you see inside Task Manager are unknown, and programs running cannot be closed.

- File sizes are different or files are completely missing (you did not delete them).

- Traffic on the Internet and network is very slow although your Internet speed is supposed to be high—in hundreds of megabits per second.

- Popups appear to advertise a product or ask you to install some software.

- Your computer restarts without your permission or crashes when you restart.

- A warning message is displayed about paying some ransom money to unlock your system within a few days of time.

- More than one user is logged into your machine, or when you log in, you receive a request to allow another user to log in.

- A new administrative account is created on your system, and you do not know who it was.

- The contents of some files have changed or have been encrypted with some unknown password.

- Your computer has a new and different search engine in the browser.

- You cannot send email from your device.

- Your system's battery drains quickly, and the system is getting hotter quickly.

- In the Internet security settings, there are new settings that you did not set up.

- When you try to go to a website, the browser always goes to another unknown site.

- The Wi-Fi connections disconnect without your consent.

- Every few minutes, you see a warning that some program needs to be installed or the system will shut down for the rest of the day.

- Your website has been defaced—the content is not what you created.

- You cannot change your registry entries or cannot run the registry editor.

- Your friends complain that you are sending them too many spam emails, and you know you did not send those emails.

- Your device's language settings have changed to a language you do not understand.

- Your credit card company calls you and says you have too many transactions from your own computer on a shopping website (you did not do any of the transactions).

Many simple things can be fixed easily by installing the correct patches for software and firmware on your computer regularly from the authenticated manufacturers. In fact, many computers are now programmed to download these automatically to protect the machines. However, spam messages, free money offers, and other such things target users with phishing and social engineering. They succeed when people are lazy or ignorant or just plain ignore all warnings. Here are some minimum fixes:

- Create a plain user account to log in and check emails. Do not use an administrative account to log in.

- Do not allow (or do not even visit) websites that have drive-by downloads.

- Do not allow Active-X components to be installed from websites.

- Do not install unknown or suspicious free software or shareware.

- Use different passwords for different sites and computer logins.

- Do not click URLs received from unknown email senders (spam).

- If you suspect an email as spam, block that user from further sending emails.

- Hover the mouse over the URLs received even from authentic or known users to confirm that the URL is an authentic link as displayed. Many spam links display a prominent and authentic URL but go to a different site upon hovering or clicking.

- Do not click links sent in emails; instead, type the address in the browser.

- Report ransomware and such activities promptly to authorities. These authorities are usually the corporatewide helpdesk, the local ISSO, or the corporate ISSO.

- Back up your files regularly for recovering data later.

- If attacked by ransomware, do not panic but plan a course of action with local law enforcement authorities.

- If attacked, try to restore your system from a restore point, if available.

- Do not keep any payment card information for automatic entry on your system.

- Continuously track your credit records and statements for unexpected billing information and confirm with the card companies where and when transactions took place and by whom, if possible. Cancel the cards if there is suspicious activity.

- Protect your government-issued documents such as passports, driving license numbers, and so on.

- Many Internet advertisements on sites such as the Facebook are spurious—promising one product but sending another after ordering. Make sure that you have adequate coverage from the credit card company or the paying tool such as PayPal for backing your purchases. Many cards and PayPal offer product warranties and purchase protection for sales when claimed within a few months.

- If nothing else works, be prepared to lose data, erase everything, and rebuild your system.

- Report to the Internet provider how and when the attack happened, and they might be able to figure out some more details.

- Be suspicious of phone calls or text messages asking for information, control of your computer via a chat message, and such. Organizations such as the FBI, IRS, Amazon, or credit card companies never call you on the phone and ask for credentials. Do not ever trust these and transfer control of your computer.

- Be wary of what information and pictures you post on social networks such as Facebook. Know that the photos can be morphed and messages can be altered and reposted on your name with a fake account by another person.

- When traveling, keep your location data safe by not posting to social engineering websites.

- After recovering from an attack, create a lessons-learned document for the future to prevent another attack. Always keep yourself abreast of current security problems in cyberspace.

- Train, retrain, and make the users aware of the dangers of suspicious phone calls, providing information to unknown callers, chat bots, and answering emails. Importantly, be very aware of the possible disgruntled employees who steal and provide information to outsiders.

- Enable logging by default for programs such as databases, email, firewalls, and networks. Watch and keep in mind who has access to those logs and what they are doing with them.

- Always remember the first line of protection is *you*. In other words, data is yours, or you have a unique identity and the data hackers want to steal.

Recovery and Salvage

Recovery happens when you have data at another site that can be brought back quickly to the primary site in some manner. Or if the primary site has a problem with data and applications, you can erase everything and restore it from a backup point. Then you also investigate to find out what happened, how it happened, and what was stolen. If something crashes due to a natural or environmental disaster, the recovery can take time, but if the problem occurs due to a short circuit that shuts down the data center and causes some data loss, backing up from the primary site itself may be sufficient to restore everything, and this can be done quickly as well. Depending on the type of business and the breach that occurred, recovery can take from a few hours to several weeks or months. The main aim of recovery is to bring the business back up and running. Can the organization do it from the primary site? Can they do it from an alternative site? It all depends on the type of disaster. If data servers and applications are down, maybe a simple restart can recover everything without losing a lot. But what if the primary site is destroyed by fire or earthquake? In such cases, recovery at the primary site can take months to years. Then the secondary hot site can be activated quickly without losing business transactions.

Think of two companies as examples: Amazon and Netflix. Both have several servers in each state, city, and country that cater to users. When a customer tries to connect, they go to the nearest site with content—also known as content servers—to fulfill a request. If the nearest content server is down, then the next nearest server tries to connect, and the information flows smoothly. An end user will not notice any difference in data transmission or a business transaction. Amazon also has hundreds and thousands of storage locations, delivery options, automated packing, returns, and other features that use a completed order to decide from where the product can be shipped efficiently. In recovery, while the secondary server keeps the business up to the minute, attempts to fix the downed primary server are made as quickly as possible. But not all organizations have the staff, resources, or money of the Amazon and Netflix organizations. Some may not even opt to have an alternative site. In such cases, business will be affected until the primary location is back up and running. In recovery, the question is, "how quickly are we back to business?" This is a time-dependent question.

In salvaging, a company tries to recover anything usable from the crashed location. Let us think of an example of a fire accident at a data center due to lightning or HVAC problem. Even after controlling the fire, if the data center servers are completely burnt, the data on hard disks might not be useful. The building itself may be insured, but what about the computers and server boxes? Can the disaster team get some or all the data back from the ashes? In such cases, what can be obtained is called salvage. Think of a car accident. If your car is completely damaged, repairs to fix cost are more than the cost of the car itself; in this case, it is declared to be totaled, the insurance company may ask you to sign a paper to transfer the car to them, and they will pay you a certain amount for your loss. With that stroke of your signature, you have given the car to the insurance company for the money they paid you. Now the insurance company may sell that damaged car in parts or as one piece to a body shop or repair person. That transaction of selling the damaged car to get some money is what is termed as salvage.

Likewise, organizations dig into the disaster after everything settles down to try to salvage something. As another example, if all the servers are locked with ransomware, and if the company has the latest backup of everything, salvage may be helpful. But if the ransom attack re-encrypts the backup data, the problem would not go away that easily. Assuming the backups are restorable and hopefully ransomware does not re-encrypt everything, the data servers can be cheerfully erased, servers reloaded to a clean base configuration, and data restored from backups. If that happens, our organization has 100% salvage capacity and can feel happy. Therefore, in salvage, the question is, "How much can be revived and reused?" at the crashed/hacked/breached location. This "how much" can be defined as a monetary amount or the size of data in question.

Getting Back to Work

When we have everything in place for a secure posture for our systems, the secure posture helps minimize the attack surface. But attackers are innovative and continue to find newer ways to infiltrate into networks, databases, and applications in all possible routes. When an attack happens, we know what to do—the basic steps of identify, protect, detect, respond, and recover. These are further divided into 10 steps, each falling into the previously mentioned five steps:

Step 1.   **Update and upgrade software immediately (identify, protect).**

Apply all available software updates using an automated update service from the vendor. Automation is a great option because attackers and threat actors first want to investigate for the latest installed patches and create exploits, often after a patch is released. These are known as N-day exploits. Also make sure that the updates are coming from an authentic source. Authentic updates have a digital signature and a verifiable hash, and they're delivered over secure connections to maintain the integrity of the patch or service pack.

Step 2.   **Defend privileges and accounts (identify, protect).**

A way to manage privilege is through change management and a hierarchy where the higher tier is provided with additional privileges, but they are limited to a few. Change management should have secure functions in place to reset credentials. Using privileged accounts and services must create logs to show who is utilizing them and at what time/day. A threat actor's main target is to create a privileged user account (for a person or a service account) so that they can come back anytime and move around the network with full access to kill, create, or stop a process, introduce a virus, or take over the entire system.

Step 3.   **Enforce signed software execution policies (protect, detect).**

Operating systems have built-in utilities to enforce signed software execution policies for scripts, executables, device drivers, system firmware, and so on. SAs should maintain a list of trusted certificates to avoid any injection of illegitimate or unknown executables. Application whitelisting is an additional step in the software execution policies to provide better security. Allowing any unsigned software to run might open a route for hackers to embed malicious code.

The Windows operating system has the following commands to check signature verification, as shown in Figure 16-2. After running the signature verification, the results are displayed as a text file in Notepad, as shown in Figure 16-3.

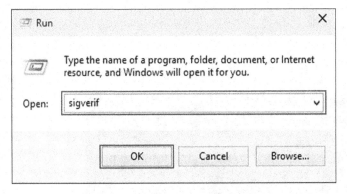

Figure 16-2   *Signature Verification Utility in Windows OS*

Windows also has other interesting tools, such as file checking and diagnostic tools. The System File Checker (SFC) utility in Windows can also scan for system files and replace the corrupted files.

The command **sfc /scannow** can also be run on a specific file rather than the entire system.files from backup. The **sfc /scannow** scans all protected system files and replaces corrupted files with a cached copy that is located in a compressed folder at %WinDir%\System32\dllcache. The %WinDir% placeholder represents the Windows operating system folder (usually Windows).

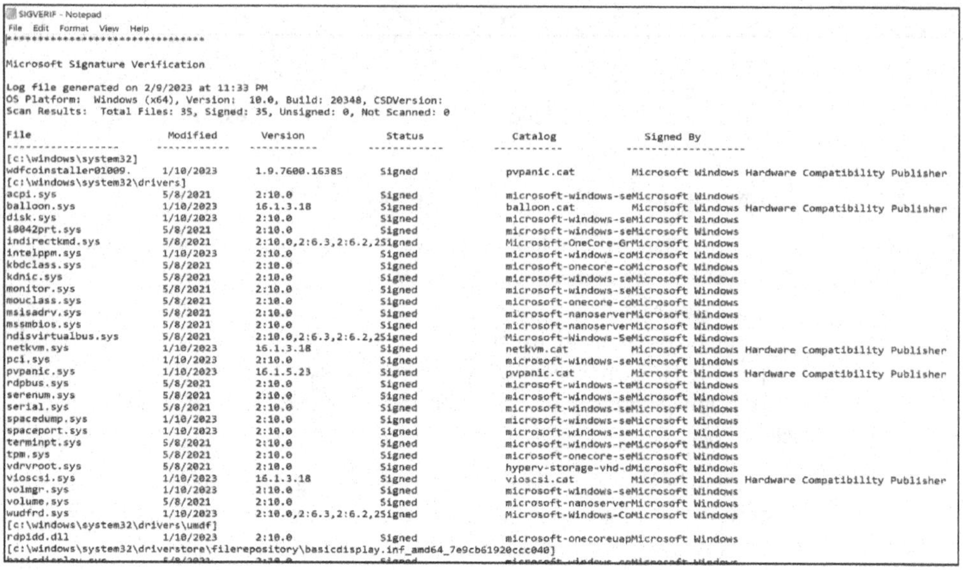

```
SIGVERIF - Notepad
File  Edit  Format  View  Help
*********************************

Microsoft Signature Verification

Log file generated on 2/9/2023 at 11:33 PM
OS Platform: Windows (x64), Version:  10.0, Build: 20348, CSDVersion:
Scan Results:  Total Files: 35, Signed: 35, Unsigned: 0, Not Scanned: 0

File                 Modified      Version          Status        Catalog          Signed By
------------------   -----------   -----------      ------------  -----------      --------------------
[c:\windows\system32]
wdfcoinstaller01009.  1/10/2023    1.9.7600.16385   Signed        pvpanic.cat      Microsoft Windows Hardware Compatibility Publisher
[c:\windows\system32\drivers]
acpi.sys             5/8/2021      2:10.0           Signed        microsoft-windows-seMicrosoft Windows
balloon.sys          1/10/2023     16.1.3.18        Signed        balloon.cat      Microsoft Windows Hardware Compatibility Publisher
disk.sys             1/10/2023     2:10.0           Signed        microsoft-windows-seMicrosoft Windows
i8042prt.sys         5/8/2021      2:10.0           Signed        microsoft-windows-coMicrosoft Windows
indirectkmd.sys      5/8/2021      2:10.0,2:6.3,2:6.2,25Signed    Microsoft-OneCore-GrMicrosoft Windows
intelppm.sys         1/10/2023     2:10.0           Signed        microsoft-windows-coMicrosoft Windows
kbdclass.sys         5/8/2021      2:10.0           Signed        microsoft-onecore-coMicrosoft Windows
kdnic.sys            5/8/2021      2:10.0           Signed        microsoft-windows-seMicrosoft Windows
monitor.sys          5/8/2021      2:10.0           Signed        microsoft-windows-seMicrosoft Windows
mouclass.sys         5/8/2021      2:10.0           Signed        microsoft-onecore-coMicrosoft Windows
msisadrv.sys         5/8/2021      2:10.0           Signed        microsoft-nanoserverMicrosoft Windows
mssmbios.sys         5/8/2021      2:10.0           Signed        microsoft-nanoserverMicrosoft Windows
ndisvirtualbus.sys   5/8/2021      2:10.0,2:6.3,2:6.2,25Signed    Microsoft-Windows-SeMicrosoft Windows
netkvm.sys           1/10/2023     16.1.3.18        Signed        netkvm.cat       Microsoft Windows Hardware Compatibility Publisher
pci.sys              1/10/2023     2:10.0           Signed        microsoft-windows-seMicrosoft Windows
pvpanic.sys          1/10/2023     16.1.5.23        Signed        pvpanic.cat      Microsoft Windows Hardware Compatibility Publisher
rdpbus.sys           5/8/2021      2:10.0           Signed        microsoft-windows-teMicrosoft Windows
serenum.sys          5/8/2021      2:10.0           Signed        microsoft-windows-seMicrosoft Windows
serial.sys           5/8/2021      2:10.0           Signed        microsoft-windows-seMicrosoft Windows
spacedump.sys        1/10/2023     2:10.0           Signed        microsoft-windows-seMicrosoft Windows
spaceport.sys        1/10/2023     2:10.0           Signed        microsoft-windows-seMicrosoft Windows
terminpt.sys         5/8/2021      2:10.0           Signed        microsoft-windows-reMicrosoft Windows
tpm.sys              5/8/2021      2:10.0           Signed        microsoft-onecore-seMicrosoft Windows
vdrvroot.sys         5/8/2021      2:10.0           Signed        hyperv-storage-vhd-dMicrosoft Windows
vioscsi.sys          1/10/2023     16.1.3.18        Signed        vioscsi.cat      Microsoft Windows Hardware Compatibility Publisher
volmgr.sys           1/10/2023     2:10.0           Signed        microsoft-nanoserverMicrosoft Windows
volume.sys           5/8/2021      2:10.0           Signed        microsoft-onecore-seMicrosoft Windows
wudfrd.sys           1/10/2023     2:10.0,2:6.3,2:6.2,25Signed    Microsoft-Windows-CoMicrosoft Windows
[c:\windows\system32\drivers\umdf]
rdpidd.dll           1/10/2023     2:10.0           Signed        microsoft-onecoreuapMicrosoft Windows
[c:\windows\system32\driverstore\filerepository\basicdisplay.inf_amd64_7e9cb61920ccc040]
basicdisplay.sys     5/8/2021      2:10.0           Signed        microsoft-windows-coMicrosoft Windows
```

Figure 16-3   *Results Displayed in Notepad After Running the Signature Verification in Windows*

Figure 16-4 shows the **sfc** command and its progress.

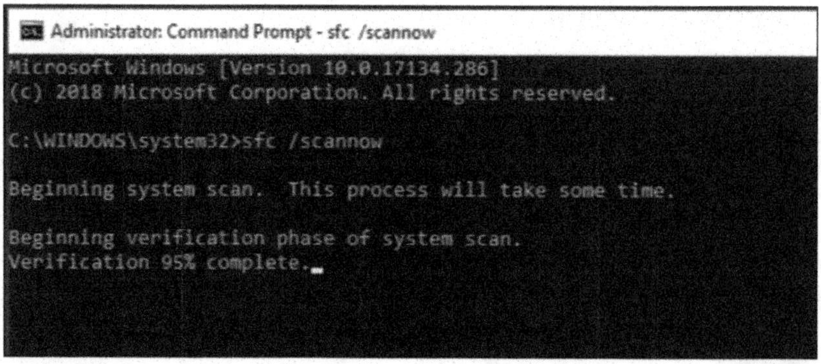

```
Administrator: Command Prompt - sfc /scannow

Microsoft Windows [Version 10.0.17134.286]
(c) 2018 Microsoft Corporation. All rights reserved.

C:\WINDOWS\system32>sfc /scannow

Beginning system scan.  This process will take some time.

Beginning verification phase of system scan.
Verification 95% complete.
```

Figure 16-4   *SFC Utility Scanning Progress in Windows*

The directX diagnostic tool (dxdiag.exe located in the C:\Windows\system32 folder) is another tool to check the details for sound, system display, and input. The details are shown in Figure 16-5. All the information displayed with the dxdiag.exe tool can be saved into text format to read later or saved for the future as a log.

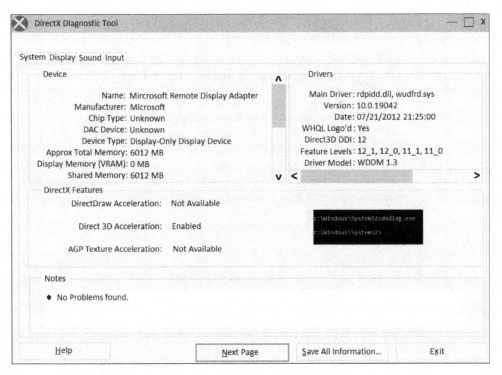

Figure 16-5   *DXDiag.exe Tool Results in Windows OS*

Step 4.   **Exercise a system recovery plan (identify, respond, recover).**

Think like a hacker, think well ahead, and be prepared with a good recovery plan. Make sure the plan protects critical data, configurations, and, importantly, all the logs to ensure continuity of operations. Backups should be encrypted, stored offsite or at a secondary site (offline if possible), and must be able to help in complete recovery. Backups stored offsite should be safe but also should be available for use very quickly in case of a trouble. Conduct a test and perform the recovery to make sure the backup copies are indeed working. The recovery plan must also include steps for natural and environmental disasters, ransomware, and other new attacks as well as known problems. All recovery plans must be tested regularly to ensure that the created disaster recovery strategy is working.

Step 5.   **Actively manage systems and configurations (identify, protect).**

Keep asset inventory of network devices and software up to date. Unwanted, unknown, unneeded, or unexpected hardware and software from the network should be removed promptly or decommissioned with proper procedures, and records should be kept. Always use a baseline configuration to reduce the attack surface. Defective devices must be reimaged and configured back with baseline configuration.

Step 6.   **Continuously hunt for network intrusions (detect, respond, recover).**

Proactively detect, contain, and remove any malicious hardware, software, or components within the network and in each system on the network. Scan the network systems regularly and use Security Information and Event Management (SIEM) products, Endpoint Detection and Response (EDR) solutions, and other data analytic capabilities or other such tools to find malicious or anomalous behaviors. Establishing proactive steps helps an organization to be prepared and enables real-time threat detection using a continuous monitoring that can optimize mitigation strategy.

Step 7.   **Leverage modern hardware security features (identify, protect).**

New hardware has security features like Unified Extensible Firmware Interface (UEFI) Secure Boot, Trusted Platform Module (TPM), and hardware virtualization. These features increase the integrity of the boot process and provide system attestation. Update the firmware as and when it is available from the authentic manufacturer as described in step 1 for software and tools.

Step 8.   **Segregate networks using application-aware defenses (protect, detect).**

Segregate critical networks and services. This was discussed at length earlier for databases and applications. Traditional intrusion detection based on known–bad signatures is not very effective due to encryption and obfuscation techniques. Threat actors now know how to hide malicious actions that can pass as genuine no-harm programs but can remove data over common protocols. This warrants a need for sophisticated, application-aware defensive mechanisms.

Step 9.   **Integrate threat reputation services (protect, detect).**

Using defense-in-depth strategy, leverage multisourced threat reputation services for files, DNS, URLs, IPs, and email addresses. Emerging threats are occurring faster than most organizations can handle, resulting in poor attention to the new threats. Defense-in-depth strategy can provide an effective security posture.

Step 10.   **Transition to multifactor authentication (identify, protect).**

Use two or more factors to let the users log in. Follow these rules strictly for all accounts with elevated privileges, remote access, and/or used on high-value assets. For example, physical smart cards or token-based systems should be used to supplement passwords and PINs.

As explained in the earlier chapters, creating a lessons learned document is important because it helps the future security strategy. This is also important for an organization because people move around branches, departments, and even out of the organization after a time.

Lessons Learned from a Ransomware Attack—Example from a ISC² Webinar

Here is another example of lessons learned from a ransom attack, which was recently a topic in a webinar conducted by ISC² (September 11, 2023). The important points are bulleted for a quick summary. These help in better preparation for proactive monitoring and getting back to normalcy after an attack:

- Understand the threat actor and their wants (usually money in huge amounts) or do research to know details about the people involved in the attack to understand their demands.

- Threat actors found a vulnerability to exploit and got into the network to lock. What vulnerability was it? Does the organization know the vulnerability existed before? If yes, why was it not mitigated by proper patching, or if not known, why did it remain unknown?

- Ransomware attackers are targeting organizations with sensitive data—like in schools, medical information that can be traumatic to patients if released publicly.

- Anybody can be a target for a ransomware security attack.

- The attackers are expert pen testers who have done these as ethical hacking tools for legitimate companies and may have some inside information already, but they've now turned to the dark side to make quick money.

- Credentials are necessary for these hackers to first get in. They have found a way to get these credentials and then create accounts and so on.

- The lesson to remember is that one must keep track of accounts created, whose account is used excessively, who is logging in at odd times of the day, who is responding to phone calls for credential information, and any inside threatening actors (disgruntled employees).

- If there is a disgruntled employee or someone who gave information to an outsider on phone calls, they may not disclose it when asked for fear of getting fired or cornered into a situation.

- Always watch the accounts, creation of new accounts, modification, and so on. These are very common in Windows operating systems.

- If the networks are not segmented (see step 8 from the earlier section about the NSA 10 step protection plan), the hacker who now has an administrative account can move around the complete organization. There is no real need for one traditional flat network for all systems.

- A ransom attack can happen with cloud providers as well. If the attackers find a way to check how the backups are made, they can alter those backup scripts and stop backups or corrupt them.

- Once the backup process is disrupted, malware is loaded by the attacker to encrypt entire data, a disk, or a part of it and lock the system.

- Encryption may sometimes not be the strategy for attacker, but they may exfiltrate data so that the organization may not be able to recover it without the demanded payment.

- When a system is locked with ransomware, looking at the malware alone is not a good strategy because there are other actors created before the malware was loaded.

- Never forget to back up logs, read those logs, and keep them up to date. A system where ransomware is injected can still save logs, but they may not be readable.

- Logs should be enabled for emails, databases, applications, and everything else. Back up logs daily and whenever possible to keep them up to date in a readable format. If that readable format had to be on a physical paper trail, it is better than nothing.

- When attackers are demanding and getting millions of dollars in ransom, they are rich and can afford to customize attacks and settings suited to a particular organization.

- If you noticed that an administrative account was already created by an attacker, the organization has already missed mitigating several vulnerabilities. It may be too late. Removing that additional account may not be helpful because the attacker knows the vulnerability, and they might come back to create another administrative account.

- At this point, the focus must be on how the attacker gained access and contain or stop that access.

- Think like a hacker and look at the following steps: the hacker has scanned the network and might have decided what machines to hit, the hacker might have found a way to create an administrative account with elevated privileges, and the hacker might have exfiltrated data. They might have uploaded malware to lock the system, corrupt backups, and so on.

- Now that we know some of these hacker ideas, we can set up some traps in those areas.

- Provide a honey net or honey pot as a fake location for hackers and attackers to log in.

- Think of the threshold time you have to take a network or system offline. Do you need permissions from managers or the CEO to do this? If the data is on cloud, who do you contact?

- Are you able to create a tabletop exercise for an attacker or attack situation simulation?

- What remote access tools are allowed on the network, and what remote access tools are actually used? Can you recognize the connections coming from remote machines and find who they are? Are they true positives or false positives (an employee might be doing overtime to complete something)?

- Keep your eyes open as you may never know if the attacker may come back again. Once an attacker has tried their skills to find a vulnerability, they may come back again to test.

- Waiting for them to come back to take some action is the worst ever. Be proactive and close the vulnerabilities so that the attacker may never have another opportunity to come back.

- Stopping an attack or blocking a hacker is not a perfect process and not set in stone. Each organization has to make its own plan and follow it to the letter.

- Consider putting default folders for operating systems and other known files in an unrecognizable path that's not the default on the hard disk and other areas (if there is no hard disk).

- Always make absolutely sure that the backups are up to date and available quickly, and they do indeed work.

- Keep a clear-cut decision with C-level managers on pay or do-not-pay situations in a ransomware attack. Does your organization have some insurance?

- Do understand that insurance may not pay 100% or may not pay in cryptocurrency. They may have their own investigation conducted before a payout can happen, and there may be a percentage of commission for buying cryptocurrency.

In conclusion, follow three golden rules for security. First, *you* are the first line of defense and you are the data or the data belongs to you. Second, everyone in the organization is equally important in protecting the assets and safeguarding the company. Three, follow the zero-trust policy with everyone. This is consistent with the adage, "if you see something, say something," because losing your most valuable asset (data) can damage the organization, the person, and destroy the company reputation in no time.

Here are the some of the latest guidelines for smart cybersecurity habits in general:

1. **Think twice, click once:** Phishing attempts and malicious links are prevalent threats. Always ensure you know the source of a link before clicking it. If it's unexpected or seems suspicious, avoid it.

2. **Verify before sharing:** Don't share sensitive information, whether personal or professional, until you're sure about the recipient's identity and their need to have that information. This applies to both digital and real-life situations.

3. Protect passwords:

■ Use strong, unique passwords for every account.

■ Change passwords regularly.

■ Consider using a password manager to keep track of your passwords securely.

4. Safeguard your data and devices:

■ Physically secure devices when they're not in use.

■ Use encryption to protect sensitive data, ensuring that even if unauthorized access occurs, the information remains unreadable.

■ Don't share your password and avoid writing it down in easily accessible places.

5. Keep it clean:

■ Regularly update your software, including the operating system and applications. These updates often contain security patches.

■ Install and regularly update a reputable antivirus and antimalware solution.

6. Keep it protected:

■ Always lock your devices when they're not in active use. This provides an additional layer of security in case the device falls into the wrong hands.

■ Use biometric security features (like fingerprint or face recognition) when available.

7. Back up regularly:

■ Always have a backup of your essential data. Use a combination of local backups (like external hard drives) and cloud-based solutions.

■ Ensure that your backups are also secure, for example, by encrypting them.

8. See something, say something:

■ If you notice any suspicious activity, report it immediately. This could be a strange email, unexpected account activity, or any signs of a potential breach.

■ Encourage a culture of security awareness among peers and colleagues.

By implementing these principles, we can safeguard our digital life against common threats. As repeatedly said in this book, cybersecurity is not a one-time effort but a continuous process of awareness, vigilance, and adaptation to new challenges.

Summary

In a large corporation, the change management process with the help of a change approval board works with various branches to approve changes and privileges for incoming and outbound employees. Each case is different and worked out by the CM branch with the zero-trust rule in mind. Physical security of the database and applications is equally important depending on the organizational resources. Business continuity and disaster recovery plans need to be planned well in advance and must have approval of the organization. Maximum Tolerable Downtime, Recovery Time Objective, and Recovery Point Objective need be set by the organization. Both business continuity and disaster recovery should have various steps and follow a step-by-step rule sheet for guidance to avoid any confusion. Recognizing attacks and loss of data or information is important because remediation depends on what is recognized and how quickly the remediation can work. In recovery, the question is, "how quickly can we go back to normal business operations?" whereas in salvage the question is, "how much can be revived or reused?" After getting back to normalcy, a lessons-learned document is created to prevent further disaster of the same kind or to act more efficiently when the scenario is repeated.

Chapter 16 Questions

1. What branch centrally manages the privileges, accounts, and security in a corporate environment?

2. What items does change management track in a corporate environment?

3. Whom do the ISSOs report to?

4. When a new person joins the organization, what are two examples of MAC and DAC?

5. Why is even an experienced employee forced to go through change management for renewals and change of computer software?

6. What are some of the rules for a visitor or vendor coming into a secure facility?

7. What are some of the physical security features for a data or application center?

8. What are some of the attack indicators in a corporate environment?

9. What is the difference between recovery and salvage?

10. What steps are recommended by the National Security Agency when a breach happens?

11. How often should a business continuity plan or disaster recovery plan be tested?

12. What are the terms MTD and RTO? How is RTO related to MTD?

13. If an attacker has gained access to the network, why would they want to create an administrative account?

14. What is sigverif in Windows OS utilities?

15. What is the use of SFC utility in Windows?

16. Why is network segregation important in corporate security posture?

Answers to Chapter 16 Questions

1. Change management branch.

2. Every change associated with hardware, software, or physical security must go through change management to keep track of assets and the changes requested.

3. ISSOs report to the CISO, who works in tandem with the CSO. Any changes happening at the lower level are passed to the C-level and expected communication on security from C-level managers is passed to ISSOs.

4. The new person joining the organization receives a baseline configured system as a part of MAC. Any additional permissions, privileges, or software are requested from the branch as DAC and go through change management for installation on the baseline machine. Any suspect machine is initially reimaged back to the original baseline configuration.

5. It is due to the fact the organization must follow a zero-trust policy, and as people move from one branch to another and one office to another, it is necessary to adjust the privileges. These adjustments are also dependent on the behavior of the employee.

6. A visitor must be accompanied by a company employee wearing the true badge, visitors cannot enter secure areas, visitors must have their visitor badge displayed, cannot carry additional electronic equipment such as USB, tablets, and so on. They must also be picked up and dropped off at the entrance by a stipulated and designated company employee.

7. Bollards for the building, CCTV cameras for visitor traffic, HVAC safety, fire alarms, water release sprinklers, and double-door man traps are some of the physical security features.

8. Slow response on systems, unknown programs running, unable to remove unknown programs, computer displaying banners or popups, changes in file contents or missing files are some of the examples of an attack.

9. Recovery is how quickly a company can come back to normalcy (the amount of time it takes to be back in business), whereas salvage is what can be accessed and reused from the primary attacked or destroyed site (amount of money, property, or data).

10. NSA recommends five steps: identify, protect, detect, respond, and recover.

11. An administrative account gives access to different areas and escalated privileges. An attacker with an administrative account can create, destroy, encrypt, or exfiltrate data and lock the entire machine with full privileges.

12. At least once a year, but as often as required.

13. MTD or the Maximum Tolerable Downtime is the amount of time an organization can accept for disruption of activities. RTO or the Recovery Time Objective is the maximum time a resource can remain unavailable. For normal business operations to resume, RTO must be shorter than MTD. If RTO exceeds MTD, it means the organization starts suffering losses and cannot remain disrupted.

14. It verifies the authentic signatures of programs, which helps make sure we have authenticated software on the machine.

15. The sfc /scannow scans all protected system files and replaces corrupted files with a cached copy that is located in a compressed folder at %WinDir%\System32\dllcache. The %WinDir% placeholder represents the Windows operating system folder.

16. New technology does not have a need for flat network connections to every system. One network connection is also dangerous in that, if a hacker can gain access to the network, they can gain access to every machine on the network. This is a great security vulnerability.

References

Rob Stubbs (2021). "Data Sovereignty and Compliancy Post Schrems." *Information Security Magazine*. https://www.infosecurity-magazine.com/opinions/data-privacy-compliance-post/.

IBM. "What Is Database Security?" https://www.ibm.com/cloud/learn/database-security.

Microsoft. "Database Design Basics." https://support.microsoft.com/en-us/office/database-design-basics-eb2159cf-1e30-401a-8084-bd4f9c9ca1f5.

Oracle. "Oracle Database 19c." https://docs.oracle.com/en/database/oracle/oracle-database/19/administration.html.

Jenn Riley (2017). "Understanding Metadata." National Information Standards Organization (NISO) Primer. https://groups.niso.org/higherlogic/ws/public/download/17446/Understanding%20Metadata.pdf.

Microsoft (2023). "Start the SQL Server Import Export Wizard." https://learn.microsoft.com/en-us/sql/integration-services/import-export-data/start-the-sql-server-import-and-export-wizard?view=sql-server-ver16.

Oracle. "2.4 Parameters Available in Data Pump Export Command-Line Mode." https://docs.oracle.com/en/database/oracle/oracle-database/19/sutil/oracle-data-pump-export-utility.html#GUID-33880357-06B1-4CA2-8665-9D41347C6705

Oracle. "Backup and Recovery Reference." https://docs.oracle.com/en/database/oracle/oracle-database/19/rcmrf/SHOW.html#GUID-6C2AF43B-FADD-41AF-9408-852A69538E2F.

Microsoft (2023). "Get Started with Virtual Smart Cards: Walkthrough Guide." https://learn.microsoft.com/en-us/windows/security/identity-protection/virtual-smart-cards/virtual-smart-card-get-started.

Chris Corum (2016). "Department of Defense Common Access Card Gets a FIPS 201 Facelift," https://www.secureidnews.com/news-item/department-of-defense-common-access-card-gets-a-fips-201-facelift/.

Oracle (2010). "Syntax of Crontab Entries." https://docs.oracle.com/cd/E19455-01/805-7229/sysrescron-62861/index.html.

Microsoft. "Send-MailMessage." https://learn.microsoft.com/en-us/powershell/module/microsoft.powershell.utility/send-mailmessage?view=powershell-7.3.

Microsoft (2023). "Send a Test Email with Database Mail." https://learn.microsoft.com/en-us/sql/relational-databases/database-mail/database-mail-sending-test-email?view=sql-server-ver16.

DoD Cyber Exchange Public. "Security Technical Implementation Guides." https://public.cyber.mil/stigs/srg-stig-tools/.

Microsoft Azure. "What is Database Security?" https://azure.microsoft.com/en-us/resources/cloud-computing-dictionary/what-is-database-security/#what-is-database-security.

Jaewon Lee (2014). "An Enhanced Risk Formula for Software Security Vulnerabilities." https://www.isaca.org/resources/isaca-journal/past-issues/2014/an-enhanced-risk-formula-for-software-security-vulnerabilities.

Microsoft (2023). "SQL Server Encryption." https://learn.microsoft.com/en-us/sql/relational-databases/security/encryption/sql-server-encryption?view=sql-server-ver16.

Microsoft (2023). "Create and Configure Datasets in the .NET Framework using Visual Studio." https://learn.microsoft.com/en-us/visualstudio/data-tools/create-and-configure-datasets-in-visual-studio?view=vs-2022.

Microsoft. "X509Certificate Class." https://learn.microsoft.com/en-us/dotnet/api/system.security.cryptography.x509certificates.x509certificate?view=net-7.0.

Microsoft (2014). "Encrypting and Decrypting Configuration Sections." https://learn.microsoft.com/en-us/previous-versions/aspnet/zhhddkxy(v=vs.100).

Microsoft (2023). "Best Practices for Deploying Passwords and Other Sensitive Data to ASP.NET and Azure App Service." https://learn.microsoft.com/en-us/aspnet/identity/overview/features-api/best-practices-for-deploying-passwords-and-other-sensitive-data-to-aspnet-and-azure.

Pas Apicella (2011). "How To: Set Up a Data Source within Tomcat 6.0 using Oracle Universal Connection Pool." https://www.oracle.com/technical-resources/articles/enterprise-manager/ucp-jdbc-tomcat.html.

Oracle. "Java Security Standard Algorithm Names." https://docs.oracle.com/en/java/javase/11/docs/specs/security/standard-names.html

Blackberry Inc. (2023). "Global Threat Intelligence Report." https://www.blackberry.com/content/dam/bbcomv4/global/pdf/0408-Threat-ReportV17.pdf.

Dave Winchers et al. "Source Code Analysis Tools." OWASP. https://owasp.org/www-community/Source_Code_Analysis_Tools.

Taylor Armerding (2021). "Securing Your Code: GDPR Best Practices for Application Security." https://www.synopsys.com/blogs/software-security/gdpr-best-practices-application-security/.

Microsoft. "Security Update Guide FAQs." https://www.microsoft.com/en-us/msrc/faqs-security-update-guide#:~:text=When%20does%20Microsoft%20release%20security,plan%20their%20deployment%20schedules%20accordingly.

DISA. "DODIN Approved Products List." https://aplits.disa.mil/processAPList.action.

ZAP. "Command Line." https://www.zaproxy.org/docs/desktop/addons/quick-start/cmdline/.

PortSwigger. "Lab: Exploiting Cross-Site Scripting to Capture Passwords." https://portswigger.net/web-security/cross-site-scripting/exploiting/lab-capturing-passwords.

Karen Scarfone et al. (2008). "Technical Guide to Information Security Testing and Assessment, 800-115." https://nvlpubs.nist.gov/nistpubs/legacy/sp/nistspecialpublication800-115.pdf.

Oracle. "Oracle Enterprise Manager Risk Matrix." https://www.oracle.com/security-alerts/cpujul2023.html#AppendixEM.

NCSC. "Understanding OPSEC: The OPSEC Cycle." https://www.dni.gov/files/NCSC/documents/nittf/Understanding_OPSEC_The_OPSEC_Cycle_Bulletin_2.pdf.

EC-Council. "What Is Digital Forensics?" https://www.eccouncil.org/cybersecurity/what-is-digital-forensics/.

STIG Viewer. "DOD Instruction 8500.2 Full Control List." https://www.stigviewer.com/controls/8500.

OWASP. "OWASPs Mobile Application Security Testing Guide (MASTG)." https://mas.owasp.org.

Okta. "OKTA Verify Guide." https://help.okta.com/eu/en-us/content/topics/end-user/ov-new-install-qr-android.htm.

NIST (2022). "Recommended Criteria for Cybersecurity Labeling of Consumer Software." https://doi.org/10.6028/NIST.CSWP.02042022-1.

Apple (2022). "Apple Platform Security." https://support.apple.com/guide/security/welcome/web.

NIST. "NIST SP 1800-21B." https://www.nccoe.nist.gov/publication/1800-21/VolB/index.html#challenge

Joshua Franklin et al. (2019). "Mobile Device Security: Cloud and Hybrid Builds 1800-4." NIST. https://nvlpubs.nist.gov/nistpubs/SpecialPublications/NIST.SP.1800-4.pdf

Kaitlin Boeckl et al. (2022). "Mobile Device Security: Bring Your Own Device (BYOD) NIST 1800-22B." NIST. https://www.nccoe.nist.gov/sites/default/files/2022-11/mdse-nist-sp1800-22b-draft-2.pdf.

Thiago Guimaraes Maraes et al. (2021). "Open Data on COVID-19 Pandemic: Anonymization as a Technical Solution for Transparency, Privacy, and Data Protection." National Library of Medicine, Oxford University Press. https://www.ncbi.nlm.nih.gov/pmc/articles/PMC8083224/.

Marit Hansen et al. (2015). "Protection Goals of Privacy Engineering." Privacy Workshops. San Jose, CA. https://ieeexplore.ieee.org/document/7163220.

Marianne Swanson et al. (2010). "Contingency Planning Guide for Federal Information Systems." NIST Publication 800-34 Rev. 1. https://nvlpubs.nist.gov/nistpubs/Legacy/SP/nistspecialpublication800-34r1.pdf.

NSA (2018). "NSA's Top Ten Cybersecurity Mitigation Strategies." https://www.nsa.gov/portals/75/documents/what-we-do/cybersecurity/professional-resources/csi-nsas-top10-cybersecurity-mitigation-strategies.pdf.

Index

D

Q

R

T

U

V